Money Moves:
The Gen Z Guide to Winning the Wealth Game

AFJAL KHAN

Copyright © 2024 Afjal Khan

All rights reserved.

ISBN: 9798342942447

DEDICATION

To the bold, ambitious, and fearless Gen Z.
This book is for you—the dreamers, the hustlers, the innovators.
May you find the courage to break the mold, the wisdom to build your own path,
and the power to create a future that is truly yours.
This is your time. Go make those money moves.

CONTENTS

ACKNOWLEDGMENTS .... *vii*

Introduction: Break the Mold and Rewrite Your Story *1*

Chapter 1: Money Doesn't Sleep—Make It Work for You *4*

Chapter 2: Understanding Financial Literacy—The Real Wealth *29*

Chapter 3: Mind Your Own Business—Building Assets, Not Liabilities *56*

Chapter 4: The Power of Financial Education—Understanding Money's Rules *84*

Chapter 5: The Rich Create Opportunities—Harnessing the Power of Initiative *115*

Chapter 6: The Rich Innovate—Creating Value in a Dynamic World *145*

Chapter 7: Overcoming Obstacles—Turning Challenges into Opportunities *176*

Chapter 8: Getting Started—Turning Ideas into Reality *206*

Chapter 9: Still Want More? Here Are Some To Do's *237*

Final Chapter: The Path Forward *268*

ACKNOWLEDGMENTS

First off, a massive shoutout to the Gen Z community—you're the reason this book exists. Your hustle, creativity, and drive to make an impact are what inspired every word on these pages. To everyone who's ever asked the tough questions, challenged the status quo, and refused to settle—you're the real MVPs.

Big thanks to my family and friends who always kept it real, especially when I needed it most. Your support means the world, and this book wouldn't be here without your love and endless encouragement.

To the mentors and motivators—both IRL and online—thank you for dropping gems of wisdom along the way. You've shown that knowledge and success are meant to be shared.

And finally, to every reader picking up this book: You're already on the path to greatness, and I'm stoked to be part of your journey. Let's keep leveling up together.

INTRODUCTION: BREAK THE MOLD AND REWRITE YOUR STORY

Life has changed. The rules that once worked for older generations don't necessarily apply to us anymore. Our parents and grandparents lived in a world where you went to school, got a degree, found a stable job, and retired with a gold watch and a decent pension. For many of them, the dream was straightforward: work hard, save diligently, and enjoy retirement. But Gen Z, you know better—times have changed, and the old playbook doesn't work anymore.

We're living in an era where the internet has become the great equalizer. Opportunities are everywhere, but they don't look like they used to. The nine-to-five grind, the traditional corporate ladder, and the "job security" that was once the golden standard aren't guaranteed anymore. We're witnessing shifts in how money is made, saved, and invested. We're challenging the idea that you must trade time for money, and instead, we're embracing the reality that wealth can be created through creativity, flexibility, and new-age thinking.

But with this freedom comes a lot of uncertainty. How do you navigate a world where the rules seem to change overnight? How do you achieve financial freedom when you're surrounded by social media influencers, flashy lifestyles, and an overwhelming flood of information about making money online? It's easy to feel lost, overwhelmed, or even tempted to give up on the idea that financial independence is possible.

Let me tell you something: it's not just possible; it's within your reach. But to get there, you'll need to break the mold. You'll need to rewrite your story, one where you're not stuck in the rat race, but instead, you're calling the shots. It's about learning how to make your money work for you, rather than the other way around. And it's about understanding the principles that have helped successful people from every walk of life—people who took control of their financial destinies instead of being controlled by them.

Now, I know what you're thinking. Isn't this just another book about money? Isn't it going to be filled with charts, graphs, and boring jargon that only makes sense to accountants and financial advisors? Not quite. What you're holding is more than a guide; it's a blueprint for a different kind of mindset, a different kind of hustle, and a different kind of freedom.

This is about more than just making a quick buck. It's about building a life where you're in control, where your time is truly your own, and where financial decisions are made with purpose and intention. It's about understanding that money, when used wisely, is a tool that can build dreams, not just pay bills. Whether you're interested in starting a business, becoming a savvy investor, or simply gaining control over your finances, you'll find that the key to success lies in your willingness to learn, adapt, and take action.

The journey won't be easy. There will be challenges along the way, from navigating the complexities of modern finance to resisting the temptations that lead to mindless spending. You'll face moments of doubt and fear—times when it feels like the whole system is rigged against you, or when you're unsure if you have what it takes to succeed. But every challenge is an opportunity. Every obstacle is a lesson waiting to be learned. And every setback is a chance to come back stronger.

There's a reason why so many people struggle to achieve financial freedom, and it's not because they lack the ability or the intelligence. It's because they've been taught to fear money instead of mastering it. They've been conditioned to believe that wealth is something that happens to a lucky few, instead of something that can be intentionally created. But here's the truth: wealth is built by those who dare to think differently, who refuse to settle for the status quo, and who take the time to learn the skills that matter.

You see, financial independence is about more than just saving and investing. It's about understanding how money flows, how to protect it, how to multiply it, and how to use it as a means to achieve your goals and fulfill your purpose. And yes, as Muslims, we are guided by principles that remind us of the importance of honesty, integrity, and earning through Halal means. It's a responsibility to ensure that our path to wealth is ethical and aligned with our values. But that doesn't mean that wealth is off-limits; in fact, it means that our approach to it is more intentional, more thoughtful, and ultimately more rewarding.

So, what does it take to start this journey? It takes courage. The courage to step outside your comfort zone, to challenge the beliefs that hold you back, and to adopt a mindset that looks beyond the paycheck. It takes the courage to invest in yourself—not just financially, but through learning, self-discipline, and a commitment to continuous improvement. And most importantly, it takes the courage to believe that you are capable of more than you've been told.

Look around you. We live in a time where innovation is at our fingertips, where you can reach people across the world with a single post, and where entire industries are being disrupted by young people with fresh ideas. It's a time when the traditional rules of wealth-building are being rewritten, and you have the power to shape your own destiny. You don't need to come from wealth, you don't need a fancy degree, and you don't need to have everything figured out. You just need the drive to keep going, even when the path is uncertain.

Imagine a life where you don't have to clock in to make ends meet, where your income isn't limited by the hours in a day, and where your efforts today create a better tomorrow. Imagine waking up each morning knowing that your decisions, your actions, and your efforts are creating something meaningful, not just for yourself but for those around you. This isn't just a fantasy—it's the reality for those who choose to live by different rules, who choose to see money not as an end, but as a means to a richer, fuller life.

As you turn these pages, remember that this is your story to write. No one else can do it for you. The tools, the strategies, and the mindset are here, but it's up to you to put them into action. It's up to you to take the first step, to embrace the challenges, and to build a life that reflects your values, your ambitions, and your vision for the future.

This isn't just a book; it's a call to action. It's a reminder that you are capable of achieving more than you think, that you have the potential to create a life that's not only financially secure but also deeply fulfilling. So, take a deep breath, let go of the doubts, and get ready to see the world—and your place in it—in a whole new light.

You're not just working for money anymore. You're working to build a life that matters. And every step you take, every lesson you learn, and every decision you make will bring you closer to that vision of freedom and purpose. It's time to take control, break the mold, and create the future you deserve.

CHAPTER 1: MONEY DOESN'T SLEEP—MAKE IT WORK FOR YOU

In today's world, the way we think about money is evolving faster than ever. It's no longer about simply clocking in at a job, waiting for a paycheck, and hoping that, by retirement, you'll have saved enough to live comfortably. The truth is, if you want financial independence, you have to learn how to make your money work for you, even when you're not actively working. Think about it—money that sleeps is money that loses potential. Every dollar you earn is an opportunity, but if that opportunity is left idle, you're missing out on what it could become.

It's time to adopt a new mindset. We've seen the stories, the viral tweets, the Instagram posts of young people turning small investments into impressive fortunes. It's easy to think they got lucky, but in reality, they've learned something fundamental: money doesn't sleep. They understand that investing, building assets, and creating multiple streams of income aren't just for the rich; they're for anyone who's willing to shift their thinking.

For too long, many of us have been taught to play it safe—get a degree, find a steady job, work hard, save a little, and hope it all pays off someday. But this approach ignores the power of passive income and the ability to create wealth that works for you 24/7. The reality is that relying solely on a paycheck is risky, especially in a world where industries are being disrupted overnight, and job security is becoming a thing of the past. What if you could change that narrative? What if, instead of working for money, you focused on ways to make money work for you?

The first step is understanding the concept of passive income. Passive income means you're earning money without needing to be physically present or actively involved in the process every single day. It's like planting a seed that grows into a tree, which continues to produce fruit season after season. Think about it: wouldn't it be better to have a system that generates money for you, even while you sleep? This is how wealth is built—by creating assets that generate income over time.

There's a common misconception that passive income is only possible if you have a lot of money to invest. But that's not true. The reality is, you can start small and scale up over time. You can begin by putting aside a small portion of your earnings into investments like stocks, real estate, or even starting a small side business. It's about making your money do the work, even if you're starting with just a little bit. As Muslims, it's important to ensure that the methods we use to grow our money are ethical and Halal (permissible). This means avoiding interest-based investments and focusing on options that align with our beliefs, like equity-based investments or real estate ventures.

It's essential to understand that passive income is not a get-rich-quick scheme. It requires patience, discipline, and a willingness to learn. But the rewards are worth it because it frees you from the limitations of time. Time is finite, but passive income gives you the ability to earn without having to exchange more hours of your life. It's about building a system that generates wealth for you, allowing you to focus on what truly matters—your family, your spiritual growth, and your passions.

One of the key principles that separate those who achieve financial independence from those who struggle is the ability to think long-term. It's easy to get caught up in the immediate gratification that comes from spending money on things you want now. But those who build real wealth understand that every dollar is a seed that can be planted and nurtured. When you put your money into assets like investments, rental properties, or even a business, you're setting yourself up for returns that compound over time. This is the power of delayed gratification.

For example, imagine you have $500. You could use that money to buy the latest phone, or you could invest it in stocks or a small side hustle that might turn that $500 into $1,000, $2,000, or more over time. It's not about avoiding enjoyment—it's about choosing investments that bring returns while allowing you to enjoy the fruits of your labor later on. This requires a shift in thinking, but it's a shift that pays dividends—literally and figuratively.

There's a hadith where the Prophet Muhammad (peace be upon him) said, "The upper hand is better than the lower hand" (Sahih Bukhari). It's a reminder that the ability to give, to be in a position where you can help others, is a blessing. And how do you get there? By building a life where you're not dependent on every paycheck but instead have created multiple streams of income. This allows you to focus on your spiritual growth, to be there for your family, and to contribute to your community in meaningful ways.

The concept of making money work for you is not new. Wealthy individuals have been using these strategies for generations. The difference is, today's technology has made these opportunities accessible to nearly everyone with an internet connection. Platforms that allow you to invest in stocks, crowdfunding real estate, and even peer-to-peer lending options have made it possible to start small and grow. But with these opportunities comes responsibility—the responsibility to do your due diligence, to learn about what you're investing in, and to make sure that your income aligns with your values.

It's easy to get caught up in the hype and jump into trends without truly understanding them. That's why it's crucial to take time to learn the basics of investing and wealth-building. Books, online courses, and mentors can provide the knowledge you need to make informed decisions. Remember, every investment has a risk, but doing your research and choosing options that align with your risk tolerance can make a significant difference.

For those of us who follow Islamic principles, it's also important to understand the concept of avoiding Riba (interest). This means being mindful about the types of investments we choose and looking for alternatives that align with our values. Shariah-compliant stocks, mutual funds, and even Islamic bonds (Sukuk) are viable options that can help you grow your wealth in a way that is ethical and permissible.

Many people are hesitant to invest because they fear losing their hard-earned money. This fear is natural, but it's important to remember that risk is a part of any worthwhile endeavor. The key is not to avoid risk altogether but to manage it wisely. Diversification is one of the best ways to do this. When you diversify, you spread your investments across different types of assets, such as stocks, real estate, and other ventures. This way, if one investment doesn't perform well, the others can balance out the impact.

Think of it like a garden: if you plant all your seeds in one spot and a storm hits, you could lose everything. But if you plant your seeds in different areas, you increase your chances of having something thrive. The same is true for your money. By spreading it across various investments, you're protecting yourself from market fluctuations and giving yourself the best chance for long-term growth.

The most important thing to remember is that you don't have to be rich to start building wealth. You can begin with whatever you have, even if it's just a small amount each month. The habit of investing and saving is more valuable than the amount you start with. Over time, those small contributions will grow, thanks to the power of compound interest and investment returns. And as your income grows, you can increase the amount you invest.

Every investment you make is a step towards financial independence, a step towards having the freedom to choose how you spend your time. It's a step towards living a life where you don't have to worry about every expense, where you have the ability to give generously, and where you're building a future that aligns with your values and dreams.

Many of us grew up with the belief that the key to financial success was saving whatever we could from our paycheck. Our parents told us to put our money in a savings account and let it grow over time. But here's the truth:

savings accounts don't make your money work hard enough. With interest rates often lagging behind inflation, the value of money in a traditional savings account can shrink over time. This is why understanding the difference between saving and investing is crucial.

Saving is important—it's your safety net. It's the money you keep for emergencies or short-term goals. But if you want to see your money multiply, you have to go beyond just saving; you have to invest. Investing is the process of putting your money into vehicles that can potentially grow in value, such as stocks, mutual funds, real estate, or a small business. When you invest, you're giving your money the opportunity to grow and produce returns that are far beyond what a savings account can offer.

Imagine this: You save $1,000 and put it into a savings account with an annual interest rate of 1%. After a year, you'll have earned about $10 in interest. But if you took that same $1,000 and invested it into a diversified stock portfolio that yields an average of 7% annually, you'd earn about $70 in the same year. Over time, the difference becomes even more significant due to the power of compounding.

But what is compounding, and why does it matter? Compounding is when the money you earn on your investment begins to earn money itself. Think of it as a snowball rolling down a hill—over time, it picks up more snow and grows larger. In the financial world, compounding means that your investment returns are reinvested to generate even more returns. The earlier you start, the more time your money has to grow, and the bigger your "snowball" can become.

Now, you might be wondering, "How do I get started with investing if I don't have a lot of money?" The beauty of investing today is that technology has made it accessible to almost everyone. With the rise of low-fee brokerage platforms and apps, you can start investing with as little as $5. The key is to start, even if you're only investing small amounts at first. It's the habit of putting money aside for investments that will build your wealth over time.

One simple way to start is by using dollar-cost averaging. This means consistently investing a fixed amount of money into the market, regardless of how the market is performing. When prices are high, your money buys fewer shares, but when prices are low, it buys more. Over time, this strategy can smooth out the ups and downs of the market, helping you to build wealth steadily without needing to time the market perfectly.

However, investing isn't just about choosing stocks or funds. It's about understanding your risk tolerance—how much risk you're willing to take on for potential returns. Some people are comfortable with the volatility of the stock market, while others prefer the stability of real estate or bonds. It's important to find the balance that works for you, so you can sleep at night knowing that your investments align with your comfort level.

Islamic finance offers guidance on how to invest ethically, focusing on investments that avoid interest (Riba) and businesses that operate in prohibited industries. Instead of looking for the highest returns, it's about seeking out investments that align with your values while still offering growth potential. This approach ensures that your wealth is not just growing, but it's growing in a way that brings peace of mind.

But let's face it—investing can be intimidating at first. There's a lot of jargon, and it's easy to feel overwhelmed by the sheer number of options. That's why education is your best ally. Take the time to learn about different types of investments, how the stock market works, and how to read financial statements. You don't need to become a financial expert, but understanding the basics will give you the confidence to make informed decisions.

Start by reading books, watching online tutorials, or even taking courses that focus on personal finance and investing. Many successful investors started with little to no knowledge, but they committed to learning, experimenting, and growing over time. Remember, you're not looking for a shortcut to wealth. You're building a foundation that will support your financial goals for the rest of your life.

As you learn, keep in mind that investing isn't a one-size-fits-all solution. What works for someone else may not be the best strategy for you. Focus on building a portfolio that aligns with your financial goals, risk tolerance, and time horizon. If you're investing for a long-term goal like retirement, you might be willing to take on more risk for higher potential returns. But if you're investing to buy a home in the next few years, a more conservative approach might be appropriate.

Patience is key when it comes to investing. There will be times when the market dips, and it's tempting to sell your investments out of fear. But the most successful investors understand that markets are cyclical—they rise and fall, but historically, they've always trended upward over time. Staying the course, especially during market downturns, can be one of the most challenging aspects of investing, but it's also one of the most important. It's about having the discipline to stick to your strategy and trust the process, even when it feels uncertain.

One of the biggest mistakes people make is trying to chase trends or "hot" investments. They hear about a stock that's skyrocketing or a new cryptocurrency that promises massive returns, and they rush to buy in without doing their research. More often than not, they end up losing money because they bought at the peak, only to watch the price plummet. This approach is driven by FOMO—fear of missing out—which can be a dangerous mindset when it comes to money.

The most successful investors don't chase trends; they focus on fundamentals. They invest in businesses that they understand, with strong management and long-term potential. They know that investing isn't about getting rich overnight; it's about growing wealth consistently over time. And they understand that sometimes, the best investment is doing nothing—letting their portfolio ride out the ups and downs of the market.

If you find yourself tempted to make impulsive investment decisions, remind yourself that true wealth-building is a marathon, not a sprint. It's about setting realistic expectations and focusing on progress, not perfection. It's about taking small steps every day, knowing that those steps will compound over time to create significant results. This mindset shift can be the difference between constantly chasing the next big thing and building a portfolio that stands the test of time.

As Muslims, we're reminded that every gain and every loss is part of Allah's plan. This doesn't mean we should avoid taking action, but it does mean that we approach our financial decisions with trust and humility. We strive to do our best, but we leave the results to Allah. This mindset not only brings peace but also encourages us to act with integrity, even when others may be cutting corners.

A common question that comes up when people start thinking about passive income is, "How much do I need to become financially free?" The answer isn't the same for everyone because financial freedom isn't just about a number—it's about what that number allows you to do. For some, financial freedom means being able to travel the world without worrying about a job. For others, it means having the time to spend with family, pursue hobbies, or engage in community work.

To determine what financial freedom looks like for you, start by considering your desired lifestyle and the costs associated with it. Calculate your monthly expenses, including necessities like housing, food, and transportation, as well as discretionary spending like entertainment and travel. Then, consider how much passive income you would need to cover those expenses without relying on a paycheck. This is your financial freedom number.

Reaching that number may seem daunting at first, especially if you're just starting out. But the key is to focus on one step at a time. If you can replace even a small portion of your income with passive income, you're already on your way. It's about creating a snowball effect—starting small, but continually adding to your investments and growing your streams of income until they cover your needs.

The journey to financial independence is unique to each person, but the principles remain the same: invest in yourself, build assets, focus on consistent growth, and stay true to your values. It's about believing that you deserve a life where money doesn't dictate your choices, where you have the freedom to pursue what matters most to you. It's about knowing that financial freedom isn't just a dream—it's a destination that you can reach with the right mindset, the right actions, and a commitment to learning along the way.

Achieving financial independence requires a fundamental change in how you think about your time and your money. We often grow up hearing that time is money, but in reality, time is far more valuable than money. You can always make more money, but you can't make more time. This is why it's so crucial to learn how to leverage your time in ways that create lasting financial benefits. When you understand how to make your money work for you, you're not just buying financial freedom—you're buying time.

Think about it this way: when you exchange your time for money in a traditional job, you're limited by the number of hours you can work. If you're working eight hours a day, that's it—there are no more hours left to earn money. But if you use those earnings to invest in assets that generate passive income, you're no longer limited by time. Your money continues to grow, even when you're spending time with family, working on a passion project, or simply resting.

This concept is at the heart of wealth-building, but many people are hesitant to take the first step because they feel like they don't have enough money to invest. The truth is, it's not about having a lot of money upfront; it's about creating habits that allow you to build wealth gradually. Even if you're starting with just $50 or $100, the habit of regularly investing is what will ultimately make the difference. It's about turning that habit into a discipline, where you consistently allocate a portion of your income towards investments, no matter how small.

Let's not overlook the importance of discipline here. Many people talk about wanting to be financially free, but when the time comes to cut back on expenses or invest in their future, they hesitate. They think that a new pair of shoes, the latest gadget, or a fancy dinner out won't make much of a difference. But over time, these little decisions compound, just like investments. Every dollar spent is a choice—a choice between instant gratification and future freedom. By choosing to invest those dollars instead of spending them, you're setting up your future self for success.

One of the most powerful tools you have at your disposal is your ability to save and invest automatically. Automation is a game-changer when it comes to building wealth because it takes the decision-making out of the equation. When you automate your investments, you're ensuring that you pay yourself first, before you have a chance to spend money on things that don't align with your long-term goals.

Imagine setting up an automatic transfer from your checking account to your investment account each month. You decide to invest $200 monthly into a diversified mutual fund or a Shariah-compliant stock portfolio. Because it's automatic, you don't have to think about it. It becomes just like any other bill you pay, but instead of draining your resources, this "bill" is helping you build wealth.

Automation also helps you stay disciplined during market fluctuations.

When the market drops, many investors panic and sell their investments, locking in their losses. But when you're investing automatically, you're buying more shares when prices are low, allowing you to take advantage of market downturns. Over time, this strategy can significantly increase the value of your portfolio as the market recovers. It's a way to remove the emotional element from investing, focusing instead on the long-term potential of your investments.

This is especially important when you're building a portfolio that aligns with your values. Shariah-compliant investments require you to avoid interest-based earnings, but there are plenty of opportunities that meet Islamic standards. Real estate, equity-based investments, and certain types of mutual funds can all provide returns while ensuring that your income remains Halal. By automating these investments, you're not just building wealth—you're building wealth in a way that aligns with your principles.

One common question that comes up when discussing financial independence is, "How do I balance saving for the future with enjoying life today?" After all, life is meant to be lived, and it's natural to want to enjoy the fruits of your labor. The key is to find a balance that allows you to live comfortably while still making sure that your future self is taken care of.

A good approach is to follow the 50/30/20 rule: allocate 50% of your income to needs (like rent, groceries, and bills), 30% to wants (like entertainment, dining out, and travel), and 20% to savings and investments. This way, you're not depriving yourself of the joys of today, but you're also ensuring that a portion of your income is working towards your future goals. You might adjust these percentages based on your lifestyle and financial goals, but the principle remains the same: save and invest intentionally, but don't forget to enjoy the journey.

The concept of balance is also deeply rooted in Islamic teachings. Islam encourages moderation in all aspects of life, including spending and saving. The Quran teaches us not to be wasteful but also not to hoard our wealth. Striking a balance allows you to live a fulfilling life while being mindful of your financial responsibilities. It's about using your wealth to improve your life and the lives of those around you without letting it become a source of pride or vanity.

It's important to remember that financial independence doesn't mean sacrificing every joy. It means making conscious choices about where your money goes, prioritizing long-term rewards over short-term pleasures. When you learn to find joy in the process of building your future, every sacrifice feels more like an investment than a loss.

As you continue to grow your income and investments, another aspect to consider is protecting your wealth. Building wealth is one thing, but protecting it is just as crucial. This involves thinking about insurance, creating a will, and having a solid plan for your financial legacy. While these topics might seem daunting or even uncomfortable, they are essential for ensuring that your hard-earned money continues to benefit you and your family for years to come.

One of the most important steps you can take is creating an emergency fund. This is a separate account with enough money to cover three to six months' worth of living expenses. It's your safety net, providing peace of mind in case of unexpected job loss, medical bills, or other emergencies. By having this fund in place, you won't have to dip into your investments or go into debt when life throws a curveball your way.

Insurance is another critical aspect of protecting your wealth. Whether it's health insurance, life insurance, or property insurance, having the right coverage ensures that you're not financially devastated by unforeseen events. While no one likes to think about worst-case scenarios, being prepared is an act of responsibility—one that protects you and those you care about.

Creating a will or a trust is also an important part of your financial plan. This ensures that your wealth is distributed according to your wishes and that your family is taken care of if something happens to you. It's not just about money—it's about providing for your loved ones and making sure they don't have to navigate a complicated legal process during a difficult time.

One of the most valuable lessons you can learn on the journey to financial independence is that it's not just about making more money—it's about managing the money you have wisely. Even if you're earning a high income, poor money management can leave you feeling like you're living paycheck to paycheck. This is why learning to budget, track your expenses, and prioritize your spending is so crucial.

Think of managing your finances like managing a business. A successful business knows where every dollar is coming from and where it's going. It plans for both short-term needs and long-term growth. You can apply the same principles to your personal finances by setting a budget that reflects your priorities and goals. This doesn't mean micromanaging every purchase; it means having a clear understanding of your financial picture so you can make informed decisions.

Start by categorizing your expenses into fixed costs (like rent, utilities, and insurance) and variable costs (like dining out, entertainment, and hobbies). Track these expenses for a few months to get a sense of where your money is going. This awareness alone can be eye-opening, helping you identify areas where you might be overspending or opportunities to save more.

But budgeting isn't just about cutting back; it's also about being intentional with your spending. It's okay to spend on things that bring you joy, as long as those expenditures align with your values and goals. The key is to make sure that you're not sacrificing your future for momentary pleasures. By being intentional, you create a balance that allows you to enjoy today while still preparing for tomorrow.

As you continue on your journey to financial independence, you'll likely encounter people who don't understand your vision. They might tell you that you're being too ambitious, that it's safer to stick with a stable job and avoid taking risks. They might question why you're spending time learning about investments or why you're choosing to save when you could be spending. But remember, this journey is yours to take, and your vision for financial freedom doesn't have to match anyone else's.

Criticism and doubt often come from a place of misunderstanding or fear. When you choose to break away from the traditional path, it can make others uncomfortable because it challenges their own beliefs about money and success. But the most successful people learn to tune out the noise and focus on their own goals. They understand that every great achievement requires stepping outside of the comfort zone, taking risks, and believing in possibilities that others might not see.

This doesn't mean you should ignore advice or reject feedback. On the contrary, it's wise to seek guidance from those who have walked the path before you, whether they are mentors, financial advisors, or successful peers. But it's also important to recognize when someone's advice is based on their own fears rather than your potential. Trust yourself and the process you're following.

Building financial independence is about having the courage to make your own decisions, even when they aren't popular. It's about staying true to your vision and not letting other people's limitations define what's possible for you. As long as you're making informed decisions and aligning your actions with your values, you're on the right path.

One of the most powerful lessons in the journey to financial independence is understanding the concept of opportunity cost. Every financial decision you make has a trade-off—choosing one path means forgoing another. Opportunity cost is the value of what you're giving up when you decide to spend money on something or when you choose not to invest it. Learning to weigh the opportunity cost of your decisions can have a profound impact on how you manage your money and time.

For example, let's say you decide to spend $1,000 on a new gadget that you've been eyeing for a while. That's one option, and there's nothing inherently wrong with enjoying the money you've earned. But if you consider the opportunity cost, you'll see that the same $1,000 could have been invested in a stock or mutual fund. If that investment averages a 7% annual return, in ten years, that $1,000 could grow to nearly $2,000. So, the real cost of buying that gadget isn't just the initial $1,000—it's also the future value of what that money could have grown into.

This isn't to say that you should never spend on things that bring you joy. Life is meant to be enjoyed, and part of financial freedom is the ability to spend on what matters to you. But understanding opportunity cost allows you to make those spending decisions more consciously. It helps you determine when it's worth splurging and when it might be better to invest that money into your future. The goal is to ensure that your financial choices align with both your short-term desires and your long-term vision.

Opportunity cost also applies to your time. Time spent watching TV or scrolling through social media is time that could be invested in learning a new skill, reading a book, or working on a side project that could generate income. This is not about eliminating leisure but about being mindful of how much time you dedicate to activities that don't add value to your life. Ask yourself: are your daily habits bringing you closer to your financial goals, or are they keeping you in the same place?

When you begin to see money as a tool rather than an end goal, you unlock a new perspective on what it means to be wealthy. True wealth isn't about how much money you have in the bank; it's about the freedom and choices that money can create for you. It's about having the ability to spend your time as you wish, whether that means traveling the world, spending more time with your loved ones, or pursuing a passion without worrying about how you'll pay the bills.

This shift in perspective is critical because it helps you focus on what you're truly working towards. If your goal is just to accumulate money for the sake of having it, you'll find that the process feels hollow. But if you see money as a way to achieve a greater purpose—whether that's financial security for your family, the ability to give to those in need, or the freedom to create without limitations—then every dollar you earn and invest has a meaning behind it.

For many, the pursuit of wealth can feel like a never-ending race. They keep working harder, chasing promotions, or expanding their businesses, hoping that the next milestone will bring satisfaction. But often, that satisfaction is short-lived because they haven't defined what "enough" means to them. Knowing what enough looks like for you is one of the most powerful ways to ensure that you're building a life that's balanced and fulfilling.

Islamic teachings remind us that while wealth is a blessing, it's also a test. We are encouraged to be grateful for what we have, to use our wealth to support others, and to avoid letting money become a source of arrogance or pride. Gratitude for what you have doesn't mean that you can't strive for more, but it keeps you grounded as you pursue your goals. It allows you to appreciate your progress while remaining humble and focused on using your blessings for good.

It's important to remember that building financial independence isn't about making sacrifices forever. It's about making strategic sacrifices now so that you can enjoy greater freedom later. This is why having a clear vision of your goals is so essential. What does financial freedom look like for you? Is it the ability to work on projects that excite you without worrying about money? Is it being able to support your family without stress or having the freedom to travel and explore the world? Knowing your "why" keeps you motivated when the journey feels challenging.

Your vision for financial freedom should be personal and specific. It's not enough to say, "I want to be rich." What does richness mean to you, and how will it change your life? Maybe it means having enough passive income to cover your living expenses, so you can spend your time volunteering or starting a passion project. Maybe it means being able to retire early and pursue hobbies that you've always dreamed of. Whatever it is, take the time to define it clearly, because your vision will guide every financial decision you make.

Setting clear goals allows you to measure your progress and adjust your strategies along the way. Without a clear goal, it's easy to get distracted by short-term desires or to lose sight of why you started in the first place. This is why vision boards, journaling, or even writing down your goals can be so powerful. When you have a tangible reminder of what you're working towards, it's easier to stay focused and make decisions that align with that vision.

Islamic principles also emphasize the importance of intention (Niyyah) in every action. When you set financial goals with a sincere intention to benefit yourself, your family, and your community, it adds a layer of purpose to your journey. You're not just building wealth for yourself; you're building a life that aligns with your values and contributes to the well-being of others. This intention can be a source of strength and motivation when the path to financial freedom feels uncertain.

Patience is often overlooked in the pursuit of financial independence, but it's one of the most powerful traits you can develop. Building wealth takes time, and it's easy to feel discouraged when progress is slow. But true wealth is built gradually, through small, consistent actions that add up over time. The key is to stay patient and trust the process, even when you don't see immediate results.

Think about planting a tree. When you first plant a seed, it looks like nothing is happening. You water it, you give it sunlight, but for weeks or months, it remains a small sprout. But beneath the surface, roots are growing, establishing a foundation that will support the tree as it grows taller and stronger. Your financial journey is much the same. The early stages might feel slow and uneventful, but the roots you're building—your knowledge, habits, and investments—are laying the foundation for future growth.

This is why it's so important to celebrate small wins. Maybe you've paid off a small debt, saved your first $1,000, or reached your first investment goal. These milestones may seem small in the grand scheme of things, but they're proof that you're moving in the right direction. Recognizing these wins keeps you motivated and reminds you that progress is being made, even when it feels slow.

It's also important to keep a long-term perspective, especially when it comes to investing. The stock market, real estate, and other investment vehicles all experience ups and downs. It's easy to panic during a market downturn and want to pull your money out. But the most successful investors understand that downturns are a normal part of the cycle. By staying invested and even buying more when prices are low, you position yourself to benefit when the market recovers.

Islam teaches us that patience (Sabr) is a virtue, and it's no different when applied to wealth-building. Patience doesn't mean sitting back and waiting—it means continuing to take action even when progress is slow. It's about having trust in Allah's plan while putting in the effort. This balance between effort and patience is what allows you to remain resilient, even when the journey feels challenging.

As you work towards financial independence, one of the most valuable skills you can develop is learning how to assess risk. Risk is a part of life, and it's certainly a part of investing. But the key to success isn't avoiding risk altogether—it's understanding which risks are worth taking and which ones are not. It's about being able to differentiate between calculated risks that have the potential for reward and reckless risks that could jeopardize your financial well-being.

For example, investing in a well-researched stock or real estate property is a calculated risk. It involves doing your homework, understanding the potential returns, and being prepared for the ups and downs of the market. On the other hand, putting all your money into a highly speculative cryptocurrency without understanding how it works is a reckless risk. While it might pay off for some, it's more akin to gambling than investing.

Understanding your own risk tolerance is crucial. Risk tolerance is your ability to withstand fluctuations in the value of your investments without panicking. Some people can handle the volatility of the stock market, knowing that the value of their investments may drop significantly before recovering. Others prefer the stability of bonds or real estate, even if the returns are more modest. Knowing your comfort level allows you to create an investment strategy that you can stick with for the long haul.

It's also wise to diversify your investments. Diversification means spreading your money across different types of investments, so you're not overly reliant on any one asset class. This could mean having a mix of stocks, real estate, bonds, and even investing in businesses. Diversification helps you manage risk because if one investment performs poorly, others can help balance out the losses.

Risk assessment isn't just about avoiding losses—it's about identifying opportunities. Every successful entrepreneur or investor has taken risks, but they've done so with a clear understanding of what's at stake. They've weighed the potential benefits against the potential downsides and made decisions that align with their long-term vision. This kind of strategic thinking allows you to take bold steps without putting your financial security at risk.

Building wealth is not just about learning how to manage money; it's also about learning how to manage yourself. Self-discipline is the foundation of any successful financial journey. It's the ability to stick to your goals, even when temptations and distractions are constantly pulling you in different directions. The reality is, there will always be things you want—new gadgets, trendy clothes, the latest entertainment options—but the discipline to say "not now" is what separates those who build wealth from those who live paycheck to paycheck.

Self-discipline doesn't mean depriving yourself of everything you enjoy. It means being mindful of your spending and making choices that reflect your values and priorities. It's about understanding the difference between needs and wants, and being honest with yourself about which category each expense falls into. For example, buying a reliable car that gets you to work is a need, while upgrading to the latest luxury model when your current car works perfectly fine might fall into the category of a want.

Developing self-discipline is like building a muscle—the more you practice it, the stronger it becomes. Start by creating small, manageable goals for yourself. Set a budget for discretionary spending each month and stick to it. If you have a goal to save or invest a certain amount, make it a non-negotiable part of your monthly routine. The more you practice making disciplined decisions, the easier it becomes to resist the urge to spend impulsively.

Islamic teachings place great emphasis on self-control and avoiding extravagance. The Quran advises believers to "eat and drink, but be not excessive. Indeed, He likes not those who commit excess" (Quran, 7:31). This principle can be applied to our financial lives as well. It's a reminder to live within our means, to avoid wastefulness, and to make choices that reflect our responsibility towards the blessings we've been given.

One of the most overlooked aspects of financial independence is the role of mental health in money management. Your mindset and emotional state play a huge role in how you handle financial challenges, make investment decisions, and even how you perceive money itself. If you view money as a source of stress, you're more likely to avoid thinking about it, which can lead to poor financial decisions. But if you see money as a tool that can bring freedom and security, you'll approach it with a mindset geared towards growth and opportunity.

Financial stress is a reality for many people, especially when they feel like they're living paycheck to paycheck or struggling to keep up with debt. It can be overwhelming to look at a mountain of bills or feel like no matter how hard you work, you're not making progress. This is why taking care of your mental well-being is just as important as taking care of your financial well-being. The two are deeply interconnected.

Practices like mindfulness, journaling, and even daily gratitude exercises can help you manage financial anxiety. When you focus on what you have, rather than what you lack, you create a mindset of abundance that allows you to see opportunities where others see obstacles. This doesn't mean ignoring your financial challenges—it means approaching them from a place of calm and confidence, rather than fear.

The concept of contentment (Qana'ah) in Islam is also relevant here. Being content doesn't mean you stop striving for better; it means you find peace with what Allah has provided while working towards your goals. It's a reminder that your worth isn't tied to the number in your bank account but to your character, your integrity, and your faith. A content heart is more likely to make wise financial decisions because it's not driven by envy, greed, or the need for external validation.

As you build your financial knowledge, one of the most important skills to develop is the ability to differentiate between good debt and bad debt. Not all debt is created equal, and understanding the difference can have a huge impact on your journey to financial freedom. Bad debt is typically consumer debt—credit card balances, personal loans, or payday loans that come with high-interest rates and offer little to no return on investment. This kind of debt drains your resources and makes it harder to build wealth.

Good debt, on the other hand, is debt that can potentially help you generate income or build an asset. This might include a mortgage for a rental property, a business loan to start or expand a business, or even a student loan that helps you acquire skills that increase your earning potential. Good debt is strategic—it's an investment in your future, and when managed correctly, it can help you achieve your financial goals faster.

However, it's crucial to approach debt with caution, especially from an Islamic perspective. Islam teaches that debt should be avoided whenever possible and that if one must take on debt, it should be repaid as soon as possible. The Quran and Hadith emphasize the importance of living within one's means and avoiding unnecessary financial burdens. This doesn't mean that all debt is inherently bad, but it does mean that taking on debt should never be done lightly. Always consider whether the debt you're taking on is truly necessary and whether it aligns with your financial goals.

If you do decide to take on debt, be strategic about how you use it and have a clear plan for repayment. This means understanding the terms of your loan, calculating the monthly payments, and making sure it fits into your budget. It's also wise to have an emergency fund in place before taking on new debt, so you're not caught off guard by unexpected expenses. This approach ensures that debt serves as a tool for growth rather than a trap that limits your options.

The journey to financial independence also involves understanding the value of your time. Many people underestimate how much time is worth, especially when they're in the habit of trading hours for dollars. But when you shift your mindset from simply earning an income to building wealth, you begin to see that your time is one of your most precious resources. The way you spend it can either contribute to your financial freedom or keep you stuck in a cycle of working just to pay the bills.

One of the most impactful shifts you can make is to start thinking about your time in terms of its return on investment (ROI). Consider the activities you engage in daily—are they helping you build skills, create value, or grow your income? Or are they simply taking up time without adding much to your life? This doesn't mean that every moment needs to be productive—rest and leisure are important—but it does mean being mindful of how you allocate your time.

For example, learning a new skill or building a side project might take time upfront, but the long-term benefits can be substantial. Skills like coding, graphic design, digital marketing, or even learning about investment strategies can increase your earning potential and open new doors. Contrast this with spending hours scrolling through social media or watching TV. While it might be enjoyable in the moment, it doesn't contribute to your long-term goals.

This shift in how you value your time can also lead to better decisions about your career. Many people stay in jobs that don't challenge them or help them grow because they're afraid of change. But sometimes, taking a risk and pursuing a new opportunity, even if it pays less initially, can be the key to unlocking a more fulfilling and lucrative path. When you see your time as an asset, you're more willing to invest it in ways that pay off in the long run.

One of the most powerful mindsets you can adopt on your journey to financial freedom is the idea of ownership. Ownership means taking full responsibility for your financial decisions, your mistakes, and your successes. It means understanding that, while external circumstances can influence your life, you ultimately have the power to shape your financial destiny through your choices.

Ownership is the difference between a victim mindset and an empowered mindset. A victim mindset looks for excuses and places blame—on the economy, on a lack of opportunities, or on past mistakes. An empowered mindset asks, "What can I do with what I have right now?" It focuses on finding solutions, learning from mistakes, and adapting to new challenges.

For example, let's say you've made financial mistakes in the past. Maybe you've racked up credit card debt or invested in a business that didn't pan out. It's easy to dwell on those mistakes and let them define your future. But taking ownership means acknowledging those mistakes, understanding why they happened, and creating a plan to move forward. It means turning those experiences into lessons that guide your future decisions, rather than letting them hold you back.

Ownership also means taking responsibility for your financial education. Many people feel overwhelmed by the complexity of investing or managing money, so they avoid learning about it altogether. But in the age of the internet, the resources you need to learn are more accessible than ever. From online courses to financial blogs and podcasts, there are countless ways to educate yourself without spending a fortune. Taking the time to learn empowers you to make informed decisions and gives you confidence in your ability to grow your wealth.

This mindset of ownership aligns with Islamic teachings about personal accountability. We are reminded in the Quran that every individual is accountable for their actions and that we should strive to make the most of the opportunities and resources that Allah has provided. Embracing this mindset means recognizing that your financial journey is a test and an opportunity to make choices that benefit you and those around you.

A common challenge that people face on the road to financial freedom is the fear of taking risks. Risk is often perceived as something negative—something that could lead to loss or failure. But in reality, risk is a necessary part of growth. Without taking risks, you remain in your comfort zone, doing the same things and getting the same results. It's only when you're willing to step outside of that comfort zone that you discover new possibilities and opportunities for success.

The key to overcoming this fear is learning how to manage and understand risk. Not all risks are equal, and some are worth taking, while others should be avoided. For example, starting a new business might be risky, but if you've done your research, developed a solid business plan, and built a support network, that risk is calculated. On the other hand, quitting your job without a backup plan or savings might be a reckless risk that could jeopardize your stability.

In the world of investing, understanding risk means knowing your own comfort level and making choices that align with it. A high-risk investment might have the potential for high returns, but if it keeps you up at night with worry, it's not worth it. Conversely, a low-risk investment might grow slowly, but if it allows you to sleep peacefully, it's a better fit for your long-term strategy. The goal is to find a balance between risk and reward that matches your financial goals and your peace of mind.

It's also helpful to reframe how you think about failure. Many people fear failure because they see it as a reflection of their worth. But failure is simply feedback—it's a way of learning what doesn't work so you can find what does. Every successful person has failed at something, but they used those failures as stepping stones to greater achievements. Embracing this mindset allows you to take risks with confidence, knowing that even if things don't go as planned, you're still moving forward.

The path to financial freedom isn't just about numbers and strategies; it's deeply rooted in the habits you build daily. Habits are the small actions that compound over time, shaping your financial reality. When you focus on building good financial habits, you're laying the foundation for long-term success. It's not the one-time actions but the consistent, daily choices that determine whether you'll achieve your goals or stay stuck in the cycle of just getting by.

Think about habits like regularly setting aside money for investments, reviewing your budget, or taking 10 minutes a day to read about financial literacy. These small actions might not seem like much, but over time, they add up to significant progress. The key is consistency. Just like brushing your teeth or exercising, your financial habits should become a part of your routine. When saving and investing become automatic, they no longer require as much mental energy, making it easier to stay on track even when life gets busy.

One powerful habit is automating your finances. By setting up automatic transfers to your savings or investment accounts, you remove the temptation to spend money before you've had a chance to invest it. It's a way of paying yourself first, ensuring that your financial goals are met before other expenses and distractions come into play. This habit helps you prioritize your future self over immediate wants and is a crucial step towards building wealth.

Another habit that can transform your financial life is tracking your spending. It's easy to lose track of where your money goes if you're not paying attention. Many people feel like they should have more money left over each month, but when they sit down and look at their expenses, they realize that small purchases—like a daily coffee or frequent takeout meals—are adding up. By tracking your spending, you gain a clear picture of your financial habits and can identify areas where you might need to cut back or adjust.

One of the most important habits for achieving financial freedom is setting regular financial goals. Just like you wouldn't go on a road trip without knowing your destination, you shouldn't navigate your financial life without clear goals. Financial goals give you a target to aim for, keeping you motivated and focused on what's important. Without them, it's easy to get sidetracked by unnecessary expenses or lose sight of the bigger picture.

Your financial goals should be specific, measurable, and realistic. Instead of saying, "I want to save more money," set a goal like, "I will save $5,000 for an emergency fund by the end of the year." This gives you a clear target and a timeline, making it easier to track your progress and stay accountable. You can set goals for different areas of your life, such as paying off debt, saving for a home, or investing in a retirement fund. The key is to break down each goal into smaller steps that you can work on consistently.

In Islam, the concept of setting goals is encouraged, as it aligns with the idea of being purposeful in our actions. The Prophet Muhammad (peace be upon him) taught us to strive for excellence in all that we do, and this applies to our financial lives as well. When you set clear goals and work towards them with intention, you're not just improving your financial situation—you're living with purpose and working towards a future that benefits both you and those around you.

Achieving your goals requires more than just writing them down; it requires a plan of action. This is where budgeting comes in. A budget is simply a plan for how you'll spend and save your money each month. It allows you to allocate your income towards your goals, ensuring that you're not spending more than you earn. Budgeting can sometimes feel restrictive, but it's actually the opposite—it gives you control over your money, allowing you to spend on what matters most while avoiding wasteful expenses.

One common mistake people make when they first start budgeting is trying to cut out all of their discretionary spending at once. This often leads to frustration and burnout, causing them to give up on their budget altogether. Instead, focus on making small, sustainable changes to your spending habits. For example, if you're used to eating out three times a week, try cutting back to once a week and cooking at home more often. Use the money you save to boost your emergency fund or add to your investment account.

It's also important to build some flexibility into your budget. Life is unpredictable, and unexpected expenses can arise at any time. A rigid budget that doesn't allow for adjustments can become a source of stress, leading you to abandon it when things don't go according to plan. Instead, set aside a small buffer in your budget for miscellaneous expenses. This gives you the freedom to adjust your spending as needed without feeling like you're breaking the rules.

Another key to successful budgeting is regular reviews. At the end of each month, take some time to look back at your spending and see how it aligned with your budget. Did you meet your savings goals? Were there any areas where you overspent? Use this information to make adjustments for the following month. This process helps you stay on track and ensures that your budget evolves with your changing needs and priorities.

In Islam, we are encouraged to practice moderation and avoid extravagance, as mentioned in the Quran: "And those who, when they spend, are neither extravagant nor miserly, but hold a medium way" (Quran, 25:67). This principle can guide us in our financial planning, reminding us to find balance between enjoying our wealth and saving for the future. A well-balanced budget allows us to live comfortably while being mindful of our responsibilities.

A critical aspect of building wealth is understanding the power of compounding. Compounding is often described as the "eighth wonder of the world" because of its ability to turn small, consistent contributions into substantial wealth over time. When you earn returns on your investments, and those returns are reinvested, they begin to generate their own returns. This process creates a snowball effect, where your money grows faster the longer you leave it invested.

For example, if you invest $1,000 at an annual return rate of 7%, after the first year, you'd have $1,070. In the second year, you earn 7% not just on the original $1,000 but also on the $70 you earned in the first year. This cycle continues, and over the years, your investment grows exponentially. This is why starting early is one of the most important factors in building wealth. Even if you can only invest small amounts at the beginning, the time you give your investments to grow can make a huge difference in the end.

Compounding isn't limited to money—it also applies to knowledge. The more you learn about investing, personal finance, and wealth-building, the more you can apply that knowledge to make smarter decisions. Reading books, taking courses, and learning from mentors all contribute to your growth, and over time, this knowledge compounds, making you a more informed and confident investor.

This principle is also reflected in the concept of continuous improvement, or "Tazkiyah" in Islamic teachings. Just as we strive to purify and improve our character and spiritual state, we can apply the same mindset to our financial lives. By consistently working towards improvement, even in small ways, we build a stronger foundation for the future.

Another important factor in building financial freedom is learning how to avoid lifestyle inflation. Lifestyle inflation happens when your expenses increase in proportion to your income. For example, if you get a raise at work and immediately upgrade to a more expensive apartment or buy a new car, you've allowed your standard of living to rise with your earnings. While there's nothing wrong with enjoying the fruits of your labor, lifestyle inflation can trap you in a cycle where, no matter how much you earn, you always feel like you're living paycheck to paycheck.

The key to avoiding lifestyle inflation is to focus on increasing your savings and investments as your income grows. Instead of letting your expenses grow alongside your earnings, maintain the same standard of living for a while and allocate the extra income towards building wealth. This approach allows you to make significant progress towards your financial goals without feeling deprived. Over time, as your investments grow, you'll have the freedom to upgrade your lifestyle without sacrificing your long-term security.

For example, let's say you receive a $5,000 bonus at work. Instead of using that money to buy a new TV or take an expensive vacation, you could invest it in a stock portfolio or put it towards paying off debt. These decisions may not provide immediate gratification, but they set you up for a stronger financial future. When you reach a point where your investments are generating significant returns, you can enjoy those luxuries without worrying about their impact on your overall financial health.

In Islamic teachings, we are reminded of the importance of moderation and not being wasteful. This applies not only to our spending habits but also to how we use the blessings we receive. By avoiding wasteful spending and focusing on building assets, we honor the resources that Allah has provided and ensure that we are prepared for whatever the future may bring.

One of the most overlooked aspects of building wealth is the role of community. Surrounding yourself with like-minded individuals who share your values and goals can be incredibly powerful. When you're around people who are also focused on financial independence, entrepreneurship, or investing, you're more likely to stay motivated and continue learning. A supportive community provides encouragement, accountability, and a space to share ideas and strategies.

This doesn't mean that you need to have friends who are all wealthy or successful. It means finding people who are committed to growth and who inspire you to become the best version of yourself. Whether it's a local investment club, an online community, or a small group of friends who meet regularly to discuss financial goals, having a network can keep you on track.

In addition to learning from others, a strong community also gives you the opportunity to give back. As you grow in your financial journey, you'll gain insights and experiences that can benefit those who are just starting out. Sharing what you've learned, offering mentorship, or even helping someone set up their first investment account are all ways to contribute to the success of others.

The Islamic concept of brotherhood and sisterhood (Ukhuwwah) emphasizes the importance of supporting one another in all aspects of life, including our financial well-being. When we share our knowledge and resources, we create a culture of empowerment that benefits everyone. The success of one person doesn't diminish the success of another—instead, it creates opportunities for growth and upliftment within the community.

Building a community around you also serves as a reminder that wealth isn't the end goal—it's a means to a greater purpose. It's a tool that allows you to make a positive impact, to create opportunities for others, and to build a legacy that goes beyond material wealth. When you see your financial success as a way to contribute to the well-being of others, you're more likely to remain grounded and focused on what truly matters.

Building wealth is as much about mastering your mindset as it is about mastering your money. One of the most significant mindset shifts you can make is moving from a scarcity mindset to an abundance mindset. A scarcity mindset is one that focuses on limitations—what you don't have, what's lacking, or what you might lose. This way of thinking can lead to fear-based decisions, like hoarding money or being afraid to invest in new opportunities because of the potential for loss.

An abundance mindset, on the other hand, is about seeing possibilities. It's about believing that opportunities are endless, that with the right effort and knowledge, you can create more value and generate more income. This doesn't mean ignoring risks or being overly optimistic; it means understanding that wealth isn't a zero-sum game. The success of others doesn't take away from your own potential for success. When you shift your focus from scarcity to abundance, you begin to see challenges as opportunities for growth.

This shift can change how you view money itself. Instead of seeing money as something that's difficult to obtain and easy to lose, you start seeing it as a tool that can work for you, create options, and open doors. This mindset makes it easier to invest, to take calculated risks, and to step outside of your comfort zone. It allows you to see money not as an end in itself but as a means to achieving the life you envision—a life where you have the freedom to spend your time in ways that are meaningful to you.

Islam teaches us about trust in Allah (Tawakkul) and understanding that sustenance (Rizq) comes from Him. Adopting an abundance mindset doesn't mean abandoning hard work or planning; it means recognizing that with every effort you make, the ultimate provision comes from Allah. This trust allows you to take steps towards financial growth without being paralyzed by fear. It's a balance between taking action and having faith that your efforts will be blessed in ways that may not always be immediately visible.

Another critical aspect of building an abundance mindset is practicing generosity. It may seem counterintuitive to give away money when you're focused on building wealth, but generosity has a unique way of shifting your perspective on abundance. When you give, whether it's through charity (Sadaqah), helping a friend in need, or supporting a cause you care about, you're reinforcing the belief that there is always enough. You're telling yourself that your wealth isn't something to be clung to out of fear, but rather something that can be shared and multiplied.

Generosity creates a positive cycle in your life. When you give with a sincere heart, you often find that blessings come back to you in unexpected ways. This doesn't mean that we give with the expectation of receiving more in return, but it's a reminder that generosity enriches both the giver and the receiver. It allows you to experience the joy of making a difference, which can be far more rewarding than any material possession.

From an Islamic perspective, giving is not just encouraged; it's a duty. The concept of Zakat—one of the Five Pillars of Islam—requires Muslims to give a portion of their wealth to those in need. This practice not only purifies your wealth but also serves as a reminder that everything you have is a trust from Allah, and it's your responsibility to use it in ways that benefit others. Beyond Zakat, voluntary charity (Sadaqah) allows you to continue giving as a way to express gratitude and to support the well-being of your community.

Generosity also shifts your focus away from materialism. When you prioritize helping others over acquiring more possessions, you become less concerned with keeping up with appearances or competing with others. Instead, you focus on building a life that feels rich on the inside—one that's defined by meaningful relationships, a sense of purpose, and the satisfaction that comes from making a positive impact.

As you continue to build wealth, it's essential to remember that financial success is about more than just accumulating money. It's about achieving balance in your life—between work and rest, between earning and giving, between ambition and contentment. This balance allows you to enjoy the journey rather than constantly striving for the next milestone, always chasing the next goal without ever taking a moment to appreciate what you've achieved.

In a world that constantly pushes for more—more income, more possessions, more recognition—it's easy to fall into the trap of thinking that success means never being satisfied. But true success comes from knowing when to push forward and when to pause, reflect, and appreciate what you have. It's about recognizing that while financial freedom can provide security and opportunities, it's not the ultimate source of happiness.

Balance also means taking care of yourself. It's about understanding that your physical, emotional, and spiritual well-being are just as important as your financial well-being. When you neglect your health or allow stress to take over, it doesn't matter how much money you have—it's difficult to enjoy it. This is why practices like taking time for self-care, maintaining a regular prayer routine, and making time for activities that nourish your soul are so vital.

From an Islamic standpoint, balance is a core principle. The Quran teaches that Allah "has set the balance, so that you do not transgress in the balance" (Quran, 55:7-8). This applies not only to the natural world but to our lives as well. Striving for balance means seeking a life where you work hard to achieve your goals but also take time to rest, to reflect, and to appreciate the blessings that you've been given.

A balanced life also means finding joy in simplicity. In a world that glorifies luxury and materialism, simplicity can be a radical act. It's about finding happiness in the little things—enjoying time with family, appreciating a beautiful sunset, or finding contentment in a home-cooked meal. When you learn to appreciate the simple joys of life, you realize that wealth isn't just about what you own; it's about how you experience the world around you.

Simplicity allows you to avoid the constant pressure of comparison. It frees you from the need to always have the latest gadgets, the biggest house, or the flashiest car. Instead, it lets you focus on what truly matters: your relationships, your faith, and your well-being. Simplicity doesn't mean living with less than you need—it means living with enough and being content with it.

Living simply can also have a direct impact on your finances. When you're content with what you have, you're less likely to overspend or fall into the trap of lifestyle inflation. You become more mindful of where your money goes, choosing to spend on experiences or investments that bring long-term value rather than short-term satisfaction. This doesn't mean you can't treat yourself to nice things; it just means that those treats are a choice rather than a habit.

The Prophet Muhammad (peace be upon him) lived a life of simplicity, even when he had the means to live luxuriously. His example teaches us that true richness lies in the heart, in being satisfied with what Allah has provided. This mindset helps us remain grounded, even as we strive for financial growth. It reminds us that while it's okay to enjoy the blessings of this world, we should never lose sight of our greater purpose.

Another crucial aspect of the journey to financial freedom is resilience. Resilience is the ability to bounce back from setbacks, to keep moving forward even when things don't go as planned. The road to financial independence is rarely a straight line—it's full of ups and downs, market fluctuations, unexpected expenses, and personal challenges. But resilience allows you to face these obstacles without giving up on your goals.

Financial resilience means having a plan for tough times. This might include building an emergency fund, diversifying your income sources, or maintaining a side hustle that can provide a cushion during economic downturns. It's about preparing for the worst while hoping for the best, knowing that life's uncertainties don't have to derail your progress.

But resilience isn't just about having a backup plan—it's also about your mindset. It's about being able to see failures as temporary setbacks rather than permanent defeats. It's about learning from your mistakes and using them as stepping stones to future success. When you adopt a mindset of resilience, you stop fearing failure and start seeing it as a natural part of growth.

In Islam, the concept of patience (Sabr) is closely tied to resilience. We are reminded that trials and challenges are a part of life, and that with every hardship comes ease (Quran, 94:6). This belief gives us the strength to persevere, knowing that no struggle is permanent and that every effort we make is seen and rewarded by Allah. Resilience is not about never feeling discouraged—it's about finding the strength to continue, trusting that your efforts will bear fruit in the right time.

As you build your financial resilience, it's also important to surround yourself with a support system. No one achieves financial freedom alone. Having people around you who believe in your vision, who encourage you when you're feeling down, and who hold you accountable can make all the difference. This support might come from friends, family, mentors, or even online communities of like-minded individuals.

A support system provides more than just encouragement—it offers perspective. When you're faced with a difficult decision or feeling uncertain about the next step, having trusted people to talk to can help you see things from a new angle. They might offer insights you hadn't considered or share their own experiences, helping you navigate your challenges with more clarity.

This is also where mentorship becomes invaluable. Finding a mentor who has already walked the path you're on can save you time and prevent costly mistakes. A mentor can provide guidance, share their knowledge, and help you stay focused on your long-term vision. Look for someone whose values align with yours and who is genuinely interested in helping you grow. A good mentor is not just a source of knowledge—they're a source of inspiration.

Supporting others on their journey is just as important. As you gain knowledge and experience, you'll have the opportunity to mentor others, to share what you've learned, and to help them avoid the pitfalls you've encountered. This is a way of giving back, of using your success to lift others up. It's a reminder that wealth is not just about what you have, but about what you're able to give.

The journey to financial independence is a marathon, not a sprint. It requires patience, dedication, and the willingness to adapt as you go. But above all, it requires a commitment to keep learning, to keep growing, and to stay true to the vision you've set for yourself. Every day, you have the opportunity to take one more step towards the life you want to create—whether that's by learning a new skill, making a small investment, or simply adjusting your mindset.

Remember, financial freedom is about creating a life where money is no longer a source of stress or limitation. It's about having the freedom to make choices that align with your values, to spend time with the people you love, and to pursue the things that bring you joy. It's about building a life that feels rich not just in terms of dollars but in terms of fulfillment, peace, and purpose.

When you focus on making your money work for you, you're not just changing your financial situation—you're changing your entire approach to life. You're taking control of your time, your future, and your potential. This journey won't always be easy, but it will be worth it. Every decision you make today, every habit you build, and every lesson you learn is bringing you closer to a life of true freedom. And that is a life worth striving for.

CHAPTER 2: UNDERSTANDING FINANCIAL LITERACY—THE REAL WEALTH

Financial literacy isn't just about crunching numbers or knowing how to balance a budget—it's about mastering a mindset that empowers you to control your money instead of letting money control you. Too often, people overlook the importance of financial literacy, thinking it's something they can learn later, or they assume it's only for those working in finance. But the reality is, financial literacy is a life skill, just like knowing how to read or write. It affects everything from the decisions you make today to the kind of life you'll be able to build for yourself and your family.

Imagine this: you have a decent job, you're earning more than enough to cover your expenses, and you feel like you're doing well financially. But at the end of each month, you find yourself wondering where all your money went. You don't have savings, your credit card bill is piling up, and there's no plan for the future. This is the reality for many people who haven't learned the basics of financial literacy. They may earn well, but without understanding how money works, they're unable to keep it, grow it, or use it in a way that serves their long-term interests.

Financial literacy involves understanding concepts like saving, investing, budgeting, and managing debt. It means knowing how to evaluate financial products like loans and insurance, understanding how interest works, and being aware of how to avoid common money traps. It's not just about being able to add up numbers—it's about making decisions that align with your goals, understanding the risks and rewards, and having a vision for where you want your money to take you.

This is why financial literacy is often considered the first step towards financial independence. It gives you the knowledge and confidence to make smart choices with your money. It's not just for the wealthy or for those working in business—it's for anyone who wants to achieve stability, peace of mind, and the ability to live life on their own terms. It's about being able to read between the lines when you're offered a loan or understanding the long-term impact of paying only the minimum on your credit card balance.

Learning about financial literacy isn't just about knowing what to do; it's about unlearning the misconceptions and myths that hold us back. Many of us grew up with the belief that debt is just a part of life, that living paycheck to paycheck is normal, or that only the rich can afford to invest. These beliefs can become self-fulfilling, keeping us stuck in cycles of financial struggle because we don't believe there's another way.

One of the most damaging myths is the idea that talking about money is somehow taboo. In many families, money is a subject that's rarely discussed openly. This silence creates a culture where people are embarrassed to ask questions, admit when they don't know something, or seek advice. But the truth is, the only way to improve your financial situation is to be willing to talk about it, learn about it, and make it a priority in your life. The more you educate yourself, the more confident you become in making decisions that impact your financial future.

Financial literacy also involves understanding the impact of interest, both when it's working for you and when it's working against you. This concept is especially important for Muslims, as interest (Riba) is prohibited in Islam. Understanding how interest works can help you navigate financial systems without falling into traps that conflict with your values. For example, knowing how compound interest works can show you why it's important to pay off debt quickly and avoid high-interest loans, but it can also help you appreciate the benefits of investing in Shariah-compliant options where your money can grow ethically.

Financial literacy isn't just about numbers—it's about your relationship with money. It's about being aware of the habits, emotions, and attitudes that shape how you earn, save, and spend. When you begin to understand these factors, you gain the power to change them. You can start making choices that align with your long-term vision rather than reacting to every financial challenge that comes your way.

One of the first steps towards building financial literacy is understanding how to budget effectively. A budget is like a blueprint for your finances—it shows you where your money is coming from, where it's going, and how much you have left to work with. But budgeting isn't just about tracking expenses; it's about aligning your spending with your values and goals. It's about making sure that your money is being used in a way that reflects what's truly important to you.

For example, let's say one of your goals is to save enough money for a down payment on a home. A budget can help you identify areas where you might be overspending—maybe it's eating out, streaming subscriptions, or impulse purchases. By reallocating those funds towards your savings goal, you're taking control of your money instead of letting it slip through your fingers. This doesn't mean you have to cut out all the things you enjoy—it means finding a balance that allows you to enjoy life today while planning for a better tomorrow.

Creating a budget can be as simple or as detailed as you like. Some people prefer to categorize every single expense, while others focus on the big picture. The most important thing is that your budget works for you and that it helps you stay mindful of where your money is going. It's not about restricting yourself—it's about being intentional with your spending so that you can reach your goals faster.

For Muslims, budgeting also involves planning for obligatory expenses like Zakat and ensuring that your spending is in line with Islamic principles. This means avoiding wastefulness, being mindful of the rights of others, and using your resources to support your family and community. Budgeting is a way of fulfilling the Islamic principle of moderation, ensuring that we neither fall into extravagance nor become miserly with what we have.

Beyond budgeting, another crucial aspect of financial literacy is understanding credit. Credit plays a major role in our modern financial system, and it affects everything from your ability to rent an apartment to the interest rates you'll pay on loans. But many people don't fully understand how credit works, leading to mistakes that can be costly in the long run.

Your credit score is a reflection of how you've handled debt in the past. It's a number that lenders use to determine how risky it is to lend you money. A high credit score can make it easier to qualify for loans and can lower the interest rates you'll pay, while a low credit score can make borrowing more expensive. Understanding what factors affect your credit score—like payment history, credit utilization, and the length of your credit history—can help you take control of your credit and use it to your advantage.

But credit isn't just about your score; it's about understanding when and how to use it. One of the biggest pitfalls people face is using credit cards as a way to fund a lifestyle they can't afford. It's easy to swipe a card without thinking about the interest that will accumulate if you don't pay off the balance each month. Before you know it, you're stuck in a cycle of debt, paying interest on things that have long since lost their value. This is why it's crucial to understand the real cost of credit and to use it only when it serves a specific purpose.

There are ways to use credit responsibly that can actually support your financial goals. For instance, using a credit card to pay for expenses you would have paid for anyway—like groceries or gas—can help you build a positive credit history, as long as you pay off the balance in full each month. This way, you're using credit as a tool to strengthen your financial position rather than allowing it to become a burden.

Debt is another area where financial literacy is essential. Not all debt is bad, but understanding the difference between productive and unproductive debt can help you make smarter choices. Productive debt is debt that helps you acquire an asset or increase your income, such as a mortgage for a rental property or a student loan that increases your earning potential. Unproductive debt, on the other hand, is debt that doesn't provide any return and often comes with high interest rates, like credit card balances or payday loans.

Paying off debt can be one of the most powerful steps you can take towards financial freedom, but it's important to have a strategy. Two popular methods for paying off debt are the debt snowball method and the debt avalanche method. The debt snowball method involves paying off your smallest debts first, giving you a sense of accomplishment that can motivate you to tackle larger debts. The debt avalanche method focuses on paying off debts with the highest interest rates first, which saves you more money in the long run. Both methods have their advantages, and the right choice depends on your personality and financial situation.

In Islam, there is a strong emphasis on paying off debts promptly. The Prophet Muhammad (peace be upon him) warned against delaying the repayment of debts when one has the means to do so. Being free of debt not only reduces stress but also allows you to use your resources more freely for investments, savings, and charitable giving. It's about being able to focus on building a better future without the burden of past financial obligations weighing you down.

Understanding the impact of interest on debt is also crucial, especially for Muslims. Interest-bearing loans can quickly become unmanageable due to compound interest, making it difficult to escape the cycle of debt. This is why it's important to seek out alternatives, like interest-free financing options or Shariah-compliant loans. Financial literacy can help you navigate these choices with confidence, ensuring that your financial decisions are aligned with your values.

Investing is another cornerstone of financial literacy, and it's one of the most effective ways to build wealth over time. But for many people, the world of investing can seem intimidating and complex. It's easy to feel overwhelmed by terms like stocks, bonds, mutual funds, and ETFs, or to be unsure about where to start. But the truth is, investing doesn't have to be complicated. With a little knowledge and the right mindset, anyone can become an investor.

At its core, investing is about putting your money into assets that have the potential to grow in value over time. This could be anything from stocks and real estate to starting a business or buying an index fund. The goal is to make your money work for you by generating returns that exceed what you could earn from a regular savings account. When you invest wisely, you're building a portfolio that can grow and compound, providing you with a source of passive income that can support your financial goals.

One of the first things to understand about investing is the concept of risk and reward. All investments come with some level of risk—the potential that you could lose money. But generally, investments that have higher potential returns also come with higher risks. Stocks, for example, tend to offer higher returns over the long term, but they can be volatile in the short term. Bonds, on the other hand, are usually more stable but offer lower returns. Understanding your own risk tolerance can help you build a portfolio that you're comfortable with and that aligns with your goals.

For Muslims, ethical investing is especially important. Shariah-compliant investing involves selecting investments that adhere to Islamic principles, such as avoiding companies that engage in prohibited activities (like alcohol or gambling) and avoiding investments that involve interest. There are mutual funds and ETFs that are specifically designed to meet these criteria, allowing Muslims to invest in a way that aligns with their beliefs while still building wealth.

One of the most powerful concepts in investing is diversification. Diversification means spreading your investments across different asset classes to reduce risk. Think of it like planting a variety of crops rather than just one—if one crop fails, the others can still provide a harvest. In the world of investing, this could mean having a mix of stocks, bonds, real estate, and other assets in your portfolio. Diversification helps protect your portfolio from market volatility because the different assets tend to perform differently under varying market conditions.

For example, when stock markets are down, bonds or real estate might hold their value or even increase, balancing out the losses from stocks. This doesn't eliminate risk entirely, but it helps manage it, providing a smoother path for your investments to grow over time. The key is to build a portfolio that aligns with your financial goals, risk tolerance, and investment horizon.

Another aspect of smart investing is understanding the difference between active and passive investment strategies. Active investing involves buying and selling stocks, trying to time the market, and selecting individual stocks that are expected to perform well. This approach requires a lot of time, research, and a willingness to take risks. Passive investing, on the other hand, is about buying into broad market indexes or funds and holding them for the long term. It's based on the belief that, over time, the market as a whole will rise, and by investing in a diversified portfolio, you can benefit from that growth without constantly managing your investments.

Passive investing is particularly popular with those who are just starting out because it doesn't require deep expertise or constant monitoring of the markets. Index funds and exchange-traded funds (ETFs) are common tools for passive investors, allowing them to buy into a broad range of stocks or bonds with a single investment. This can be an excellent way to gain exposure to the market while keeping costs low, as index funds often have lower fees than actively managed mutual funds.

Understanding the power of compounding is crucial when it comes to investing. Compounding is the process where the returns on your investments generate their own returns, creating exponential growth over time. It's often said that compounding is the most powerful force in the financial world because it allows small investments to grow into substantial sums over the years. The longer your money stays invested, the more it can compound, making time one of your most valuable assets.

To illustrate, imagine investing $1,000 in an index fund with an average annual return of 7%. After one year, you'd have $1,070. In the second year, you'd earn 7% not just on the original $1,000 but also on the $70 you gained in the first year. Over decades, this effect can lead to significant growth, especially if you're consistently adding to your investments. This is why starting early, even with small amounts, can have a huge impact on your financial future.

Compounding isn't just about returns; it's also about reinvesting dividends. When a company makes a profit, it often pays a portion of that profit to shareholders in the form of dividends. Instead of taking these dividends as cash, you can choose to reinvest them back into purchasing more shares of the stock. This reinvestment can help boost the compounding effect, as you're using the returns generated by your investments to buy more assets, which in turn generate even more returns.

The magic of compounding underscores the importance of patience in investing. Many people get discouraged when they don't see immediate returns and are tempted to pull their money out when the market dips. But those who understand compounding know that the real gains often come in the later years, as the snowball effect of growth kicks in. This is why staying the course, even during market downturns, can be so rewarding.

A critical aspect of financial literacy is knowing how to protect your wealth once you start building it. Protecting your wealth means having strategies in place to safeguard your assets from risks like market downturns, inflation, and unexpected life events. One of the most basic ways to protect your wealth is through an emergency fund. An emergency fund is a stash of money set aside to cover unexpected expenses, such as medical bills, car repairs, or a sudden loss of income.

Financial experts often recommend having three to six months' worth of living expenses saved in an easily accessible account. This money acts as a financial cushion, allowing you to handle emergencies without having to dip into your investments or go into debt. The peace of mind that comes from having an emergency fund can't be overstated—it allows you to focus on your long-term goals without the constant worry of being derailed by unexpected expenses.

Another important aspect of protecting your wealth is insurance. Insurance isn't about getting something for nothing—it's about managing risk. It's a way to transfer the financial burden of a major loss to an insurance company in exchange for a premium. Types of insurance that are crucial for financial stability include health insurance, life insurance, and property insurance. Health insurance ensures that a medical emergency doesn't wipe out your savings, while life insurance provides financial security for your family if something happens to you. Property insurance protects your home or other valuable assets from damage or loss.

When choosing insurance, it's important to understand the terms and conditions, so you know what is and isn't covered. Not all policies are created equal, and some may have exclusions or limits that could leave you unprotected when you need it most. Taking the time to review your coverage ensures that you're not paying for insurance you don't need while making sure you're protected in areas where it matters most.

Taxes are another area where financial literacy plays a crucial role. Understanding how taxes work can help you make smarter financial decisions, keep more of what you earn, and avoid costly mistakes. Taxes affect almost every aspect of your financial life—from your income and investments to the purchases you make and the property you own. Learning how to manage your taxes efficiently can save you a significant amount of money over time.

One way to reduce your tax burden is through tax-advantaged accounts like retirement savings accounts. These accounts allow you to invest money before it's taxed, letting it grow tax-free until you withdraw it in retirement. This can provide a double benefit—helping you save for the future while reducing your taxable income today. Examples of tax-advantaged accounts include traditional retirement accounts, which allow you to defer taxes until withdrawal, and Roth accounts, where contributions are made with after-tax dollars, but withdrawals are tax-free.

Another important concept to understand is capital gains tax. When you sell an investment like a stock or real estate for a profit, that profit is considered a capital gain, and it's subject to taxes. The rate at which you're taxed depends on how long you held the asset before selling it. Short-term capital gains, from assets held for less than a year, are usually taxed at a higher rate than long-term capital gains. This means that holding investments for a longer period can be more tax-efficient.

Tax planning isn't just about paying less tax—it's about making decisions that align with your overall financial goals. For example, knowing that a large withdrawal from an investment account could push you into a higher tax bracket might encourage you to spread out withdrawals over several years. Similarly, understanding tax deductions and credits can help you maximize your savings when filing your taxes each year.

One of the most empowering aspects of financial literacy is learning how to assess investment opportunities. The world is full of investment options, from traditional assets like stocks and bonds to alternative investments like real estate and digital currencies. Each of these options has its own risks, potential rewards, and considerations. By understanding how to evaluate these opportunities, you can make decisions that align with your risk tolerance and financial goals.

When assessing an investment, one of the first things to consider is its risk-reward profile. Every investment has a level of risk associated with it, and understanding that risk is essential before making a commitment. Stocks, for example, can offer higher returns than bonds, but they also come with greater volatility. Real estate can provide steady cash flow through rental income, but it requires more upfront capital and ongoing management. The key is to balance higher-risk investments with more stable options, creating a portfolio that can weather different market conditions.

It's also important to understand the concept of liquidity—how quickly you can convert an investment into cash without affecting its value. Stocks and bonds are generally considered liquid because they can be sold relatively quickly on exchanges. Real estate, on the other hand, is less liquid because selling a property can take time and may involve significant transaction costs. Understanding liquidity is important when building a portfolio, especially if you anticipate needing access to cash in the near future.

Another factor to consider is the time horizon of your investment. Short-term investments are those you expect to cash out within a few years, while long-term investments are those you plan to hold for five, ten, or even twenty years. Your time horizon affects the types of investments that are suitable for you. Long-term investments have more time to recover from market downturns, making them better suited for higher-risk assets like stocks, while short-term goals may be better served by more stable investments like bonds or money market funds.

Diversifying your knowledge about different types of investments can help you make smarter choices, but it's also important to keep an eye on the broader economic environment. The state of the economy, changes in interest rates, inflation, and geopolitical events can all impact your investments, sometimes in ways that are difficult to predict. Staying informed about economic trends and understanding how they might affect different asset classes can give you an edge when making investment decisions.

For example, when interest rates rise, borrowing becomes more expensive, which can slow down economic growth and impact the stock market. At the same time, higher interest rates can make bonds more attractive, as new bonds will offer higher yields. Inflation, on the other hand, can erode the value of cash savings but may increase the value of tangible assets like real estate and commodities. Understanding these dynamics helps you anticipate changes and adjust your portfolio accordingly.

Another way to stay informed is by following market news and reading financial reports. While it's not necessary to become an expert in economics, having a basic understanding of key indicators like GDP growth, unemployment rates, and consumer confidence can help you make sense of market movements. This awareness allows you to make more informed decisions about when to buy or sell investments, which sectors to focus on, and how to position your portfolio for different market conditions.

Keeping a long-term perspective is crucial when navigating economic changes. The stock market has historically recovered from downturns, and the overall trend has been upward. Trying to time the market—buying low and selling high—can be extremely difficult, even for seasoned investors. Instead, focusing on the fundamentals of your investments and maintaining a diversified portfolio can help you weather the ups and downs of the market, allowing you to benefit from long-term growth.

One of the keys to financial success is understanding how inflation affects your money. Inflation is the gradual increase in prices over time, which means that the purchasing power of your money decreases as the cost of goods and services goes up. While inflation is a natural part of any economy, it can significantly impact your ability to save and invest for the future if you don't account for it in your financial planning.

For example, if you keep all your savings in a standard bank account that earns little to no interest, you might feel like you're protecting your money, but you're actually losing value each year due to inflation. Imagine that inflation is 3% per year, and your savings account offers an interest rate of 1%. Even though your account balance might technically grow, its real value—what you can buy with that money—actually decreases over time.

This is why investing is so important. By putting your money into assets that have the potential to grow faster than the rate of inflation, you can preserve and even increase your purchasing power. Stocks, real estate, and other assets with growth potential tend to outpace inflation over time, making them a crucial part of any long-term financial plan. The goal is to ensure that your investments are growing at a rate that keeps up with or surpasses inflation, so that your future wealth isn't eroded.

But investing to beat inflation isn't just about choosing high-growth assets. It's also about maintaining a balanced portfolio that matches your risk tolerance and time horizon. For example, younger investors might choose to have a higher proportion of their portfolio in stocks because they have time to recover from market downturns. As you get closer to your financial goals, such as retirement, you might shift towards more stable investments like bonds to protect the gains you've made.

Understanding inflation also helps you make better decisions when it comes to setting financial goals. Let's say you want to save enough money to buy a house or send your child to college in 10 years. It's important to account for how inflation might affect the cost of those goals over time. A house that costs $200,000 today might be significantly more expensive a decade from now, and the same goes for education costs, medical expenses, and other major purchases. By planning with inflation in mind, you can set more realistic savings targets and avoid being caught off guard when prices rise.

One strategy to protect against inflation is investing in assets that tend to do well when prices rise. Real estate, for example, often holds its value during inflationary periods because property prices and rents tend to increase as the cost of living goes up. Commodities like gold and silver can also serve as a hedge against inflation, as their value tends to rise when the purchasing power of currency decreases. Treasury inflation-protected securities (TIPS) are another option; these government bonds are designed to adjust with inflation, providing a safer way to preserve value over time.

Another way to outpace inflation is through investing in yourself. Increasing your skills and earning potential is one of the best ways to ensure that your income keeps up with or exceeds inflation. Whether it's gaining new certifications, learning new technologies, or expanding your professional network, investing in your human capital can pay dividends throughout your career. When your skills are in demand, you're in a better position to negotiate for higher pay, promotions, or new opportunities that can keep you ahead of rising costs.

Inflation can be a challenge, but it doesn't have to be a roadblock. With the right strategies, you can ensure that your money grows in a way that keeps up with the changing economic environment. The key is to stay informed, adapt to changes, and make financial decisions that prepare you for the future rather than just reacting to the present.

An important part of financial literacy is learning how to navigate the emotional side of money. Money is often tied to feelings of security, status, and self-worth, and these emotions can sometimes lead to irrational decisions. Understanding your emotional triggers when it comes to money can help you make better financial choices and avoid common pitfalls that can derail your progress.

For example, many people experience "lifestyle creep" when they start earning more money. As their income increases, so do their spending habits. They upgrade their cars, move to bigger homes, or spend more on luxuries. This is a natural response to having more disposable income, but it can be dangerous if left unchecked. Lifestyle creep can prevent you from building wealth because every time you earn more, you're spending just as much—or even more. Recognizing this tendency and making a conscious effort to maintain your standard of living, even as your income grows, can help you save and invest more for the future.

Fear is another common emotion that affects financial decisions. When the stock market takes a downturn, it's easy to panic and want to sell your investments to avoid further losses. This fear-based decision-making can be costly because it often means selling low and missing out on the market's recovery. History has shown that the market tends to recover over time, and those who stay invested during downturns often benefit from the subsequent upswings. Developing the discipline to stick to your investment strategy, even when emotions are running high, is key to long-term success.

On the flip side, greed can lead to taking on too much risk in the hopes of earning quick profits. This might involve putting all your money into a trendy stock or investing heavily in a single asset class without proper research. When driven by greed, it's easy to overlook the risks and focus solely on potential gains. A balanced approach involves recognizing the excitement of potential opportunities while maintaining a level-headed view of the risks involved.

Learning how to manage emotions around money is also about understanding the psychology of spending. Retailers and advertisers spend billions of dollars each year learning how to trigger your spending instincts. From sales tactics to creating a sense of urgency with limited-time offers, there are countless ways that companies try to convince you to part with your hard-earned cash. By becoming more aware of these tactics, you can make more deliberate choices about when and where you spend your money.

For example, have you ever noticed how many online stores use countdown timers to create a sense of urgency? They want you to feel like you'll miss out if you don't buy right now, pushing you to make a decision without taking the time to think it through. The same goes for special offers like "buy one, get one free" or "limited time discounts." While these deals can sometimes offer genuine savings, they can also lead to impulse purchases that you wouldn't have made otherwise.

To counteract this, try implementing a 24-hour rule before making major purchases. When you feel the urge to buy something, give yourself a full day to think it over. This cooling-off period can help you determine whether you truly need the item or if it's just a momentary impulse. Many people find that after waiting 24 hours, the desire to purchase fades, allowing them to make more thoughtful decisions.

Another way to manage spending habits is by focusing on experiences rather than things. Research has shown that spending on experiences—like travel, concerts, or even a nice dinner with friends—tends to bring more lasting happiness than buying material goods. This is because experiences create memories and connections that can enrich your life in ways that a new gadget or a piece of clothing never could. By prioritizing spending that aligns with your values, you can enjoy your money while still making progress towards your financial goals.

Understanding financial literacy also involves recognizing the role of gratitude in your financial journey. Gratitude might not seem like a financial principle at first glance, but it has a powerful impact on how you view and manage money. When you practice gratitude, you shift your focus away from what you lack and towards what you already have. This change in perspective can help reduce the urge to spend impulsively, as you become more content with what you possess.

Gratitude helps you recognize the abundance in your life, even if you're not yet where you want to be financially. It encourages you to appreciate the small wins—like paying off a credit card, saving a little more each month, or making progress towards your investment goals. This sense of appreciation can fuel your motivation to continue working towards financial freedom, helping you maintain a positive outlook even when the journey feels slow or challenging.

Gratitude can also improve your relationship with money by reducing feelings of envy or comparison. In a world where social media constantly showcases other people's lifestyles, it's easy to fall into the trap of comparing your financial situation to others'. But when you focus on gratitude, you're less likely to measure your success by someone else's standards. Instead, you learn to define success based on your own values and progress.

Incorporating gratitude into your daily routine can be simple. It might involve keeping a journal where you write down things you're thankful for, taking a few moments each day to reflect on the good in your life, or expressing appreciation to those who have helped you along the way. This habit doesn't just make you feel better—it can change the way you approach spending and saving, making you more mindful and intentional with your resources.

Building a strong financial future requires a commitment to lifelong learning. The world of finance is constantly evolving, with new investment opportunities, technologies, and economic trends emerging all the time. Staying informed and continuing to educate yourself is essential for making smart financial decisions and adapting to changes in the market.

One of the best ways to stay on top of financial trends is by reading books, listening to podcasts, and following credible financial news sources. There's a wealth of information available online, but it's important to distinguish between quality content and hype. Look for resources that focus on long-term principles rather than get-rich-quick schemes. Understanding the difference between solid financial advice and short-lived fads can help you avoid costly mistakes.

Attending workshops or taking online courses can also be a great way to deepen your knowledge. Whether you're learning about the basics of investing, understanding real estate markets, or diving into the nuances of tax strategies, there's always more to explore. The more you know, the more confident you'll become in navigating your financial journey. Knowledge empowers you to take control of your decisions, rather than relying on others to manage your money.

Learning from others' experiences is another valuable part of financial education. Seek out mentors who have achieved the kind of financial success you aspire to. Ask them about the mistakes they've made, the lessons they've learned, and the strategies that have worked for them. While everyone's journey is unique, hearing about the experiences of those who have been where you want to go can provide valuable insights and inspiration.

The pursuit of knowledge is not just about gaining more information; it's about building wisdom that allows you to make better choices. When you approach your finances with a mindset of curiosity and a willingness to learn, you're better equipped to handle the challenges that come your way. You become more adaptable, more resilient, and more capable of turning opportunities into lasting success.

One of the most powerful aspects of financial literacy is learning how to align your money with your values. It's easy to get caught up in the hustle and bustle of life, making financial decisions based on convenience or habit. But when you take the time to reflect on what truly matters to you, you can begin to make financial choices that support those priorities. This approach not only helps you feel more in control of your finances but also ensures that your money is being used in ways that bring you genuine satisfaction.

Start by thinking about your core values and what makes you feel fulfilled.

Is it the sense of security that comes from knowing you have a solid savings cushion? Is it the freedom to travel and experience new cultures? Or perhaps it's the ability to support causes and communities that are important to you? Understanding what drives you can help you identify where you want to allocate your resources and what you're willing to cut back on.

For example, if giving back to the community is one of your core values, you might decide to prioritize charitable donations or volunteer work over spending on luxury items. If family is a key priority, you might choose to invest in experiences that strengthen your bond with loved ones, such as family trips or quality time at home. Aligning your spending with your values helps ensure that each dollar you spend is contributing to the life you want to live.

Aligning money with values also extends to how you choose to invest. Investing isn't just about making a profit—it's also about supporting companies and industries that reflect your beliefs. For instance, you might choose to invest in sustainable businesses that prioritize environmental responsibility or support local enterprises that uplift the communities they serve. This approach, often referred to as socially responsible investing, allows you to grow your wealth while contributing to causes that matter to you.

Another aspect of aligning your money with your values is understanding the concept of opportunity cost. Every time you make a financial decision, you're also choosing what you're giving up. For example, when you spend money on a night out, you're giving up the opportunity to put that money towards your savings or an investment. When you choose to work extra hours, you might be sacrificing time that could have been spent with friends or family. Recognizing these trade-offs helps you make decisions that align more closely with your long-term goals.

Opportunity cost isn't about guilt—it's about being mindful. It's about asking yourself whether the decisions you're making today are moving you closer to or further from the life you envision. This doesn't mean you can't enjoy your money or treat yourself, but it does mean being aware of how those choices fit into the bigger picture. When you make financial decisions with this kind of awareness, you become more intentional with your spending and saving habits.

This awareness can also help you avoid common money traps. For instance, it's easy to justify small expenses like daily coffee runs or new clothes, thinking that they don't make much of a difference. But over time, these small purchases can add up, eating into your ability to save or invest. By considering the opportunity cost of those small expenses—like what that money could become if it were invested instead—you might find that you're more willing to make adjustments and focus on what truly matters.

When you align your money with your values and understand the opportunity costs of your decisions, you gain a sense of control over your finances that is both empowering and liberating. You're no longer at the mercy of marketing tactics or social pressures; instead, you're making decisions that feel right for you, driven by a clear sense of purpose.

One of the most challenging but rewarding aspects of financial literacy is learning how to set boundaries around money. Setting boundaries is about knowing when to say no, whether that's to yourself or to others. It means being able to decline an invitation to an expensive outing when it doesn't fit within your budget or turning down a loan request from a friend or relative when it would strain your finances. It's about recognizing that your financial well-being is a priority and that you have the right to protect it.

Setting boundaries doesn't mean being selfish or unkind—it means being realistic about what you can afford and what aligns with your goals. For many, it's difficult to say no because they fear disappointing others or being seen as stingy. But in reality, setting boundaries is one of the healthiest things you can do for your relationships and your financial future. It allows you to give and share when you genuinely can, without putting yourself in a position of stress or financial strain.

For example, if you have a monthly budget for entertainment and you've already reached your limit, it's okay to suggest a more affordable way to spend time with friends. If a family member asks for financial help, but you know that giving them the money would disrupt your savings goals, you might offer to help in other ways, like providing support or advice. These boundaries ensure that you're not constantly sacrificing your own financial stability for the sake of others' expectations.

Boundaries also extend to how you manage your time and energy around money. It's easy to get caught up in the endless pursuit of more—more money, more investments, more success. But sometimes, the best thing you can do for your financial well-being is to set limits on how much time you spend worrying about money. This might mean giving yourself permission to unplug from work, to enjoy time with loved ones, or to pursue hobbies that have nothing to do with your financial goals. These boundaries help ensure that your pursuit of wealth doesn't come at the cost of your well-being.

One of the most empowering shifts you can make in your financial journey is developing a mindset of abundance over scarcity. A scarcity mindset is rooted in the belief that there's never enough—enough money, enough opportunities, enough resources. It's a mindset that can lead to hoarding, excessive worrying, and a constant fear of missing out. An abundance mindset, on the other hand, believes that there are plenty of opportunities for everyone and that wealth is not a zero-sum game.

When you adopt an abundance mindset, you start seeing opportunities instead of obstacles. For example, instead of viewing a market downturn as a loss, you might see it as a chance to buy assets at a lower price. Instead of seeing someone else's success as a threat, you might see it as proof that achieving financial goals is possible. This perspective shift allows you to approach challenges with creativity and optimism, turning setbacks into stepping stones.

An abundance mindset also encourages generosity. When you believe that there is enough for everyone, you're more likely to share your knowledge, your time, and even your financial resources. This generosity creates a positive cycle in your life, where the act of giving opens up more opportunities for growth and connection. It's about trusting that what you put out into the world will come back to you, even if it's in unexpected ways.

Cultivating an abundance mindset takes time, especially if you've spent years thinking in terms of scarcity. It might involve changing the way you talk about money, focusing on gratitude for what you have rather than dwelling on what you lack, and seeking out stories of people who have overcome challenges to build lives of freedom and fulfillment. This mindset isn't about ignoring reality or pretending that challenges don't exist—it's about choosing to focus on what's possible and believing that your efforts will be rewarded.

Another essential skill in financial literacy is understanding how to negotiate. Negotiation isn't just for business deals—it's a life skill that can have a major impact on your financial situation. Whether you're negotiating a salary, the price of a car, or the terms of a contract, knowing how to advocate for yourself can save you money and open up new opportunities. But many people are uncomfortable with negotiation, either because they don't know where to start or because they fear rejection.

The first step in becoming a better negotiator is knowing your worth. When negotiating a salary, for example, it's important to research the market rate for your position and experience level. This gives you a clear understanding of what others in your field are earning, which allows you to make a case for why you deserve a certain salary. Confidence is key here—if you know that you bring value to the table, you're more likely to communicate that effectively during negotiations.

Negotiation also involves being willing to walk away when terms don't align with your goals. This can be difficult, especially when it comes to job offers or major purchases. But understanding that you have the power to say no gives you leverage. It allows you to hold out for opportunities that truly meet your needs and goals, rather than settling for less. This mindset shift can lead to better financial outcomes because you're not allowing fear or desperation to dictate your decisions.

The art of negotiation isn't just about getting what you want; it's about finding solutions that work for everyone involved. This means approaching negotiations with a win-win mindset, where both parties feel like they're getting a fair deal. It's about listening, understanding the other person's needs, and being willing to make compromises that still protect your interests. This approach not only leads to better financial outcomes but also helps build stronger relationships in both professional and personal settings.

Financial literacy also involves understanding the importance of networking and building relationships. The people you know and the connections you make can have a profound impact on your financial journey. Networking isn't just about advancing your career or finding new job opportunities—it's about creating a support system, learning from others, and discovering new possibilities for growth.

Effective networking starts with a genuine interest in others. It's not about handing out business cards or collecting contacts—it's about building meaningful relationships based on mutual respect and shared interests. This might mean taking the time to attend industry events, joining professional groups, or simply reaching out to people whose work you admire. The key is to approach networking with the mindset of giving rather than just looking for what you can gain.

For example, if you come across an article or opportunity that you think might benefit someone in your network, don't hesitate to share it with them. Small gestures like these build trust and show that you're invested in their success. Over time, these relationships can lead to opportunities you might never have discovered on your own—like job offers, investment advice, or partnerships that help you reach your goals faster.

Building a strong network also provides you with access to mentorship. Having a mentor who has already walked the path you're on can be incredibly valuable. They can offer insights, share their experiences, and help you avoid common mistakes. Mentors can provide encouragement when you're facing challenges and celebrate with you when you reach milestones. Finding the right mentor is about seeking someone whose values align with yours and who is genuinely interested in helping you grow.

Mentorship and networking aren't just about what you can gain—they're also about paying it forward. As you grow in your financial journey, you'll have the opportunity to mentor others and share what you've learned. This creates a ripple effect, where your success inspires others and contributes to a culture of growth and empowerment.

Another essential part of financial literacy is learning how to navigate major life transitions. These transitions can range from starting a new job, moving to a new city, getting married, having children, or even planning for retirement. Each of these milestones comes with financial implications that can either strengthen your financial position or strain your resources if not managed properly. Preparing for these moments in advance allows you to face them with confidence and ensures that your financial goals remain on track.

Starting with the basics, when transitioning to a new job, one of the most important financial decisions you'll make is negotiating your salary. Many people, especially early in their careers, underestimate the long-term impact of starting salary negotiations. A small difference in starting salary can compound over the years, affecting not just your annual income but your retirement savings, investment contributions, and overall financial trajectory. Negotiating doesn't just stop at salary; it's also important to consider benefits like health insurance, retirement contributions, and even flexibility in work arrangements. These perks may seem secondary to salary, but they can significantly affect your long-term financial well-being.

Getting married is another significant life event with major financial implications. When two people merge their lives, they also merge their financial situations. This requires open communication and planning. Couples need to discuss their financial goals, spending habits, and any debt they might be bringing into the relationship. One of the most important conversations to have is whether you'll combine your finances or keep them separate. Both approaches can work, but the key is to find a system that aligns with your shared goals and ensures transparency.

Financial transitions don't stop with getting married. If you're planning to have children, it's essential to start thinking about the costs associated with raising a family, from medical bills and childcare to education savings plans. Even if having children feels like a distant future goal, starting a college fund early can give your money time to grow through investments, making education more affordable in the long run. Additionally, having adequate life and health insurance ensures that your family is protected financially in case of unexpected events.

When it comes to planning for retirement, the key is to start as early as possible. The sooner you begin contributing to a retirement fund, the more time your money has to grow through compounding interest. Many people delay saving for retirement, thinking they can make up for lost time later. But in reality, the earlier you start, the less you have to save each month to reach your goals. Even if you're only able to contribute a small amount, the magic of compounding works in your favor, multiplying your savings over time.

Retirement planning involves more than just setting aside money in a savings account. It's important to invest those savings in vehicles that provide long-term growth, such as stocks, bonds, and retirement-specific accounts like IRAs or 401(k)s. These accounts offer tax advantages that can make a big difference in how much you're able to save. For example, contributions to a traditional IRA or 401(k) are often tax-deductible, meaning you pay less in taxes upfront, allowing more of your money to grow. Roth IRAs, on the other hand, offer tax-free withdrawals in retirement, making them a great option for those who anticipate being in a higher tax bracket later in life.

Retirement planning isn't just about money; it's also about lifestyle. One of the most overlooked aspects of retirement is understanding how you want to spend your time once you're no longer working full-time. Some people dream of traveling the world, while others want to focus on hobbies, volunteer work, or spending more time with family. Whatever your vision for retirement is, it's important to ensure that your financial plan aligns with it. This might mean adjusting your savings rate, investing more aggressively, or even considering part-time work during retirement to supplement your income.

Additionally, as you near retirement, you'll need to start thinking about how to convert your savings into a steady income stream. This could involve selling investments, withdrawing from retirement accounts, or purchasing annuities. It's essential to create a withdrawal strategy that ensures you don't outlive your savings, especially considering factors like inflation and unexpected medical expenses.

As you move through life's various stages, estate planning becomes another critical component of financial literacy. Estate planning is about more than just writing a will; it's about ensuring that your assets are managed and distributed according to your wishes after you're gone. This includes naming beneficiaries for your accounts, setting up trusts for your heirs, and appointing a power of attorney or health care proxy to make decisions on your behalf if you're unable to do so.

Many people avoid estate planning because it feels morbid or overwhelming, but failing to plan can leave your loved ones in a difficult position. Without a clear plan, the courts may decide how your assets are divided, which could lead to legal battles, delays, and additional costs for your family. Having a will in place is the first step in making sure your wishes are respected. It allows you to designate who will inherit your assets, appoint guardians for minor children, and specify how any remaining debts should be paid.

Trusts can also be a valuable tool in estate planning, especially if you want to protect your assets from probate or ensure that they are managed responsibly over time. For example, a trust can be set up to provide for a child's education or to care for a family member with special needs. Trusts offer flexibility and control over how your assets are used, even after you're no longer around to manage them yourself.

In addition to setting up a will or trust, it's essential to review and update your beneficiary designations regularly. These designations override what's written in your will, meaning that the individuals you list on accounts like life insurance policies or retirement plans will receive the assets directly, regardless of your will's contents. This is especially important if your circumstances change—such as after a marriage, divorce, or the birth of a child.

Another key component of estate planning is considering your end-of-life wishes and healthcare decisions. No one likes to think about these situations, but having a plan in place can provide peace of mind for both you and your loved ones. This might include creating a living will, which outlines the types of medical care you want to receive if you become incapacitated. You can also designate a healthcare proxy, someone who can make medical decisions on your behalf if you're unable to do so. These documents ensure that your wishes are followed and that your family doesn't have to make difficult decisions without guidance.

Estate planning is also an opportunity to think about your legacy and how you want to be remembered. For some, this might involve leaving a financial inheritance for future generations. For others, it could mean supporting causes or charities that are meaningful to you. Charitable giving can be incorporated into your estate plan through donations, establishing a charitable trust, or creating a foundation that supports causes you care about long after you're gone. This allows you to leave a lasting impact on the world while also potentially reducing estate taxes for your heirs.

While estate planning might seem complex, it doesn't have to be overwhelming. Working with an attorney who specializes in estate law can help ensure that your plan is thorough and legally sound. It's important to start the process early and to update your estate plan as your circumstances change. Whether you're just starting to accumulate assets or are nearing retirement, having a plan in place is an essential part of long-term financial security.

Estate planning is about protecting not just your financial assets but also your loved ones' emotional well-being. One of the most valuable gifts you can give your family is the peace of mind that comes with knowing everything is in order. This means that in addition to legal documents like wills and trusts, you should also create an organized system for all your financial accounts, insurance policies, and other important documents. Many families face confusion and stress when they don't know where to find critical information after a loved one passes away.

Consider creating a "legacy binder" or digital file where you keep all the important information your family will need, such as account numbers, passwords, the contact information for financial advisors and attorneys, and instructions for accessing safe deposit boxes or digital assets. Having all this information in one place can make the process much smoother for your loved ones during what is already an emotionally difficult time.

In addition to organizing your financial information, it's essential to have conversations with your family about your estate plan. While these conversations can be uncomfortable, they are necessary to ensure that everyone is on the same page and to avoid misunderstandings later. Being transparent about your wishes helps prevent conflicts and ensures that your loved ones know how to carry out your final plans. It's also an opportunity to explain your values and the reasoning behind your decisions, which can be especially important when it comes to charitable giving or dividing assets among heirs.

Estate planning isn't just about preparing for the end of life—it's about creating a legacy that reflects your values, protects your loved ones, and ensures that your hard-earned wealth is used in ways that matter to you. It's a process that evolves over time, just as your financial goals and family dynamics evolve. By taking the time to plan thoughtfully, you can leave a positive, lasting impact that extends far beyond your lifetime.

An often overlooked but critical aspect of financial literacy is protecting yourself against identity theft and fraud. In today's digital age, where more and more of our financial transactions and personal information are conducted online, the risk of having your identity stolen or falling victim to fraud is higher than ever. Being proactive about safeguarding your financial information is a key part of maintaining long-term security.

Identity theft occurs when someone uses your personal information—like your Social Security number, bank account details, or credit card information—without your permission to commit fraud. This can lead to unauthorized charges, drained bank accounts, or even loans taken out in your name. Resolving identity theft can be time-consuming and stressful, which is why prevention is so important.

One of the simplest ways to protect yourself is by regularly monitoring your bank and credit card statements. Keep an eye out for any transactions that you don't recognize, no matter how small. Thieves often start with small charges to see if they go unnoticed before moving on to larger purchases. Most banks and credit card companies offer alerts that can notify you of any unusual activity, giving you the chance to act quickly if something doesn't seem right.

Using strong, unique passwords for each of your financial accounts is another critical step. Avoid using easily guessed information, such as birthdays or common words. Consider using a password manager, which can create and store complex passwords for you. Additionally, enable two-factor authentication whenever it's available, as this adds an extra layer of security by requiring a second form of verification before accessing your accounts.

Another way to protect yourself is by being cautious about sharing personal information online. Be wary of phishing scams, which are fraudulent attempts to obtain sensitive information by pretending to be a trustworthy entity. These scams can come in the form of emails, text messages, or phone calls that appear to be from your bank, a government agency, or a well-known company. Always verify the identity of the sender before clicking on links or providing any personal information.

In today's world, another critical skill for financial literacy is understanding the power and pitfalls of credit. Credit is a tool that can either open doors or become a burden, depending on how it's used. While credit cards, loans, and financing options can offer a way to access opportunities like education or homeownership, they can also lead to a cycle of debt if not managed carefully. Knowing how to use credit wisely is a fundamental part of taking control of your financial future.

At its core, credit allows you to borrow money with the agreement that you will pay it back over time, often with interest. This can be incredibly useful when you need to make a significant purchase or cover an emergency expense. But the ease of access to credit can also make it tempting to spend money you don't have. This is why understanding interest rates is so crucial. Even a small interest rate can add up significantly over time, especially if you're only making minimum payments on credit card debt.

For instance, if you have a credit card balance of $1,000 with an interest rate of 18%, making only the minimum payment could mean paying hundreds of dollars in interest over the course of a few years. By paying more than the minimum each month, you can reduce the total interest paid and pay off the balance much sooner. This is why it's important to read the fine print before taking out any form of credit and to have a strategy for paying it back as quickly as possible.

Building a positive credit history is about more than just avoiding debt. It's about demonstrating that you can manage borrowed money responsibly. This involves paying bills on time, keeping your credit utilization low (ideally under 30% of your available credit), and not opening too many new credit accounts at once. A strong credit score can save you money in the long run, as it allows you to qualify for better interest rates on loans and mortgages, potentially saving you thousands over the life of a loan.

Another aspect of credit management is understanding the difference between good debt and bad debt. Good debt is debt that has the potential to increase your net worth or provide long-term benefits. This could include a mortgage on a home that appreciates in value, student loans that lead to higher earning potential, or a business loan that allows you to expand your entrepreneurial ventures. When managed properly, good debt can be a tool that helps you build wealth and achieve your financial goals.

Bad debt, on the other hand, is debt that doesn't offer a return on investment. This typically includes high-interest consumer debt, such as credit card balances, personal loans for discretionary spending, or financing for depreciating assets like cars and luxury items. While these purchases might bring temporary satisfaction, they can hinder your financial progress in the long run, as the interest paid on these debts takes away from money that could be used for savings or investments.

A key part of managing debt is knowing when to use credit and when to save up for a purchase instead. For example, while financing a home might make sense due to the potential for property appreciation, financing a vacation or new clothes might not be the best use of credit. By understanding the long term impact of debt on your financial health, you can make more strategic decisions about when to borrow and when to pay out of pocket.

One of the best strategies for avoiding the trap of bad debt is to build an emergency fund. Having a financial cushion allows you to handle unexpected expenses without relying on credit cards or loans. This can prevent you from accumulating debt that could take months or even years to pay off. An emergency fund acts as a buffer, giving you time to recover from financial setbacks without jeopardizing your long-term goals.

A significant part of financial literacy also involves learning how to save effectively. Saving is often thought of as the first step towards building wealth, but not all saving strategies are created equal. Understanding the difference between saving for short-term needs, like an upcoming vacation or a new appliance, and saving for long-term goals, like buying a house or retirement, can help you choose the right savings vehicles for your needs.

For short-term savings, a regular savings account or a high-yield savings account can be ideal. These accounts keep your money safe while earning a bit of interest, making them a good choice for goals that are a few months to a few years away. It's important to look for accounts with no fees and a competitive interest rate to ensure that your money is working as hard as possible for you.

For long-term goals, investing is often a more effective way to grow your savings. While investments come with risks, they also offer the potential for higher returns than a savings account. For example, putting your money in a diversified portfolio of stocks and bonds can help it grow significantly over a period of 10, 20, or even 30 years. This makes investing a powerful tool for goals like retirement, where the effects of compound growth can make a substantial difference.

Automating your savings can make the process easier. By setting up automatic transfers from your checking account to your savings or investment accounts, you ensure that you're consistently putting money away without having to think about it. This "set it and forget it" approach can help you build savings steadily over time, making it easier to reach your goals without feeling like you're sacrificing your lifestyle.

In addition to automating your savings, it's crucial to understand the role of inflation in your savings strategy. Inflation is the gradual increase in the cost of goods and services over time, which means that the value of money decreases as prices rise. If your savings are earning a lower interest rate than the rate of inflation, the purchasing power of your money is actually shrinking, even if the balance in your account is growing.

For example, if inflation is at 2% per year and your savings account earns 1% interest, the real value of your savings is decreasing. This is why it's important to balance your savings between safe, easily accessible accounts and investments that have the potential to outpace inflation. By doing so, you can ensure that your money retains its value over time, allowing you to reach your financial goals without being caught off guard by rising costs.

This understanding of inflation can also help you make better decisions when it comes to long-term financial planning. For instance, when saving for retirement, it's essential to account for how inflation will affect the cost of living in the future. What might seem like a comfortable retirement savings goal today could fall short decades from now if you don't account for rising prices. This is why many financial advisors recommend investing a portion of your retirement savings in assets that tend to appreciate over time, like stocks and real estate.

In addition to managing the impact of inflation, understanding how to protect your savings from unnecessary fees is also important. Many banks and financial institutions charge fees for everything from maintaining an account to making transfers. These fees might seem small, but over time, they can add up and eat away at your savings. Taking the time to shop around for fee-free accounts or negotiating with your bank can help you keep more of your hard-earned money.

As you develop your financial literacy, it's also important to understand the concept of building multiple streams of income. Relying solely on a single source of income, such as a full-time job, can leave you vulnerable if that income stream dries up. Building multiple streams of income allows you to diversify your earnings and create a financial safety net that can support you through changes in your career or economic downturns.

There are many ways to create additional income streams, and the right choice depends on your skills, interests, and available time. For some, this might mean starting a side business or freelancing in their field of expertise. For others, it could involve investing in dividend-paying stocks, rental properties, or starting an online store. The key is to choose income streams that align with your strengths and that you can manage alongside your primary job without burning out.

Building multiple streams of income isn't just about making more money—it's also about creating more freedom and flexibility in your life. When you have diverse income sources, you're not as dependent on any one job or client, which means you can afford to be more selective about the work you take on. This can lead to a better work-life balance and give you the freedom to pursue projects or opportunities that are more aligned with your passions and values.

Diversifying your income also means being prepared for periods when one income stream might slow down. For example, a freelancer might have periods with fewer clients or a rental property might have a vacancy. Having other income streams in place can help you ride out these slow periods without having to dip into your savings or take on debt. This approach provides stability, allowing you to focus on growth rather than constantly worrying about making ends meet.

Creating multiple streams of income also encourages you to think like an entrepreneur. Even if you have no intention of starting a full-time business, the mindset of an entrepreneur can help you spot opportunities, manage risks, and think creatively about how to add value to others. This might involve identifying skills or hobbies that could be turned into a profitable venture or learning about new markets that you could invest in.

For example, if you enjoy writing or creating content, you might consider starting a blog or a YouTube channel. While it takes time to build an audience, these platforms can eventually become sources of passive income through ad revenue, sponsorships, and affiliate marketing. Similarly, if you have a talent for photography, you might sell your photos online through stock photography websites. The key is to think beyond the traditional nine-to-five job and explore how your skills and passions can generate income in new ways.

Investing in real estate is another popular way to build multiple streams of income. Owning rental properties can provide a steady cash flow, as tenants pay rent each month. Real estate also offers the potential for appreciation, where the value of the property increases over time, allowing you to sell it for a profit in the future. However, being a landlord also comes with responsibilities like property maintenance, dealing with tenants, and managing expenses, so it's important to go into this venture with a clear understanding of the time and effort involved.

While it's tempting to focus solely on the most lucrative income opportunities, it's also important to choose options that align with your long-term goals and interests. Not every income stream needs to be directly tied to your day job or require a large initial investment. By focusing on what you enjoy and are good at, you can build income streams that feel rewarding and sustainable, allowing you to maintain a healthy balance between work and life.

Another critical skill in financial literacy is learning how to set financial goals that inspire and motivate you. Setting goals is about more than just deciding to save a certain amount or pay off debt—it's about creating a vision for the life you want and mapping out the steps to achieve it. Well-defined goals give you a sense of purpose and direction, turning abstract dreams into concrete actions that you can take every day.

When setting financial goals, it's important to be specific. Vague goals like "I want to be rich" or "I want to save more" don't provide a clear target to aim for. Instead, try setting goals that are specific, measurable, attainable, relevant, and time-bound (SMART). For example, instead of saying "I want to save money," you might say, "I will save $5,000 for an emergency fund by the end of the year." This goal is clear, has a deadline, and allows you to track your progress along the way.

Breaking larger goals into smaller, more manageable steps can also make the process less overwhelming. If your goal is to pay off $10,000 in debt, for example, break it down into monthly or weekly targets. Focus on paying off one credit card or loan at a time, and celebrate each milestone you reach. These small wins keep you motivated and make the journey to achieving your goals feel more achievable.

Setting goals isn't just about focusing on financial milestones—it's also about creating balance in other areas of your life. For example, you might set a goal to reduce work stress by exercising regularly, or to improve your financial literacy by reading one finance book each month. These goals contribute to your overall well-being, making it easier to stay focused on your larger financial ambitions. When you take a holistic approach to goal-setting, you're more likely to achieve lasting success and create a life that feels rich in every sense of the word.

Setting financial goals is not just about focusing on numbers; it's about understanding the *why* behind those goals. Why do you want to save a certain amount of money? Why is investing important to you? Why are you striving for financial independence? These questions help you connect your goals to your deeper motivations, making it easier to stay committed when the journey gets tough. When your goals are tied to a sense of purpose, they become more than just targets—they become a part of your identity.

For example, if your goal is to build an emergency fund, think about why that goal matters. Maybe it's about providing security for your family, ensuring that you can handle unexpected medical bills, or simply giving yourself the peace of mind that comes from knowing you have a safety net. This sense of purpose transforms saving from a chore into an act of self-care and responsibility. It reminds you that every dollar saved is a step towards a more secure and stable life.

Similarly, if your goal is to invest for retirement, it's important to visualize what that retirement looks like for you. Do you see yourself traveling the world, starting a small business, or spending more time with loved ones? The clearer your vision, the easier it is to make the sacrifices needed to reach it. This clarity can help you stay focused when you're tempted to spend on things that don't align with your long-term vision.

A sense of purpose also helps you navigate the emotional side of money. It can be challenging to stay disciplined with your budget, especially when you see friends or influencers living lifestyles that seem unattainable on your current income. But when you're grounded in your own vision and values, you're less likely to be swayed by external pressures. You understand that the sacrifices you're making today are building towards a future that you've chosen for yourself, not one that's dictated by the expectations of others.

One of the most empowering aspects of financial literacy is understanding the role of delayed gratification. In a world that constantly promotes instant pleasure and immediate results, learning how to delay gratification can set you apart from the crowd. Delayed gratification means choosing long-term rewards over short-term pleasures—saving and investing today so that you can enjoy greater financial freedom in the future.

Delayed gratification isn't about depriving yourself; it's about making conscious choices that align with your goals. For instance, instead of splurging on a brand-new gadget, you might decide to put that money into your investment account, knowing that it will grow over time. Instead of going out for dinner every week, you might cook at home and use the savings to pay down your debt faster. These choices might not bring immediate satisfaction, but they contribute to a stronger financial foundation.

The ability to delay gratification is closely tied to self-discipline. It's about being able to say no to the things you don't truly need so that you can say yes to the things that matter most. It's about recognizing that every dollar you save or invest today is a vote for your future self. This mindset shift can change the way you view spending, making it easier to prioritize your long-term vision over momentary desires.

Research shows that those who are able to delay gratification tend to have better financial outcomes over their lifetime. This makes sense when you consider that building wealth is often a slow, steady process rather than a quick win. The stock market takes time to grow, real estate investments appreciate gradually, and even building a successful business requires years of effort. Delayed gratification allows you to stay patient and persistent, even when progress feels slow.

The practice of delaying gratification doesn't mean that you never get to enjoy life in the present. It's about finding balance—treating yourself when you reach milestones, celebrating small wins, and taking joy in the journey. The difference is that your enjoyment is intentional and earned, not a reaction to every impulse or external pressure. This approach ensures that when you do indulge, it's meaningful and aligned with your overall goals.

A final piece of the financial literacy puzzle is learning how to cultivate a mindset of lifelong growth. The financial world is constantly evolving, with new technologies, investment opportunities, and economic challenges emerging all the time. Staying adaptable and open to learning is crucial for maintaining your financial health over the long term. This mindset isn't just about acquiring new information; it's about embracing change, being willing to adjust your strategies, and never becoming complacent with what you already know.

One of the best ways to maintain a growth mindset is by setting aside time for continuous education. This might involve reading books on personal finance, following reputable financial blogs, or taking online courses on investing and money management. Staying curious allows you to keep up with the latest trends and best practices, ensuring that your strategies remain effective as the market changes. It also keeps you from falling into the trap of thinking that you've learned everything there is to know.

Being part of a community of like-minded individuals can also fuel your growth. Surrounding yourself with people who are focused on improving their financial lives can keep you motivated and inspired. This might mean joining investment clubs, attending seminars, or participating in online forums where people share their experiences and strategies. These communities provide a space to ask questions, get feedback, and learn from others' successes and mistakes.

Another aspect of lifelong growth is being willing to learn from your own experiences. Not every financial decision will work out as planned, and that's okay. The key is to view mistakes as opportunities for learning rather than as failures. If an investment doesn't perform as expected, take the time to analyze what went wrong and how you can adjust your approach in the future. If you find yourself struggling to stick to a budget, look for patterns in your spending habits and think about what changes you can make.

Ultimately, financial literacy is a journey rather than a destination. It's about continuously refining your understanding, adapting to new circumstances, and staying committed to your vision of financial freedom. By approaching your financial life with a mindset of growth and curiosity, you can build a future that is not only secure but also rich in opportunities for fulfillment, freedom, and purpose.

CHAPTER 3: MIND YOUR OWN BUSINESS— BUILDING ASSETS, NOT LIABILITIES

The phrase "mind your own business" takes on a whole new meaning when it comes to financial success. While it's often used as a way to tell others to stay out of personal matters, in the world of money, it's about something deeper. It means taking control of your financial life, treating your personal finances like a business, and focusing on building assets instead of liabilities. Successful people don't just work for a paycheck—they work to create income streams that grow, even when they're not working.

The key to achieving this lies in understanding the difference between assets and liabilities. An asset is something that puts money in your pocket, while a liability is something that takes money out of your pocket. Sounds simple, right? But many people confuse liabilities with assets. For example, a house might seem like an asset because it's valuable, but if it's costing you more in mortgage payments, maintenance, and interest than it's bringing in, it's actually a liability. This doesn't mean you shouldn't own a house—it just means that true financial freedom comes from understanding how to balance these costs with assets that generate income.

Assets come in many forms. They can be stocks, bonds, real estate, businesses, intellectual property, or anything else that earns you money over time. Liabilities, on the other hand, are things like loans, credit card debt, or even purchases that lose value over time, such as cars or luxury goods. To build wealth, you have to focus on acquiring assets and minimizing liabilities.

When you shift your mindset from working for money to making money work for you, you open up a world of possibilities. Instead of just earning a paycheck and spending it, you start thinking about how to use that money to buy assets that will grow. This might mean investing in the stock market, purchasing rental properties, or starting your own business. The goal is to create multiple streams of income so that you're not dependent on one source, such as a job. When your assets generate enough income to cover your living expenses, you've achieved financial independence.

The journey toward building assets starts with understanding where you are financially. Just like a business owner reviews their financial statements to assess the health of their company, you need to take stock of your personal finances. This means tracking your income, expenses, assets, and liabilities. Many people avoid doing this because they're afraid of what they might find, but the reality is that you can't fix what you don't measure.

Start by listing out all of your current assets—everything that puts money in your pocket. This might include savings accounts, investment accounts, real estate, or even side hustles that generate extra income. Next, make a list of your liabilities—everything that takes money out of your pocket. This includes your mortgage, student loans, credit card debt, car payments, and any other regular expenses.

Once you have a clear picture of your financial situation, it's time to focus on how to grow your assets and reduce your liabilities. If you have high-interest debt, paying that off should be a priority because it's a significant liability. At the same time, you want to start thinking about how to build your asset column. One of the easiest ways to begin is by investing in stocks or index funds. While the stock market can be volatile in the short term, historically, it has been one of the best ways to grow wealth over time.

Real estate is another powerful asset class, especially if you're able to purchase properties that generate rental income. Owning rental properties not only provides you with a steady stream of income but also allows you to benefit from property appreciation over time. The key is to approach real estate as an investment, not just a home to live in. This means looking at cash flow, property management, and long-term growth potential when making a decision to buy.

Entrepreneurship is one of the most effective ways to build assets, and in today's digital age, starting your own business has never been easier. Whether you're interested in e-commerce, creating digital products, or offering freelance services, there are countless opportunities to turn your skills and passions into income-generating assets. The advantage of owning a business is that it allows you to scale your income beyond the limits of a traditional job. You're no longer trading time for money—you're building something that can grow and generate income on its own.

When thinking about starting a business, the first step is identifying a problem that you can solve. The most successful businesses are built around solving real problems for people. It could be as simple as offering a service that makes people's lives easier or creating a product that fills a gap in the market. Once you've identified a problem to solve, the next step is to create a business plan. This plan doesn't have to be complicated, but it should outline your goals, target audience, and how you plan to make money.

Running a business also teaches you valuable lessons about money management, risk, and growth. You quickly learn the importance of keeping your expenses low while focusing on increasing revenue. Just like with personal finances, the goal is to create a positive cash flow—where your business earns more money than it spends. As your business grows, you can reinvest profits into expanding your operations, hiring employees, or developing new products and services. Over time, a successful business can become one of your most valuable assets, providing you with income long after the initial work is done.

Starting a business isn't for everyone, but even if you're not ready to go all-in on entrepreneurship, having a side hustle or a part-time venture can be a great way to begin building assets. Whether it's freelancing in your spare time, creating digital products, or investing in real estate, the goal is to create multiple streams of income that complement your primary job.

A critical aspect of building assets is understanding how to protect them. Just as a business owner safeguards their company from risks, you need to protect your personal assets from financial setbacks. This means having the right types of insurance, such as health, life, and property insurance, to protect yourself and your family from unexpected expenses. It also means creating an emergency fund to cover three to six months' worth of living expenses in case you lose your job or face a significant financial challenge.

But protecting your assets goes beyond insurance and emergency funds. It's also about ensuring that your investments are diversified. Diversification is a strategy that involves spreading your money across different types of investments—stocks, bonds, real estate, and even businesses—so that your risk is minimized. The idea is that if one investment underperforms, others may do well, balancing out your overall returns. For example, if the stock market takes a downturn, you might have real estate investments that continue to generate rental income.

Another way to protect your assets is by staying informed and continuously learning about personal finance and investing. The more you know, the better equipped you are to make informed decisions and avoid common financial mistakes. This might mean reading books on investing, following financial news, or even taking courses on wealth-building strategies. Knowledge is one of the most valuable assets you can have because it empowers you to make choices that lead to long-term financial security.

Finally, protecting your assets also involves planning for the future. Estate planning is often overlooked, but it's essential if you want to ensure that your wealth is passed down to your loved ones according to your wishes. This might involve creating a will, setting up trusts, or designating beneficiaries for your investment accounts. Estate planning not only protects your assets but also gives you peace of mind, knowing that your financial legacy is secure.

One of the most overlooked aspects of building assets is investing in yourself. While stocks, real estate, and businesses are important, your most valuable asset is your ability to learn, adapt, and grow. Investing in your education, skills, and personal development can have a profound impact on your financial success. The more you know and the more skilled you become, the more opportunities you'll have to increase your income and build wealth.

In today's fast-paced world, continuous learning is essential. Whether it's staying up to date on the latest trends in your industry, learning new skills, or exploring new business opportunities, the ability to adapt is key to staying ahead. This might mean taking courses, attending workshops, or even investing in personal coaching to develop specific skills. The goal is to become the best version of yourself so that you can take full advantage of the opportunities that come your way.

Investing in yourself also means taking care of your health and well-being. After all, you can't build wealth if you're not physically and mentally well enough to enjoy it. Prioritizing self-care, whether it's through regular exercise, healthy eating, or taking time to recharge, is just as important as managing your finances. When you're healthy and focused, you're better able to make sound financial decisions and stay committed to your goals.

Additionally, building a strong network of mentors, peers, and advisors is another way to invest in yourself. Surrounding yourself with people who are successful in areas where you want to grow can provide valuable insights and guidance. Mentors can offer advice based on their own experiences, helping you avoid common pitfalls and fast-track your success. A strong network also opens doors to new opportunities, whether it's through business partnerships, job offers, or investment deals.

Another key aspect of building assets is mastering the art of delayed gratification. In a world where instant gratification is often celebrated, those who can wait for bigger rewards tend to achieve more substantial financial success. Delayed gratification is the ability to resist the temptation for immediate rewards in favor of larger, more meaningful gains in the future. It's about making smart financial choices today that will pay off tomorrow.

For example, instead of spending all of your disposable income on luxury goods or vacations, you might choose to invest that money in the stock market or put it towards buying a rental property. While the payoff isn't immediate, these investments have the potential to grow over time, providing you with income and financial security down the road. The more you practice delaying gratification, the easier it becomes to prioritize long-term goals over short-term pleasures.

Delayed gratification also involves understanding the concept of opportunity cost. Every dollar you spend today is a dollar that you're not investing in your future. This doesn't mean that you should never spend money on things that make you happy, but it does mean being mindful of how your spending aligns with your financial goals. By thinking in terms of opportunity cost, you can make more intentional decisions about when to spend, save, or invest.

Developing the ability to delay gratification can be a game-changer when it comes to building assets. It allows you to stay focused on your goals even when distractions arise, and it helps you build the patience needed to stick with your investments during market fluctuations. It's not about denying yourself joy—it's about creating a life where you have the freedom to enjoy the things that matter most to you, without the stress of financial uncertainty.

One of the most important steps in building assets is understanding the power of passive income. Passive income refers to money that you earn without having to actively work for it on a day-to-day basis. Unlike a regular job, where you trade your time for money, passive income allows you to earn while you sleep, travel, or spend time with family. This is a fundamental concept for anyone who wants to achieve financial freedom because it allows you to decouple your time from your earnings.

There are many different ways to generate passive income, and the best approach depends on your interests, skills, and resources. One of the most popular methods is investing in dividend-paying stocks. When you own shares of a company, you're entitled to a portion of its profits, which are paid out as dividends. These payments can be reinvested to buy more shares, or they can be taken as cash to supplement your income. Over time, as you accumulate more shares, the dividend payments can become a significant source of income.

Real estate is another common way to build passive income, especially if you invest in rental properties. Owning a property that generates rental income each month can provide a steady cash flow, allowing you to cover your mortgage and expenses while earning additional profit. Real estate also has the potential to appreciate in value, meaning that you could sell the property for a profit down the line. However, being a landlord does require some work, such as maintaining the property and managing tenants, so it's important to weigh the time and effort involved.

Digital products are another avenue for creating passive income, especially in today's digital world. This could include writing an e-book, creating an online course, or developing a software application. Once these products are created and put online, they have the potential to earn money indefinitely as people continue to purchase them. The initial investment of time and effort can pay off in the form of ongoing income with little additional work required.

Creating passive income streams requires a shift in mindset. It's about learning to think like an investor rather than just a consumer. Instead of asking, "How can I spend this money?" you start asking, "How can I use this money to make more money?" This shift is what separates those who struggle to make ends meet from those who build wealth and financial security over time. It's about turning every dollar into an opportunity to generate more income.

One way to think like an investor is to focus on building assets that appreciate in value. For example, instead of buying a brand-new car that will lose value the moment you drive it off the lot, you might invest in stocks or real estate that have the potential to grow over time. This doesn't mean you can't enjoy nice things, but it does mean being strategic about which purchases are assets and which are liabilities. By prioritizing assets, you're setting yourself up for long-term financial growth.

It's also important to understand the concept of cash flow when building passive income streams. Cash flow is the money that comes in and out of your pocket, and it's the lifeblood of any investment. Positive cash flow means that your investments are earning more than they cost to maintain, while negative cash flow means that your expenses are greater than your earnings. When it comes to real estate, for example, a property with positive cash flow is one where the rental income covers all expenses, including mortgage payments, maintenance, and property management.

The goal is to build a portfolio of assets that produce positive cash flow. This could include rental properties, dividend stocks, or businesses that generate income without requiring you to be involved in the day-to-day operations. As your passive income grows, you can use it to reinvest in more assets, creating a snowball effect where your wealth continues to grow over time. This is how many of the world's wealthiest individuals have built their fortunes—by focusing on creating and acquiring assets that generate income.

One of the challenges of building assets and creating passive income is overcoming the fear of taking risks. Investing in assets often means putting your money into opportunities that have the potential to grow, but there's always a chance that things won't go as planned. This fear can be paralyzing, especially if you're not used to thinking like an investor. But taking calculated risks is a necessary part of building wealth, and learning how to manage those risks can help you make smarter decisions.

The key to taking smart risks is understanding the difference between calculated risks and reckless gambles. A calculated risk is one that you've thoroughly researched, where you understand the potential rewards as well as the risks involved. It's a decision that's based on data, analysis, and a clear understanding of your goals. For example, investing in a well-diversified index fund might be considered a calculated risk because it spreads your investment across many different companies, reducing the chance of losing all your money.

Reckless gambles, on the other hand, are decisions made without adequate knowledge or preparation. This could include putting all your savings into a single stock without understanding the company's financials, or investing in a real estate property without knowing the local market. These types of risks can lead to significant losses, which is why it's so important to do your homework before making any investment. Knowledge is your best defense against making reckless decisions, and it allows you to take risks that are more likely to pay off.

One way to build confidence in taking risks is to start small. Instead of putting all your money into a new venture, you might start by investing a small amount in the stock market or purchasing a rental property that's within your budget. This allows you to learn the ropes without putting everything on the line. As you gain experience and see the results of your decisions, you'll become more comfortable with taking larger risks that have the potential for greater rewards.

Another key to building assets is learning how to leverage other people's money (OPM). This concept might sound intimidating at first, but it's actually one of the most powerful tools for building wealth. OPM refers to using borrowed money to invest in opportunities that have the potential to generate returns greater than the cost of the loan. When used wisely, this strategy can help you acquire assets that you might not have been able to purchase with your own cash alone.

For example, most people use OPM when they take out a mortgage to buy a home. Instead of saving up hundreds of thousands of dollars, you use a bank's money to buy the property, paying them back over time with interest. If the property appreciates in value and you're able to rent it out for more than the monthly mortgage payment, you're effectively using the bank's money to build your wealth. The key is ensuring that the cash flow generated by the asset is greater than the cost of the loan, so you're not losing money.

Leveraging OPM can also be applied to starting or expanding a business. Many successful entrepreneurs use business loans or investment capital to fund their ventures, allowing them to scale faster than if they relied solely on their own savings. This approach does come with risks, as you're responsible for paying back the borrowed money even if the business doesn't succeed. But when done thoughtfully, leveraging can be a way to accelerate your growth and build assets more quickly.

Understanding how to use debt strategically is crucial when leveraging OPM. Not all debt is bad, and when used to purchase income-producing assets, debt can be a valuable tool. The goal is to avoid high-interest consumer debt that doesn't contribute to your financial growth and focus on low-interest loans that enable you to invest in assets that will pay off in the long run. This might mean taking out a mortgage to buy a rental property or using a small business loan to purchase equipment that will increase your production capacity.

When it comes to building assets, timing is everything. Understanding market cycles and knowing when to buy or sell can have a huge impact on your ability to grow wealth. This doesn't mean trying to predict the market—something even the most seasoned investors struggle with—but rather having a basic understanding of how different markets operate and how they tend to move over time. This knowledge allows you to make more informed decisions about when to enter or exit an investment.

For example, the real estate market tends to move in cycles, with periods of rapid appreciation followed by corrections or downturns. Buying real estate during a market downturn, when prices are lower, can provide an opportunity to purchase properties at a discount. As the market recovers, the value of those properties can increase, allowing you to sell them for a profit or enjoy higher rental income. The same principle applies to stocks, where downturns can present opportunities to buy quality companies at lower prices.

However, timing the market doesn't mean rushing to buy whenever there's a dip. It's important to consider your long-term strategy and not get caught up in the hype or panic of short-term market movements. For example, if you're investing for retirement, a temporary drop in the stock market might be an opportunity to buy more shares at a discount, rather than a reason to sell in fear. Having a long-term perspective helps you stay calm during market fluctuations and focus on the bigger picture.

This is why having a plan is so crucial when investing. A solid investment plan outlines your goals, your risk tolerance, and your time horizon. It helps you stay focused on your objectives, even when the market is volatile. It also allows you to make decisions based on logic rather than emotion, which is essential for building long-term wealth. A well-thought-out plan can help you determine when to buy, when to hold, and when to sell, ensuring that you're always moving towards your financial goals.

Patience is one of the most underrated traits when it comes to building assets. In a world that celebrates quick wins and overnight success, it can be easy to forget that true wealth is often built slowly over time. Patience allows you to stay invested during market downturns, to wait for the right investment opportunities, and to stick with your financial plan even when progress feels slow. It's the ability to resist the urge to chase the latest trends or jump on every new opportunity that promises fast returns.

One of the best examples of the power of patience is the stock market. Historically, the stock market has trended upward over the long term, even though there have been many short-term dips and crashes. Investors who panic during downturns and sell their stocks often lock in losses, while those who hold steady are able to benefit from the market's recovery. This is why the most successful investors are often those who are willing to wait, letting time and compound growth do the heavy lifting.

Patience also plays a role in real estate investing. Property values don't always increase overnight, and it can take years for a rental property to generate significant cash flow. But over time, as the mortgage is paid down and rental rates increase, the income from a rental property can become a substantial source of passive income. This long-term perspective is what separates successful investors from those who give up too soon.

Even in entrepreneurship, patience is key. Building a business takes time, and there will be setbacks along the way. It's easy to get discouraged when things don't go as planned or when profits don't come in as quickly as you hoped. But those who are willing to stay committed, to learn from their mistakes, and to keep pushing forward are often the ones who ultimately succeed. Patience allows you to focus on the process rather than the outcome, knowing that the results will come if you stay consistent.

Building assets requires a solid understanding of cash flow management. Cash flow is the movement of money in and out of your financial life, and it's a key factor that determines whether you're building wealth or struggling to make ends meet. Positive cash flow means that more money is coming in than going out, while negative cash flow means that your expenses exceed your income. Managing cash flow effectively is crucial for creating a financial foundation that allows you to invest in assets and pursue your financial goals.

The first step in managing cash flow is creating a detailed budget. A budget isn't just a list of expenses; it's a tool that helps you understand where your money is going and how you can make adjustments to align your spending with your priorities. Start by tracking all your income sources and expenses for a month. This includes everything from rent or mortgage payments, utilities, and groceries to entertainment, dining out, and subscriptions. By breaking down your expenses into categories, you can see where you might be overspending and identify areas where you can cut back.

For example, you might discover that you're spending a significant amount on takeout and coffee, which could be redirected towards paying off debt or investing in the stock market. Making small changes, like cooking more meals at home or canceling subscriptions you don't use, can free up money that can be used to build assets. These adjustments don't have to feel like sacrifices—they're choices that reflect your commitment to your financial future.

Once you have a budget in place, the next step is to automate your savings. Automation takes the guesswork out of saving by ensuring that a portion of your income is automatically directed to your savings or investment accounts each month. This is often referred to as "paying yourself first." By setting up automatic transfers to your savings or brokerage account, you ensure that you're consistently building your asset base before you have a chance to spend that money on discretionary expenses. It's a simple yet powerful way to prioritize your financial goals.

Cash flow management also involves understanding the difference between fixed and variable expenses. Fixed expenses are those that remain the same each month, such as rent, insurance premiums, and loan payments. These expenses are often non-negotiable, meaning that you have limited control over their amount. Variable expenses, on the other hand, can fluctuate from month to month and often include things like dining out, entertainment, and travel. Managing your variable expenses effectively is one of the quickest ways to improve your cash flow.

For instance, if you find that your entertainment spending is higher than you'd like, consider finding free or low-cost activities that align with your interests. This could mean exploring local parks, attending community events, or hosting movie nights at home. Similarly, shopping for groceries with a list and sticking to it can help reduce impulse purchases and cut down on food waste. These small changes can add up over time, allowing you to save more money and invest in income-generating assets.

Another aspect of managing cash flow is being prepared for unexpected expenses. Life is full of surprises, and unexpected costs can throw even the best-laid financial plans off track. This is why having an emergency fund is so crucial. An emergency fund acts as a buffer, giving you the flexibility to handle unexpected expenses without having to rely on credit cards or loans. Aim to save three to six months' worth of living expenses in an easily accessible account. This safety net allows you to stay focused on your long-term financial goals even when life throws you a curveball.

As your cash flow improves, it's also important to regularly revisit your budget and make adjustments as needed. Your financial situation will change over time—your income may increase, your expenses may shift, and your goals may evolve. Regularly reviewing your budget ensures that it continues to serve you as a roadmap to financial success. It's not about being rigid with your spending; it's about being intentional with your choices and making sure that your money is working for you.

Building assets also means understanding the value of time. Time is one of the most important factors in wealth building, and it's a resource that we all have in equal measure. The difference between those who achieve financial freedom and those who don't often comes down to how they use their time, particularly when it comes to investing. The earlier you start investing, the more time your money has to grow through the power of compounding.

Compounding is the process where the returns on your investments generate their own returns. It's like a snowball effect—your initial investment earns returns, those returns are reinvested, and then those reinvested returns generate even more returns. Over time, this process can turn small, regular contributions into a substantial nest egg. This is why starting early, even with a small amount, can make a huge difference in the long run.

For example, if you invest $200 per month starting at age 25 and earn an average annual return of 7%, you could have over $400,000 by the time you turn 65. But if you wait until age 35 to start investing the same amount, your total would be closer to $200,000. The difference isn't because you invested more money—it's because your investments had more time to compound. This illustrates the power of starting early and the value of time when it comes to building wealth.

However, time is not just about when you start—it's also about how you manage your time while building assets. Many people get caught up in the daily grind of working long hours without taking the time to think about how they can make their money work for them. It's important to carve out time to educate yourself, analyze your investments, and strategize about your financial future. Whether it's reading books, attending seminars, or seeking advice from financial experts, investing time in learning about money is one of the best investments you can make.

In addition to investing time in your financial education, it's also essential to understand the time value of money (TVM). The time value of money is a financial principle that states that a dollar today is worth more than a dollar in the future. This concept is based on the potential earning capacity of money—money you have today can be invested to earn interest or returns, making it more valuable than the same amount received later.

For instance, if you receive a bonus at work, you have a choice: you can spend it immediately, or you can invest it and let it grow over time. If you choose to invest it in an asset that earns a 5% annual return, that money will grow each year, becoming more valuable over time. Understanding the time value of money can help you make better decisions about when to spend, when to save, and when to invest.

This principle is also why it's so important to start paying off debt as soon as possible. Interest works both ways—just as it can help your investments grow, it can also cause your debts to grow if you don't pay them off quickly. High-interest debt, like credit card balances, can erode your financial progress, making it harder to build assets. By focusing on paying off high-interest debt early, you free up more money that can be directed towards savings and investments.

The time value of money is a reminder that every financial decision you make today has a ripple effect on your future. It encourages you to think beyond immediate desires and consider the long-term impact of your choices. This perspective shift can help you stay focused on building a solid financial foundation, knowing that the sacrifices you make today will pay off in the form of financial freedom and security down the road.

Building assets is not just about making money—it's about understanding how to use money as a tool to create the life you want. One of the most effective ways to use money as a tool is through strategic reinvestment. Reinvesting means taking the profits or returns from an investment and putting them back into the same or new investment opportunities. This approach allows you to accelerate the growth of your assets by compounding your returns over time.

For example, if you own a rental property and earn rental income each month, you could use that income to pay off the mortgage faster, invest in upgrades to increase the property's value, or save up for another rental property. Each of these strategies involves reinvesting the income you earn to create even more value. By reinvesting, you're allowing your assets to grow exponentially rather than just relying on a single stream of income.

Reinvesting isn't limited to real estate—it applies to stocks, mutual funds, and even business profits. When you receive dividends from a stock, you have the option to reinvest those dividends into purchasing more shares. This reinvestment allows you to buy additional shares without having to use new money from your pocket. Over time, as you accumulate more shares, the dividends you earn also increase, creating a virtuous cycle of growth.

In a business context, reinvesting might mean using a portion of your profits to expand your operations, develop new products, or hire additional staff. While it can be tempting to take profits and use them for personal expenses, reinvesting allows you to build a business that can generate even greater returns in the future. This is how many successful entrepreneurs have turned small businesses into thriving enterprises—by being disciplined about reinvesting their profits for long-term growth.

Strategic reinvestment also applies to your own skills and personal development. Just as you might reinvest profits from a business, reinvesting in yourself can pay off in the form of higher earning potential and greater career opportunities. This might involve pursuing additional education, obtaining professional certifications, or learning new skills that make you more valuable in the job market. The more you invest in your own abilities, the more opportunities you have to increase your income and build wealth.

For example, if you're working in a field like technology or finance, staying up to date with industry trends and learning new software can make you more competitive in your field. This can translate to higher salaries, more job opportunities, or even the ability to start your own consulting business. The key is to view personal development as an investment rather than an expense. While the upfront cost of courses or certifications might seem high, the long-term return on investment can be significant.

Reinvesting in yourself also means taking care of your health and well-being. Financial success is closely tied to your ability to stay focused, productive, and resilient. Prioritizing activities like exercise, mindfulness, and self-care can boost your overall well-being, allowing you to maintain the energy and drive needed to pursue your goals. Just as you wouldn't let a valuable asset go without maintenance, it's important to take care of yourself as you work towards building wealth.

In every aspect of life, reinvestment is about thinking long-term. It's about recognizing that the actions you take today can create opportunities for growth tomorrow. This mindset allows you to make decisions that are aligned with your future goals rather than being limited by immediate desires. When you adopt this approach, you're not just building wealth—you're building a life that reflects your values, your vision, and your purpose.

One of the most important aspects of building assets is learning how to scale. Scaling means growing your assets or business in a way that increases revenue or value without a corresponding increase in costs. This concept is essential because it allows you to create more wealth without necessarily working harder or spending more time. Scaling can apply to businesses, investments, and even personal finances, and it's one of the most effective ways to achieve long-term financial success.

In a business context, scaling often involves finding ways to serve more customers or expand into new markets without dramatically increasing overhead. For example, if you run an e-commerce store, you might scale by automating your inventory management, using social media to reach more customers, or outsourcing customer service to save time. These strategies allow your business to grow and increase profits while keeping expenses relatively stable. The result is that your profit margins improve, and your business becomes more efficient.

In investing, scaling often refers to reinvesting profits or dividends to buy more of the same asset or to diversify into new assets. For instance, if you own rental properties, you could use the income from one property to save up for another, thereby growing your portfolio without taking on additional debt. Similarly, in the stock market, reinvesting dividends allows you to accumulate more shares over time, which leads to greater dividend payments in the future. This process of compounding creates a snowball effect, where your assets continue to grow without requiring additional investment from your primary income.

Scaling can also apply to personal finance strategies. For example, as you pay off debt and free up more of your monthly income, you can "scale" your savings by directing that extra money into investment accounts. Over time, this approach allows you to build a larger financial cushion and gives you more opportunities to invest in assets that generate passive income. The key to scaling is finding ways to increase your financial output without proportionally increasing your financial input.

One of the best ways to scale your financial efforts is by leveraging technology. In today's digital world, there are countless tools and platforms that make it easier than ever to manage your money, automate your investments, and grow your business. Whether it's using budgeting apps to track your spending, investing platforms to manage your portfolio, or social media to grow your business, technology is a powerful ally in your journey to financial success.

For example, investing platforms like robo-advisors allow you to automate your investment strategy. These platforms use algorithms to create and manage a diversified portfolio for you, based on your risk tolerance and financial goals. By automating the process, you eliminate the need to constantly monitor the market, rebalance your portfolio, or make complex investment decisions. This not only saves time but also reduces the emotional stress that can come with market volatility.

Similarly, budgeting apps like YNAB (You Need A Budget) or Mint make it easy to track your income and expenses in real-time. These apps can help you identify areas where you might be overspending, set financial goals, and stay on track with your savings plan. By automating your budgeting process, you free up mental energy that can be better spent on building assets and growing your income streams.

If you're an entrepreneur, technology can also help you scale your business. E-commerce platforms like Shopify or Etsy allow you to reach customers around the world without needing a physical storefront. Social media marketing tools let you advertise your products or services to a global audience with minimal upfront costs. And customer relationship management (CRM) systems can help you automate interactions with your customers, ensuring that you provide great service without having to personally handle every interaction. These tools allow you to focus on what matters most—growing your business—while the technology handles many of the day-to-day tasks.

Scaling your financial life isn't just about making more money—it's also about protecting what you've built. As your assets grow, so do the risks associated with managing them. This is why it's essential to have a strategy for risk management in place. Risk management is about identifying potential threats to your financial well-being and taking steps to mitigate those risks. Whether it's through insurance, diversification, or legal protections, managing risk is a critical part of building and preserving wealth.

One of the most important risk management tools is insurance. As you accumulate assets, it's essential to protect them with the right types of insurance. This includes health insurance to protect you from unexpected medical bills, life insurance to provide for your family in the event of your death, and property insurance to protect your home, car, or other valuable assets. Having adequate insurance ensures that an unforeseen event doesn't wipe out everything you've worked so hard to build.

Another key aspect of risk management is diversification. As the saying goes, "Don't put all your eggs in one basket." Diversification means spreading your investments across different asset classes, industries, and geographies so that your portfolio is less vulnerable to market fluctuations. For example, if you're heavily invested in the stock market, you might want to balance your portfolio with real estate or bonds, which tend to be less volatile. Diversification helps ensure that if one area of the market takes a hit, your entire portfolio doesn't suffer.

Legal protections are also an important part of risk management. As you build assets, it's important to think about how they will be passed on to your heirs or beneficiaries. Estate planning tools like wills, trusts, and powers of attorney can help ensure that your assets are distributed according to your wishes. If you own a business, setting up the right legal structure—such as an LLC or corporation—can protect your personal assets from business liabilities. These legal protections provide peace of mind, knowing that your wealth is secure no matter what challenges may arise.

As you scale and grow your financial life, it's also important to keep your mindset in check. Many people assume that once they start earning more money or building assets, all of their financial problems will disappear. But the truth is, wealth building brings its own set of challenges. Managing larger amounts of money, making complex investment decisions, and protecting your assets from risks can all create new pressures. This is why maintaining a healthy financial mindset is crucial to long-term success.

One of the most common pitfalls for people who begin to build wealth is lifestyle inflation. Lifestyle inflation occurs when your expenses increase as your income increases. You might start upgrading your car, moving to a bigger house, or spending more on luxury goods simply because you can afford it. While there's nothing wrong with enjoying the fruits of your labor, lifestyle inflation can quickly erode your wealth if you're not careful. The key is to resist the temptation to overspend and instead focus on reinvesting your money into assets that will continue to grow your wealth.

Another mindset trap is the fear of losing what you've built. As your assets grow, it's natural to feel more protective of them, but this fear can sometimes lead to overly conservative decisions. For example, you might avoid investing in the stock market because you're afraid of losing money, or you might hesitate to take calculated risks that could accelerate your financial growth. While it's important to be prudent, it's equally important not to let fear hold you back from pursuing opportunities that align with your financial goals.

To maintain a healthy financial mindset, it's important to stay grounded in your values and long-term vision. Wealth should be a tool to help you achieve your goals and live a fulfilling life, not an end in itself. Regularly revisiting your goals, staying educated about personal finance, and surrounding yourself with people who share your values can help you stay focused on what truly matters. This mindset ensures that as your wealth grows, so does your sense of purpose and satisfaction.

As you continue building assets and scaling your financial life, one of the most powerful lessons is learning how to leverage other people's expertise. While it's important to educate yourself about personal finance and investing, no one can be an expert in everything. This is where financial advisors, accountants, lawyers, and mentors come in. These professionals can provide you with valuable insights, help you navigate complex financial situations, and ensure that you're making the best possible decisions for your long-term success.

Working with a financial advisor can be particularly helpful if you're managing a diverse portfolio of assets. A good advisor will help you create a comprehensive financial plan that aligns with your goals and risk tolerance. They can also assist with tax strategies, retirement planning, and estate planning, ensuring that you're taking advantage of all available opportunities to grow and protect your wealth. The key is to find an advisor who understands your goals and who can provide personalized advice based on your unique financial situation.

Accountants are another essential resource as you scale your finances. As your income and assets grow, so do your tax responsibilities. An experienced accountant can help you navigate the complexities of tax laws, identify deductions and credits you might qualify for, and create strategies to minimize your tax liability. They can also help you with business finances if you're an entrepreneur, ensuring that your bookkeeping and tax filings are accurate and compliant with the law.

In addition to financial professionals, mentors can play a pivotal role in your financial journey. A mentor who has already achieved the level of financial success you aspire to can provide guidance, support, and encouragement as you work towards your goals. They can help you avoid common mistakes, introduce you to valuable connections, and provide insights based on their own experiences. Building relationships with mentors and learning from their expertise can fast-track your success and provide you with a sense of community on your wealth-building journey.

As you grow your assets and scale your wealth, one of the most fulfilling aspects is the ability to give back. Financial success isn't just about accumulating wealth for yourself—it's also about using your resources to make a positive impact on the world. Whether it's through charitable giving, supporting causes you care about, or helping others achieve their financial goals, giving back can be one of the most rewarding parts of your financial journey.

Charitable giving can take many forms, from donating to non-profit organizations to setting up a scholarship fund or supporting local community projects. Giving back doesn't always have to involve large sums of money—sometimes, your time and expertise can be just as valuable. Volunteering with organizations that align with your values, mentoring young entrepreneurs, or sharing your financial knowledge with those who are just starting out can create a ripple effect that goes beyond monetary contributions.

One way to give back while also growing your wealth is through impact investing. Impact investing involves putting your money into companies or projects that generate both financial returns and positive social or environmental impact. For example, you might invest in renewable energy companies, social enterprises, or funds that focus on affordable housing. This approach allows you to grow your assets while also supporting initiatives that align with your values. It's a way to use your wealth as a force for good while still achieving your financial goals.

Giving back also provides a sense of purpose that goes beyond financial gain. It reminds you that wealth is not just a number in a bank account—it's a tool that can be used to uplift others and create a better future. This sense of purpose can be a powerful motivator, keeping you focused and grounded even as your financial life becomes more complex. By making generosity a part of your financial plan, you create a legacy that extends far beyond your lifetime.

As you continue to scale your wealth-building efforts, a crucial concept to master is the importance of liquidity. Liquidity refers to how quickly and easily an asset can be converted into cash without losing its value. Liquidity is important because it determines your ability to access cash in times of need or when investment opportunities arise. While building a portfolio of assets like real estate, stocks, and businesses is key to wealth, maintaining a level of liquidity ensures that you remain financially flexible and can take advantage of unexpected opportunities or emergencies.

Cash is the most liquid asset, as it can be used immediately for any purpose. Savings accounts and money market accounts are also highly liquid, allowing you to access funds quickly if needed. These accounts are ideal for emergency savings because they offer immediate access to cash while providing a small return in the form of interest. Having three to six months of living expenses in a liquid savings account is often recommended to provide a financial buffer in case of unexpected expenses like medical bills, car repairs, or job loss.

However, while liquidity is essential, keeping too much of your wealth in cash or low-interest savings accounts can actually be a missed opportunity for growth. Cash doesn't earn much in terms of returns, and over time, inflation can erode its purchasing power. This is why it's important to strike a balance between maintaining enough liquidity for emergencies and investing the rest of your money in assets that have the potential for higher returns. Investments like stocks, bonds, and real estate are less liquid than cash but offer greater opportunities for growth over time.

Liquidity also plays a role in how you structure your investment portfolio. For example, it might be wise to keep a portion of your investments in more liquid assets like stocks, which can be sold quickly if you need to free up cash. Real estate, while potentially very profitable, is less liquid because it takes time to sell a property, and you may not always get the price you want. Understanding this trade-off allows you to make more informed decisions about where to allocate your money, depending on your financial goals and time horizon.

In addition to liquidity, understanding leverage is another key concept for building assets. Leverage involves using borrowed capital to increase the potential return on an investment. While it can amplify gains, it can also amplify losses, so it's important to use leverage wisely and understand the risks involved. When used strategically, leverage can be a powerful tool that allows you to invest in assets you wouldn't be able to afford otherwise, accelerating your path to financial freedom.

One of the most common forms of leverage is a mortgage. When you take out a mortgage to buy a home or investment property, you're using the bank's money to purchase an asset that can appreciate in value. If you buy a property for $200,000 with a down payment of $40,000 and the property increases in value to $300,000, your equity has grown significantly more than if you had paid the entire purchase price in cash. This leverage allows you to benefit from the appreciation of the entire property while only investing a portion of the capital yourself.

Leverage can also be used in the stock market through margin trading, where investors borrow money from their brokerage to purchase additional shares. While this can increase potential returns, it also comes with significant risks. If the value of the stocks you've purchased with borrowed money drops, you could be required to sell shares to repay the margin loan, potentially locking in losses. This is why margin trading is typically recommended only for experienced investors who understand the risks and have a strategy in place.

For business owners, leverage might involve taking out a loan to expand operations, purchase equipment, or hire additional staff. If the investment leads to increased revenue that exceeds the cost of the loan, then leverage has worked in your favor. However, it's important to have a clear plan for how borrowed funds will generate returns and to ensure that you have a buffer in place in case things don't go as planned. Using leverage responsibly means understanding how much debt you can handle and being prepared for both the ups and downs that come with borrowing.

A key part of building assets and scaling your wealth is understanding the role of taxes. Taxes can have a significant impact on your financial success, but with the right knowledge and strategies, you can minimize your tax burden and keep more of your hard-earned money. Tax planning is not about avoiding taxes altogether; it's about being smart with how you manage your investments, income, and expenses so that you pay what is legally required while taking advantage of available tax breaks and deductions.

One of the most effective tax strategies is to invest in tax-advantaged accounts like IRAs (Individual Retirement Accounts) and 401(k)s. These accounts offer tax benefits that can make a big difference in your long-term savings. For example, contributions to a traditional IRA or 401(k) are often tax-deductible, meaning you can reduce your taxable income for the year. This not only helps you save for retirement but also lowers your tax bill in the short term. Roth IRAs, on the other hand, allow for tax-free withdrawals in retirement, making them a great option if you expect to be in a higher tax bracket in the future.

Real estate investors can benefit from deductions related to property ownership. These include mortgage interest deductions, depreciation, and expenses related to property maintenance and management. Depreciation allows you to deduct a portion of the cost of the property each year, even though the property may be appreciating in value. This can significantly reduce your taxable rental income, allowing you to keep more of your rental earnings while building equity in the property.

If you own a business, there are numerous deductions available that can help reduce your taxable income. This includes deductions for office space, supplies, equipment, travel expenses, and even a portion of your home if you use it for business purposes. Understanding which expenses are deductible and keeping detailed records can make a significant difference come tax time. A qualified accountant can help you navigate the complexities of business tax laws and ensure that you're taking advantage of all available deductions.

In addition to taking advantage of tax-advantaged accounts and deductions, another strategy for managing your tax burden is through strategic timing of income and expenses. For example, if you expect your income to be higher this year than next, you might delay certain expenses or charitable contributions until next year, allowing you to take those deductions when they will provide a greater tax benefit. Similarly, if you expect to be in a lower tax bracket in the future, you might delay withdrawals from retirement accounts to reduce the taxes owed.

Tax-loss harvesting is another strategy that can help investors minimize their tax liability. This involves selling investments that have lost value to offset the gains from other investments that have appreciated. By doing this, you can reduce the amount of capital gains tax you owe while maintaining a diversified investment portfolio. After selling the losing investment, you can reinvest the proceeds in a similar asset to maintain your overall investment strategy. This approach can be particularly effective during market downturns, allowing you to turn a loss into a long-term tax benefit.

Understanding how to manage capital gains is also important for investors. Capital gains are the profits you earn from selling an asset for more than you paid for it. Short-term capital gains, which apply to assets held for less than a year, are typically taxed at a higher rate than long-term capital gains. Holding onto an investment for more than a year before selling it can significantly reduce the amount of taxes you owe on the sale. This is why having a long-term investment strategy not only makes sense from a growth perspective but also from a tax efficiency standpoint.

Effective tax planning is not just about reducing your tax bill for the current year—it's about making decisions that minimize your tax burden over the long term. By being proactive and staying informed about tax laws, you can make strategic choices that help you keep more of your wealth as it grows. This might mean working with a tax professional, keeping up with changes in tax policy, or using software that helps you optimize your deductions and credits.

Another crucial element of building assets is having a clear exit strategy for your investments. An exit strategy is a plan for how and when you will sell or liquidate an investment. It's important because it helps you lock in gains, minimize losses, and ensure that your investments align with your long-term financial goals. Whether you're investing in real estate, stocks, or a business, having an exit strategy ensures that you're not just focused on acquiring assets but also on how to eventually turn those assets into cash when the time is right.

In real estate, an exit strategy might involve selling a rental property after it has appreciated in value, using the proceeds to invest in a larger property or diversify into other investments. Alternatively, you might choose to refinance the property to take out some of the equity while maintaining ownership. This allows you to access cash without selling the asset, potentially using those funds to invest in new opportunities while continuing to generate rental income from the original property.

For stock market investors, an exit strategy might involve selling shares when they reach a certain price target or when the fundamentals of the company change. Some investors set stop-loss orders, which automatically sell a stock if it drops to a certain price, helping to limit potential losses. Others might have a long-term plan to gradually sell shares as they approach retirement or another financial goal. The key is to have a plan in place before you make the investment, so you're not making decisions based on emotion or market hype.

In business, an exit strategy might involve selling your company to another entrepreneur, merging with a larger business, or even going public through an IPO (Initial Public Offering). If you're a business owner, it's important to think about how you want to exit the business from the beginning, even if you don't plan to sell for many years. This ensures that you're building a business that is attractive to potential buyers and that you have a plan for how to maximize the value of your hard work when the time comes.

One of the often-overlooked aspects of building assets is understanding the role of estate planning in preserving wealth for future generations. Estate planning involves making arrangements for how your assets will be managed and distributed after your passing. While this might seem like a distant concern, it's an essential part of a comprehensive financial plan, especially if you want to ensure that your wealth benefits your loved ones and continues to support your values even after you're gone.

A will is one of the most basic estate planning tools, and it allows you to specify how your assets will be divided among your heirs. Without a will, your estate will be distributed according to state laws, which might not align with your wishes. A will also allows you to name a guardian for any minor children, ensuring that they are cared for by someone you trust. While creating a will might seem daunting, it's a critical step in ensuring that your assets are distributed according to your wishes.

Trusts are another powerful tool in estate planning, especially for those with significant assets. A trust allows you to transfer assets to a trustee who manages them for the benefit of your beneficiaries. Trusts can help minimize estate taxes, avoid probate, and ensure that your assets are used in a way that aligns with your values. For example, you might create a trust that provides for your children's education or supports a charitable cause you care about. Trusts offer more flexibility than a will, making them a valuable tool for those with more complex financial situations.

Estate planning also involves considering how taxes will affect your heirs. The federal estate tax can take a significant portion of a large estate, but there are strategies to minimize its impact. For example, gifting a portion of your assets to your heirs while you're still alive can reduce the size of your estate and provide them with financial support when they need it most. Working with an estate planning attorney can help you understand the best options for your situation and ensure that your wealth is preserved for future generations.

Another crucial factor to consider when building assets is understanding market cycles. Markets, whether they are stock markets, real estate markets, or broader economic cycles, tend to move in patterns of growth and contraction. These cycles are a natural part of economic systems, influenced by factors such as interest rates, consumer sentiment, technological advancements, and geopolitical events. By understanding how market cycles work, you can better time your investments, avoid costly mistakes, and maximize your returns over the long term.

Market cycles generally consist of four phases: expansion, peak, contraction, and trough. During the expansion phase, economic activity increases, businesses grow, employment rates are high, and consumer spending rises. This phase is typically characterized by a bull market in stocks, where share prices rise, and investors are optimistic about future growth. In real estate, expansion might mean rising property values and increased demand for housing, which can be a great time to buy investment properties before prices peak.

The peak phase occurs when growth slows, and the economy reaches its maximum output. In this phase, asset prices often hit their highest point, and signs of overheating may become evident—such as overvalued stocks, excessive speculation, or a housing bubble. Investors who recognize these signs might begin to take profits, selling assets that have appreciated significantly. While it's difficult to time the exact peak of a market, understanding the signals can help you avoid buying assets at their highest prices.

Contraction follows the peak, leading to a slowdown in economic activity. During this phase, businesses might reduce their spending, unemployment may rise, and consumer confidence tends to drop. In the stock market, this is often referred to as a bear market, where prices decline, and investors become more risk-averse. Real estate values might also fall during this period as demand decreases. While it can be tempting to sell during a downturn, savvy investors understand that contractions can create opportunities to buy assets at a discount, setting the stage for future gains.

The final phase of the market cycle is the trough, which is the low point before the next expansion begins. During the trough, economic activity stabilizes at a lower level, and asset prices may bottom out. This phase often presents some of the best opportunities for investors who have cash on hand and are willing to take advantage of low prices. For example, during a stock market downturn, stocks may be undervalued, presenting a chance to buy quality companies at a lower cost. Similarly, in real estate, a market downturn might offer opportunities to purchase properties at reduced prices before demand and prices pick up again.

Understanding market cycles isn't about trying to predict every twist and turn in the market; rather, it's about recognizing the general trends and adjusting your strategy accordingly. For long-term investors, market downturns can be a time to buy and hold assets, while periods of market exuberance may be a good time to take profits or reallocate your portfolio. This approach helps you stay disciplined and focused on your long-term goals, rather than getting caught up in the emotions of market volatility.

Patience is essential when navigating market cycles. It's easy to become anxious during a downturn or overly optimistic during a boom, but successful investors maintain a long-term perspective. They understand that markets move in cycles and that staying invested through the ups and downs is often the best strategy for building wealth over time. For example, during the financial crisis of 2008, many investors panicked and sold their stocks at a loss, only to miss out on the market recovery that followed. Those who stayed the course, or even bought more during the downturn, saw significant gains in the years that followed.

This is why having a clear investment plan is so important. Your plan should outline your investment goals, your time horizon, and your tolerance for risk. It should also include guidelines for when you might rebalance your portfolio or take profits, ensuring that you don't let short-term market movements derail your long-term strategy. By sticking to your plan, you can weather market cycles with confidence, knowing that you're taking a disciplined approach to building assets.

A major component of building assets is learning how to balance risk and reward. Every investment comes with a certain level of risk, and understanding how to manage that risk is key to achieving long-term success. The goal is not to avoid risk altogether—because doing so would mean missing out on many opportunities—but to manage it in a way that aligns with your financial goals and allows you to sleep well at night.

One way to balance risk and reward is through asset allocation. Asset allocation is the process of dividing your investments among different asset classes, such as stocks, bonds, real estate, and cash. The right mix of assets depends on your risk tolerance, investment time horizon, and financial goals. For example, a young investor with a long time horizon might allocate more of their portfolio to stocks, which have higher potential returns but also come with more volatility. An investor nearing retirement, on the other hand, might prefer a more conservative allocation with a greater emphasis on bonds, which tend to be less risky.

Diversification is another important tool for managing risk. By spreading your investments across different asset classes and sectors, you reduce the impact of a poor-performing investment on your overall portfolio. For example, if you own stocks in different industries—such as technology, healthcare, and energy—a downturn in one sector won't necessarily drag down your entire portfolio. Diversification can help smooth out the bumps in the market and provide more consistent returns over time.

It's also important to consider your risk tolerance, which is your ability to handle the ups and downs of the market without making emotional decisions. Some people are naturally more risk-averse, while others are comfortable with taking on more risk in pursuit of higher returns. Understanding your own risk tolerance helps you build a portfolio that you're comfortable with, reducing the likelihood that you'll panic-sell during a market downturn. If you're unsure of your risk tolerance, working with a financial advisor can help you assess your comfort level and create a strategy that matches your needs.

Risk management also involves having a plan for handling market volatility. Market volatility refers to the rapid price changes that can occur in financial markets, often triggered by economic events, geopolitical developments, or shifts in investor sentiment. Volatility is a normal part of investing, but it can be unnerving for those who aren't prepared. By having a strategy in place, you can navigate these periods with greater confidence and avoid making decisions driven by fear or panic.

One approach to managing volatility is dollar-cost averaging, which involves investing a fixed amount of money at regular intervals, regardless of market conditions. This strategy can help smooth out the impact of market fluctuations because you're buying more shares when prices are low and fewer when prices are high. Over time, dollar-cost averaging can reduce the average cost of your investments, allowing you to benefit from long-term market growth without trying to time the market.

Another strategy is to maintain a diversified portfolio with a mix of assets that tend to perform differently under various market conditions. For example, during periods of economic growth, stocks may perform well, while bonds may provide stability during downturns. By holding a range of assets, you can reduce the impact of volatility on your portfolio and ensure that you're not overly exposed to any single investment. This approach allows you to stay invested through market cycles without having to make drastic changes every time the market shifts.

It's also helpful to focus on your long-term goals rather than the daily ups and downs of the market. While it's important to stay informed about market trends, obsessing over short-term movements can lead to stress and impulsive decisions. Instead, focus on the big picture—what are you investing for, and how do your current actions align with those goals? Keeping your eye on the long-term horizon can help you stay disciplined during periods of volatility and maintain the patience needed for building assets.

When building assets, it's also important to understand the concept of liquidity risk. Liquidity risk refers to the difficulty of selling an asset without affecting its price. For example, stocks in large, well-established companies are typically very liquid, meaning you can buy or sell them quickly without significantly impacting their price. Real estate, on the other hand, is less liquid because it can take time to find a buyer, and selling quickly might require accepting a lower price.

Liquidity risk can become a problem if you need to access cash quickly and your assets are tied up in investments that are difficult to sell. This is why it's important to balance your portfolio with a mix of liquid and illiquid assets, depending on your cash flow needs. For example, if you have a significant portion of your wealth invested in real estate, you might want to maintain a cash reserve or invest in more liquid assets like stocks or bonds to ensure that you can access funds when needed.

Liquidity risk can also affect the value of your investments during market downturns. In times of economic stress, investors often rush to sell their holdings, leading to a lack of buyers and falling prices. This can make it difficult to sell illiquid assets at a fair price, potentially resulting in losses if you're forced to sell during a downturn. Being aware of liquidity risk allows you to plan for these scenarios and ensures that you're not caught off guard when market conditions change.

One way to mitigate liquidity risk is by maintaining an emergency fund that covers at least three to six months' worth of living expenses. This fund should be kept in a highly liquid account, such as a savings account or money market account, where it's easily accessible in case of unexpected expenses. By having a cash reserve, you reduce the need to sell investments at an inopportune time, allowing you to stay invested through market cycles and maintain a long-term perspective.

Another strategy for managing liquidity risk is to plan your investment time horizon carefully. Your time horizon is the amount of time you expect to hold an investment before needing to access the funds. For example, if you're saving for a down payment on a house that you plan to buy in the next two years, you'll want to keep those savings in a liquid and low-risk account, such as a high-yield savings account or short-term bonds. This ensures that your money is available when you need it, without the risk of market fluctuations.

If you're investing for a long-term goal like retirement, you can afford to take on more illiquid investments, such as real estate or private equity, because you won't need to access the funds for many years. The longer your time horizon, the more you can ride out market volatility and benefit from the potential growth of higher-risk investments. Understanding your time horizon helps you choose investments that match your needs and allows you to balance the benefits of liquidity with the potential for higher returns.

Liquidity is also important when considering investment opportunities in private markets, such as investing in small businesses, startups, or real estate projects. While these investments can offer attractive returns, they are often more illiquid than publicly traded stocks or bonds. It's important to evaluate the terms of the investment and understand how easily you can exit before committing your capital. This ensures that you're making informed decisions about how much of your portfolio to allocate to illiquid investments.

Ultimately, managing liquidity risk is about ensuring that you have the flexibility to adapt to changing circumstances. By maintaining a balance of liquid and illiquid assets, planning your time horizon, and keeping a cash reserve, you can build a portfolio that supports your long-term goals while also providing the stability you need to navigate life's unexpected twists and turns. This approach allows you to stay focused on building assets and creating wealth, even when the markets and the economy are uncertain.

One of the most powerful tools for building wealth and managing financial growth is the art of negotiation. Whether you're negotiating the price of a home, discussing salary with a new employer, or working out a business deal, negotiation skills can directly impact your financial success. It's about learning to recognize value, advocate for your interests, and create agreements that benefit all parties involved. Mastering negotiation not only helps you save money but also enables you to build stronger relationships and seize opportunities that might otherwise pass you by.

The first step to successful negotiation is preparation. Before entering any negotiation, it's essential to know exactly what you want and what you're willing to compromise on. This means doing your research to understand the market value of what you're negotiating for—whether it's the price of a car or a business partnership. For example, if you're negotiating the purchase of a rental property, you should understand the local real estate market, the going rate for comparable properties, and the potential rental income the property could generate. This information gives you a baseline and helps you identify a fair price.

In addition to knowing your desired outcome, it's important to understand the other party's perspective. What are their needs and priorities? What might they be willing to compromise on? This empathy can help you craft a win-win scenario where both parties feel satisfied with the outcome. For instance, if you're negotiating a salary, understanding the company's budget constraints and what skills or experiences they value most can help you position yourself as the right candidate who deserves a higher offer. By focusing on the benefits you bring to the table, you increase the likelihood of reaching an agreement that meets your needs.

Confidence is another critical element of negotiation. Many people shy away from negotiating because they fear conflict or worry about being perceived as demanding. However, negotiation is not about confrontation—it's about advocating for your worth. Being confident in your value can make a big difference in the outcomes you achieve. Practicing assertive communication, maintaining good posture, and speaking clearly can all help convey confidence, even if you feel nervous inside. Remember, the worst outcome of a negotiation is often a "no," and that's not a failure—it's simply an opportunity to refine your approach and try again.

A key strategy in negotiation is knowing when to walk away. This is often referred to as having a "BATNA"—Best Alternative to a Negotiated Agreement. Your BATNA is your fallback plan if the negotiation doesn't go as expected, and it gives you the power to walk away if the terms aren't in your favor. For example, if you're negotiating the price of a property, your BATNA might be the other comparable properties you've researched. If the seller refuses to budge on the price, knowing that you have other options can give you the leverage to walk away without feeling pressured to accept a bad deal.

Having a strong BATNA also changes the dynamics of a negotiation. It shifts the balance of power, giving you more confidence and preventing you from feeling desperate to reach an agreement. It's easier to stay firm on your terms when you know that you have alternatives. This mindset can be particularly valuable in business negotiations, where the stakes are high, and emotions can run hot. By focusing on the strength of your alternatives, you can stay calm and rational, even when the other party pushes back.

Negotiation is also about creating value. Sometimes, it's possible to reach an agreement that benefits both parties more than they initially expected. This is known as "expanding the pie." For example, if you're negotiating with a potential business partner, you might find a way to collaborate on additional projects or share resources in a way that benefits both of you. By being creative and looking for ways to add value, you can often reach agreements that exceed the expectations of both parties.

Listening is a crucial skill in this process. Many people focus so much on what they're going to say next that they miss valuable information from the other side. Listening carefully allows you to pick up on subtle clues about the other party's priorities and concerns. This can help you find solutions that address their needs while still achieving your goals. When you listen more than you speak, you show respect for the other party, which can help build trust and make them more open to your proposals.

Another important aspect of negotiation is managing emotions—both yours and those of the other party. Negotiations can become tense, especially when money is on the line, and it's easy to let emotions get in the way of a good deal. Staying calm and composed allows you to think more clearly and avoid making impulsive decisions that you might regret later. If you feel yourself becoming frustrated or angry during a negotiation, take a moment to pause, breathe, and refocus on your goals.

Emotional intelligence can also help you connect with the other party on a human level, making them more likely to be receptive to your proposals. For example, showing empathy when the other party expresses concerns or frustrations can help de-escalate tension and foster a more collaborative atmosphere. This doesn't mean conceding on your terms, but rather acknowledging the other party's perspective and showing that you understand where they're coming from. A little bit of empathy can go a long way in building rapport and reaching a mutually beneficial agreement.

It's also important to keep your ego in check during negotiations. Sometimes, people get so caught up in "winning" that they lose sight of the bigger picture. But negotiation isn't a zero-sum game—both parties can win if they focus on creating value rather than simply outsmarting each other. For instance, if you're negotiating a business deal, securing slightly better terms might feel like a win in the short term, but if it leads to a strained relationship or future disagreements, it could cost you more in the long run. Prioritizing long-term relationships and shared success is often a better strategy than seeking to "win" at any cost.

Preparation, confidence, listening, and emotional intelligence all come together to form the foundation of successful negotiation. These skills are not just valuable in the boardroom or during salary discussions—they're applicable to everyday life, from negotiating with service providers to discussing terms with landlords or even working out household budgets with family members. The more you practice, the more natural these skills become, and the more opportunities you'll find to create value in your life.

The art of negotiation also extends to negotiating with yourself. Self-negotiation is about setting boundaries, holding yourself accountable, and making decisions that align with your long-term goals rather than succumbing to short-term desires. It's about being your own advocate, pushing yourself to achieve more while also knowing when to take a step back and recharge. This internal dialogue is just as important as any external negotiation because it determines the trajectory of your financial and personal growth.

One of the most common areas of self-negotiation is budgeting. Creating a budget is essentially a negotiation between your present self and your future self—deciding how much to spend today versus how much to save for tomorrow. It requires discipline and honesty, recognizing where you might be overspending and finding ways to adjust. For example, if you find yourself spending too much on takeout each month, self-negotiation might involve setting a realistic goal for how many times you'll cook at home instead. It's about finding a balance that allows you to enjoy life while staying committed to your financial goals.

Self-negotiation also involves setting realistic yet ambitious goals. It's easy to dream big, but achieving those dreams requires breaking them down into actionable steps and holding yourself accountable for making progress. For example, if your goal is to save $10,000 for an investment property, you'll need to negotiate with yourself about how much you'll save each month and what sacrifices you're willing to make to reach that goal. This might mean cutting back on non-essential expenses or finding ways to increase your income. It's not about being hard on yourself—it's about being intentional with your choices.

The ability to negotiate with yourself also helps you stay focused during challenging times. Life doesn't always go according to plan, and setbacks are inevitable. When these setbacks occur, it's easy to become discouraged and give up on your goals. But by negotiating with yourself, you can find a way to adapt your plans and stay committed to your vision. For example, if you face an unexpected medical expense that sets back your savings goal, self-negotiation might involve revising your timeline while finding new ways to make up for the shortfall. This flexibility allows you to keep moving forward, even when the path is not straightforward.

Self-negotiation also means knowing when to reward yourself for your efforts. Just as it's important to hold yourself accountable, it's equally important to celebrate your achievements along the way. These rewards don't have to be extravagant—a small treat, a day off, or a special outing can serve as a way to recognize your progress and maintain your motivation. By balancing discipline with celebration, you create a sustainable approach to personal growth and financial success.

CHAPTER 4: THE POWER OF FINANCIAL EDUCATION—UNDERSTANDING MONEY'S RULES

Financial education is the foundation upon which wealth is built. Understanding how money works is not just about learning to save or invest; it's about gaining the knowledge to navigate a complex financial world and make decisions that align with your goals. Many people think that financial literacy is only about math, but it's more about understanding the principles that govern wealth creation, risk management, and the strategies that successful people use to grow their resources.

One of the first lessons in financial education is understanding the flow of money. Money doesn't grow by sitting in a savings account or under a mattress—it grows by being put to work. This is why the wealthy focus on investing their money rather than just saving it. Investing allows your money to generate returns, whether through stocks, bonds, real estate, or business ventures. The key is to understand the different types of investments, their risks, and how they can fit into your overall strategy.

But before diving into investments, it's crucial to understand the basics of income and expenses. Income can come from multiple sources, including wages, rental income, investment returns, and side businesses. Expenses, on the other hand, include everything that takes money out of your pocket, like rent, groceries, utilities, and discretionary spending. Understanding the relationship between income and expenses is the first step to managing cash flow and ensuring that you're living within your means while building a surplus that can be invested.

A common mistake is to focus only on increasing income without managing expenses. While earning more money is important, it's equally important to ensure that your expenses don't grow at the same rate. Many high earners find themselves living paycheck to paycheck because they allow their spending to keep pace with their earnings. This phenomenon is known as lifestyle inflation, and it can prevent you from building wealth even as your salary grows. True financial success comes from maintaining a gap between income and expenses and using that gap to invest in assets that generate additional income.

One of the core concepts of financial education is understanding the power of compound interest. Albert Einstein is often credited with calling compound interest the "eighth wonder of the world," and for good reason. Compound interest is the process where your investment gains generate their own returns, leading to exponential growth over time. It's the reason why starting to invest early can be so powerful—because even small amounts of money can grow significantly if given enough time.

For example, if you invest $1,000 at an annual interest rate of 7%, it would grow to about $1,967 in ten years. But if you leave it invested for 20 years, it would grow to about $3,870, and after 30 years, it would be worth approximately $7,612. The initial amount stays the same, but the returns become larger as time goes on because each year, you earn interest on both your original investment and the interest that has already accumulated. This exponential growth is what makes compound interest so powerful, turning small, consistent investments into a significant nest egg over time.

Compound interest works both ways, though, and it's equally important to understand how it affects debt. Just as compound interest can help your investments grow, it can also make debt more expensive over time. Credit card debt, for example, is notorious for its high-interest rates, which can quickly turn a small balance into a financial burden. If you carry a balance on a credit card with an 18% interest rate, that balance can double in just four years if you make only the minimum payments. This is why it's so important to pay off high-interest debt as quickly as possible—because compound interest can work against you just as easily as it can work in your favor.

Understanding the principles of compound interest allows you to make smarter decisions about saving, investing, and managing debt. It helps you recognize the value of starting early, even if you can only invest a small amount. It also underscores the importance of avoiding debt traps that can hold you back from building wealth. When you understand the power of compound interest, you start to see money as a tool that can either work for you or against you, depending on how you use it.

Another critical element of financial education is learning about the different types of investment vehicles and how they can help you achieve your goals. Stocks, bonds, mutual funds, ETFs (Exchange-Traded Funds), and real estate are all common options, but each comes with its own set of risks and potential rewards. Understanding the basics of each allows you to make informed choices about where to put your money and how to diversify your portfolio.

Stocks represent ownership in a company, and when you buy a stock, you become a part-owner of that company. Stocks offer the potential for high returns, especially if the company grows and increases in value. However, they are also more volatile, meaning their value can rise and fall quickly based on market conditions, company performance, and broader economic trends. For those willing to accept this volatility, stocks can be an effective way to grow wealth over the long term.

Bonds, on the other hand, are considered more conservative investments. When you buy a bond, you are essentially lending money to a company or government in exchange for regular interest payments and the return of your principal at maturity. Bonds tend to be less volatile than stocks, but they also offer lower returns. They are often used to provide stability to an investment portfolio, especially as investors approach retirement and want to reduce their exposure to market fluctuations.

Mutual funds and ETFs allow you to invest in a diversified basket of stocks or bonds without having to pick individual securities yourself. They are managed by professional fund managers and can be an excellent option for those who want a diversified portfolio without having to do extensive research. Mutual funds often have higher fees than ETFs, but they can offer a wide range of investment strategies, from aggressive growth funds to conservative bond funds.

Real estate is another popular investment vehicle, offering the potential for rental income and long-term appreciation. Real estate can provide a steady cash flow if you invest in rental properties, and it also serves as a tangible asset that tends to appreciate over time. However, real estate requires more hands-on management than stocks or bonds, as you'll need to deal with tenants, maintenance, and property taxes. Understanding the risks and rewards of real estate investing is essential if you want to make it a part of your asset-building strategy.

In addition to understanding investment vehicles, it's also essential to learn about investment strategies that align with your financial goals and risk tolerance. Some investors prefer a more passive approach, such as investing in index funds, which track the performance of a specific market index like the S&P 500. Index funds offer a simple way to achieve broad market exposure with lower fees, making them a popular choice for long-term investors who want to benefit from overall market growth without having to pick individual stocks.

Active investing, on the other hand, involves selecting individual stocks, bonds, or other assets with the goal of outperforming the market. This approach requires more research, analysis, and time commitment, as you'll need to stay up-to-date with market trends, company performance, and economic indicators. While active investing has the potential for higher returns, it also comes with greater risks, as individual stock picks may not always perform as expected.

One of the most effective investment strategies for beginners is dollar-cost averaging, which involves investing a fixed amount of money at regular intervals, regardless of market conditions. This strategy takes the emotion out of investing and ensures that you're buying more shares when prices are low and fewer shares when prices are high. Over time, this approach can help smooth out the impact of market volatility and build wealth steadily.

Diversification is another crucial strategy that helps manage risk by spreading your investments across different asset classes, industries, and geographical regions. A diversified portfolio might include a mix of stocks, bonds, real estate, and cash, as well as international investments that offer exposure to different markets. Diversification helps protect your portfolio from major losses, as the performance of one investment can offset the losses of another. For example, if your stock investments are experiencing a downturn, your bonds might be performing better, helping to balance your overall returns.

Rebalancing is a strategy that involves adjusting your investment portfolio periodically to maintain your desired asset allocation. For example, if your target allocation is 60% stocks and 40% bonds, but a market rally causes the stock portion of your portfolio to grow to 70%, rebalancing would involve selling some stocks and buying more bonds to return to the original allocation. Rebalancing helps ensure that your portfolio stays aligned with your risk tolerance and long-term goals, allowing you to maintain a consistent strategy even as markets fluctuate.

Understanding financial education also means learning about the psychological aspects of investing. Emotions like fear, greed, and overconfidence can influence decision-making and lead to mistakes that hinder financial progress. Recognizing these psychological factors and learning how to manage them can help you become a more disciplined and successful investor.

Fear is one of the most common emotions that can affect investors, especially during market downturns. When the market drops, it's natural to feel anxious about losing money, but selling investments out of fear can lock in losses and prevent you from benefiting from future market recoveries. Successful investors learn to manage their fear by focusing on the long-term and understanding that market corrections are a normal part of the investment cycle. By maintaining a long-term perspective and sticking to your plan, you can avoid making impulsive decisions that could harm your portfolio.

Greed can also be a powerful motivator, leading investors to take on more risk than they can handle or to chase after "hot" investments that promise quick gains. This can be especially tempting when markets are booming, and it seems like everyone else is making money. However, chasing after high-risk investments without fully understanding the risks can lead to significant losses. The key is to remain disciplined, stick to your investment strategy, and avoid the temptation to jump into investments without proper research.

Overconfidence can be another trap for investors, especially those who have experienced some early success. It's easy to assume that a few winning stock picks mean you have the Midas touch, but the reality is that markets are unpredictable, and even the best investors make mistakes. Overconfidence can lead to taking on excessive risk, failing to diversify, or ignoring the need for a well-rounded financial plan. By staying humble, acknowledging what you don't know, and continuing to learn, you can avoid the pitfalls of overconfidence and make more thoughtful investment decisions.

Patience and discipline are two of the most valuable traits for any investor. Building wealth through investing takes time, and it's important to resist the urge to constantly check your portfolio or make changes based on short-term market movements. Instead, focus on your long-term goals and remember that true wealth is built through consistent, disciplined action over time. By mastering the psychological aspects of investing, you can create a mindset that supports your financial success.

A critical part of financial education is understanding how taxes impact your investments and overall financial strategy. Taxes can take a significant chunk out of your returns, but with the right knowledge, you can minimize your tax burden and keep more of your money working for you. Tax planning is not just for the wealthy; it's an essential skill for anyone who wants to build long-term wealth. By learning how to navigate the tax code, you can make informed decisions that align with your financial goals.

One of the most basic concepts in tax planning is the difference between earned income and investment income. Earned income comes from wages, salaries, and business profits, while investment income comes from sources like dividends, interest, and capital gains. Understanding how these types of income are taxed differently allows you to plan strategically. For example, capital gains from investments held for more than a year are often taxed at a lower rate than ordinary income, making long-term investing a tax-efficient way to grow wealth.

Dividends, which are payments made by companies to their shareholders, can be a valuable source of passive income. However, not all dividends are taxed the same. Qualified dividends, which come from shares of U.S. corporations or certain foreign companies, are taxed at the lower long-term capital gains rate, while non-qualified dividends are taxed at your regular income tax rate. Knowing the difference can help you select investments that offer more favorable tax treatment and enhance your overall returns.

Retirement accounts offer another powerful way to reduce your tax liability. Contributions to accounts like 401(k)s and traditional IRAs are often tax-deductible, meaning you can reduce your taxable income for the year by contributing to these accounts. This not only helps you save for retirement but also allows you to benefit from tax-deferred growth, meaning you won't pay taxes on your investment earnings until you withdraw the money in retirement. This strategy can be particularly effective if you expect to be in a lower tax bracket when you retire, as it allows you to pay taxes when your income is lower.

Roth IRAs provide a different kind of tax advantage. Unlike traditional IRAs, contributions to a Roth IRA are made with after-tax dollars, meaning you don't get a tax deduction upfront. However, the trade-off is that qualified withdrawals in retirement are tax-free, including any investment gains. This can be a huge advantage if you expect to be in a higher tax bracket when you retire or if you want to minimize your tax burden during your retirement years. Roth IRAs also offer more flexibility, as they don't require mandatory withdrawals like traditional IRAs, allowing your money to grow longer if you don't need it immediately.

Tax-loss harvesting is another strategy that can help investors minimize their tax liability. It involves selling investments that have declined in value to offset gains from other investments. For example, if you have stocks that have appreciated, but you also have stocks that have lost value, selling the losing investments can help offset the taxable gains, reducing the amount of capital gains tax you owe. The key is to understand the "wash-sale" rule, which prevents you from buying a substantially identical investment within 30 days of selling it, as this would disqualify the tax benefit. Tax-loss harvesting can be especially valuable during years when the market is down, allowing you to turn a loss into a long-term benefit.

Another aspect of tax planning involves understanding how state and local taxes affect your overall financial picture. In some states, income taxes can be as high as 10% or more, while other states have no state income tax at all. This can have a big impact on where you choose to live and retire, as well as where you decide to invest in real estate or start a business. If you're planning to move, it's worth considering how the tax rates in different states could affect your overall financial plan. While taxes shouldn't be the only factor in your decision, they can be a significant consideration when comparing the cost of living in different areas.

For those who own their own businesses, understanding the available tax deductions is crucial. Business expenses like office space, supplies, travel, and even a portion of your home if you use it as a home office can be deducted from your taxable income. This reduces the amount of income you pay taxes on, allowing you to keep more of your hard-earned money. Staying organized and keeping detailed records of your expenses can make tax time much easier and help ensure that you're not missing out on valuable deductions. Working with a tax professional can also help you identify deductions that you might not be aware of.

Financial education is not just about understanding numbers; it's also about understanding human behavior and the role it plays in financial decisions. Behavioral finance is a field that examines how psychological factors influence investors' actions, often leading to mistakes that can be costly. Recognizing these behavioral biases can help you avoid common pitfalls and make more rational decisions when it comes to managing money.

One common bias is *loss aversion*, which refers to the tendency to feel the pain of a loss more acutely than the pleasure of a gain. For example, the discomfort of losing $100 can feel more intense than the satisfaction of gaining $100. This bias can lead investors to hold on to losing investments for too long, hoping to avoid realizing a loss, even when it would be wiser to cut their losses and invest in a more promising opportunity. By understanding loss aversion, you can learn to focus on the long-term potential of your investments rather than reacting emotionally to short-term losses.

Another behavioral bias is *overconfidence*, which can lead people to overestimate their knowledge or abilities when making investment decisions. Overconfident investors might trade too frequently, believing they can time the market or pick winning stocks consistently. However, studies have shown that frequent trading often leads to lower returns, as transaction costs and market timing mistakes erode gains. Recognizing the limits of your knowledge and the unpredictability of markets can help you adopt a more disciplined approach, such as sticking to a diversified, long-term investment plan.

Herd mentality is another common bias that can affect investors, causing them to follow the crowd without fully understanding why. This can lead to buying assets that are overpriced because "everyone else is doing it," or selling in a panic during a market downturn. History is full of examples where herd mentality has led to market bubbles and crashes, from the dot-com bubble of the late 1990s to the housing market crash of 2008. Understanding this tendency can help you stay grounded and resist the urge to follow trends blindly, instead focusing on your own research and long-term strategy.

An often-overlooked part of financial education is the importance of building financial resilience. Financial resilience is the ability to withstand and recover from unexpected financial setbacks, such as a job loss, medical emergency, or economic downturn. It's about being prepared for the uncertainties of life and having a plan in place to navigate challenges without derailing your long-term financial goals. Building financial resilience is not just a safety net—it's a foundation that gives you the confidence to take calculated risks and pursue opportunities.

An emergency fund is the cornerstone of financial resilience. It's a pool of money set aside specifically for unplanned expenses, providing you with a buffer that allows you to cover costs without going into debt. Most financial experts recommend having three to six months' worth of living expenses in an easily accessible savings account. This ensures that if you experience a job loss or an unexpected medical bill, you can continue to meet your financial obligations without resorting to high-interest credit cards or loans. The peace of mind that comes from having an emergency fund can be invaluable, allowing you to stay focused on your long-term goals even when life throws a curveball.

Insurance is another critical part of building financial resilience. Health insurance, life insurance, and disability insurance are all designed to protect you and your family from financial hardship in case of illness, injury, or death. While no one likes to think about these scenarios, being prepared ensures that you're not left financially vulnerable if the worst happens. For example, life insurance can provide your loved ones with the resources they need to maintain their standard of living, pay off debts, and cover final expenses in the event of your passing.

Disability insurance is equally important, especially for those who rely on their income to support their families. It replaces a portion of your income if you're unable to work due to illness or injury, ensuring that you can continue to pay your bills and support your loved ones during a difficult time. Many employers offer disability insurance as part of their benefits package, but it's worth considering additional coverage if your employer's plan doesn't provide sufficient protection. Investing in the right types of insurance is a way of protecting your wealth-building efforts and ensuring that you have the resources to recover from setbacks.

Building financial resilience also involves creating multiple streams of income. Relying on a single source of income can leave you vulnerable if that source dries up. Diversifying your income streams allows you to maintain financial stability even if one stream is disrupted. This might involve having a full-time job while also running a side business, investing in rental properties, or earning passive income through dividends or royalties. By creating a mix of active and passive income sources, you can increase your financial security and build wealth more effectively.

Side hustles are one way to create additional income, and in today's gig economy, there are countless opportunities to earn money outside of a traditional job. From freelance writing and graphic design to tutoring or offering services like pet sitting, side hustles can provide a valuable supplement to your primary income. The key is to choose a side hustle that aligns with your skills and interests, allowing you to enjoy the work while also building your financial resilience.

Passive income sources, such as rental properties or dividend-paying stocks, are another way to diversify your income. Unlike active income, where you trade time for money, passive income allows you to earn money with minimal ongoing effort. For example, investing in dividend-paying stocks means you receive regular payouts without having to manage the companies directly. Rental properties require more involvement, but they can provide a steady stream of cash flow if managed properly. By focusing on building passive income, you create a financial safety net that supports you even if your active income is disrupted.

Creating multiple streams of income is not just about earning more money—it's about creating options and flexibility. It gives you the freedom to make choices based on what's best for you and your family, rather than feeling trapped by financial constraints. Whether it's taking time off to care for a loved one, pursuing a passion project, or exploring new career opportunities, having multiple income streams allows you to live life on your own terms.

Understanding debt and how to manage it is a crucial part of financial education. Not all debt is created equal, and knowing the difference between "good debt" and "bad debt" can help you make decisions that support your long-term financial goals. Debt can be a tool for building wealth when used strategically, but it can also be a trap that keeps people in a cycle of financial struggle when mismanaged.

Good debt is generally considered debt that is used to purchase assets that appreciate or generate income. For example, taking out a mortgage to buy a home or rental property can be considered good debt if the property increases in value over time or provides rental income. Similarly, student loans can be considered good debt if they allow you to gain skills or credentials that lead to higher earning potential. The key to managing good debt is ensuring that the asset you're purchasing will generate enough value to justify the cost of borrowing.

Bad debt, on the other hand, is debt used to purchase items that lose value over time or that don't contribute to your financial growth. This includes high-interest credit card debt, personal loans for non-essential purchases, or borrowing to buy expensive items like cars that depreciate quickly. Bad debt can create a burden on your finances, making it harder to save, invest, and build wealth. Understanding the difference between good and bad debt helps you make choices that support your financial well-being and avoid borrowing for things that don't offer long-term value.

One of the first steps in managing debt is understanding interest rates. The interest rate determines how much you'll pay in addition to the principal amount you borrowed, and it can vary widely depending on the type of debt and your creditworthiness. For example, credit cards often have interest rates above 20%, while mortgages and student loans might have much lower rates. Focusing on paying off high-interest debt first can save you a significant amount of money over time, as the compounding effect of high interest can make your debt grow quickly if left unpaid.

Creating a debt repayment plan is essential for regaining control over your finances. Two popular methods for paying off debt are the debt snowball and the debt avalanche methods. The debt snowball method involves paying off your smallest debts first, regardless of interest rate. This approach gives you quick wins and a sense of accomplishment, which can provide the motivation needed to tackle larger debts. The idea is that as you pay off smaller balances, you free up more money to put towards the next debt, gradually building momentum like a snowball rolling downhill.

The debt avalanche method, on the other hand, focuses on paying off the debt with the highest interest rate first. This approach is mathematically more efficient because it minimizes the total interest paid over time. By targeting the most expensive debt first, you can reduce the amount of money you lose to interest, which helps you become debt-free more quickly. While the avalanche method might take longer to see progress in the beginning, it can save you more money in the long run. Choosing the method that works best for you depends on your personality and what will keep you motivated to stay the course.

Debt consolidation is another strategy that can make managing debt easier. It involves combining multiple high-interest debts into a single loan with a lower interest rate. This can simplify your payments and reduce the overall interest you pay, making it easier to pay down the balance. For example, if you have several credit cards with high balances, you might consider a personal loan with a lower interest rate to pay off those cards. The key is to avoid using the newly freed-up credit to accumulate more debt, as this can undo the progress you've made.

It's also important to avoid using debt to fund lifestyle inflation. Lifestyle inflation occurs when your expenses increase as your income grows, often leading to using credit cards or loans to finance a more luxurious lifestyle. This can be a major obstacle to financial freedom, as it keeps you in a cycle of working to pay off debt rather than using your income to build assets. By focusing on living within your means and avoiding unnecessary debt, you can create a financial foundation that allows you to save and invest for the future.

An often-overlooked aspect of financial education is the impact of credit scores on your financial life. Your credit score is a numerical representation of your creditworthiness, and it plays a major role in your ability to borrow money, the interest rates you receive, and even your ability to rent an apartment or get a job in some cases. A good credit score can save you thousands of dollars in interest over your lifetime, while a poor credit score can limit your financial options and make borrowing more expensive.

Credit scores are based on several factors, including your payment history, credit utilization, length of credit history, new credit inquiries, and the mix of credit accounts you have. Payment history is the most significant factor, accounting for about 35% of your score. This means that making on-time payments is crucial for maintaining a healthy credit score. Even one missed payment can have a negative impact, so it's important to prioritize paying your bills on time, whether they're credit cards, student loans, or utility bills.

Credit utilization, which refers to the percentage of your available credit that you're using, is another critical factor. It's generally recommended to keep your credit utilization below 30% to maintain a good score. For example, if you have a total credit limit of $10,000, you should aim to keep your balance below $3,000. High credit utilization can signal to lenders that you're relying too heavily on credit, making you appear riskier. Paying down balances and requesting credit limit increases can help lower your credit utilization and improve your score.

The length of your credit history is also important, as it shows lenders how long you've been managing credit. The longer your history, the more data lenders have to assess your creditworthiness. For this reason, it's generally a good idea to keep older credit accounts open, even if you're not using them frequently, as closing them can shorten your credit history and potentially lower your score. Understanding these factors allows you to take proactive steps to build and maintain a strong credit score, opening up more financial opportunities.

One of the most powerful benefits of financial education is the ability to recognize and seize opportunities for growth. The world is full of investment opportunities, side hustles, and entrepreneurial ventures that can help you build wealth, but recognizing these opportunities requires a certain mindset. It's about being curious, staying informed, and developing a willingness to step outside of your comfort zone when the right opportunity comes along.

Opportunities often come disguised as challenges or changes. For example, economic downturns can be a difficult time for many, but they can also present opportunities to buy undervalued stocks or real estate. When markets decline, quality assets can go on sale, allowing those with the right mindset and a bit of capital to invest for future gains. The key is to have a long-term perspective and to focus on the intrinsic value of the investments rather than being swayed by market sentiment.

Entrepreneurial opportunities can also arise from identifying gaps in the market. This could mean starting a business that solves a problem you've encountered or offering a service that is in high demand. For example, the rise of digital tools and platforms has made it easier than ever to start a side business, whether it's offering online courses, providing consulting services, or creating content for social media. The most successful entrepreneurs are often those who can identify emerging trends and adapt quickly to meet new demands.

Networking is another way to uncover opportunities. Building relationships with people in your industry or area of interest can open doors that might otherwise remain closed. Attending conferences, joining online communities, and participating in networking events can introduce you to mentors, investors, and potential business partners. These connections can provide valuable insights, support, and even investment capital that can help you take your financial ventures to the next level.

Building a strong foundation in financial education also means developing a deep understanding of cash flow management. Cash flow refers to the movement of money in and out of your personal finances or business, and it's one of the most critical indicators of financial health. Positive cash flow means that more money is coming in than going out, while negative cash flow means that you're spending more than you're earning. Managing cash flow effectively is essential for maintaining financial stability, making investments, and achieving long-term financial goals.

One of the most important aspects of cash flow management is tracking your income and expenses. This might sound simple, but many people overlook this basic step, leading to confusion about where their money is going. By tracking every dollar you earn and spend, you can identify patterns, spot areas where you might be overspending, and make adjustments to align your spending with your priorities. This process can be as simple as using a spreadsheet or a budgeting app to categorize your expenses and monitor your progress over time.

Creating a budget is a powerful tool for managing cash flow. A budget helps you allocate your income towards necessary expenses, savings, and investments, ensuring that you're living within your means and setting money aside for future goals. For example, you might use the 50/30/20 rule, where 50% of your income goes towards needs like housing and utilities, 30% goes towards wants like dining out and entertainment, and 20% goes towards savings and investments. This framework can help you balance enjoying life today with planning for tomorrow.

Another aspect of managing cash flow is understanding the timing of your income and expenses. This is especially important for entrepreneurs, freelancers, or those with irregular income. If you're paid on a project basis, you might have months with high earnings followed by slower periods. Planning for these fluctuations by setting aside a portion of your income during good months can help you maintain stability during leaner times. Similarly, timing your expenses—such as paying bills right after receiving income—can help you avoid cash flow gaps that might require you to dip into savings or take on debt.

Financial education also involves learning how to navigate different economic cycles. Understanding how the economy affects your personal finances, investments, and job prospects is key to making smart decisions, especially during periods of economic change. The economy moves through cycles of growth, peak, contraction, and recovery, and each phase presents different challenges and opportunities for building and preserving wealth.

During periods of economic growth, job opportunities tend to be plentiful, wages often rise, and businesses thrive. This is typically a time when stock markets perform well, consumer spending is high, and real estate markets appreciate. For individuals, this can be an ideal time to focus on increasing savings, investing in stocks or property, and taking advantage of low unemployment rates to negotiate higher salaries. It's also a time to prepare for the future by building an emergency fund and paying down debt, so you're better positioned when the cycle shifts.

Economic peaks occur when growth reaches its highest point, and signs of overheating in the economy can start to appear. Inflation may rise, asset prices may become overvalued, and central banks might increase interest rates to cool down the economy. For investors, this is a time to exercise caution, as markets can become more volatile and the risk of a downturn increases. It's important to review your portfolio, ensure that it's well-diversified, and consider taking profits from investments that have grown significantly. Staying vigilant and prepared during economic peaks can help you protect your wealth as the cycle moves into the contraction phase.

The contraction phase, or recession, is characterized by slowing economic activity, rising unemployment, and declining asset values. This can be a challenging time, but it can also present opportunities for those who are prepared. Recessions often lead to lower stock and real estate prices, making it a good time to invest if you have a long-term perspective and the financial stability to withstand short-term losses. Having an emergency fund and maintaining a conservative approach to debt can provide a cushion during this period, allowing you to take advantage of lower prices without putting your financial security at risk.

During the recovery phase, the economy begins to grow again, businesses start to hire, and consumer confidence improves. This is a time when investment markets often rebound, making it important to stay invested during downturns so you can benefit from the recovery. It's also a time to reassess your financial goals and adjust your strategy to align with the new economic landscape. For example, if you used a recession to buy undervalued stocks or real estate, the recovery phase may be a time to hold those assets as they appreciate in value.

Understanding economic cycles allows you to take a proactive approach to your finances, rather than reacting out of fear or excitement when markets change. It helps you maintain perspective during downturns, knowing that they are a natural part of the economic landscape, and it allows you to recognize opportunities when others are hesitant to act. By aligning your financial strategy with the current phase of the economic cycle, you can make decisions that position you for long-term success.

In addition to understanding the broader economic cycle, it's also important to be aware of how interest rates impact your financial life. Interest rates affect everything from mortgage payments and car loans to credit card debt and investment returns. When interest rates rise, borrowing becomes more expensive, which can slow down spending and investment. Conversely, when interest rates are low, borrowing becomes cheaper, encouraging spending and making it easier for businesses to invest in growth.

For homeowners, rising interest rates can mean higher monthly mortgage payments if they have an adjustable-rate mortgage (ARM). It can also lead to lower property values, as potential buyers may find it more difficult to afford homes. On the other hand, higher interest rates can benefit savers, as savings accounts, CDs (Certificates of Deposit), and bonds tend to offer better returns during these periods. Understanding how interest rates affect different aspects of your finances allows you to adjust your strategy based on current conditions, whether that means refinancing a mortgage, shifting your investment focus, or building up savings.

Interest rates also play a crucial role in the stock market and investment decisions. When interest rates are low, borrowing costs are lower, making it easier for businesses to take out loans to expand operations, invest in new projects, and increase profitability. This often leads to higher stock prices, as investors are willing to pay more for shares of companies that are growing. Conversely, when interest rates rise, the cost of borrowing increases, which can lead to slower business growth and lower stock valuations. Investors may shift their money from stocks to bonds or savings accounts, which become more attractive as interest rates increase.

For bond investors, understanding the relationship between interest rates and bond prices is particularly important. When interest rates rise, the prices of existing bonds tend to fall because new bonds offer higher yields, making older bonds with lower yields less attractive. This means that if you own bonds and interest rates go up, the value of your bonds may decrease.

However, if you hold those bonds until maturity, you will still receive the face value. On the other hand, when interest rates fall, the value of existing bonds tends to rise, making them more valuable to investors.

Interest rates also impact the exchange rates between currencies, which can affect anyone who invests in foreign markets or travels internationally. For example, when a country raises its interest rates, its currency often becomes stronger because higher rates attract foreign investors looking for better returns on their investments. A stronger currency can make imported goods cheaper, but it can also make exports more expensive, which can affect businesses that rely on global markets. Understanding these dynamics can help you make informed decisions if you're investing in foreign stocks or bonds or if you're planning to travel or work abroad.

In addition to economic cycles and interest rates, inflation is another critical factor to consider in financial planning. Inflation is the general increase in prices over time, and it can erode the purchasing power of your money if your income and investments don't keep pace. For example, if inflation is 3% per year, an item that costs $100 today would cost about $103 next year. This might not seem like much, but over time, inflation can significantly reduce the value of your savings if you're not earning a return that outpaces it.

To protect against inflation, it's important to invest in assets that have the potential to grow in value over time. Stocks, real estate, and certain types of bonds are often considered good hedges against inflation because they tend to increase in value as prices rise. For example, companies can often pass on higher costs to consumers by raising prices, which can help maintain their profitability and support stock prices. Real estate values often rise with inflation as the cost of building materials and labor increases, making property ownership a way to preserve purchasing power over time.

Inflation also affects fixed-income investments like bonds and savings accounts. When inflation is high, the real return on bonds can be negative if the interest paid on the bonds is lower than the rate of inflation. This is why some investors choose to include Treasury Inflation-Protected Securities (TIPS) in their portfolios. TIPS are government bonds that are designed to keep up with inflation, providing a way to protect your principal against rising prices. Including TIPS in your investment strategy can help balance the risks associated with traditional bonds during periods of high inflation.

Understanding how inflation affects different aspects of your finances can also inform your approach to saving and budgeting. During times of high inflation, it's especially important to be mindful of how rising prices affect your daily expenses, such as groceries, transportation, and housing. Adjusting your budget to account for these changes can help you maintain control over your spending and avoid dipping into savings to cover increased costs. Being proactive about managing inflation allows you to make adjustments that keep you on track towards your financial goals.

Another way to combat inflation is by focusing on increasing your earning potential. This could mean seeking out opportunities for career advancement, pursuing additional education or certifications, or starting a side business that provides extra income. By focusing on ways to grow your income, you can ensure that your earning power keeps up with or exceeds the rate of inflation, allowing you to maintain your standard of living and continue building wealth over time. The ability to adapt to changing economic conditions is a valuable skill, and it can make a significant difference in your financial success.

One of the most empowering aspects of financial education is learning how to achieve financial independence. Financial independence means having enough income from investments, savings, or passive income sources to cover your living expenses without relying on a traditional job. It's about having the freedom to choose how you spend your time, pursue your passions, and make decisions based on what is best for you and your family, rather than being tied to a paycheck.

The journey to financial independence starts with a clear understanding of your expenses and how much you need to maintain your desired lifestyle. This involves calculating your monthly living expenses, including housing, utilities, food, transportation, and any other costs that are essential to your day-to-day life. Once you have a clear picture of your expenses, you can set a target for how much passive income or investment returns you need to achieve financial independence.

Building a portfolio of income-generating assets is key to achieving this goal. This might include stocks that pay dividends, rental properties that provide cash flow, or businesses that generate passive income. The idea is to create a diverse stream of income sources that can support your lifestyle without requiring active work. For example, if your living expenses are $3,000 per month, you might aim to build a portfolio that generates $3,000 per month in passive income. This could come from a combination of stock dividends, rental income, and interest from bonds.

One popular strategy for achieving financial independence is the FIRE movement—Financial Independence, Retire Early. FIRE advocates focus on aggressively saving and investing a large portion of their income, often aiming for savings rates of 50% or more. The idea is to reach a point where investment returns can cover living expenses, allowing them to retire from traditional work much earlier than the typical retirement age. While the FIRE lifestyle requires a high level of discipline and frugality, it can offer a path to freedom for those who are willing to make sacrifices in the short term for greater flexibility in the future.

Achieving financial independence isn't just about building wealth; it's about changing the way you think about money. It requires shifting from a mindset of dependency—relying on a paycheck or employer—to a mindset of empowerment, where you're in control of your financial future. This shift is fundamental because financial independence is as much a mental journey as it is a financial one. It's about rethinking how you approach spending, saving, and investing, and developing the discipline to prioritize long-term goals over short-term gratification.

One of the first steps towards this shift is developing a *scarcity to abundance* mindset. A scarcity mindset focuses on limitations—constantly worrying about not having enough money, opportunities, or resources. This can create a sense of fear and urgency that leads to impulsive financial decisions. On the other hand, an abundance mindset focuses on possibilities, growth, and the potential to create wealth through strategic actions. It encourages you to see money as a tool that can be used to generate more opportunities rather than something to be feared.

With an abundance mindset, you're more likely to take calculated risks, such as starting a side business, investing in real estate, or learning new skills that can increase your earning potential. You see challenges as opportunities for growth rather than as insurmountable barriers. For example, instead of thinking, "I'll never be able to save enough to buy a house," you might think, "What steps can I take to increase my savings and make homeownership a reality?" This shift in thinking is powerful because it opens up new pathways for achieving your goals and helps you stay motivated through setbacks.

Another important mindset shift is focusing on *delayed gratification*. This means making sacrifices in the short term for the sake of greater rewards in the future. It's the willingness to live below your means, save diligently, and invest wisely, even when it means forgoing certain luxuries today. For instance, choosing to live in a smaller apartment or drive an older car might allow you to save more money that can be invested in assets that appreciate over time. Delayed gratification is what enables you to build a financial cushion, take advantage of investment opportunities, and eventually reach a point where you're no longer dependent on a paycheck.

Building financial independence also means being intentional about where you put your money. It's about recognizing that every dollar is a potential employee, and just like a good manager, you want to put your dollars to work in the most efficient way possible. This is where budgeting, goal-setting, and tracking your progress become essential tools. By giving each dollar a job—whether it's saving, investing, or paying down debt—you ensure that your money is always working towards your goals, not being wasted on mindless spending.

A zero-based budget can be particularly effective for those working towards financial independence. This budgeting method involves assigning every dollar of income a specific purpose until you reach zero. For example, if you earn $4,000 per month, you would allocate every dollar towards expenses, savings, and investments until you've accounted for the full $4,000. This approach forces you to be intentional with your spending and helps you avoid the trap of lifestyle inflation, ensuring that any increases in income go towards building wealth rather than unnecessary purchases.

Automating your finances is another powerful tool for staying on track towards financial independence. Automating means setting up automatic transfers to savings accounts, investment accounts, and bill payments, so that you don't have to rely on willpower to make smart financial decisions. For example, you might set up an automatic transfer to a high-yield savings account each time you receive a paycheck, ensuring that you're consistently saving a portion of your income before you have a chance to spend it. Automation helps you stay consistent, even during busy periods when it's easy to let financial discipline slip.

Tracking your progress is also crucial for staying motivated on the path to financial independence. This might involve calculating your net worth regularly—adding up the value of all your assets (like cash, investments, and real estate) and subtracting your liabilities (such as mortgages, credit card debt, and student loans). Watching your net worth grow over time can provide a sense of accomplishment and reinforce your commitment to making smart financial choices. It's a reminder that every small step you take—every dollar saved, every debt paid off—brings you closer to your goal.

A significant part of financial education is understanding the concept of *financial freedom* versus *financial security*. While the two terms are often used interchangeably, they represent different stages in the journey towards controlling your financial destiny. Financial security is the point at which your basic living expenses are covered by passive income, savings, or investments, allowing you to meet your needs without financial anxiety. Financial freedom, on the other hand, is the stage where your passive income or investments generate enough money to support your desired lifestyle without needing to work unless you choose to.

Reaching financial security is the first milestone, and it involves building a solid emergency fund, paying off high-interest debt, and ensuring that your investments can generate enough income to cover essential expenses like housing, utilities, and groceries. For many, achieving financial security is a huge relief, as it means no longer living paycheck to paycheck or worrying about how to handle an unexpected expense. It gives you the confidence to take risks, whether that means starting a new career, launching a business, or pursuing personal passions that might not generate immediate income.

Financial freedom goes beyond security by providing the means to live life on your own terms. It allows you to travel, pursue hobbies, spend time with family, or contribute to causes that matter to you without being constrained by financial obligations. For some, financial freedom means retiring early, while for others, it means having the flexibility to work part-time, take sabbaticals, or explore creative endeavors. The definition of financial freedom is personal, but it always involves a sense of autonomy and the ability to make choices based on what brings fulfillment rather than what pays the bills.

To move from financial security to financial freedom, it's important to focus on building *scalable income streams*. Scalable income refers to earnings that can grow without a corresponding increase in time or effort. This could include investment income, such as dividends or rental income, or building a business that generates revenue even when you're not actively involved in day-to-day operations. For example, creating digital products, such as e-books, courses, or software, can provide scalable income because once the initial work is done, you can sell the product repeatedly without significant additional effort.

Developing the mindset and skills to achieve financial freedom also involves learning to differentiate between *assets* and *liabilities*. Robert Kiyosaki, the author of *Rich Dad Poor Dad*, popularized the idea that assets are things that put money into your pocket, while liabilities are things that take money out of your pocket. This simple distinction can change the way you think about purchases and investments, encouraging you to focus on acquiring assets that generate cash flow rather than liabilities that drain your resources.

For example, a car might be considered a liability because it requires ongoing expenses for fuel, maintenance, and insurance, and it depreciates in value over time. However, if you use that car for a business, like offering rideshare services, it can become an asset because it generates income that exceeds the cost of ownership. Real estate, when rented out to tenants, is another example of an asset, as it can provide a steady stream of rental income while appreciating in value over time.

It's important to note that assets can also be intangible, such as skills, knowledge, and relationships that create opportunities for earning and growth. Investing in education, attending industry conferences, or building a strong professional network can be seen as building intangible assets that contribute to your overall financial success. These investments in yourself can open doors to higher-paying jobs, business opportunities, or new ways to generate passive income.

Liabilities, on the other hand, often involve debt or obligations that require regular payments, such as a mortgage, car loan, or credit card balance. While some liabilities, like a mortgage, can be part of a wealth-building strategy if managed carefully, others can be a drag on your financial progress. High-interest debt, like credit card balances, can quickly spiral out of control if not addressed, eating away at the money that could otherwise be invested in building assets. This is why paying down high-interest debt is often a priority for those working towards financial independence—it frees up cash flow that can be redirected towards wealth-building activities.

Achieving financial independence requires developing a strong *wealth-building mindset*. This mindset is about seeing opportunities where others see obstacles, staying persistent in the face of setbacks, and continually seeking ways to improve your financial situation. It's about being willing to put in the effort to learn new skills, adapt to changing circumstances, and make decisions that align with your long-term vision for your life. A wealth-building mindset doesn't come naturally to everyone, but it can be developed through consistent effort and a commitment to growth.

One of the most important aspects of this mindset is *self-discipline*. Building wealth is a marathon, not a sprint, and it requires the ability to make smart decisions consistently over time. This might mean saying no to impulse purchases, choosing to invest extra money rather than spending it, or sticking to a budget even when it feels restrictive. Self-discipline allows you to stay focused on your goals and make decisions that bring you closer to financial freedom, even when those decisions aren't easy.

Another key trait is *resilience*. The path to financial independence is rarely a straight line, and setbacks are inevitable. You might experience job loss, investment losses, or unexpected expenses that throw your plans off course. Developing resilience means being able to bounce back from these setbacks and continue moving forward. It's about maintaining a long-term perspective, recognizing that a single setback doesn't define your financial future, and being willing to adjust your plans as needed.

Finally, a wealth-building mindset is about being *proactive*. It means taking responsibility for your financial life and actively seeking out opportunities for improvement. This could involve learning new investment strategies, finding ways to reduce expenses, or exploring new income streams. Being proactive also means not waiting for perfect conditions before you start—whether it's investing your first dollar, launching a side hustle, or learning about real estate. The sooner you take action, the more time you have to benefit from the power of compound growth and the more opportunities you can create for yourself.

A key component of financial education is understanding the importance of *self-investment*. Investing in yourself means dedicating time, money, and energy into improving your skills, knowledge, and well-being. It's one of the most effective ways to increase your earning potential and set yourself up for long-term success. While many people focus on external investments like stocks and real estate, self-investment can often provide the highest return because it directly impacts your ability to create and seize new opportunities.

Education is one of the most powerful forms of self-investment. This doesn't necessarily mean going back to school for a degree—though that can be a valuable path—but rather continually seeking out opportunities to learn. This could involve taking online courses, attending workshops, reading books on personal finance and entrepreneurship, or finding mentors who can guide you through new challenges. The digital age has made it easier than ever to access knowledge on a wide range of topics, from coding and digital marketing to real estate investing and stock analysis. By dedicating time each day or week to learning, you can stay ahead of trends and adapt to changes in the job market or investment landscape.

Developing soft skills like communication, leadership, and emotional intelligence is also a crucial part of self-investment. These skills are often what separate those who can climb the career ladder or succeed as entrepreneurs from those who struggle to advance. For example, being able to communicate effectively can help you negotiate a higher salary, secure a promotion, or attract investors to your business. Leadership skills allow you to inspire and manage a team, while emotional intelligence helps you navigate interpersonal challenges, both at work and in personal relationships. Investing in these areas can enhance your effectiveness in almost any field.

Physical and mental well-being is another area of self-investment that is often overlooked. Health is foundational to every other aspect of life, including your ability to work, earn, and enjoy the fruits of your labor. Regular exercise, a balanced diet, and time for relaxation and mental clarity can increase your energy levels and productivity, making you more effective in your personal and professional life. Investing in your health might mean spending money on a gym membership, investing in quality nutrition, or taking time to meditate and manage stress. The returns on these investments are less tangible but can significantly impact your quality of life and ability to achieve financial success.

Self-investment also involves building a strong personal brand, especially in today's digital age. A personal brand is how you present yourself to the world—your skills, expertise, values, and the unique qualities that make you stand out. Building a strong personal brand can open doors to new job opportunities, business partnerships, and a broader network of like-minded individuals. It's about creating a reputation that aligns with your goals and allows you to position yourself as a valuable resource in your field.

Social media has become a powerful tool for building a personal brand. Platforms like LinkedIn, Instagram, and even TikTok can be used to showcase your knowledge, share your journey, and connect with others in your industry. For example, if you're passionate about personal finance, you could create content that educates others about budgeting, investing, or achieving financial independence. This not only helps you build a following but also positions you as an expert in your niche, which can lead to speaking opportunities, consulting work, or collaborations with brands.

It's important to approach personal branding with authenticity. People are drawn to stories and experiences that feel real, and they can quickly spot insincerity. Sharing your successes is important, but so is sharing the challenges and lessons learned along the way. This authenticity helps build trust with your audience and makes you more relatable, whether you're seeking a new job, attracting clients to your business, or simply building a network of supportive peers. Personal branding isn't about creating a false image—it's about highlighting your strengths and being open about your journey.

Your personal network is another area where self-investment pays dividends. Building relationships with mentors, peers, and industry leaders can provide you with guidance, support, and access to opportunities that might not be available otherwise. A strong network can be a source of encouragement when you're facing challenges, as well as a pool of knowledge and resources that can help you overcome obstacles. For example, a mentor might introduce you to potential clients or provide feedback on your business ideas, while peers can offer insights into industry trends and best practices. Networking is not just about what others can do for you, but also about how you can provide value to them, creating a mutually beneficial relationship.

A crucial part of financial education is learning how to navigate *financial setbacks* and failures. No matter how carefully you plan, life has a way of throwing unexpected challenges your way, whether it's a job loss, a market downturn, or an unexpected medical expense. The key is not to avoid setbacks altogether—because that's impossible—but to learn how to recover and come back stronger. Resilience in the face of financial setbacks is what separates those who achieve lasting success from those who give up when things get tough.

One of the most important steps in managing financial setbacks is to maintain an *emergency mindset*. This means recognizing that setbacks are a normal part of life and being prepared for them before they happen. This is why having an emergency fund is so important—it provides a financial cushion that allows you to cover unexpected expenses without going into debt or selling off your investments at a loss. An emergency fund gives you breathing room to navigate challenges without feeling panicked, allowing you to make thoughtful decisions about how to move forward.

During financial setbacks, it's also important to focus on what you can control. When the stock market is down or the economy is in a recession, it's easy to feel overwhelmed by factors that are outside of your control. However, focusing on small, actionable steps can help you regain a sense of agency and start to rebuild. This might mean creating a new budget, finding ways to reduce expenses, or looking for side hustles that can provide extra income. By taking control of your daily actions, you can begin to turn the tide, even if progress feels slow at first.

Another strategy for navigating financial setbacks is to *embrace flexibility*. Flexibility means being willing to adapt your plans and adjust your goals in response to changing circumstances. For example, if you lose your job, you might need to pivot to a new industry or take on a temporary role while you search for a better opportunity. If an investment doesn't perform as expected, you might need to adjust your portfolio or explore new asset classes. Flexibility allows you to see setbacks not as failures, but as opportunities to learn, grow, and find new paths forward.

One of the hardest parts of dealing with financial setbacks is managing the emotional toll they can take. Money is deeply tied to our sense of security, identity, and self-worth, and financial difficulties can lead to feelings of anxiety, shame, or hopelessness. Understanding that these feelings are normal is the first step towards managing them in a healthy way. It's important to give yourself grace during challenging times and remember that setbacks don't define your worth or your potential for future success.

Building a *support system* can make a big difference during tough times. This might include talking to friends or family members who understand your situation, joining a support group, or even seeking advice from a financial counselor. Sometimes, just knowing that you're not alone can provide the strength you need to keep going. A support system can also offer practical advice, such as tips for budgeting, job hunting, or finding community resources that can help you get back on your feet.

Practicing *mindfulness and gratitude* is another way to manage the stress that comes with financial setbacks. Mindfulness involves staying present and accepting your current situation without judgment, rather than getting caught up in worries about the future. Gratitude, on the other hand, involves focusing on what you still have, rather than what you've lost. For example, even if you're struggling financially, you might still have a supportive family, good health, or skills that can help you rebuild. Focusing on these positive aspects can provide a sense of perspective and remind you that challenges are temporary.

It's also important to maintain a focus on the long-term, even when facing short-term difficulties. This means keeping your financial goals in mind and remembering that setbacks don't mean you have to abandon those goals entirely. For example, if you're working towards financial independence but experience a job loss, you might need to adjust your timeline, but that doesn't mean you have to give up on the dream. Staying focused on your vision for the future can provide motivation and a sense of direction, even when the path forward feels uncertain.

Rebuilding after a financial setback often requires *reassessing your priorities* and making adjustments to your lifestyle. This might mean cutting back on discretionary spending, finding ways to live more frugally, or redefining what is truly important to you. While these changes can feel difficult in the moment, they can also lead to a simpler, more intentional way of living. Many people find that simplifying their lives after a setback helps them focus on what truly matters, whether that's spending time with loved ones, pursuing hobbies, or finding a sense of purpose outside of material success.

Living frugally doesn't mean depriving yourself of joy—it means being mindful about how you spend your money and making sure that your spending aligns with your values. For example, you might find that cutting back on dining out allows you to save more for future investments, or that canceling unused subscriptions frees up cash for a family trip that you value more. Frugality is about making trade-offs that support your long-term goals, rather than mindlessly spending on things that don't add real value to your life.

As you rebuild, it's also an opportunity to *redefine your relationship with money*. Instead of seeing money as an end goal, you might start to see it as a tool that enables you to create the life you want. This shift in perspective can change the way you approach earning, saving, and investing, making the process more meaningful and less stressful. It allows you to focus on building a life that aligns with your values, rather than constantly chasing a higher income or the next material possession.

Finding new sources of inspiration can be a powerful motivator during the rebuilding process. This might involve reading books or listening to podcasts about people who have overcome similar challenges, or seeking out stories of entrepreneurs who started from nothing and built successful businesses. Inspiration can remind you that setbacks are not the end of the story—they are simply a chapter in a much longer journey. By surrounding yourself with stories of resilience, you can reignite your sense of hope and determination to create a brighter financial future.

As you rebuild and refocus after a financial setback, it's essential to embrace the concept of *financial agility*. Financial agility means being adaptable, open to new opportunities, and willing to adjust your strategy as circumstances change. It's about not being rigidly tied to a single plan but being ready to pivot when necessary. Financial agility is a mindset that enables you to navigate the ups and downs of the financial landscape with confidence, always keeping your long-term goals in sight.

One aspect of financial agility is staying current with trends and changes in the economy, job market, and investment opportunities. The world of work and finance is constantly evolving, and new technologies, industries, and ways of making money can emerge rapidly. For example, the rise of the gig economy has created new opportunities for freelance work, allowing people to earn income outside of traditional employment. Similarly, advancements in technology have opened up new investment opportunities in fields like cryptocurrency, renewable energy, and digital assets.

Staying informed about these trends doesn't mean chasing every new opportunity that comes along, but it does mean being open to learning and adapting. This might involve following financial news, reading books by experts, or taking courses to understand new investment vehicles or market shifts. The goal is to keep your knowledge up-to-date so that when opportunities arise, you're ready to take advantage of them. Financial agility allows you to be proactive rather than reactive, positioning yourself ahead of changes rather than struggling to catch up.

Having multiple income streams is another key component of financial agility. When your income comes from more than one source, you're less vulnerable to changes in any single area. For example, if you lose a job, having a side hustle or passive income from investments can provide a financial cushion while you search for new opportunities. Diversifying your income not only provides stability but also gives you the flexibility to pursue passions and interests that might not immediately pay off. This could mean building a business on the side, investing in rental properties, or creating content that generates ad revenue over time.

Financial agility also means being willing to take *calculated risks*. In the pursuit of financial independence and growth, playing it safe all the time can limit your potential. Calculated risks are risks that you've carefully considered, where the potential rewards outweigh the downsides. This doesn't mean making reckless decisions but rather being willing to step outside of your comfort zone after weighing the pros and cons. Calculated risks often come with the possibility of significant rewards, such as starting a new business, investing in a promising startup, or entering a new market.

For instance, investing in real estate can be a calculated risk. It requires a significant upfront investment and a willingness to manage tenants or properties, but it also offers the potential for long-term cash flow and appreciation. By doing thorough research, understanding market trends, and ensuring you have a financial buffer in place, you can take on such risks in a way that is measured and thoughtful. The same goes for stock market investments—while they can be volatile in the short term, understanding market fundamentals and choosing a diversified portfolio can turn the risk into a strategic opportunity for growth.

Building a risk-taking mindset often involves shifting your perception of failure. Many people fear failure to the point that they avoid taking any risks at all, but the most successful individuals understand that failure is often a stepping stone to growth. Each setback provides valuable lessons that can help you refine your strategy and make better decisions in the future. By viewing failure as part of the learning process, you become more willing to take calculated risks, knowing that even if you don't succeed immediately, you'll gain insights that will be useful down the line.

Having a plan for *risk management* is crucial when taking calculated risks. Risk management involves identifying potential risks and creating strategies to minimize their impact. For example, if you're investing in stocks, you might use stop-loss orders to limit potential losses, or if you're starting a business, you might keep a part-time job until your business is profitable. This approach allows you to pursue ambitious goals while still maintaining a safety net, reducing the likelihood that a single misstep will derail your progress. Risk management is about balancing ambition with caution, ensuring that you remain on a stable path even as you strive for growth.

Building and maintaining *financial resilience* requires a strong focus on long-term planning, even as you adapt to short-term changes. Long-term planning is about setting clear goals and creating a roadmap for achieving them, but it's also about being willing to adjust those goals as your situation evolves. For example, your plan for retirement might include a target savings amount and a desired lifestyle, but as the economy changes or as your family's needs shift, you might need to adjust that target or reallocate your investments.

Creating a long-term financial plan begins with identifying your *financial goals*. These could include saving for a down payment on a home, building an education fund for your children, or reaching a specific net worth by a certain age. It's important to make your goals specific and measurable, such as "save $20,000 for a home down payment within three years" rather than a vague goal like "save more money." Specific goals give you a clear target to work towards and allow you to track your progress over time.

After identifying your goals, the next step is breaking them down into smaller, actionable steps. If your goal is to save $20,000 for a down payment, this might involve setting up automatic transfers to a dedicated savings account, reducing discretionary spending, and finding ways to increase your income through a side hustle. Breaking down big goals into smaller steps makes them feel more achievable and helps you stay motivated by providing regular progress checks. It also allows you to adjust your plan if you encounter obstacles along the way, ensuring that you stay on track even when circumstances change.

A successful long-term plan also includes *regular reviews and adjustments*. This means setting aside time to review your financial situation, track your progress towards your goals, and make adjustments as needed. For example, you might review your investment portfolio annually to ensure that it remains diversified and aligned with your risk tolerance. Or you might adjust your budget if your income changes or if you discover new expenses that need to be accounted for. Regular reviews help you stay focused and make sure that your actions are aligned with your evolving priorities.

One of the key elements of financial resilience and long-term planning is preparing for *retirement*. Retirement planning involves setting aside enough money during your working years to support yourself once you're no longer earning a regular paycheck. It's a process that requires careful thought, as the amount you need will depend on factors like your desired lifestyle, healthcare needs, and how long you expect to live. Retirement planning is about more than just saving—it's about creating a sustainable plan for maintaining your standard of living over time.

Understanding the different retirement accounts available to you is a critical part of this process. In many countries, there are tax-advantaged retirement accounts like 401(k)s, IRAs, or pension plans that allow you to save and invest money with specific tax benefits. For example, contributions to a traditional 401(k) are often tax-deductible, reducing your taxable income in the year you make the contribution. The money in the account then grows tax-deferred until you withdraw it in retirement. Roth accounts, on the other hand, don't offer an upfront tax break, but withdrawals in retirement are tax-free, which can be a huge advantage if you expect to be in a higher tax bracket later in life.

Diversifying your retirement investments is also essential for managing risk. While stocks might provide the potential for high returns, bonds offer more stability and predictable income, making them a key component of many retirement portfolios. Real estate can also play a role in retirement planning, either through owning rental properties that provide income or by owning your primary residence outright, reducing your living expenses. Diversification helps ensure that your retirement savings aren't overly dependent on the performance of any one type of asset, providing a more stable foundation for the future.

It's also important to plan for *healthcare expenses* in retirement. Medical costs tend to rise as we age, and having a strategy for covering these expenses can prevent them from eating into your retirement savings. This might involve contributing to a Health Savings Account (HSA), which offers tax advantages for medical expenses, or purchasing long-term care insurance to cover the costs of in-home care or assisted living. Factoring in healthcare costs helps ensure that you're prepared for whatever the future holds, allowing you to focus on enjoying your retirement without financial worries.

Another critical aspect of long-term planning is creating an *estate plan*. Estate planning involves making arrangements for how your assets will be distributed after your passing, ensuring that your wishes are carried out and that your loved ones are taken care of. While it might not be the most comfortable topic to think about, estate planning is essential for protecting your family's future and preventing disputes over your assets. It can also help reduce the amount of taxes your heirs may have to pay, preserving more of your wealth for the people you care about.

A *will* is one of the most basic tools in estate planning. A will allows you to specify how your assets, such as your home, investments, and personal belongings, will be distributed. It also allows you to name a guardian for any minor children, ensuring that they will be cared for by someone you trust. Without a will, the state will determine how your assets are divided, which may not align with your wishes. Creating a will is a simple but important step in ensuring that your legacy is preserved.

Trusts are another powerful estate planning tool, especially for those with more complex financial situations. A trust allows you to transfer assets to a trustee who manages them for the benefit of your beneficiaries. Trusts can be used to provide for family members, support charitable causes, or manage assets for individuals who may not be able to manage them on their own. They also offer privacy, as the terms of a trust do not become public like a will does. Trusts can help reduce estate taxes and avoid probate, making them a valuable tool for protecting your assets.

Power of attorney and healthcare directives are also important components of an estate plan. A power of attorney allows someone you trust to make financial decisions on your behalf if you become incapacitated, while a healthcare directive outlines your wishes for medical care in case you're unable to communicate them yourself. These documents ensure that your wishes are respected and that your affairs are managed according to your values, even if you're unable to make decisions on your own.

As you think about long-term financial planning, it's essential to consider the impact of *legacy building*. Legacy isn't just about the money or assets you leave behind; it's about the values, lessons, and opportunities you create for the next generation. Legacy building involves a broader view of wealth—not just material wealth, but also the knowledge, principles, and sense of purpose that you pass down. For many, this means not only securing their own financial future but also ensuring that their children, family, or community have the tools they need to thrive.

A key aspect of legacy building is *educating the next generation* about financial literacy. It's one thing to amass wealth, but it's another to ensure that those who inherit it know how to manage it wisely. Teaching your children or younger relatives about budgeting, investing, and the value of hard work can empower them to build on what you leave behind rather than squandering it. This might involve having open conversations about money, involving them in family financial decisions, or even starting investment accounts in their name to teach them about compounding.

Creating a culture of financial responsibility within a family can set the stage for a strong legacy. This doesn't mean imposing strict rules or micromanaging every decision, but rather fostering an environment where financial goals are discussed openly, and everyone understands the importance of planning for the future. It could mean setting up family meetings to review budgets or investment plans, discussing the importance of giving back through charitable contributions, or encouraging each other to pursue entrepreneurial ventures. By making financial responsibility a part of family culture, you create a foundation that supports generational success.

Charitable giving and philanthropy are also important components of legacy building. Many people find fulfillment in using their wealth to support causes that align with their values, whether that means contributing to local community projects, supporting educational programs, or funding initiatives that address global challenges. Setting up a charitable foundation or making regular donations can be a way to extend the impact of your wealth beyond your lifetime. It also provides a powerful example for your children or successors, showing them the importance of using resources to make a positive difference in the world.

For those who run their own businesses, *succession planning* is a critical part of legacy building. Succession planning involves preparing for the day when you step back from the business and ensuring that it continues to thrive under new leadership. Whether you plan to pass the business down to a family member, sell it to an outside party, or transition it to employee ownership, having a clear succession plan helps preserve the value of what you've built and ensures a smooth transition.

Succession planning starts with identifying potential successors and providing them with the training and experience they need to take over. This might mean involving family members in the business from a young age, giving them opportunities to learn different aspects of the operation, or grooming key employees who have shown the potential to lead. It's important to create a culture where leadership skills are developed, and the next generation is encouraged to bring their own vision to the business while respecting its foundational values.

In addition to choosing a successor, it's important to consider the financial aspects of transitioning a business. This might involve setting up a buy-sell agreement, where the terms of transferring ownership are outlined in advance, or working with financial advisors to structure a sale in a way that minimizes tax liabilities. Properly valuing the business and understanding its financial health is crucial for setting fair terms and ensuring that the new leadership is set up for success. This planning ensures that the business can continue to thrive even as it changes hands.

Communicating your vision for the future of the business is also a key part of succession planning. It's not just about handing over the keys; it's about passing on a sense of mission and purpose. This might involve documenting the company's core values, its commitment to customers, and its long-term goals. Sharing this vision with your successors helps ensure that the business remains aligned with its original principles, even as new leadership brings their own ideas and innovations. A well-thought-out succession plan helps ensure that your business remains a part of your legacy, continuing to create opportunities and impact long after you've stepped back.

For those who focus on personal investments, *strategic philanthropy* can be a way to leave a lasting impact while also providing tax benefits that enhance your overall financial plan. Strategic philanthropy involves carefully planning charitable contributions to maximize their impact. Rather than simply writing a check, it means working with non-profits or community organizations to ensure that donations are used effectively to create meaningful change. This could involve funding scholarships, supporting social enterprises, or creating endowments that continue to generate support for a cause over time.

Donor-advised funds (DAFs) are one tool that many people use for strategic philanthropy. A DAF allows you to make a charitable contribution, receive an immediate tax deduction, and then recommend grants to charitable organizations over time. The money in the DAF can be invested, allowing it to grow and support future charitable giving. This approach offers flexibility, as you can decide where to direct your donations at a later date, while also benefiting from the tax deduction at the time of the initial contribution. DAFs can be a powerful way to involve family members in charitable decisions, making philanthropy a shared value and part of your family's legacy.

Planned giving is another aspect of strategic philanthropy that involves making arrangements for charitable contributions as part of your estate plan. This could include leaving a percentage of your estate to a favorite charity, setting up a charitable remainder trust, or designating a non-profit as a beneficiary of a retirement account. Planned giving allows you to make a significant impact on causes that matter to you, while also potentially reducing estate taxes and ensuring that more of your assets go towards supporting your values.

Beyond the financial benefits, strategic philanthropy offers a sense of purpose and fulfillment that goes beyond personal wealth. It's an opportunity to align your resources with your values and to make a lasting contribution to the causes you care about. This can be especially rewarding as you approach retirement or later stages of life, providing a sense of meaning that transcends the accumulation of money. Strategic philanthropy allows you to use your financial knowledge and resources to create positive change in a way that reflects your unique vision for the world.

One of the most rewarding aspects of financial education is understanding the concept of *financial empowerment*. Financial empowerment goes beyond knowing how to save, invest, or budget—it's about gaining the confidence to take control of your financial destiny and the freedom to make choices that align with your values. It's about breaking free from the limitations that might have held you back in the past, whether that's debt, lack of knowledge, or a fear of taking risks. Financial empowerment is the feeling of being in the driver's seat of your financial life, able to steer it in the direction you choose.

Achieving financial empowerment often involves challenging the beliefs and narratives you hold about money. Many people grow up with limiting beliefs, such as "I'm not good with money," or "Investing is too risky for me." These beliefs can become self-fulfilling prophecies, holding you back from reaching your potential. Part of the process of financial empowerment is recognizing these beliefs and replacing them with more empowering thoughts, such as "I am capable of learning about money," or "Investing can be a tool for building my future." Shifting these internal narratives can open up new possibilities for growth and success.

Empowerment also comes from *taking ownership* of your financial decisions. This means being proactive about learning, asking questions, and seeking out resources that help you make informed choices. It means not relying solely on financial advisors or family members to make decisions for you, but instead working in partnership with them, using their expertise as a guide rather than a crutch. When you take ownership of your finances, you gain a sense of autonomy and control that translates into greater confidence in other areas of your life as well.

Building a community of like-minded individuals can also be a source of financial empowerment. Surrounding yourself with people who are committed to financial growth, whether through local meetups, online forums, or mastermind groups, provides support, encouragement, and accountability. A community can offer different perspectives, share investment ideas, or simply serve as a sounding board when you're facing a tough financial decision. Knowing that you're not alone on the journey to financial independence can provide motivation and remind you that the challenges you face are surmountable.

Financial empowerment ultimately leads to the ability to *live life on your own terms*. It's about having the freedom to choose your path, whether that means pursuing a passion project, spending more time with family, or giving back to your community. It's about creating a life that reflects your deepest values and desires, rather than one that is dictated by financial constraints. For some, this might mean retiring early and traveling the world, while for others, it might mean starting a non-profit or spending time mentoring others on their financial journeys.

One of the greatest benefits of financial empowerment is the ability to take *calculated risks* without fear. When you're no longer dependent on a single source of income or constantly worried about making ends meet, you can afford to pursue opportunities that might not have seemed possible before. This could mean starting your own business, exploring creative projects, or investing in new and innovative areas. Financial empowerment gives you the flexibility to explore your passions without the pressure of immediate financial returns, allowing you to take a long-term view of your personal and professional growth.

Living life on your own terms also means having the freedom to *prioritize experiences over possessions*. Many people find that once they achieve financial security, their priorities shift from accumulating material wealth to creating meaningful experiences, whether that's traveling, spending time with loved ones, or investing in personal growth. Experiences often provide more lasting fulfillment than possessions, as they shape who we are and leave us with memories that enrich our lives. Financial empowerment allows you to focus on what truly matters to you, without being constrained by the need to constantly chase after more.

At its core, financial empowerment is about realizing that you have the power to shape your future. It's about understanding that money is not just a means to an end, but a tool that can help you build the life you want. It's the realization that, with the right knowledge, mindset, and support, you have the ability to overcome any financial challenge and create opportunities for yourself and others. Financial empowerment is the culmination of everything learned through the journey of financial education, leading to a life of freedom, choice, and fulfillment.

CHAPTER 5: THE RICH CREATE OPPORTUNITIES—HARNESSING THE POWER OF INITIATIVE

The difference between those who build wealth and those who don't often comes down to one trait: initiative. Taking initiative means acting without being prompted, spotting opportunities that others overlook, and being willing to take the first step even when the path ahead isn't entirely clear. It's a mindset that transforms the way you see the world, turning challenges into chances to grow and adversity into a springboard for success. Initiative is the driving force that helps you build something from nothing, and it's a trait that every successful person has in common.

Initiative doesn't require having all the answers or waiting for the perfect moment. In fact, the most successful people understand that there's rarely a "perfect time" to start. They recognize that progress is better than perfection and that taking even small steps forward can lead to big results over time. By focusing on action rather than waiting for ideal conditions, they create momentum that propels them closer to their goals. This willingness to move forward, even in uncertainty, is what separates those who create opportunities from those who miss them.

The ability to see potential where others see problems is a hallmark of taking initiative. It's about looking at a vacant lot and seeing a thriving business, or recognizing a gap in the market that you can fill with your skills or expertise. For example, during economic downturns, many people see only risk and uncertainty. But those with initiative see opportunities to invest in undervalued assets, start businesses that address new needs, or learn skills that position them for the next wave of growth. It's not about being reckless—it's about being willing to act when others hesitate.

Taking initiative often starts with a simple question: "What can I do right now to move closer to my goals?" This question shifts your focus from obstacles to possibilities, from what you don't have to what you can leverage. Maybe you can reach out to a potential mentor, start learning a new skill online, or set up a small savings plan that will eventually fund a bigger investment. The key is to take action, no matter how small, and trust that each step will bring you closer to your vision. Initiative turns dreams into plans and plans into reality.

One of the most powerful aspects of initiative is that it creates a ripple effect. When you take action, you inspire others around you to do the same, whether it's within your family, your circle of friends, or your community. This is particularly true in the digital age, where sharing your journey on social media or through a blog can reach thousands of people who are looking for inspiration. By taking the first step, you become a catalyst for change, showing others that it's possible to take control of their financial future.

Initiative isn't just about big moves; it's also about the everyday choices you make. It's about deciding to read a book that expands your understanding of finance, choosing to spend a weekend learning a new skill instead of binge-watching TV, or taking the time to draft a business plan for an idea that's been on your mind. These small actions, repeated consistently, build habits that lead to significant results over time. It's a reminder that every big success story is made up of countless small steps, each taken with intention and purpose.

The habit of taking initiative also changes the way you handle setbacks. When you're used to taking action, a setback isn't seen as a failure—it's seen as feedback. It's an opportunity to reassess, pivot, and try a different approach. For example, if a business idea doesn't gain traction, someone with initiative doesn't give up. They look for what went wrong, gather feedback from potential customers, and tweak their offering until it meets a real need. This resilience is what allows them to succeed where others might have given up after the first setback.

Initiative is closely tied to a sense of *ownership*. When you take initiative, you take ownership of your life and your outcomes. You don't wait for others to give you permission to pursue your goals, and you don't blame external circumstances for where you are. Instead, you focus on what you can control and take responsibility for your progress. This mindset empowers you to shape your own future rather than being at the mercy of external events. It's about realizing that while you can't control everything, you can always control how you respond and what actions you take next.

The willingness to take initiative also plays a crucial role in building relationships and expanding your network. Whether you're seeking out a mentor, connecting with like-minded peers, or reaching out to potential clients, it's initiative that makes the difference. It's the willingness to make the first move, to introduce yourself, or to ask for a meeting. In today's connected world, many opportunities come from who you know, and taking initiative helps you build those connections.

For example, if you admire someone's career path or business acumen, reaching out with a thoughtful message can open doors you never imagined. It might be as simple as sending a direct message on social media, commenting thoughtfully on their posts, or attending an event where they're speaking. The key is to be genuine and show that you value their perspective. Many people are willing to share their experiences or offer advice if you show a genuine interest. By taking the first step, you can build relationships that provide guidance, support, and new opportunities.

Taking initiative in networking isn't just about reaching out to those who are already successful—it's also about building relationships with peers who are on a similar path. These relationships can provide mutual support, accountability, and opportunities for collaboration. For example, partnering with a fellow entrepreneur on a joint project or co-hosting an online workshop can help both of you reach a larger audience. Initiative allows you to create win-win situations, where your efforts benefit not only you but also those around you.

Initiative also means being willing to seize opportunities even when they come in unexpected forms. For example, a chance conversation with a stranger at a coffee shop could lead to a business partnership, or a hobby you've been pursuing could become a profitable side hustle. The willingness to say "yes" to opportunities, even when they don't fit neatly into your plan, can lead to some of the most rewarding experiences. It's about keeping an open mind and being willing to explore new paths, knowing that even if one door closes, another might open.

An important part of developing initiative is building the *courage to take risks*. Many people are held back by the fear of failure or the fear of what others might think. They wait for permission or for someone else to tell them it's okay to pursue their dreams. But those who take initiative understand that the greatest risk is often doing nothing. They know that by staying in their comfort zone, they miss out on the potential for growth, learning, and success.

Building courage doesn't mean being fearless; it means acting despite the fear. It's normal to feel uncertain when stepping into new territory, whether that's starting a business, making a big investment, or learning a new skill. But instead of letting fear hold them back, those with initiative focus on what they stand to gain. They ask themselves, "What's the worst that could happen if I try this?" and "What's the best that could happen if it works?" By focusing on the potential upside rather than the risks, they find the courage to move forward.

Taking small risks can be a way to build up your confidence and prepare for bigger challenges. For example, if you're hesitant to start a business, you might begin with a small side project that requires minimal investment. This allows you to test your ideas, gain experience, and build a customer base without putting everything on the line. As you gain confidence, you can gradually take on bigger risks, such as scaling up the business or exploring new markets. This approach allows you to grow your risk tolerance over time, making each new challenge feel more manageable.

The courage to take risks also involves being willing to *challenge the status quo*. Many opportunities are missed because people accept things as they are rather than asking how they could be better. For example, if you see inefficiencies in the way a process works at your job, taking the initiative to suggest improvements could lead to a promotion or even inspire you to start your own business. It's about questioning why things are done a certain way and being willing to propose new solutions. Challenging the status quo requires courage, but it also opens the door to innovation and progress.

Another critical aspect of initiative is the ability to *embrace a proactive mindset*. A proactive mindset means anticipating future needs and taking steps to prepare for them rather than waiting for challenges to arise. It's about being one step ahead, whether that's in your career, your investments, or your personal development. Those with a proactive mindset don't wait for the right opportunity to come along—they create their own opportunities through careful planning and forward-thinking.

For example, a proactive approach to career growth might involve learning new skills before they're required for a promotion, or building relationships with key players in your industry before you need a job. This way, when an opportunity does arise, you're already prepared to seize it. A proactive investor, meanwhile, might study market trends and research new investment opportunities before they become mainstream, allowing them to invest early in high-potential assets. This approach means you're not constantly reacting to changes but are instead positioned to benefit from them.

A proactive mindset also applies to managing personal finances. Rather than waiting for financial emergencies to happen, those with initiative build emergency funds, set up automatic savings plans, and make a habit of reviewing their budgets regularly. They plan for retirement early, knowing that the sooner they start, the more time their money has to grow. This forward-thinking approach creates a sense of stability and security, allowing them to focus on long-term goals without being derailed by short-term setbacks.

Embracing a proactive mindset also means setting clear goals and working towards them consistently. Those with initiative don't just wish for a better future—they create a roadmap to get there. This might mean setting specific savings targets, outlining a plan for paying off debt, or breaking down a big goal into smaller, manageable steps. They track their progress, adjust their strategies as needed, and celebrate their achievements along the way. This sense of direction gives them a clear purpose and helps them stay focused even when faced with distractions or challenges.

Developing a strong sense of initiative often involves understanding the difference between *reactive* and *proactive* thinking. Reactive thinkers wait for events to unfold and respond to them as they happen, often feeling like they're constantly putting out fires or dealing with unexpected challenges. Proactive thinkers, on the other hand, anticipate challenges before they arise and take steps to prepare for them. This shift from reacting to creating can change the trajectory of your financial life and help you build a foundation for success.

Proactive thinking starts with *visualizing your future goals* and identifying the steps needed to reach them. It means thinking beyond the immediate needs of today and considering where you want to be in five, ten, or even twenty years. For example, if you envision owning a home, traveling the world, or reaching a certain level of financial freedom, proactive thinking pushes you to map out a strategy to achieve those goals. It might mean creating a savings plan, building a diversified investment portfolio, or learning new skills that increase your earning potential.

Proactive thinkers also build *contingency plans* for potential setbacks. They recognize that life doesn't always go as planned, and they prepare for the unexpected. This could involve setting up an emergency fund that covers six months of living expenses, maintaining a diversified investment portfolio to balance risks, or having insurance to protect against unexpected medical costs. By planning for worst-case scenarios, they ensure that even if challenges arise, they won't be completely derailed. This forward-thinking approach is what allows them to stay focused on their long-term goals, even when faced with obstacles.

A key aspect of being proactive is learning to *see opportunities in every situation*, even those that might initially seem negative. For example, losing a job can be a stressful experience, but a proactive individual might see it as an opportunity to pursue a new career path, start a business, or take time to develop new skills. Similarly, a market downturn might be seen as a chance to buy investments at lower prices or to reevaluate and strengthen their financial strategy. This mindset shift allows them to remain optimistic and adaptable, seeing challenges as temporary detours rather than dead ends.

Taking initiative also means *being willing to ask for what you want*. Many people miss out on opportunities because they're afraid to speak up or because they assume that others will automatically recognize their value. However, those who take initiative understand that sometimes, you have to create your own opportunities by asking for them. Whether it's negotiating a higher salary, requesting more responsibility at work, or seeking investment from potential backers for a business idea, being willing to ask is often the first step towards achieving your goals.

Learning to negotiate is a critical skill in this process. Negotiation is not about demanding what you want without compromise; it's about finding a solution that benefits both parties. It starts with understanding your own value—knowing what you bring to the table and being able to articulate that clearly. It also involves understanding the needs and motivations of the other party, whether it's an employer, a client, or a potential business partner. By focusing on how your skills or ideas can provide value to them, you can frame your request in a way that makes it easier for them to say yes.

Effective negotiators are also skilled at *framing their requests*. They understand that how you present an idea can be just as important as the idea itself. For example, rather than simply asking for a raise, a proactive individual might present a list of their recent accomplishments, the value they've added to the company, and the market rate for their position. This approach provides evidence and makes it easier for the employer to see why the request is reasonable. By taking the time to prepare and present your case thoughtfully, you increase your chances of getting what you want.

In addition to negotiation, being willing to *reach out for help or mentorship* is a powerful way to create opportunities. Many people are hesitant to ask for guidance because they fear being perceived as inexperienced or because they don't want to impose on others. However, those who take initiative understand that seeking mentorship is a sign of strength, not weakness. It's about recognizing that you don't have to have all the answers and that learning from those who have more experience can help you reach your goals faster. Mentors can provide valuable insights, introduce you to new networks, and offer feedback that helps you grow.

Building initiative also involves *developing a strong sense of curiosity*. Curiosity is what drives people to ask questions, explore new ideas, and seek out knowledge that can help them improve. It's the desire to understand how things work and why they are the way they are. In the context of financial success, curiosity might lead you to explore new investment strategies, learn about emerging industries, or understand the dynamics of global markets. It's about being open to learning and constantly seeking out new information that can help you make better decisions.

Curiosity often leads to innovation. When you're willing to ask, "What if?" or "How could this be better?" you open the door to creative problem-solving. For example, if you notice that a particular service is missing in your community, curiosity might drive you to investigate whether starting a business to fill that gap could be profitable. If you see inefficiencies in a process at work, your curiosity might inspire you to propose a new solution that saves time or money. This mindset turns challenges into puzzles to be solved rather than barriers to be accepted.

Curiosity also plays a role in *networking and relationship-building*. When you're genuinely interested in others, you ask more thoughtful questions, listen attentively, and build deeper connections. People appreciate when you take an interest in their work, their challenges, and their successes. This approach not only helps you learn from others' experiences but also makes you more memorable in their minds. As a result, when opportunities arise, they're more likely to think of you because you've taken the time to build a genuine connection.

One of the best ways to cultivate curiosity is to make *learning a daily habit*. This could involve reading books on business and personal development, listening to podcasts that explore new ideas, or taking online courses to build new skills. Even setting aside 15 to 30 minutes each day to learn something new can have a compounding effect over time, expanding your knowledge and opening up new possibilities. Curiosity-driven learning keeps you engaged with the world around you, making it easier to spot trends and opportunities that others might miss.

Developing a habit of *taking initiative* also means becoming comfortable with *experimentation*. Experimentation is about trying new things, testing different approaches, and being willing to learn through trial and error. It's about recognizing that there is often more than one way to achieve a goal and that the best path forward might not be clear until you've tested a few options. This willingness to experiment is what allows people to innovate, find new solutions, and adapt quickly to change.

For example, if you're interested in starting a business, experimentation might involve testing different product ideas, launching small-scale campaigns to see what resonates with customers, or trying different pricing models to see which is most profitable. Rather than waiting until you have a perfect plan, you start with a small pilot and adjust based on feedback. This approach allows you to learn what works and what doesn't without committing all your resources upfront. It's a way to reduce risk while still taking action.

Experimentation is not just for entrepreneurs; it's a valuable approach in many areas of life. For example, if you're trying to improve your productivity, you might experiment with different time management techniques to see which ones work best for you. If you're learning to invest, you might start with a small portfolio, testing different strategies before committing larger sums. The key is to approach each experiment with an open mind, seeing it as a learning experience rather than a pass-or-fail test. This mindset makes it easier to adapt and iterate as you discover what works best.

A critical part of successful experimentation is *learning to embrace failure* as part of the process. Failure is often seen as something to avoid, but those who take initiative understand that it's an inevitable part of trying new things. Every failure provides valuable feedback that can be used to improve your approach. It's a chance to refine your ideas, build resilience, and develop a deeper understanding of what it takes to succeed. When you stop seeing failure as a negative outcome and start seeing it as an opportunity for growth, you become more willing to take the risks that lead to innovation.

Another fundamental aspect of taking initiative is *mastering time management*.

Time is one of the most valuable resources you have, and how you use it can determine the success or failure of your efforts. Those who take initiative understand that time is limited, and they make conscious choices about how to spend it. They prioritize activities that bring them closer to their goals and eliminate or delegate tasks that don't. Mastering time management allows them to focus on what matters most, making their actions more effective and impactful.

Effective time management starts with *setting clear priorities*. It's about knowing what tasks will have the greatest impact on your goals and focusing your energy on those. For example, if you're building a business, activities like product development, marketing, and customer engagement should take precedence over less critical tasks like administrative work. Prioritizing high-impact tasks ensures that your efforts are aligned with your goals, making the most of your limited time.

One popular time management technique is the *Pareto Principle*, also known as the 80/20 rule. This principle suggests that 80% of your results come from 20% of your efforts. By identifying the tasks that fall into that 20%, you can focus your time on the activities that produce the most significant outcomes. For example, if you're an investor, 20% of your portfolio might generate 80% of your returns. By focusing on these high-performing investments, you can maximize your gains while minimizing time spent on less productive areas.

Time management also involves learning to *avoid distractions* and stay focused. In a world filled with constant notifications, social media, and digital distractions, maintaining focus can be a challenge. Those who take initiative set boundaries around their time, such as turning off notifications during work sessions or setting specific times for checking email. They use tools like time-blocking to schedule their day and ensure that each task gets the attention it deserves. By creating an environment that supports focus, they can work more efficiently and make progress faster.

Mastering time management is not just about organizing your schedule—it's also about understanding the *value of time* itself. Time is a finite resource, and unlike money, once it's spent, you can't earn it back. Recognizing this truth is what drives those with initiative to be intentional about how they spend their time. They understand that every minute spent scrolling through social media or watching mindless television is a minute that could have been invested in something more valuable—whether that's learning, building, creating, or simply resting to recharge for the next challenge.

This mindset shift often leads to a focus on *high-value activities*. High-value activities are the tasks that move the needle in your life, whether it's building skills that increase your earning potential, nurturing relationships that bring joy and opportunity, or working on projects that have a lasting impact. It's about shifting your energy away from activities that provide short-term gratification but little long-term benefit and instead prioritizing those that align with your bigger vision. For example, spending time developing a side hustle, networking with industry professionals, or studying market trends can have a far greater impact on your financial future than indulging in fleeting entertainment.

The concept of *time investing* can be a helpful way to think about how you allocate your hours. Just as you would invest money in assets that appreciate over time, you can invest your time in activities that compound in value. For example, time spent learning a new skill, such as coding or digital marketing, can pay dividends over your entire career by opening up new opportunities for higher-paying jobs or freelance work. Time spent nurturing a relationship with a mentor can lead to guidance, introductions, and advice that help you avoid costly mistakes. When you think of time as an investment, you become more intentional about how you spend it, focusing on activities that create long-term value.

Another aspect of mastering time management is understanding the difference between *being busy* and *being productive*. Many people equate busyness with effectiveness, filling their days with endless tasks and meetings, but those who take initiative know that not all tasks are created equal. Being productive means focusing on the tasks that have a meaningful impact on your goals, even if it means doing less overall. It's about recognizing that sometimes, saying no to certain commitments allows you to say yes to the things that truly matter.

The power of saying *no* is a critical skill for those who take initiative. While it might seem counterintuitive, learning to say no can actually increase your ability to create opportunities. This is because saying no allows you to protect your time and energy, ensuring that you have the bandwidth to pursue the projects and goals that are most important to you. It's about setting boundaries that keep you from getting spread too thin, and focusing on quality over quantity in both your professional and personal life.

Saying no can be challenging, especially if you're used to being a people-pleaser or if you fear missing out on opportunities. However, those who excel in taking initiative understand that not every opportunity is the right one. For example, if a new project at work doesn't align with your career goals or if a social engagement will take away time from your business, it might be better to decline. By being selective about where you focus your energy, you ensure that the commitments you do make are the ones that matter most.

Learning to say no also means being able to *prioritize your mental and physical well-being*. Burnout is a real risk for people who are constantly pushing forward without taking time to rest and recharge. Those who take initiative know that their best work comes from a place of balance, where they have the energy and focus needed to tackle their most important tasks. This might mean scheduling regular downtime, taking breaks during work sessions, or engaging in activities that help them relax and reset. By prioritizing self-care, they ensure that they have the stamina to sustain their efforts over the long term.

Another key part of time management and initiative is embracing the concept of *deep work*. Deep work refers to periods of focused, uninterrupted work where you tackle complex tasks that require concentration and creativity. It's in these moments that you make the most progress on challenging projects, whether it's developing a business strategy, writing a book, or learning a new skill. Deep work requires eliminating distractions, setting aside dedicated time, and being fully present in the task at hand. It's about valuing quality over speed and recognizing that true progress often comes from intense focus rather than multitasking.

Developing the ability to engage in deep work can significantly increase your productivity and effectiveness. To cultivate this skill, many people find it helpful to use techniques like *time blocking*. Time blocking involves dividing your day into blocks of time, each dedicated to a specific task or activity. For example, you might set aside the first two hours of your morning for deep work on a major project, followed by a block for emails and administrative tasks, and then another block for meetings or networking. This approach helps you stay focused on one thing at a time, reducing the mental fatigue that comes from constantly switching between tasks.

Time blocking can also be used to ensure that you're dedicating time to activities that contribute to your long-term goals. By scheduling time for exercise, learning, or building relationships, you make sure that these important but often neglected areas of life get the attention they deserve. It's a way of aligning your daily actions with your broader vision, ensuring that each day brings you a little closer to your dreams. Time blocking makes it easier to stay disciplined and avoid the temptation to procrastinate or waste time on low-value activities.

Another technique that can enhance deep work is the *Pomodoro method*. This involves working for a set period, typically 25 minutes, followed by a short break. After completing four Pomodoro sessions, you take a longer break. This approach helps maintain focus and prevents burnout by breaking tasks into manageable chunks. It can be especially helpful for those who find it difficult to concentrate for long periods, as the frequent breaks provide a chance to recharge and come back to the task with renewed energy.

Deep work isn't just about professional tasks; it can also apply to personal development and creativity. For example, if you're learning a new language, practicing an instrument, or working on a passion project, setting aside time for focused practice can lead to significant improvement over time. The key is to treat these activities with the same level of seriousness as you would a work project, recognizing that they are an investment in your personal growth and fulfillment. By dedicating time to deep work, you create space for progress and innovation in all areas of your life.

Taking initiative is also about *embracing a mindset of continuous improvement*.

Continuous improvement means always looking for ways to get better, whether that's in your work, your personal finances, or your relationships. It's about understanding that no matter how much you've accomplished, there is always room for growth. This mindset is a hallmark of those who create their own opportunities because it drives them to seek out new skills, refine their strategies, and learn from their experiences.

Continuous improvement starts with being open to *constructive feedback*. Feedback from mentors, peers, or customers can provide valuable insights into areas where you can improve. It's important to see feedback as an opportunity for growth rather than a personal critique. For example, if a client suggests a change in your service offering, or a mentor points out a weakness in your presentation skills, embracing that feedback can help you make meaningful adjustments that improve your performance. It's about seeing feedback as a tool for getting better rather than as a judgment.

Learning from *past experiences* is another key aspect of continuous improvement. Every success and every setback contains lessons that can inform your future decisions. For example, if you've launched a product that didn't sell well, analyzing what went wrong—whether it was the marketing, pricing, or product fit—can help you adjust your approach the next time around. Similarly, reflecting on the habits that contributed to your past successes can help you identify which practices to continue. This process of reflection and adjustment ensures that each new effort builds on the lessons of the past.

Continuous improvement also involves *investing in education*. Whether it's through formal courses, online learning platforms, or attending workshops, those who are committed to self-improvement understand the value of expanding their knowledge. This might involve deepening your expertise in a particular field, learning about new industries, or acquiring soft skills like leadership and communication. Education is a lifelong process, and those who keep learning remain adaptable and relevant, even as industries and markets evolve.

One of the most important elements of continuous improvement is *setting goals that stretch your abilities*. Stretch goals are ambitious targets that push you beyond your comfort zone and force you to develop new skills or approaches. They are not about achieving perfection, but rather about pushing yourself to see what you're capable of. For example, if you've been saving 10% of your income, setting a stretch goal of saving 20% might challenge you to find new ways to cut expenses or increase your earnings. If you're a freelancer, setting a goal to double your client base might push you to improve your marketing strategy or refine your services.

Stretch goals can be motivating because they give you a sense of purpose and direction. They create a sense of excitement and urgency, making each day feel like a step towards something bigger. The key is to break these ambitious goals down into smaller milestones, allowing you to track your progress and celebrate each win along the way. This approach keeps you focused and prevents you from feeling overwhelmed by the magnitude of the goal. It also allows you to adjust your strategy as you learn more about what it takes to succeed.

It's also essential to *celebrate progress* on the journey of continuous improvement. Acknowledging your achievements, no matter how small, can boost your motivation and remind you of how far you've come. This might mean taking a moment to reflect on the skills you've developed, the challenges you've overcome, or the new opportunities you've created through your efforts. Celebrating progress helps you stay positive and committed, even when the path to your larger goals feels long.

The journey of continuous improvement is never finished, but that's what makes it so rewarding. It's about finding joy in the process of becoming better, rather than only focusing on the end result. It's about knowing that each day, you're taking steps to become a more skilled, knowledgeable, and capable version of yourself. This mindset of growth and improvement is what drives those who take initiative to keep striving, keep learning, and keep creating new opportunities, no matter where they are on their journey.

A major part of taking initiative is *embracing the power of ownership*—not just in a literal sense, such as owning assets or businesses, but in the sense of taking full responsibility for your actions, decisions, and outcomes. Ownership is about understanding that you are the primary driver of your success. When you adopt an ownership mindset, you stop waiting for others to provide opportunities and start creating them yourself. This approach shifts your perspective from seeing yourself as a passenger in life's journey to becoming the driver.

This sense of ownership leads to a mindset where challenges become personal projects. Instead of seeing obstacles as reasons to give up, you start to see them as puzzles to solve. For example, if your savings aren't growing as fast as you'd like, taking ownership might mean researching new investment opportunities, learning about compound interest, or consulting with a financial advisor to adjust your strategy. When you own the problem, you also own the solution, which empowers you to act rather than feeling stuck.

Ownership also means *taking accountability* for your choices and their outcomes, whether they lead to success or failure. It's about being honest with yourself about where you might have fallen short and using that self-reflection to fuel improvement. For instance, if a business venture doesn't succeed, someone with an ownership mindset doesn't blame the market, the competition, or bad luck. Instead, they ask, "What could I have done differently?" and "What lessons can I take from this experience?" This kind of accountability allows you to learn from every experience, turning mistakes into stepping stones for future growth.

Owning your journey also means being proactive about *self-motivation*.

When you adopt an ownership mindset, you recognize that no one else is going to push you towards your goals. It's up to you to stay disciplined, even when motivation fades. This might involve setting daily routines that keep you on track, finding sources of inspiration like books or podcasts, or creating a vision board that reminds you of what you're working towards. The key is to find what keeps you focused and use it to stay committed to your long-term vision, even when progress feels slow.

The power of ownership extends beyond individual success—it also impacts the way you build *collaborative relationships*. When you approach collaborations with an ownership mindset, you focus on how you can add value, take initiative in communication, and ensure that the project moves forward smoothly. This approach makes you a valuable partner in any team setting, whether it's in a professional environment, a business venture, or a community project. When others see that you are committed to delivering results and taking responsibility for your role, it builds trust and opens doors to new opportunities.

In business, this ownership mindset can make a significant difference when working with clients or customers. For example, rather than just delivering what was asked, someone with initiative might look for ways to exceed expectations or suggest improvements that provide additional value. This might mean offering extra insights on a project, suggesting ways to streamline processes, or identifying potential issues before they become problems. By taking ownership of the outcome, you differentiate yourself from those who are simply following instructions, positioning yourself as a strategic partner rather than just a service provider.

Ownership in relationships is also about *leading by example*. When you take responsibility for your own growth, others are inspired to do the same. This is especially true in leadership roles, where your willingness to take initiative sets the tone for those around you. If you're leading a team, your approach to challenges, your attitude towards setbacks, and your commitment to continuous learning will influence how your team members approach their own work. By embodying the principles of initiative and ownership, you create a culture where everyone is empowered to take action and strive for excellence.

This mindset also applies to personal relationships, where taking ownership means being proactive in maintaining connections, resolving conflicts, and nurturing mutual understanding. Rather than waiting for others to reach out, you take the initiative to keep in touch, express appreciation, or address misunderstandings before they escalate. This proactive approach helps strengthen relationships, whether it's with family, friends, or professional contacts, creating a network of support that can be invaluable as you pursue your goals.

Taking initiative also requires the ability to *adapt to change*. The world is constantly evolving, and those who succeed are the ones who can adjust their strategies when circumstances shift. Adaptability is about being flexible in your approach while remaining focused on your overall vision. It means knowing when to pivot and when to stay the course, and being willing to try new methods when old ones no longer work. Adaptability ensures that you can thrive in any environment, turning unexpected challenges into opportunities for innovation.

One of the most important aspects of adaptability is *staying informed*. In a rapidly changing world, those who keep up with new trends, technologies, and industry developments are better positioned to seize opportunities as they arise. This might involve reading industry reports, following thought leaders on social media, or attending webinars and conferences. By staying current, you can spot shifts in the market, anticipate changes in consumer behavior, or recognize emerging trends that others might overlook. This knowledge allows you to adjust your strategy before it's too late, keeping you ahead of the curve.

Adaptability also means being willing to *experiment with new ideas*. When you encounter a problem or a roadblock, an adaptable mindset encourages you to try different solutions until you find one that works. For example, if a marketing strategy isn't delivering the results you hoped for, an adaptable person might test different messaging, explore new platforms, or try a completely different approach. This willingness to experiment and learn from trial and error ensures that you don't get stuck in outdated methods, allowing you to continue growing even when the landscape changes.

Being adaptable also involves *letting go of attachment to past successes*. It's easy to fall into the trap of relying on methods that have worked in the past, even when they're no longer effective. However, those who take initiative understand that what worked yesterday may not work tomorrow, and they remain open to evolving their approach. For example, a business that thrived through traditional retail methods might need to shift to e-commerce to stay competitive. By being willing to let go of the old and embrace the new, you ensure that you remain relevant and capable of taking advantage of new opportunities.

Adapting to change is closely tied to the concept of *resilience*. Resilience is the ability to bounce back from setbacks, to keep going when things get tough, and to maintain a positive outlook even in the face of adversity. It's an essential trait for anyone who takes initiative because the path to success is rarely a straight line. There will be challenges, failures, and unexpected obstacles, and it's resilience that allows you to continue moving forward despite them.

Building resilience starts with *developing a strong sense of purpose*. When you have a clear understanding of why you're working towards your goals, it's easier to stay motivated during difficult times. This purpose can be anything from providing for your family, achieving financial independence, or making a difference in your community. Whatever it is, having a purpose gives you a reason to keep going, even when progress is slow or setbacks make it feel like you're moving backward. It's the fuel that keeps your initiative alive, even when the road gets rough.

Resilience also involves *managing stress effectively*. Taking initiative often means taking on more responsibilities and facing higher levels of pressure, whether that's in your career, your business, or your personal life. Developing healthy ways to cope with stress—such as through regular exercise, mindfulness practices, or spending time with supportive friends and family—ensures that you have the energy and mental clarity needed to stay focused on your goals. It's about maintaining balance, so that you can continue to perform at your best without burning out.

Another aspect of resilience is *learning to reframe challenges* as opportunities for growth. Instead of seeing a setback as a sign that you've failed, those with resilience view it as a chance to learn, adapt, and become stronger. For example, a financial loss might be seen as an opportunity to develop better budgeting skills or to explore new investment strategies. A professional setback might prompt you to develop new skills or pivot to a more fulfilling career path. By reframing challenges in this way, you transform them into opportunities for development, allowing you to grow stronger through adversity.

Building resilience and adaptability also involves cultivating a *growth mindset*. A growth mindset, as popularized by psychologist Carol Dweck, is the belief that abilities and intelligence can be developed through effort, learning, and persistence. It's the opposite of a fixed mindset, where people believe that their talents and intelligence are set in stone. Those with a growth mindset see challenges as opportunities to grow, embrace effort as a path to mastery, and learn from criticism rather than being discouraged by it. This mindset is essential for taking initiative because it encourages you to keep pushing forward, even when the going gets tough.

A growth mindset allows you to see *potential* in every situation, rather than being limited by what's currently possible. It's the belief that, with enough effort and time, you can improve your skills, adapt to new environments, and achieve your goals. For example, if you're new to investing, a growth mindset helps you see every research session and every market analysis as a step towards becoming a savvy investor. It keeps you focused on progress rather than perfection, allowing you to build competence through consistent effort.

To develop a growth mindset, it's important to focus on *the process, not just the outcome*. Instead of measuring success solely by the results you achieve, those with a growth mindset take pride in the effort they put in, the skills they develop, and the progress they make along the way. This perspective makes it easier to stay motivated during the early stages of any new endeavor, when results might not yet be visible. It's about enjoying the journey of learning, knowing that each step, no matter how small, brings you closer to mastery.

A growth mindset also means being *open to feedback* and using it as a tool for improvement. It's about recognizing that constructive criticism is not a personal attack but a valuable source of information that can help you get better. For example, if a mentor points out an area where you could improve your communication skills, a person with a growth mindset would see it as an opportunity to refine their approach, rather than feeling discouraged. This openness to learning ensures that you continue evolving, no matter how much experience you have or how successful you become.

Another crucial aspect of taking initiative is *building a mindset of abundance*. An abundance mindset is the belief that there are enough opportunities, resources, and success for everyone. It contrasts with a scarcity mindset, where people see the world as a zero-sum game, believing that someone else's gain means their loss. Adopting an abundance mindset can profoundly impact how you approach opportunities, challenges, and relationships. It allows you to act without fear, knowing that new possibilities are always available if you are open to finding them.

An abundance mindset shifts your focus from competition to collaboration. When you believe that there's enough success to go around, you're more likely to help others, share your knowledge, and build partnerships. For example, rather than seeing other businesses in your niche as rivals, you might explore ways to collaborate on projects, cross-promote products, or share best practices. This collaborative approach can lead to new insights, expanded networks, and opportunities that you might never have discovered on your own.

In contrast, a scarcity mindset can lead to *fear-based decisions*, such as hoarding resources, avoiding risks, or becoming overly competitive. Those with a scarcity mindset might hesitate to invest in themselves or their ideas because they fear losing money. They might be reluctant to share their expertise, worrying that others will surpass them. However, this mentality often limits growth and innovation, keeping them stuck in the same patterns. An abundance mindset, on the other hand, encourages you to invest in opportunities, knowing that even if one venture doesn't succeed, others will come along.

To cultivate an abundance mindset, it's important to *focus on gratitude*. Gratitude helps shift your attention away from what you lack and towards what you already have. It creates a sense of contentment that makes it easier to take risks, as you're not constantly driven by a fear of losing what you have. For example, taking a few minutes each day to reflect on the things you're grateful for—whether it's your skills, your health, or the support of loved ones—can create a positive outlook that fuels your initiative. Gratitude helps you recognize the abundance that already exists in your life, making it easier to see new opportunities.

An abundance mindset also encourages *creative problem-solving*. When you believe that there's always a way to make things work, you become more resourceful in finding solutions to challenges. For example, if you're starting a business but lack the capital to launch, an abundance mindset might prompt you to look for alternative funding sources like crowdfunding, strategic partnerships, or pre-sales. It encourages you to think outside the box, finding ways to achieve your goals even when the path forward isn't obvious.

Creative problem-solving often involves *leveraging what you have* to create new opportunities. This might mean using your existing network to open doors, finding new uses for skills you already possess, or identifying untapped potential in resources you currently have. For example, a graphic designer might leverage their design skills to create a digital product that generates passive income, while a teacher might use their expertise to develop online courses. By focusing on what you can do with what you have, you turn limitations into possibilities, creating a pathway to success.

Developing an abundance mindset also means *embracing opportunities for learning*. When you believe that there's always more to gain, you become eager to acquire new knowledge and skills. This could involve taking courses, attending workshops, or learning from those who have already achieved what you aspire to. An abundance mindset helps you see education as an investment in your future, rather than a cost. It motivates you to continually expand your capabilities, knowing that the more you learn, the more you'll be able to achieve.

Learning also extends to *seeking out new perspectives*. An abundance mindset encourages you to listen to others' experiences and viewpoints, recognizing that different perspectives can provide valuable insights. This could mean joining a mastermind group, participating in online communities, or simply reaching out to people in your field for virtual coffee chats. By being open to diverse perspectives, you gain new ideas and strategies that can help you overcome challenges or spot opportunities that you hadn't considered before. It's about recognizing that there's always more to learn and more ways to grow.

Embracing an abundance mindset also has a significant impact on your *relationship with money*. Rather than seeing money as something that must be tightly controlled or hoarded, those with an abundance mindset see it as a tool that can be used to create more wealth and opportunity. They understand that while it's important to save and manage finances wisely, it's also important to use money to invest in growth—whether that's through education, starting a business, or investing in assets that appreciate over time.

This perspective encourages a *balance between saving and investing*. Rather than keeping all their money in a savings account, those with an abundance mindset seek out ways to make their money work for them. They understand the power of compounding—how investments grow over time—and they're willing to put their money into stocks, real estate, or other ventures that have the potential for long-term returns. They don't view spending on education or professional development as a loss but as an investment in their future earning potential.

An abundance mindset also changes how you approach *spending decisions*. Instead of making decisions based on fear or scarcity, you make them based on what will add value to your life. For example, you might choose to spend money on tools that help you be more productive, like a high-quality laptop or software that automates tasks. Or you might invest in experiences that enrich your life, such as travel or courses that expand your skills. This approach ensures that your spending is aligned with your values and goals, making each purchase a step towards a better future.

This doesn't mean being reckless with money—on the contrary, those with an abundance mindset are often more mindful about their spending because they recognize the value of what they have. They're willing to spend on things that contribute to their growth, but they're also careful to avoid wasteful spending that doesn't align with their priorities. This balance between mindfulness and generosity allows them to enjoy the present while still building for the future, creating a lifestyle that is both fulfilling and sustainable.

An abundance mindset can also transform your approach to *building wealth*. When you believe in abundance, you're more willing to take a long-term view of wealth creation. This involves focusing not just on making money, but on building assets that generate passive income, such as rental properties, dividend-paying stocks, or digital products. It's about creating streams of income that continue to flow even when you're not actively working, allowing you to achieve financial freedom over time.

One of the most important steps in building wealth with an abundance mindset is *identifying opportunities for passive income*. Passive income streams can come from a variety of sources, such as investing in real estate, creating online courses, or building a portfolio of dividend-paying stocks. The key is to focus on income-generating activities that align with your skills and interests. For example, if you have a talent for writing, creating e-books or blogging can provide a source of income that continues to grow with each new piece of content. If you're interested in real estate, learning about rental properties or real estate crowdfunding could open up new possibilities.

Building passive income is not an overnight process—it requires time, effort, and a willingness to learn. However, those with an abundance mindset understand that the effort is worth it because it leads to greater financial independence in the long run. They're willing to put in the work upfront, knowing that it will pay off down the road. For example, a blogger might spend months creating content before seeing significant ad revenue, but the passive income generated once the content gains traction can continue for years. This long-term perspective is what allows them to persevere through the initial challenges and build a stable foundation for the future.

Another key to building wealth with an abundance mindset is *reinvesting your gains*. Rather than spending all of the money they earn, those with initiative understand the importance of putting a portion of their profits back into their businesses, investments, or personal development. This might involve purchasing new equipment for a business, expanding into a new market, or taking courses that enhance their skills. Reinvesting allows your money to continue growing, creating a snowball effect that accelerates your progress towards financial independence.

An abundance mindset also encourages a *focus on long-term goals* over short-term gratification. While it's tempting to prioritize immediate pleasures, those who are successful in building wealth understand that true abundance comes from making decisions that create value over time. This might mean choosing to invest in a business idea rather than spending on luxury items, or putting money into a retirement fund instead of splurging on a vacation. By focusing on long-term rewards, they ensure that their efforts today will pay off in a more secure and fulfilling future.

This focus on long-term goals is closely tied to the concept of *delayed gratification*. Delayed gratification is the ability to resist the temptation of immediate rewards in favor of larger, more meaningful goals. It's a skill that is critical for building wealth, as it enables you to save and invest rather than spending impulsively. For example, choosing to drive a used car instead of buying a new one might allow you to save thousands of dollars that can be invested in stocks or real estate. Over time, these investments grow, creating far more value than the temporary pleasure of a new car.

However, delayed gratification doesn't mean living a life of constant sacrifice. It's about making choices that align with your values and goals, rather than being swayed by societal pressure to keep up with appearances. It's about understanding that the freedom and security that come from financial independence are worth far more than any material possession. Those with an abundance mindset find joy in the journey of building wealth, knowing that each small decision to save, invest, or learn brings them closer to their vision of a better future.

Developing the habit of *goal-setting* is one of the most effective ways to stay focused on long-term objectives. Goal-setting allows you to break down your vision into specific, actionable steps, making it easier to track your progress and stay motivated. For example, if your goal is to reach financial independence, you might set milestones like saving a certain percentage of your income each month, investing in a rental property, or achieving a specific net worth. By breaking down big goals into smaller targets, you create a roadmap that guides your daily actions and ensures that each step you take is moving you closer to your vision.

Taking initiative is also about *understanding the power of leverage*. Leverage means using resources, skills, and opportunities in a way that amplifies your efforts. It allows you to achieve more with less time and effort, whether it's leveraging money, time, or relationships. Those who master leverage can accelerate their path to success, creating opportunities that might have seemed out of reach otherwise. Understanding how to use leverage effectively is a game changer in both personal and financial growth.

Financial leverage is one of the most common types of leverage and involves using borrowed money to increase your potential returns. For example, many real estate investors use leverage to purchase properties by taking out a mortgage. By using a small amount of their own money and borrowing the rest, they can control a larger asset and benefit from any appreciation or rental income it generates. If the investment is successful, the returns can be significantly higher than if they had purchased the property outright with cash. However, financial leverage also comes with risks, as borrowed money needs to be repaid regardless of whether the investment performs well. This makes it crucial to understand both the benefits and risks before using leverage in any financial decision.

Another form of leverage is *leveraging time*. Time leverage involves finding ways to multiply your productivity, such as through outsourcing, automation, or delegation. For example, if you run a small business, you might hire virtual assistants to handle administrative tasks, freeing up your time to focus on high-value activities like business development or strategic planning. Automation tools can handle repetitive tasks like scheduling social media posts or managing customer emails, allowing you to accomplish more in less time. Time leverage allows you to focus on what you do best, while other tasks are handled efficiently.

Leveraging relationships is another powerful way to create opportunities. Building a strong network of mentors, peers, and collaborators can open doors that might otherwise remain closed. For example, a connection with a mentor might lead to a job referral or introduce you to investors for your startup. Networking with peers in your industry can help you stay informed about trends and best practices, giving you a competitive edge. It's about understanding that you don't have to do everything alone; by working with others, you can achieve more than you ever could on your own.

Leveraging relationships is not just about *taking*—it's about *giving* as well. Building meaningful connections means being willing to offer value without expecting anything in return. This might involve sharing your expertise, helping others solve problems, or simply being a supportive listener. When you approach relationships with a mindset of generosity, you build trust and goodwill, making people more likely to think of you when opportunities arise. This reciprocity is at the heart of successful networking and is what turns casual acquaintances into long-term collaborators or business partners.

Generosity also extends to *mentoring others* once you've reached a certain level of success. Many people who have achieved their goals find fulfillment in helping others along the way, sharing the lessons they've learned and guiding others through their challenges. Mentoring is not only a way to give back but also an opportunity to deepen your own understanding of what you've learned. Teaching others can reinforce your own knowledge and provide new perspectives on familiar challenges. It's a way of building a legacy that goes beyond financial success, leaving a lasting impact on the lives of others.

Leverage also comes into play when *scaling a business*. Scaling means expanding your business in a way that increases revenue without a corresponding increase in costs. It's about finding systems and processes that allow you to grow efficiently. For example, if you run a product-based business, you might use e-commerce platforms to reach a larger audience without needing to open a physical store. Or, if you're a freelancer, you might create digital products, such as online courses or e-books, that allow you to reach more clients without needing to trade more hours for dollars. Scaling through leverage allows you to build a business that can grow beyond the limits of your time and energy.

Another way to leverage resources is through *partnerships*. Strategic partnerships can help you access new markets, expand your product offerings, or pool resources for a larger impact. For example, a partnership between a software company and a hardware manufacturer might allow both to offer a more complete solution to customers, creating a win-win situation. By combining strengths, each partner can achieve more than they could alone. Partnerships are a way to leverage not only financial resources but also knowledge, skills, and market reach.

The concept of leverage is also closely tied to *building scalable systems*. Systems are repeatable processes that allow you to achieve consistent results with less effort. Whether you're managing your personal finances, running a business, or working on a creative project, having systems in place can save time, reduce errors, and improve efficiency. Those who take initiative understand that building systems is a way to multiply their efforts and create a more sustainable path to success.

A simple example of a scalable system is *automating your savings*. By setting up automatic transfers from your checking account to a savings or investment account, you ensure that you're consistently building your financial future without having to think about it each month. This system takes advantage of the power of compounding, allowing your savings to grow over time with minimal effort on your part. It's a way of leveraging the predictability of automation to achieve long-term goals.

Systems can also be applied to *business processes*. For example, if you're an entrepreneur, you might create a standard operating procedure (SOP) for tasks like customer service, product fulfillment, or social media marketing. SOPs ensure that these tasks are completed consistently, even as your business grows and you bring on new team members. This allows you to maintain quality and efficiency while focusing your attention on higher-level strategic decisions. Systems are the backbone of any scalable business, allowing you to grow without losing control over the details.

In your personal life, building systems can help you stay focused on your goals. For example, if you're committed to learning a new skill, you might create a system for studying each day, such as setting aside 30 minutes each morning for reading or practice. This consistency helps you make steady progress without needing to rely on willpower alone. By turning your goals into habits through systems, you ensure that you continue moving forward, even when motivation is low. Systems help you take initiative by making progress feel effortless over time.

Taking initiative often means being *willing to invest in relationships and networks*. Relationships are one of the most valuable assets you can build, offering support, inspiration, and access to opportunities that money alone can't buy. Investing in relationships means making time for others, showing genuine interest in their success, and being willing to lend a hand when needed. It's about building a network of mutual respect and trust, where everyone supports each other's growth.

One of the most effective ways to build strong relationships is by *being present*. In today's digital world, where communication is often reduced to text messages and social media likes, being present means taking the time to have real conversations, whether in person or through a video call. It means listening attentively, asking thoughtful questions, and showing that you value the other person's perspective. When people feel heard and understood, they're more likely to open up and share opportunities or collaborate on projects.

Another key to building a strong network is *following up*. It's easy to make connections at events or through social media, but maintaining those connections requires effort. Following up with a thank-you message after a meeting, sending occasional updates on your progress, or sharing articles that might be of interest are simple ways to keep the relationship active. This approach shows that you're genuinely interested in staying connected and that you value the other person's time and insights. Consistent follow-up can turn a casual introduction into a meaningful professional relationship over time.

Investing in relationships also means being willing to *share your own journey*. People are often drawn to authenticity and transparency, and sharing your story—both the successes and the struggles—can create deeper connections. This might involve writing a blog post about a challenge you overcame, sharing your thoughts on a topic you're passionate about, or speaking at an industry event. By being open about your experiences, you make it easier for others to relate to you and see you as someone who is both knowledgeable and approachable. It's about building connections through honesty, rather than trying to impress others with a perfect image.

An important part of creating opportunities through relationships is *understanding the value of mentorship*. Mentorship is a powerful form of leverage because it allows you to learn from someone else's experiences, avoiding common pitfalls and accelerating your own growth. A good mentor can provide guidance, introduce you to key contacts, and offer insights that you might not find in books or online courses. They can help you see the big picture, offering a perspective that comes from years of experience in your field.

Finding a mentor doesn't have to be a formal process—it can start with a simple conversation. Reaching out to someone you admire and asking for advice on a specific challenge or sharing your appreciation for their work can be the first step towards building a mentorship relationship. It's important to approach potential mentors with respect for their time, being clear about what you hope to learn and how you're willing to put in the effort. Many people are willing to mentor others when they see that the mentee is serious about learning and committed to applying the advice they receive.

Being a good mentee involves *being coachable*. This means being open to feedback, willing to admit when you don't know something, and ready to take action on the advice you receive. It's about showing that you value the mentor's time by making the most of their guidance. This attitude of humility and eagerness to learn is what makes mentorship relationships thrive, turning them into valuable sources of growth for both the mentor and the mentee.

Mentorship is not just about what you can gain; it's also about *paying it forward*. As you grow in your own journey, you'll have the opportunity to mentor others who are just starting out. Sharing what you've learned, offering encouragement, and guiding someone through their challenges can be incredibly rewarding. It creates a ripple effect, where the knowledge and opportunities you've gained are passed on to others, helping to build a community where everyone is empowered to take initiative. This cycle of giving and receiving mentorship is what keeps the spirit of growth and opportunity alive.

A critical part of taking initiative is *developing a strong work ethic*. Success doesn't come from ideas alone—it requires consistent, focused effort over time. Those who build wealth and create opportunities understand that hard work is the foundation upon which all other strategies rest. While many people focus on finding shortcuts to success, those with a strong work ethic are willing to put in the time and energy to achieve their goals, knowing that the rewards will come through perseverance and dedication.

A strong work ethic starts with *discipline*. Discipline means doing what needs to be done, even when you don't feel like it. It's about sticking to your commitments and following through on your plans, regardless of external distractions or internal resistance. For example, if you've set a goal to work on your business for two hours each day, discipline is what keeps you at your desk even when you're tempted to watch TV or scroll through social media. Over time, discipline becomes a habit, making it easier to stay on track and maintain momentum.

In addition to discipline, having a strong work ethic means *embracing the grind*. The grind refers to the daily effort that often goes unnoticed—the long hours spent learning, practicing, and building. It's the unglamorous side of success, the part that happens behind the scenes. Those who succeed understand that the grind is what separates those who talk about their goals from those who achieve them. Whether you're starting a business, learning a new skill, or working your way up in a career, the grind is where real progress is made.

However, hard work alone isn't enough—it must be combined with *smart work*. Smart work means focusing on the tasks that have the greatest impact on your goals, rather than simply staying busy. It's about prioritizing high-value activities that move the needle, such as developing a new product, improving your marketing strategy, or learning a critical skill. For example, an entrepreneur who spends hours tweaking their website design but neglects customer acquisition is working hard but not smart. Smart work involves knowing where to direct your efforts for maximum results.

One of the keys to working smarter, not just harder, is *understanding the concept of opportunity cost*. Opportunity cost refers to the value of what you give up when you choose one option over another. Every time you spend time, money, or energy on a task, you're choosing not to spend those resources on something else. Those who take initiative are constantly aware of opportunity costs, ensuring that they're investing their time and resources in activities that provide the highest return on investment (ROI).

For example, if you're a freelancer, you might face the choice between spending an hour doing administrative tasks or using that hour to pitch new clients. While both tasks are necessary, the opportunity cost of doing the administrative work is the potential income you could generate by bringing in new business. In this case, outsourcing the administrative tasks might be a smarter use of your resources, allowing you to focus on higher-value activities. By being mindful of opportunity costs, you can make more strategic decisions about how to allocate your time and effort.

Another important aspect of working smart is *learning to optimize your workflow*. Optimizing your workflow means finding ways to streamline your processes, reduce inefficiencies, and eliminate distractions. This might involve using productivity tools like project management software, setting up automated systems, or batching similar tasks together to minimize context-switching. For example, rather than checking email sporadically throughout the day, you might set aside specific blocks of time for responding to messages, allowing you to stay focused on more important tasks in between. Optimizing your workflow ensures that you're getting the most out of your efforts and making steady progress towards your goals.

Developing a strong work ethic also involves *managing your energy*, not just your time. While time management is essential, energy management is equally important because it determines how effectively you can use the hours you have. Those who are committed to taking initiative understand that they need to protect and replenish their energy in order to perform at their best. This might involve prioritizing sleep, eating a healthy diet, exercising regularly, and taking breaks throughout the day to recharge. Managing your energy allows you to maintain focus and productivity over the long haul, avoiding burnout and ensuring that you have the stamina to achieve your goals.

Building a strong work ethic also means being willing to *do what others won't*. Many people shy away from tasks that are difficult, tedious, or outside their comfort zone, but those who take initiative understand that these tasks often present the greatest opportunities for growth. Whether it's making cold calls, handling difficult conversations, or learning a new skill that's outside your area of expertise, being willing to tackle tough challenges is what sets you apart from those who play it safe. It's about being willing to do the hard work that others avoid, knowing that it will pay off in the long run.

One of the most powerful ways to develop a strong work ethic is by *setting ambitious goals*. Ambitious goals push you to stretch beyond your current capabilities and tap into your full potential. They challenge you to grow, learn, and become better, even when the path forward is difficult. For example, setting a goal to double your income in the next year might seem daunting, but it forces you to think creatively, seek out new opportunities, and work harder than ever before. Ambitious goals provide a sense of purpose and direction, motivating you to keep going even when the road gets tough.

However, ambitious goals must be accompanied by *consistent action*. It's not enough to set big goals—you also need to take small, daily steps towards achieving them. This is where many people fall short; they set lofty goals but fail to put in the consistent effort needed to reach them. Those who take initiative understand that progress is made through consistent, disciplined action over time. Whether it's working on your business every day, setting aside time for learning, or saving a portion of your income each month, it's the small actions that add up to big results.

A strong work ethic also means *staying committed* even when things don't go as planned. It's easy to stay motivated when everything is going well, but true commitment is tested during tough times. Whether it's a failed project, a rejected proposal, or a market downturn, those with a strong work ethic keep pushing forward, knowing that setbacks are a natural part of the journey. They don't let obstacles stop them—they use them as fuel to work even harder.

This level of resilience is what allows them to create opportunities even in the face of adversity.

Resilience is closely tied to *grit*, which psychologist Angela Duckworth defines as passion and perseverance for long-term goals. Grit is the ability to keep going, even when progress is slow, results are uncertain, and the path ahead is filled with challenges. Those who are gritty don't give up when things get tough—they dig deeper, find new solutions, and continue moving forward. Grit is one of the most important qualities for anyone who wants to take initiative and create lasting success because it enables you to push through the inevitable setbacks and failures that come with ambitious goals.

Building grit involves *embracing discomfort*. Many people avoid discomfort, whether it's the discomfort of taking a risk, facing failure, or simply putting in long hours. However, those with grit understand that discomfort is a sign of growth. They're willing to step outside their comfort zone and tackle difficult tasks because they know that's where the real progress happens. For example, an entrepreneur might feel uncomfortable pitching their business to investors, but they do it anyway because they know it's necessary for growth. Embracing discomfort allows you to develop the resilience needed to keep going, even when the journey is challenging.

Grit also involves *maintaining a long-term perspective*. Those with grit are able to delay gratification, focusing on their long-term goals rather than seeking immediate rewards. They understand that success doesn't happen overnight and that the journey is often slow and filled with setbacks. However, they keep their eyes on the bigger picture, knowing that each small step they take brings them closer to their ultimate vision. For example, someone who is saving for a down payment on a house might make sacrifices in the short term—such as cutting back on dining out or vacations—in order to achieve their goal. By staying focused on the long-term reward, they're able to persevere through the short-term challenges.

One of the most effective ways to build grit is by *celebrating small wins*. While it's important to stay focused on your long-term goals, it's equally important to recognize and celebrate the progress you're making along the way. Celebrating small wins—whether it's completing a challenging task, reaching a financial milestone, or learning a new skill—helps keep you motivated and reinforces the belief that you're capable of achieving your goals. These small victories provide a sense of accomplishment and fuel your desire to keep going, even when the bigger goal feels far away.

Grit also involves *cultivating optimism*. Those with grit are able to maintain a positive outlook, even in the face of adversity. They believe that their efforts will eventually pay off, even if the results aren't immediate. This optimism allows them to stay motivated and keep working towards their goals, even when the journey is tough. It's about maintaining a belief in your own ability to succeed and refusing to give up, no matter how many setbacks you face. Optimism provides the emotional energy needed to persevere, keeping you focused on the possibilities rather than the obstacles.

Optimism doesn't mean ignoring challenges or pretending that everything is perfect—it means *facing challenges with a positive mindset*. For example, if a business owner faces a difficult financial quarter, they don't dwell on the failure. Instead, they look for ways to improve, learn from the experience, and adjust their strategy for the next quarter. This positive mindset helps them maintain momentum, even when the situation is challenging. It's about seeing setbacks as temporary and believing that you have the ability to overcome them.

To maintain optimism, many people find it helpful to *focus on what they can control*. Rather than worrying about external factors like the economy or market trends, they focus on the actions they can take to improve their situation. This might mean focusing on improving their skills, building new relationships, or finding ways to reduce costs. By focusing on what you can control, you regain a sense of agency and empowerment, making it easier to stay positive and motivated. It's about recognizing that while you can't control everything, you can always control your response and your actions.

Grit and optimism are powerful when combined because they allow you to keep moving forward with a positive attitude, even when the road is long and difficult. They give you the strength to persevere, the belief that your efforts will pay off, and the ability to find joy in the journey. These qualities are what enable those who take initiative to create opportunities where others see only challenges, and to turn setbacks into stepping stones towards their goals.

Another essential component of taking initiative is *embracing the power of creativity*. Creativity is not limited to artistic expression; it's a crucial skill in problem-solving, innovation, and building unique solutions that can give you a competitive edge. Those who take initiative understand that creativity allows them to see the world differently, to challenge conventional thinking, and to come up with ideas that others might overlook. Creativity is about being willing to imagine new possibilities and to act on those visions with confidence.

Creativity is often sparked by *asking better questions*. Instead of accepting things as they are, those with a creative mindset ask, "What if?" and "Why not?" They question assumptions and look for ways to improve existing systems or create new ones. For example, a creative entrepreneur might look at a common problem in their industry and ask, "What would happen if we approached this from a completely different angle?" This kind of thinking leads to breakthrough ideas that can redefine markets and open up new opportunities.

One of the most effective ways to cultivate creativity is through *exposure to diverse experiences and perspectives*. Creativity thrives when you step outside your comfort zone and encounter new ideas, cultures, and ways of thinking. This might involve traveling, reading books outside your usual genre, or attending events and workshops in fields that are different from your own. For example, an engineer might gain new insights into problem-solving by studying art, or a marketer might find inspiration by exploring psychology. By broadening your horizons, you create a fertile ground for innovative ideas to grow.

Creativity also involves *embracing failure as part of the process*. Many people avoid taking risks because they fear failure, but those who are creative understand that failure is often a necessary step towards finding a successful solution. For example, Thomas Edison is famous for saying that he didn't fail 10,000 times when inventing the light bulb; he simply found 10,000 ways that didn't work. This mindset allows creative individuals to experiment freely, knowing that each attempt, even if it doesn't succeed, brings them closer to the breakthrough they're looking for. It's about being willing to try, fail, and try again until you find what works.

Creativity is also about *connecting the dots in new ways*. Steve Jobs once said that creativity is simply connecting things—seeing relationships between concepts that others might miss. This ability to see connections allows you to bring together ideas from different fields, creating innovative solutions that others might not have considered. For example, many of the most successful tech startups are built on the combination of existing technologies in a new way. Uber didn't invent GPS or smartphones, but they combined these tools to create a new way of providing transportation services. By seeing the potential in connecting existing elements, creative thinkers can create new value and opportunities.

To enhance your ability to connect the dots, it's important to *stay curious*. Curiosity drives you to explore new ideas, ask questions, and seek out knowledge that others might overlook. It's about being interested in how things work and why they work that way, and using that understanding to fuel innovation. For example, a curious entrepreneur might spend hours researching consumer behavior, looking for insights that could lead to a new product idea. Curiosity keeps you engaged with the world around you, making it easier to spot opportunities that others might miss.

One powerful way to cultivate curiosity is through *mindful observation*. Mindful observation means paying attention to the details of your environment, whether it's the way customers interact with a product, the patterns of behavior in a market, or the design elements that make a website user-friendly. This attention to detail can reveal insights that lead to creative solutions. For example, a fashion designer might notice a growing trend in sustainable materials and use that insight to create a new line of eco-friendly clothing. Mindful observation allows you to see opportunities in the everyday, turning ordinary experiences into sources of inspiration.

Creativity also involves *reimagining limitations*. Instead of seeing constraints as obstacles, creative thinkers see them as opportunities to innovate. For example, if a startup has a limited budget, they might find creative ways to market their product using social media or collaborate with influencers rather than relying on expensive ad campaigns. This ability to work within constraints is often what drives the most innovative solutions, as it forces you to think outside the box and find new ways to achieve your goals.

One of the most important aspects of creativity is the willingness to *think for yourself*. Independent thinking is a crucial trait for those who take initiative because it allows you to form your own opinions, make your own decisions, and pursue your own path, even when it goes against the grain. Independent thinkers are not swayed by popular opinion or trends—they're willing to challenge the status quo and explore ideas that others might dismiss. This ability to think for yourself is what allows creative individuals to create something truly unique.

Thinking for yourself requires *confidence in your ideas*, even when others don't immediately see their value. Many of the world's most successful innovators faced skepticism and criticism when they first introduced their ideas. For example, when Jeff Bezos started Amazon, many people doubted the potential of an online bookstore. However, his willingness to pursue his vision, despite the naysayers, allowed him to build one of the most successful companies in history. Independent thinking requires a strong sense of self-belief and the courage to pursue your vision, even when it's not widely accepted.

Independent thinking also means being willing to *challenge your own assumptions*. Just because an idea has worked in the past doesn't mean it will work in the future, and just because something is commonly accepted doesn't mean it's the best way to do things. Those who think for themselves are constantly questioning their beliefs and seeking new information. For example, a business owner might challenge their assumptions about their target market by conducting surveys or focus groups, leading them to discover new customer needs and preferences. This openness to rethinking and refining ideas is what keeps creative thinkers adaptable and innovative.

Being an independent thinker doesn't mean rejecting others' opinions outright—it means *critically evaluating* the information you receive and making decisions based on your own analysis. It's about listening to feedback, considering different perspectives, and then making a choice that aligns with your own values and goals. This approach ensures that your decisions are well-informed and thought out, rather than being based on trends or external pressures. It allows you to stay true to your vision, while remaining open to the insights and ideas of others.

Creativity and initiative are also deeply connected to *embracing the power of storytelling*. Storytelling is a powerful tool that allows you to communicate your ideas, inspire others, and build connections. Whether you're pitching a business idea, building a brand, or sharing your journey, storytelling allows you to convey the value of what you're doing in a way that resonates with others. It's about turning information into a narrative that engages the emotions and imagination, making your message more memorable and impactful.

A good story doesn't just share facts—it *creates an experience*. It takes the listener on a journey, showing them the challenges you faced, the lessons you learned, and the vision you're working towards. For example, an entrepreneur pitching their startup to investors might not just talk about market size and revenue projections; they might share the story of how they discovered the problem they're solving, the people they've helped, and the impact they hope to create. This story makes the business more relatable, showing the human side of what might otherwise be seen as a series of numbers and data points.

Storytelling is not just for entrepreneurs—it's a valuable skill for anyone looking to *influence and inspire*. Whether you're a leader motivating a team, a teacher engaging students, or an activist rallying support for a cause, storytelling allows you to convey your passion and vision in a way that moves others. It helps you build a connection with your audience, showing them why your message matters. By mastering the art of storytelling, you can make your ideas more persuasive, your brand more memorable, and your mission more compelling.

A key part of storytelling is *understanding your audience*. Effective storytellers tailor their message to the needs, interests, and values of the people they're speaking to. They understand that the same story can be told in different ways, depending on who is listening. For example, a social entrepreneur might tell one version of their story when speaking to potential investors, focusing on the financial sustainability of their model, and a different version when speaking to a community group, focusing on the social impact. By understanding your audience, you can shape your story in a way that resonates most deeply with them.

Storytelling is also a way to *connect with your own purpose*. Sharing your story helps you reflect on your journey, understand the challenges you've faced, and remind yourself of why you started. This can be especially important during difficult times, when it's easy to lose sight of your motivation. By reflecting on your story, you can reconnect with the passion that drives you, making it easier to persevere through setbacks. It's about remembering that your journey has meaning and that each step, no matter how small, is part of a larger narrative.

When you share your story, you also create an opportunity to *inspire others*. Your experiences, struggles, and successes can be a source of motivation for people who are facing similar challenges. By being open about your journey, you show others that they're not alone and that it's possible to overcome obstacles. For example, an entrepreneur who shares their story of overcoming failure might inspire others to keep going, even when their own ventures don't go as planned. Storytelling is a way of passing on the lessons you've learned, helping others to grow and succeed.

At its core, storytelling is about *authenticity*. People connect with stories that feel real, that show vulnerability, and that are grounded in genuine experiences. This means being willing to share not just the highlights but also the struggles, the mistakes, and the moments of doubt. Authentic storytelling builds trust, because it shows that you're not trying to present a perfect image—you're sharing a true and honest account of your journey. This honesty makes your story more relatable, allowing others to see themselves in your experiences and to believe that they too can achieve their goals.

The power of storytelling lies in its ability to *create change*. Stories have the power to shift perspectives, challenge assumptions, and inspire action. They can change the way people think about a problem, the way they see themselves, and the way they approach their own goals. By sharing your story, you become a catalyst for change, not only in your own life but in the lives of those who hear it. This is why storytelling is such an important part of taking initiative—because it allows you to turn your journey into a source of inspiration, and to use your voice to make a difference in the world.

CHAPTER 6: THE RICH INNOVATE—CREATING VALUE IN A DYNAMIC WORLD

Innovation is often seen as the domain of tech companies, scientists, and entrepreneurs, but the truth is that innovation belongs to anyone willing to embrace change and think creatively. Innovation is about taking an idea, product, or process and making it better. It's the spark that drives progress and allows individuals to create value in their personal and professional lives. In a fast-paced, ever-changing world, those who learn how to innovate continuously position themselves at the forefront of opportunity.

At its core, innovation is about solving problems. It's the ability to identify a need, pain point, or gap in the market and come up with a solution that adds value. For example, ride-sharing apps like Uber solved the problem of inefficient taxi services, while streaming platforms like Netflix solved the issue of limited access to entertainment. These innovations didn't create entirely new markets—they simply improved existing ones, making life easier and more enjoyable for consumers. By focusing on how you can solve problems, you open the door to countless opportunities for innovation in any field.

Innovation doesn't always require coming up with something completely new. In fact, many of the most successful innovations are *iterations*—improvements on existing products or services. This is often referred to as "incremental innovation," and it can be just as valuable as groundbreaking, disruptive ideas. For example, the evolution of smartphones over the past decade has largely been driven by incremental innovations—better cameras, faster processors, and improved battery life. Each improvement adds value to the user experience, even if it doesn't completely change the device.

One of the keys to being innovative is the ability to see *possibilities where others see limitations*. While many people see problems as barriers, innovative thinkers view them as opportunities for growth. For example, the constraints imposed by a tight budget might push an entrepreneur to find more creative, cost-effective ways to deliver a product or service. By viewing obstacles as challenges to be overcome, rather than roadblocks, innovators are able to find solutions that others might overlook.

Innovation also requires a deep understanding of the *market and the people you serve*. It's not enough to come up with a great idea—you need to ensure that it addresses a real need or desire in the market. This is where customer feedback, market research, and trend analysis come into play. The most successful innovators are those who take the time to understand their target audience, identifying their pain points, preferences, and buying behaviors. By deeply understanding your market, you can tailor your innovations to meet real-world needs, making them more likely to succeed.

Listening to customer feedback is an essential part of the innovation process. Many of the best ideas come directly from customers who point out problems or suggest improvements. For example, a software company might release a new app, only to find that users are frustrated with its interface. By listening to customer feedback and making the necessary changes, the company can turn a mediocre product into a great one. Innovation isn't about getting it right the first time—it's about being willing to adapt and improve based on feedback.

In addition to understanding your market, innovation requires a willingness to *take risks*. All innovation involves some level of uncertainty, and there's always a possibility that your idea might not work out as planned. However, those who innovate successfully are willing to take calculated risks, knowing that the potential rewards are worth it. For example, launching a new product or entering a new market can be risky, but it can also lead to significant growth if the innovation resonates with consumers. The key is to manage risk by doing your research, testing your ideas, and being willing to pivot if necessary.

A key element of innovation is *experimentation*. Experimentation allows you to test new ideas in a low-risk environment, gathering data and feedback before making a full commitment. For example, a company might release a beta version of a new app to a small group of users, collecting feedback and making improvements before launching it to the public. This approach allows innovators to refine their ideas and reduce the risk of failure. By experimenting, you can discover what works and what doesn't, allowing you to innovate more effectively.

One of the most powerful tools for innovation is *collaboration*. While innovation often starts with a single idea, it's rarely achieved in isolation. Some of the most successful innovations come from teams of people who bring different perspectives, skills, and experiences to the table. Collaboration allows you to tap into the collective intelligence of your team or network, leading to ideas and solutions that you might not have thought of on your own. For example, a marketing team might work with a design team to create a more user-friendly app, or a business development team might collaborate with engineers to find more efficient ways to produce a product.

Collaboration also opens the door to *cross-industry innovation*. Many groundbreaking ideas come from applying concepts from one industry to another. For example, the principles of lean manufacturing, which were originally developed in the automotive industry, have been successfully applied to industries as diverse as healthcare, software development, and education. By learning from other industries and collaborating with people outside your immediate field, you can discover new ways of thinking and problem-solving that lead to innovation.

In addition to collaboration, innovation requires a mindset of *continuous learning*. The world is constantly changing, and those who innovate successfully are those who commit to learning and adapting throughout their careers. This means staying curious, seeking out new information, and being open to new ideas. For example, an entrepreneur might attend industry conferences, read books on business trends, or take online courses to stay up to date with the latest developments in their field. By constantly learning, you keep your mind open to new possibilities, making it easier to spot opportunities for innovation.

Another critical aspect of innovation is *embracing failure*. Failure is an inevitable part of the innovation process, and those who are afraid to fail often miss out on opportunities to learn and grow. Rather than viewing failure as a setback, successful innovators see it as a learning experience. For example, if a product launch doesn't go as planned, an innovative entrepreneur will analyze what went wrong, gather feedback, and use that information to improve the product. Failure isn't the end of the road—it's a stepping stone to future success.

Innovation also thrives in an environment of *open-mindedness*. Those who are willing to entertain unconventional ideas and think beyond the status quo are the ones most likely to come up with creative solutions. Open-mindedness means being willing to consider new perspectives, even if they challenge your existing beliefs or methods. It's about creating a culture where ideas can flow freely and where experimentation is encouraged. This openness to new ideas is what allows innovators to break free from traditional ways of thinking and discover groundbreaking solutions.

One way to cultivate open-mindedness is by *surrounding yourself with diverse voices*. Diversity in thought, background, and experience leads to richer discussions and more creative problem-solving. For example, a company that includes people from different cultural backgrounds might come up with innovative products that appeal to a global audience. A team that includes people with different skill sets—such as marketers, engineers, and designers—will approach a problem from multiple angles, leading to more comprehensive solutions. By embracing diversity, you create an environment where innovation can thrive.

Another important aspect of open-mindedness is the ability to *let go of your ego*. Sometimes, innovators fall into the trap of becoming too attached to their ideas, even when they're not working. Successful innovators, however, are willing to let go of ideas that aren't delivering results and pivot to something new. This flexibility allows them to innovate more effectively, as they're not bogged down by their own pride or attachment to a particular idea. It's about being willing to fail fast, learn from the experience, and move on to the next idea.

Innovation also involves *being resourceful*. Resourcefulness is the ability to make the most of what you have, even when resources are limited. Many of the world's most successful innovations were born out of constraints—whether it was a lack of funding, time, or materials. For example, many startups begin with very little capital, yet they find creative ways to market their products, reach customers, and build their brands. By being resourceful, innovators can achieve remarkable results even in the face of limitations.

Resourcefulness often leads to the creation of *disruptive innovations*. Disruptive innovations are those that challenge the existing market and change the way things are done. They typically start with a small niche market and eventually expand to disrupt established industries. For example, when Airbnb was first launched, it was a resourceful solution for people who wanted to rent out their spare rooms to travelers. Today, it has grown into a global platform that has disrupted the traditional hotel industry. Disruptive innovations are often born out of necessity, where resourceful entrepreneurs find creative solutions to unmet needs.

Disruptive innovation often requires *thinking differently* about the value you offer. Rather than competing directly with established players, disruptors find new ways to deliver value to consumers. This might mean offering a more affordable option, simplifying a complex process, or providing a more personalized experience. For example, when streaming services like Netflix and Hulu first emerged, they didn't try to compete with cable companies by offering traditional TV packages. Instead, they disrupted the market by offering on-demand content that allowed viewers to watch shows and movies on their own schedule. This new way of delivering value completely changed the entertainment industry.

Another powerful driver of disruptive innovation is *technology*. Technology has the ability to transform industries and create entirely new markets. For example, the rise of e-commerce disrupted the retail industry, while the advent of smartphones changed the way we communicate, shop, and consume content. Innovators who understand how to harness the power of technology can create products and services that meet the evolving needs of consumers. Whether it's through automation, artificial intelligence, or data analytics, technology offers countless opportunities for innovation.

Disruptive innovation also involves *anticipating trends* and staying ahead of the curve. Successful innovators are always looking for signs of change in their industry and adapting their strategies accordingly. For example, a real estate developer might notice a shift in consumer preferences towards sustainable living and invest in eco-friendly housing projects. By staying ahead of trends, they position themselves as leaders in the market, ready to meet the needs of the next generation of consumers. Anticipating trends allows innovators to stay relevant, even as the market evolves.

Disruptive innovation thrives on *rethinking customer experiences*. Rather than focusing solely on the product or service itself, innovative thinkers pay close attention to the way their customers interact with what they offer. This means asking questions like, "How can I make this easier for my customers?" or "What would make this experience more enjoyable?" By focusing on the customer journey, innovators can create solutions that resonate deeply with their audience, building loyalty and long-term success.

A key part of improving customer experience is *removing friction points*. Friction points are the small annoyances or inconveniences that make a customer's experience less enjoyable. For example, a long checkout process on an e-commerce website can cause frustration, leading customers to abandon their purchase. An innovator might simplify the process, offering options like one-click purchasing or guest checkout to make it faster and easier. Removing friction can be the difference between a customer choosing your product or going to a competitor, making it a crucial focus for anyone looking to innovate.

Improving customer experience also means *personalizing interactions*. Today's consumers expect products and services to be tailored to their specific needs and preferences. This is where data can play a significant role. By analyzing customer data—such as past purchases, browsing behavior, and feedback—innovators can create personalized experiences that make customers feel understood and valued. For example, streaming services use algorithms to recommend content based on users' viewing history, while e-commerce platforms suggest products based on past purchases. Personalization turns a generic experience into something uniquely tailored, building a stronger connection between the brand and the customer.

Another aspect of innovation is *creating memorable experiences*. Memorable experiences go beyond the functional benefits of a product—they create an emotional connection with the customer. For example, brands like Apple don't just sell products; they create a sense of excitement and belonging through their sleek designs, minimalist stores, and engaging product launches. This experience makes customers feel like they're part of something special, turning them into loyal advocates. By focusing on the emotional side of customer interactions, innovators can create experiences that stand out in a crowded market.

Innovation is also about *finding new markets and opportunities*. While many businesses focus on competing for a share of an existing market, true innovators look for ways to expand into new areas that others might overlook. This often involves identifying unmet needs or underserved audiences and creating products or services that cater specifically to them. For example, when ride-sharing apps like Uber and Lyft first emerged, they weren't just competing with traditional taxis—they were creating an entirely new market for convenient, app-based transportation.

Finding new markets often requires *observing trends and shifts in behavior*. For example, the rise of remote work has created new needs in the tech industry, leading to innovations in video conferencing, project management tools, and online collaboration platforms. Innovators who recognize these shifts early can position themselves to meet the evolving needs of consumers, tapping into new markets before they become saturated. It's about being attuned to changes in society, culture, and technology, and using that knowledge to identify new opportunities.

One of the most effective ways to identify new markets is through *geographic expansion*. While many businesses focus on their local market, innovators often find success by expanding into new regions or countries where their product or service is in demand. For example, a startup that develops an app for cashless payments might start in a country where digital banking is common, but expand into markets where the transition from cash to digital payments is still underway. This approach allows innovators to reach new customers and diversify their revenue streams, making their business more resilient.

Geographic expansion is not without its challenges—it requires understanding the cultural, economic, and regulatory differences in each new market. However, those who are willing to do their research and adapt their approach can find enormous success. For example, a restaurant chain might need to adjust its menu to suit local tastes, or a tech company might need to navigate different data privacy laws in various regions. The key is to see these challenges as opportunities to innovate, rather than obstacles to be avoided.

Innovation is also deeply connected to the concept of *sustainability*. In today's world, consumers are increasingly concerned about the impact of their choices on the environment, and businesses that can provide sustainable solutions have a significant advantage. Innovators who focus on sustainability are able to attract a growing base of environmentally conscious consumers while also contributing to a better future. This involves thinking creatively about how to reduce waste, use resources more efficiently, and develop products that have a minimal impact on the planet.

Sustainability can be a powerful driver of product innovation. For example, companies in the fashion industry have begun using recycled materials, organic fabrics, and sustainable production methods to create clothing that appeals to eco-conscious consumers. In the food industry, plant-based alternatives to meat and dairy have emerged as innovative solutions that cater to people looking to reduce their environmental footprint. By focusing on sustainable practices, innovators can differentiate themselves in the market, offering products that not only meet customer needs but also align with their values.

Sustainability is not just about products—it's also about *rethinking business models*. For example, some companies have shifted to a circular economy model, where products are designed to be reused, refurbished, or recycled at the end of their lifecycle. This approach reduces waste and ensures that materials are kept in use for as long as possible. A smartphone manufacturer, for instance, might offer trade-in programs that encourage customers to return their old devices, which are then refurbished or recycled. This not only reduces waste but also creates a new revenue stream for the business.

Another way to embrace sustainability is by *reducing energy consumption* and making operations more efficient. For example, companies might invest in renewable energy sources like solar or wind power, implement energy-saving technologies, or adopt more efficient manufacturing processes. These changes can lead to significant cost savings over time, while also reducing the company's carbon footprint. Innovators who focus on energy efficiency are able to position themselves as leaders in their industry, appealing to both cost-conscious and environmentally minded consumers.

Innovative thinking is also about *embracing digital transformation*. The digital age has fundamentally changed the way we live, work, and communicate, and those who are willing to adapt to these changes are the ones who can create new opportunities. Digital transformation is not just about adopting new technologies—it's about reimagining the way you do business in a digital world. This might involve automating processes, using data analytics to make better decisions, or creating digital platforms that connect with customers in new ways.

One of the most important aspects of digital transformation is *embracing data-driven decision-making*. Data provides valuable insights into customer behavior, market trends, and operational efficiency, allowing businesses to make more informed decisions. For example, an e-commerce company might use data analytics to understand which products are most popular with customers, optimize its inventory, and improve its marketing strategies. By using data to guide decisions, innovators can reduce guesswork, making their efforts more effective and targeted.

Digital transformation also involves *creating seamless digital experiences* for customers. In today's world, consumers expect to be able to interact with brands online, whether it's through social media, websites, or apps. This means providing a user-friendly digital presence that makes it easy for customers to find information, make purchases, and connect with customer support. For example, a restaurant might create an app that allows customers to order food online, track their delivery, and earn loyalty rewards. By providing a seamless digital experience, businesses can enhance customer satisfaction and build stronger relationships.

Another aspect of digital transformation is *automating repetitive tasks*. Automation allows businesses to streamline their operations, reduce costs, and free up time for more strategic activities. For example, a company might use chatbots to handle customer inquiries, automated email marketing tools to nurture leads, or software that manages inventory levels. Automation not only improves efficiency but also allows businesses to scale more effectively, making it possible to serve a larger customer base without a corresponding increase in workload.

Digital transformation is also about *adapting to new forms of communication*. In a world where people are constantly connected through social media and messaging apps, businesses need to find new ways to reach and engage their audience. This means embracing platforms like Instagram, TikTok, and YouTube, where millions of potential customers spend their time. Innovators who understand how to create content that resonates on these platforms can build a loyal following and reach new audiences in ways that traditional advertising can't match.

One of the most effective ways to engage with digital audiences is through *storytelling and content creation*. By creating content that tells a story or provides value, businesses can build a connection with their audience, turning followers into loyal customers. For example, a fitness brand might create videos that offer workout tips, healthy recipes, and motivational stories, creating a community around their brand. This approach goes beyond selling products—it's about building a relationship with your audience and creating a sense of belonging.

Digital transformation also requires *staying agile* in a rapidly changing landscape. The digital world moves quickly, and what works today might not work tomorrow. This means being willing to experiment with new platforms, adapt to changes in algorithms, and stay on top of emerging trends. For example, a company that relies heavily on social media for marketing might need to adapt its strategy when a new platform becomes popular or when algorithms change. Staying agile ensures that you can continue to reach your audience, even as the digital landscape evolves.

Another critical aspect of digital transformation is *investing in cybersecurity*. As businesses move more of their operations online, the risk of cyberattacks increases. Innovators who prioritize cybersecurity are able to protect their customers' data, build trust, and avoid the reputational damage that comes with data breaches. This might involve implementing encryption, conducting regular security audits, or using multi-factor authentication. By taking cybersecurity seriously, businesses can ensure that their digital transformation is both effective and secure.

Digital transformation is also about *leveraging data to predict future trends*. Data is often called the new oil, and for a good reason—it can provide a wealth of insights into market trends, customer preferences, and emerging opportunities. Innovators who know how to analyze and interpret data can spot patterns that others might miss, allowing them to anticipate shifts in the market and stay ahead of the competition. Predictive analytics, which uses data to forecast future outcomes, is a powerful tool for making strategic decisions.

For example, an online retailer might use predictive analytics to determine which products will be in high demand during the holiday season. By analyzing past purchasing trends, search data, and social media chatter, they can identify the items that are likely to be popular and stock up accordingly. This allows them to maximize sales while minimizing the risk of overstocking less popular items. Predictive analytics can be applied to various industries, from finance to healthcare, helping businesses make more informed decisions.

Another way data can drive innovation is through *personalized marketing*. With access to detailed information about customer behavior, businesses can create highly targeted marketing campaigns that speak directly to individual preferences. This level of personalization can significantly improve conversion rates, as customers are more likely to respond to messages that feel tailored to their needs. For example, an online streaming service might use data to recommend shows based on a user's viewing history, making it more likely that the user will find something they enjoy. Personalized marketing creates a more engaging experience, helping businesses build stronger relationships with their customers.

Data-driven innovation is also crucial for *optimizing operations*. By analyzing data from various parts of their business, companies can identify inefficiencies and find ways to improve. For example, a logistics company might use data from GPS tracking devices to optimize delivery routes, reducing fuel consumption and delivery times. A restaurant chain might analyze sales data to determine which menu items are most popular and adjust their offerings accordingly. This kind of data analysis allows businesses to operate more efficiently, reducing costs and increasing profitability.

In addition to leveraging data, innovation is about *fostering a culture of creativity within your organization*. A culture of creativity encourages employees to think outside the box, share their ideas, and experiment with new solutions. When people feel empowered to contribute their creative thoughts, they're more likely to come up with innovative ideas that can benefit the entire organization. This culture doesn't just happen on its own—it requires deliberate effort from leaders to create an environment where creativity is valued and rewarded.

One of the most effective ways to foster a creative culture is by *encouraging collaboration across departments*. When people from different backgrounds and skill sets come together, they bring diverse perspectives that can lead to more creative problem-solving. For example, a marketing team might collaborate with product developers to come up with a new way to position a product, or a sales team might work with customer service to identify pain points that could be addressed through innovation. These cross-departmental collaborations create a flow of ideas that can lead to breakthroughs.

Creativity also flourishes when *people feel safe to take risks*. In a culture of creativity, failure is seen as a natural part of the learning process, rather than something to be punished. When employees know that they won't be penalized for trying new things, they're more likely to experiment and take bold steps that could lead to innovation. For example, a software company might create a "fail fast" policy, encouraging developers to test new features quickly and learn from the results, even if the feature doesn't work out. This approach speeds up the innovation process by allowing teams to iterate rapidly.

In addition to encouraging risk-taking, a creative culture is built on *open communication*. When people feel comfortable sharing their ideas and feedback, it creates an environment where innovation can thrive. This might involve regular brainstorming sessions, suggestion boxes, or informal meetings where employees can share their thoughts. Leaders play a crucial role in fostering this open communication by actively listening to their teams, encouraging dialogue, and creating a space where all voices are heard. By promoting open communication, businesses create a pipeline of ideas that can fuel innovation.

A culture of creativity also involves *investing in ongoing education and skill development*. When employees have access to resources that help them grow, they're better equipped to come up with innovative solutions. This might involve offering workshops, online courses, or access to industry conferences where employees can learn about the latest trends and best practices. For example, a company might provide training in design thinking, a problem-solving framework that encourages creative approaches to challenges. By investing in education, businesses ensure that their teams have the skills needed to stay innovative.

Skill development is not just about formal training—it's also about *encouraging curiosity and self-directed learning*. In a culture of creativity, employees are encouraged to explore new ideas, read widely, and experiment with new tools and technologies. For example, a graphic designer might take the initiative to learn a new design software, or a marketer might explore emerging trends in social media advertising. This culture of continuous learning ensures that the team stays adaptable and open to new ideas, making it easier to respond to changes in the market.

Creativity also benefits from *a focus on well-being and work-life balance*. When employees are overworked and stressed, their creativity tends to suffer. In contrast, when people feel energized and have time to recharge, they're more likely to come up with fresh ideas. This might involve offering flexible work hours, encouraging regular breaks, or providing access to wellness programs. For example, a company might create a relaxation space where employees can take a break or offer remote work options to reduce commuting stress. By prioritizing well-being, businesses can create an environment where creativity can thrive.

A creative culture is also about *celebrating innovative thinking*. Recognizing and rewarding employees who come up with creative ideas helps reinforce the importance of innovation within the organization. This might involve hosting innovation challenges where employees can pitch new ideas, offering bonuses for successful projects, or simply acknowledging creative contributions in team meetings. When people feel that their creativity is valued, they're more likely to continue thinking outside the box, leading to a continuous flow of fresh ideas.

Another key element of innovation is *adapting to change with agility*. Agility is the ability to pivot quickly in response to new information or changing conditions. In a world where markets, technologies, and consumer preferences can shift rapidly, agility is what allows businesses to stay relevant and competitive. Agility is not about abandoning your plans at the first sign of trouble—it's about being flexible enough to adjust your strategy when new opportunities or challenges arise.

Agility often requires *rapid decision-making*. In a fast-paced environment, waiting too long to make decisions can mean missing out on opportunities. Agile organizations empower their teams to make decisions quickly, based on the best information available at the time. This might involve giving team leaders the authority to make tactical decisions without needing approval from upper management, or creating a framework that allows teams to experiment with new ideas without going through a lengthy approval process. By speeding up decision-making, businesses can respond more quickly to changes in the market.

Agility is also about *embracing feedback loops*. Feedback loops allow businesses to gather information quickly, learn from their experiences, and make adjustments in real time. For example, a software company might use customer feedback to release updates and fixes on a regular basis, rather than waiting for a major annual release. This approach ensures that the product stays in line with customer needs and that issues are addressed promptly. Feedback loops allow businesses to iterate and improve continuously, making them more responsive to changes in the market.

Another aspect of agility is *being willing to change course when necessary*. While it's important to have a vision and long-term goals, it's equally important to recognize when a strategy isn't working and to make adjustments. This might involve pivoting to a new product line, adjusting your marketing strategy, or even changing the focus of your business entirely. For example, a company that initially focused on brick-and-mortar retail might shift to e-commerce in response to changing consumer behavior. The ability to pivot ensures that businesses can stay relevant, even as the world around them changes.

Agility also involves *empowering teams to innovate*. In an agile organization, innovation isn't confined to a single department—it's a mindset that permeates the entire company. This means giving teams the autonomy to come up with new ideas, experiment with different approaches, and take ownership of their projects. When teams have the freedom to innovate, they're more likely to come up with creative solutions that drive the business forward. This approach is especially important in industries where speed and adaptability are crucial for staying ahead of the competition.

Empowering teams requires *trust and accountability*. Leaders in agile organizations trust their teams to make decisions and take risks, knowing that they have the skills and knowledge to deliver results. This trust creates a sense of ownership among team members, motivating them to take initiative and push the boundaries of what's possible. At the same time, accountability ensures that everyone stays focused on the end goal and is held responsible for their contributions. This balance between trust and accountability creates a high-performance environment where innovation can thrive.

Agility is also about *embracing simplicity*. In a world where complexity can slow down decision-making and create bottlenecks, simplicity allows businesses to move quickly. This means streamlining processes, reducing bureaucracy, and focusing on the core elements that deliver value. For example, a startup might focus on a single product feature that solves a specific problem, rather than trying to build a complex suite of features from the start. By keeping things simple, businesses can launch products faster, gather feedback, and iterate based on real-world data.

An agile approach also means being open to *continuous improvement*. Rather than aiming for perfection, agile innovators focus on making incremental improvements over time. This mindset allows them to adapt quickly, test new ideas, and learn from their mistakes. For example, a software company might release a minimum viable product (MVP) to gather feedback from users, then use that feedback to improve the product over multiple iterations. This approach allows businesses to bring new ideas to market faster, while continuously refining their offerings.

Agility is also about *embracing a mindset of resilience*. In the process of innovation, setbacks are inevitable. New ideas may not always work out as expected, and market conditions can change suddenly. Those who innovate successfully understand that resilience is essential for navigating these challenges. Resilience is the ability to bounce back from failures, adapt to new realities, and keep moving forward with determination. It's about maintaining a positive attitude even when things get tough, and using each setback as an opportunity to learn and grow.

Resilience starts with *accepting uncertainty*. Innovation is inherently uncertain because it involves venturing into new territory. There are no guarantees that a new product will succeed, that a new market will be profitable, or that a new strategy will work. Accepting this uncertainty allows innovators to remain calm and focused, even when results are not immediate. Rather than being paralyzed by fear of the unknown, they are able to embrace uncertainty as part of the journey. This mindset allows them to take calculated risks, knowing that failure is not a reflection of their abilities, but a step on the path to eventual success.

Resilience also involves *developing mental toughness*. Mental toughness means staying focused on your long-term vision, even when you encounter obstacles. It's about not letting short-term setbacks derail your progress or diminish your motivation. For example, an entrepreneur who experiences a financial loss might be tempted to give up, but those with resilience will find ways to cut costs, pivot their business model, or seek new sources of revenue. Mental toughness allows you to stay committed to your goals, no matter how difficult the journey becomes.

A crucial part of building resilience is *practicing self-care*. Innovation requires a lot of energy, both mental and physical, and it's important to take care of yourself to maintain that energy over the long haul. This might involve getting enough sleep, eating a balanced diet, exercising regularly, and finding time for activities that bring you joy. Self-care is not a luxury—it's a necessity for maintaining the focus, creativity, and drive needed to innovate. By taking care of your well-being, you ensure that you have the stamina to overcome challenges and keep pushing forward.

Innovation also involves *adopting a global perspective*. In a connected world, opportunities for innovation are not limited by geography. Those who are willing to think globally can find new markets, new partners, and new sources of inspiration that others might overlook. A global perspective allows you to understand trends and changes on a broader scale, identifying opportunities that are emerging in different parts of the world. It's about being open to the fact that the next big idea might come from a different culture or a distant market.

A global perspective can be particularly valuable when it comes to *cultural adaptation*. Products and services that succeed in one region might need to be adapted to meet the preferences and needs of consumers in another. For example, fast-food chains that expand into international markets often adjust their menus to include local flavors, ensuring that they appeal to local tastes. By understanding cultural differences and adapting your approach accordingly, you can ensure that your innovations resonate with a global audience. This adaptability is key to creating products that have widespread appeal.

In addition to adapting to different cultures, a global perspective means *being aware of international trends*. By keeping an eye on what's happening in different parts of the world, you can spot trends that may not have reached your local market yet. For example, trends in technology, fashion, or entertainment often start in one region and gradually spread to others. Innovators who are aware of these trends can introduce new ideas to their market before the competition, positioning themselves as leaders in their industry.

Having a global perspective also involves *building international partnerships*. Partnering with companies, organizations, or individuals in different regions can open up new opportunities for growth and collaboration. For example, a tech startup in Europe might partner with a manufacturing company in Asia to produce hardware components, while a consulting firm in North America might collaborate with experts in emerging markets to gain insights into new customer behaviors. These partnerships allow businesses to leverage the strengths and expertise of others, creating a win-win situation where both parties benefit from shared knowledge and resources.

A global perspective is also about *understanding the impact of global events* on markets and industries. Events like economic recessions, political changes, and public health crises can have far-reaching effects on consumer behavior and business environments. Those who innovate successfully are able to anticipate these changes and adjust their strategies accordingly. For example, the rise of remote work during the COVID-19 pandemic created new opportunities for digital collaboration tools, while economic shifts in certain regions can influence where businesses choose to invest or expand.

Being aware of global events also means *staying informed about international regulations and standards*. For businesses that operate across borders, understanding the regulatory environment in different regions is essential for compliance and success. This might involve keeping up with changes in trade policies, data privacy regulations, or environmental standards. Innovators who understand these regulations can navigate international markets more smoothly, avoiding costly mistakes and ensuring that their products meet the necessary requirements. This knowledge allows businesses to expand confidently, knowing that they're prepared for the legal and regulatory challenges of each market.

Innovation with a global perspective also means *embracing diversity and inclusion*. Diverse teams bring a wider range of perspectives, experiences, and ideas to the table, making it easier to develop products that appeal to a broader audience. For example, a company that includes people from different cultural backgrounds might be better equipped to understand the needs of international customers. By prioritizing diversity and inclusion, businesses can create a culture where everyone feels valued and empowered to contribute their best ideas. This inclusive approach fosters innovation by ensuring that all voices are heard.

Diversity also extends to *thought diversity*. In a world where innovation is often driven by unconventional thinking, it's important to include people who bring different perspectives and approaches. This might involve hiring people with backgrounds in different industries or creating teams with a mix of analytical thinkers, creatives, and practical problem-solvers. By bringing together people with diverse ways of thinking, businesses can tackle challenges from multiple angles, leading to more innovative solutions. Thought diversity ensures that innovation is not limited by a single way of thinking.

Another important aspect of innovation is *understanding the role of ethics and social responsibility*. In today's world, consumers expect businesses to operate in a way that is ethical, transparent, and socially responsible. Innovators who take these values seriously can create products and services that resonate with consumers on a deeper level, building trust and loyalty. Ethical innovation is not just about doing what's legally required—it's about going above and beyond to ensure that your business has a positive impact on society.

One area where ethics and innovation intersect is in *fair labor practices*. As supply chains become more global, businesses have a responsibility to ensure that their products are produced in a way that respects the rights and dignity of workers. This might involve conducting audits of suppliers, ensuring fair wages, and providing safe working conditions. For example, many companies in the fashion industry have faced scrutiny over the working conditions in factories. Innovators who prioritize ethical labor practices can differentiate themselves by offering transparency about how their products are made, appealing to consumers who care about social justice.

Ethical innovation also involves *environmental responsibility*. As awareness of climate change grows, businesses are increasingly expected to minimize their environmental impact. This might involve reducing waste, using sustainable materials, or investing in renewable energy. For example, a company that manufactures consumer electronics might implement a take-back program, allowing customers to return old devices for recycling. By reducing the environmental footprint of their products, businesses can appeal to consumers who prioritize sustainability, while also contributing to a healthier planet.

Another aspect of ethical innovation is *data privacy and security*. In an age where personal data is often collected and used for various purposes, consumers are increasingly concerned about how their information is handled. Innovators who prioritize data privacy can build trust with their customers, ensuring that their data is stored securely and used transparently. For example, a tech company might implement encryption to protect user data, or provide clear explanations of how data is collected and used. By taking data privacy seriously, businesses can differentiate themselves in a crowded market, building loyalty among privacy-conscious consumers.

Ethical innovation also extends to *creating products that improve quality of life*. Innovators who focus on solving real-world problems can create products that make a meaningful difference in people's lives. This might involve developing healthcare solutions that improve patient outcomes, creating educational tools that make learning more accessible, or designing products that make everyday tasks easier. For example, the development of telemedicine platforms has made it easier for people in remote areas to access healthcare, while online learning tools have expanded educational opportunities for students around the world.

Creating products that improve quality of life requires *empathy and understanding*. Innovators who are able to put themselves in the shoes of their customers are better equipped to design solutions that truly meet their needs. This might involve conducting interviews, surveys, or focus groups to understand the challenges that people face, and then using that information to guide product development. By starting with empathy, businesses can create products that are not only functional but also genuinely helpful.

Another important aspect of ethical innovation is *transparency*. Consumers today expect businesses to be open about how they operate, from their supply chains to their pricing. Transparency helps build trust, as it shows that a company has nothing to hide. For example, a food company might provide detailed information about where its ingredients are sourced, or a financial service might be clear about its fees and charges. This transparency allows consumers to make informed decisions and builds a sense of trust between the brand and its customers.

Transparency is also important when it comes to *acknowledging mistakes*. No business is perfect, and mistakes are inevitable. However, how a company responds to mistakes can make a big difference in how it's perceived. Innovators who are willing to admit when they've made an error, apologize, and take steps to make things right can turn a negative situation into an opportunity to build trust. For example, if a product is recalled due to a safety issue, a company that acts quickly, communicates openly with customers, and offers a solution can maintain customer loyalty even in the face of challenges.

Ethical innovation also means *engaging with communities*. Businesses don't operate in a vacuum—they are part of larger communities, and those that give back can create a positive impact that extends far beyond their bottom line. Community engagement allows companies to build strong relationships with the people they serve, fostering loyalty and goodwill. It's about recognizing that businesses have a role to play in improving the lives of those around them, whether through local initiatives, charitable contributions, or by providing opportunities for growth and development.

One way to engage with communities is through *corporate social responsibility (CSR) programs*. CSR initiatives can take many forms, from volunteering efforts to support local schools and nonprofits, to programs aimed at reducing environmental impact or supporting underprivileged groups. For example, a tech company might sponsor coding workshops for young students in underserved communities, helping to inspire the next generation of innovators. These initiatives not only benefit the community but also provide employees with a sense of purpose, knowing that their work contributes to a larger cause.

Community engagement also involves *listening to community needs*. Many companies assume they know what's best for the communities they serve, but true engagement starts with listening. This might involve holding town hall meetings, conducting surveys, or partnering with local leaders to understand the most pressing challenges facing the community. For example, a company planning to build a new facility might engage with local residents to understand their concerns about environmental impact or job opportunities. By listening first, businesses can ensure that their actions align with the needs and desires of the community, creating a more positive and lasting impact.

Another important aspect of community engagement is *supporting local economies*. When businesses invest in local suppliers, hire locally, and contribute to the economic development of their communities, they help create a more sustainable and inclusive economy. For example, a restaurant chain that sources its ingredients from local farmers not only supports those farmers but also offers customers fresher and more sustainable options. This approach helps build a network of mutual support, where businesses and communities grow together, each benefiting from the other's success.

Innovation is also about *building a legacy that lasts*. While many people think of innovation as something that drives immediate results, the most impactful innovations are those that stand the test of time. Building a legacy means creating products, services, or ideas that continue to provide value long after they are introduced. It's about thinking beyond short-term gains and focusing on the long-term impact that your work will have on future generations. Innovators who build legacies are remembered not just for their success, but for the difference they made in the world.

Building a legacy involves *creating products that solve timeless problems*. While trends come and go, some challenges are universal, and finding solutions to these problems can create lasting value. For example, innovations in healthcare that improve patient outcomes or make care more accessible will always be in demand. Similarly, products that promote sustainability, education, or economic empowerment can have a lasting impact, as they address fundamental needs that transcend changes in the market. By focusing on creating solutions that are relevant in any era, innovators can ensure that their work remains valuable over time.

Creating a legacy also means *mentoring the next generation of innovators*. Those who have achieved success have a responsibility to share their knowledge and experience with others who are just starting out. Mentorship allows experienced innovators to pass on their lessons, helping to build a new generation of leaders who are equipped to tackle the challenges of the future. For example, a successful entrepreneur might mentor young founders, providing guidance on everything from fundraising to product development. This transfer of knowledge ensures that the spirit of innovation continues, even as new challenges arise.

Mentorship is not just about formal relationships—it's also about *inspiring others through your example*. Innovators who lead with integrity, resilience, and a commitment to positive change serve as role models for those around them. Their actions set a standard for what is possible and show others that they too can make a difference. For example, a business leader who prioritizes sustainability might inspire other companies to adopt greener practices, creating a ripple effect that extends far beyond their own organization. By living their values and staying true to their mission, innovators can inspire others to follow in their footsteps.

Another key to building a legacy is *continuously adapting to change*. The world doesn't stay the same, and those who want to create lasting impact must be willing to evolve along with it. This means staying open to new ideas, being willing to pivot when necessary, and always looking for ways to improve. Innovators who build legacies are those who never rest on their laurels—they're always seeking the next opportunity to make a difference. For example, a company that started by manufacturing physical products might adapt to the digital age by developing software solutions or investing in e-commerce platforms.

Adaptability also involves *embracing new technologies*. Technological advancements continue to reshape industries, from artificial intelligence to blockchain to renewable energy. Those who are willing to explore these new technologies can find ways to integrate them into their existing models, creating new value and staying ahead of the curve. For example, a logistics company might use AI to optimize delivery routes, reducing fuel consumption and delivery times. By staying on the cutting edge of technology, businesses can ensure that they remain relevant, even as the world changes around them.

Building a legacy also means *focusing on long-term relationships with customers*. While many companies prioritize short-term sales, those that build legacies understand the importance of customer loyalty. This means going beyond the transaction and building relationships based on trust, transparency, and a commitment to delivering value. For example, a software company might offer exceptional customer support, ensuring that users feel valued and heard. Over time, these relationships become a source of resilience, as loyal customers are more likely to stick with a brand through ups and downs.

Customer loyalty is often built through *consistency and reliability*. When customers know that they can count on a brand to deliver quality products and services, they are more likely to continue doing business with them. This might involve maintaining high standards of product quality, delivering on promises, and being responsive to customer feedback. For example, a company that manufactures home appliances might build a reputation for durability and customer support, earning the trust of homeowners who rely on their products. This consistency creates a sense of stability, making the brand a preferred choice in a competitive market.

Another important aspect of building a legacy is *leaving a positive impact on the environment*. As concerns about climate change continue to grow, businesses that take responsibility for their environmental impact are positioned to leave a lasting legacy. This means going beyond regulatory requirements and finding innovative ways to reduce carbon footprints, conserve resources, and protect ecosystems. For example, a company that manufactures consumer goods might invest in biodegradable packaging, reducing plastic waste and appealing to eco-conscious consumers. By prioritizing environmental responsibility, businesses can create a legacy that future generations will respect.

Environmental innovation often involves *rethinking supply chains*. Traditional supply chains can be wasteful and energy-intensive, but innovators are finding ways to make them more efficient and sustainable. This might involve sourcing materials from ethical suppliers, reducing transportation emissions, or using renewable energy in production processes. For example, a clothing brand might switch to organic cotton, reducing the environmental impact of its raw materials. By rethinking supply chains, businesses can ensure that their products are not only high quality but also aligned with the values of sustainability.

Another way to leave a positive environmental legacy is through *education and advocacy*. Many companies are in a unique position to raise awareness about environmental issues and inspire positive change. For example, a brand that produces outdoor gear might use its platform to promote conservation efforts, encouraging customers to respect and protect natural spaces. By using their influence to advocate for sustainability, businesses can create a ripple effect that extends beyond their own operations, inspiring others to take action.

In addition to environmental responsibility, building a legacy involves *contributing to social progress*. Innovators have the power to address social issues and create solutions that improve quality of life for people around the world. This might involve developing affordable healthcare solutions, creating educational opportunities for marginalized communities, or supporting economic development in underserved regions. For example, a company that creates water filtration systems for communities without access to clean drinking water is not just building a business—it's making a difference in people's lives. By focusing on social impact, innovators can create a legacy that benefits society as a whole.

Creating a lasting legacy also means *being true to your values*. In a world where trends and market pressures can shift rapidly, it's easy to get caught up in the pursuit of profits or popularity. However, those who build legacies are those who remain grounded in their principles, even when it's not the easiest or most profitable path. Staying true to your values means making decisions that align with your beliefs, treating people with respect, and maintaining a sense of purpose in everything you do. This integrity is what gives a legacy its strength, making it a source of inspiration for others.

Being true to your values involves *making ethical decisions, even when it's difficult*. This might mean turning down a lucrative business deal that conflicts with your principles or choosing to support a cause that might not be popular with all stakeholders. For example, a company that prioritizes fair labor practices might refuse to work with suppliers that exploit their workers, even if it means higher costs. By making these tough choices, businesses demonstrate that their commitment to their values is genuine, earning the respect of customers, employees, and partners alike.

Values-driven innovation is also about *creating a positive workplace culture*. A company's culture reflects its values, and a positive culture can become a key part of its legacy. This means creating an environment where employees feel valued, supported, and empowered to do their best work. For example, a company might offer flexible work arrangements, provide opportunities for professional development, and create a culture of recognition and appreciation. A positive culture not only improves employee satisfaction but also enhances productivity and creativity, making it easier to innovate and grow.

Creating a positive culture also involves *promoting diversity and inclusion*. When people from different backgrounds feel welcome and valued, they bring their unique perspectives and ideas to the table, enriching the organization. This diversity leads to better problem-solving, more innovative thinking, and a more inclusive product or service offering. For example, a tech company that actively recruits women and people of color might develop products that better serve a diverse user base. By promoting diversity, businesses ensure that their legacy is one of inclusivity and empowerment.

Building a lasting legacy also means *investing in people*. The most successful innovators understand that their greatest asset is not technology or capital—it's the people who bring their vision to life. Investing in people means creating opportunities for growth, recognizing talent, and providing the resources that allow individuals to reach their full potential. When employees feel valued and supported, they're more likely to be engaged, creative, and committed to the organization's success. This investment in people is what creates a culture of innovation that can sustain a company over the long term.

Investing in people often involves *offering mentorship and guidance*. Just as mentorship is important for entrepreneurs and innovators, it's equally crucial within an organization. By providing mentorship opportunities, companies can help employees develop their skills, build confidence, and achieve their career goals. For example, a tech firm might establish a mentorship program where senior engineers guide newer team members, offering insights into problem-solving and career development. This kind of mentorship creates a supportive environment where knowledge is shared, and employees feel empowered to take on new challenges.

Another way to invest in people is through *continuous learning and development*. The business world is constantly evolving, and those who keep up with the latest trends, technologies, and methodologies are better equipped to innovate. This might involve providing access to online courses, hosting in-house training sessions, or encouraging employees to attend industry conferences. For example, a marketing team might learn about new digital advertising tools, while a product development team might stay updated on advancements in user experience design. By fostering a culture of learning, businesses ensure that their teams are always at the cutting edge, ready to adapt and innovate.

Investing in people also means *creating a culture of recognition and appreciation*.

Recognizing the contributions of team members, no matter how small, can have a big impact on morale and motivation. This might involve celebrating team achievements, offering bonuses for innovative ideas, or simply taking the time to thank employees for their hard work. For example, a company might hold monthly meetings to highlight the accomplishments of different departments or recognize individuals who went above and beyond. This recognition creates a positive work environment where people feel valued, leading to greater engagement and a stronger commitment to innovation.

Innovation is also about *building resilience into your organization*. Resilient organizations are those that can withstand challenges, adapt to changes, and emerge stronger from setbacks. Building resilience requires a combination of strategic planning, flexibility, and a positive mindset. It's about preparing for uncertainty, being willing to pivot when necessary, and maintaining a sense of optimism even in difficult times. Resilience is what allows companies to navigate economic downturns, shifts in consumer behavior, and industry disruptions without losing sight of their long-term goals.

One of the most important aspects of building resilience is *developing a strong foundation*. This means ensuring that the core aspects of your business—such as financial stability, customer relationships, and operational efficiency—are solid. For example, a company might build up a cash reserve to weather economic downturns or focus on maintaining strong relationships with key clients. By having a stable foundation, businesses are better equipped to handle unexpected challenges, allowing them to focus on innovation rather than just survival.

Building resilience also involves *creating a culture of adaptability*. In a resilient organization, employees are encouraged to think creatively, adapt to new situations, and embrace change. This might involve cross-training team members so they can take on different roles as needed, or encouraging teams to experiment with new approaches to their work. For example, a company that traditionally relied on in-person sales might shift to a digital-first strategy, adapting to changes in consumer behavior. By fostering adaptability, businesses can ensure that their teams are ready to respond to whatever challenges arise.

Another key to building resilience is *prioritizing transparency and communication*. During times of uncertainty, clear and honest communication helps maintain trust and morale. This might involve keeping employees informed about the company's financial situation, sharing updates on strategic decisions, or being open about the challenges the company is facing. For example, a CEO might hold regular town hall meetings with employees to discuss the impact of a market downturn and the steps the company is taking to adapt. This transparency helps create a sense of unity, as employees understand that they are all working towards the same goals.

Resilience also involves *developing a long-term vision*. While it's important to focus on immediate challenges, those who build resilient organizations are always thinking about the future. A long-term vision provides a sense of purpose and direction, helping companies stay focused on their goals even when the path is difficult. For example, a renewable energy company might have a vision of creating a carbon-neutral future, guiding its decisions and investments even when facing short-term market challenges. This vision helps keep the company on track, ensuring that its efforts are aligned with its larger mission.

A long-term vision also allows companies to *invest strategically in innovation*. Rather than chasing every new trend, resilient organizations focus on the innovations that are most likely to drive long-term growth. This might involve investing in research and development, building partnerships with universities, or supporting internal innovation labs. For example, a pharmaceutical company might invest in research for new treatments, knowing that the process could take years but ultimately lead to breakthroughs that improve patient outcomes. By focusing on strategic innovation, businesses can ensure that their efforts are building towards a brighter future.

In addition to focusing on long-term vision, resilience is about *embracing change with a growth mindset*. A growth mindset is the belief that abilities and intelligence can be developed through hard work, learning, and perseverance. This mindset allows individuals and organizations to see challenges as opportunities for growth, rather than as threats. For example, a team that embraces a growth mindset might view a failed product launch as a learning experience, using the feedback to create a better version. This perspective makes it easier to stay motivated and engaged, even when faced with setbacks.

Developing a growth mindset involves *encouraging a culture of experimentation*. When people feel free to test new ideas without fear of failure, they are more likely to come up with creative solutions. This might involve running pilot programs, conducting small-scale tests, or encouraging "what if" thinking. For example, a company might allow employees to spend a portion of their time on passion projects or new ideas, creating a space where innovation can flourish. By creating a culture that values experimentation, businesses can ensure that they remain flexible and open to new possibilities.

Another essential element of resilience is *building a network of support*. Just as individuals benefit from having a support system, businesses thrive when they build strong relationships with partners, suppliers, and other stakeholders. A network of support provides access to resources, knowledge, and opportunities that can help businesses navigate challenges more effectively. For example, during a supply chain disruption, a company with strong relationships might be able to secure alternative sources for materials, while a company without those connections might struggle.

Building a network of support often involves *nurturing strategic partnerships*. Strategic partnerships allow businesses to leverage each other's strengths, creating synergies that benefit both parties. For example, a software company might partner with a hardware manufacturer to create a more integrated user experience, or a restaurant chain might collaborate with a local farm to source fresh ingredients. These partnerships create a sense of interdependence, where both parties work together to achieve shared goals. This network of relationships creates resilience, as businesses are able to draw on the support of their partners when needed.

In addition to external partnerships, a resilient organization also focuses on *internal collaboration*. By breaking down silos and encouraging collaboration across departments, businesses can create a more cohesive and adaptive team. This might involve regular cross-departmental meetings, collaborative projects, or creating spaces where employees from different teams can share ideas. For example, a product development team might collaborate closely with customer support to ensure that new features address real user needs. This internal collaboration ensures that the organization can move quickly and adapt to changes as a unified front.

A network of support is also about *building strong relationships with customers*. Loyal customers can be a company's greatest advocates, providing valuable feedback and spreading the word about products and services. Building customer loyalty involves going beyond transactional relationships and creating a sense of connection and community. For example, a fitness brand might create an online community where customers can share their progress, offer tips, and encourage each other. This sense of community creates a deeper connection between the brand and its customers, making them more likely to stick around even during challenging times.

Resilience is also about *embracing the power of storytelling*. Storytelling allows businesses to connect with their audience on an emotional level, creating a sense of shared identity and purpose. In times of uncertainty, storytelling can provide hope, inspire action, and reinforce the values that guide a company. For example, a company that faces a major challenge might share the story of its founding, reminding employees and customers of the original vision and the journey that led to its success. This story can serve as a source of motivation, helping everyone stay focused on the bigger picture.

Storytelling also plays a role in *building a strong brand identity*. A brand's story is more than just a marketing tool—it's a way of communicating what the brand stands for, what it values, and why it exists. A strong brand story can differentiate a company from its competitors, making it more memorable and appealing to customers. For example, a brand that focuses on sustainability might share the story of how it sources materials ethically, reducing its environmental impact. This story helps customers feel good about their choice, knowing that they are supporting a company that aligns with their values.

In addition to external storytelling, resilience also involves *internal storytelling*. Within an organization, storytelling can be a powerful way to communicate vision, celebrate successes, and maintain a sense of unity. For example, leaders might share stories of how the company overcame past challenges, reinforcing the message that resilience is part of the company's DNA. These stories can serve as a reminder that the team has faced difficult times before and emerged stronger, helping to maintain morale during periods of uncertainty.

Resilience is not just about bouncing back—it's about *growing stronger through adversity*. Those who are truly resilient don't just survive challenges—they use them as an opportunity to grow, improve, and innovate. This means being willing to learn from mistakes, adapting to new circumstances, and using setbacks as fuel for future success. For example, a business that experiences a downturn might use that time to invest in training, refine its processes, or develop new products. This approach ensures that when the challenges pass, the company is stronger and more capable than ever before.

Resilience is also about *embracing a culture of accountability*. Accountability is the backbone of any strong organization, and it's a critical aspect of resilience because it ensures that every team member takes responsibility for their actions and contributes to the organization's success. In a culture of accountability, people are not afraid to own their mistakes, learn from them, and take the necessary steps to improve. This creates an environment where continuous improvement becomes the norm, making the organization more adaptable and capable of handling challenges.

A culture of accountability starts with *clear expectations*. When employees understand what is expected of them, they are better equipped to take ownership of their roles. This might involve setting specific goals, defining key performance indicators (KPIs), and regularly reviewing progress. For example, a sales team might have clear targets for monthly revenue, while a customer service team might be measured on customer satisfaction scores. By providing clarity around what success looks like, leaders can create a framework where accountability is built into the daily operations of the company.

Accountability also requires *transparency and openness*. When leaders are transparent about their decisions and the reasons behind them, it creates a sense of trust and encourages others to be open about their own actions. For example, a company might hold regular meetings where leadership shares updates on financial performance, strategic decisions, and upcoming projects. This openness sets the tone for a culture where people feel comfortable sharing their own progress, challenges, and ideas for improvement. Transparency ensures that everyone is working with the same information, making it easier to align efforts towards common goals.

In addition to transparency, fostering accountability involves *providing constructive feedback*. Feedback is a powerful tool for growth, but it must be delivered in a way that is respectful and focused on improvement.

Constructive feedback helps individuals understand where they can improve and provides guidance on how to achieve their goals. For example, a manager might provide feedback on a project presentation, highlighting what went well and offering suggestions for making future presentations more effective. This feedback loop creates an environment where people are constantly learning, growing, and taking responsibility for their performance.

Another crucial aspect of resilience is *embracing change as a constant*. Many organizations struggle with change, preferring to stick to familiar routines and strategies. However, those who understand that change is inevitable are better prepared to adapt when new challenges or opportunities arise. Rather than resisting change, they see it as an opportunity to innovate and grow. Embracing change means being willing to let go of outdated practices, adopt new technologies, and explore new markets, even when it means stepping outside of your comfort zone.

Embracing change starts with *developing a mindset of flexibility*. Flexibility is the ability to adapt your approach based on new information or circumstances. It's about being open to trying new things and not becoming too attached to a particular way of doing things. For example, a company that traditionally relied on in-store sales might shift to e-commerce as more consumers move to online shopping. This flexibility allows businesses to stay relevant, even as consumer behavior shifts. Being flexible doesn't mean abandoning your vision—it means finding new ways to achieve it.

A flexible mindset also involves *experimenting with new ideas*. Experimentation allows you to test different approaches and find out what works best, without committing all your resources to a single strategy. For example, a marketing team might run A/B tests on different ad campaigns to see which message resonates most with their audience. This willingness to test and learn helps businesses find innovative solutions more quickly, as they can pivot based on the results of their experiments. Experimentation ensures that you're not just guessing—you're using data to guide your decisions.

Embracing change also means *building a team that is adaptable*. In a world that is constantly evolving, having a team that can adapt to new challenges is a key competitive advantage. This might involve hiring people who are comfortable with ambiguity, providing training in new skills, or fostering a culture where people are encouraged to think creatively. For example, a company might prioritize hiring employees who are eager to learn and open to taking on new responsibilities, even if they don't have experience in a particular area. By building an adaptable team, businesses can ensure that they are ready to face whatever changes come their way.

Innovation is also about *cultivating an entrepreneurial spirit within the organization*. An entrepreneurial spirit means thinking like a founder, even if you're not the one who started the company. It's about taking ownership of your work, seeking out opportunities, and being willing to take risks to achieve your goals. When employees feel empowered to think like entrepreneurs, they're more likely to come up with creative solutions, take initiative, and contribute to the company's growth in meaningful ways. This entrepreneurial mindset is what drives innovation, as it encourages people to constantly look for ways to improve and create value.

Cultivating an entrepreneurial spirit involves *giving employees autonomy*. Autonomy allows people to make decisions about how they approach their work, which can lead to greater engagement and innovation. For example, a company might give team members the freedom to explore new projects, take on leadership roles in their area of expertise, or develop new processes that improve efficiency. This sense of ownership motivates employees to take pride in their work and to think creatively about how they can contribute to the organization's success.

An entrepreneurial spirit is also fueled by *encouraging calculated risk-taking*. Innovation often requires stepping into the unknown, and those who are afraid to take risks are unlikely to achieve breakthrough results. However, it's important that risk-taking is calculated, meaning that decisions are made based on careful analysis and an understanding of the potential outcomes. For example, a company might encourage employees to propose new product ideas, but also guide them through a process of evaluating market demand, production costs, and potential risks. This approach ensures that risk-taking is balanced with strategic thinking, leading to more successful outcomes.

Creating an entrepreneurial culture also means *celebrating initiative*. When people take initiative, they are often going beyond their regular duties to make a positive impact. For example, an employee might notice a bottleneck in a process and take the lead in developing a solution, even if it's not part of their job description. Recognizing and celebrating this kind of initiative helps to reinforce the value of an entrepreneurial spirit within the organization. It sends the message that innovation is not just the responsibility of leadership—it's something that everyone can contribute to.

An entrepreneurial spirit is also closely linked to *problem-solving*. Entrepreneurs are, by nature, problem-solvers—they see challenges not as obstacles but as opportunities to create solutions. This mindset is essential for innovation because it allows individuals and teams to tackle complex problems with creativity and determination. For example, when faced with a decline in customer satisfaction, a team with an entrepreneurial mindset might conduct surveys, analyze feedback, and develop a new customer service strategy that addresses the issues. This proactive approach to problem-solving helps businesses stay ahead of challenges and continue to provide value to their customers.

Problem-solving in an innovative organization often involves *approaching challenges from different angles*. This might mean bringing together people from different departments to brainstorm solutions or looking for inspiration outside your industry. For example, a design team might look to nature for inspiration when creating a new product, or a logistics team might study the operations of a successful e-commerce company to find ways to improve delivery times. This willingness to explore different perspectives ensures that problems are not approached with a one-size-fits-all mentality, leading to more innovative solutions.

Another key to problem-solving is *focusing on the root cause rather than just the symptoms*. Many organizations make the mistake of addressing the symptoms of a problem without digging deeper to find the underlying issue. For example, if a company is struggling with high employee turnover, it might try to fix the problem by offering higher salaries. However, the root cause might be a lack of career development opportunities or a toxic work environment. By focusing on the root cause, businesses can create solutions that address the real issue, leading to more lasting improvements.

Problem-solving also involves *staying persistent*. Some challenges don't have easy answers, and it can take time to find the right solution. Those with an entrepreneurial spirit understand that persistence is key—they're willing to keep trying, even when progress is slow. For example, an engineer working on a new product might encounter multiple setbacks before finally finding a design that works. This persistence is what allows innovators to overcome obstacles and achieve breakthroughs. It's about believing that every problem has a solution, and being willing to put in the effort to find it.

Innovation is also deeply tied to *creating a vision that inspires*. A compelling vision provides a sense of direction and purpose, guiding the decisions and actions of everyone involved. It's what unites people around a common goal, motivating them to work together to create something bigger than themselves. A strong vision is more than just a mission statement—it's a story about the impact you want to make in the world. For example, a tech startup might have a vision of making the internet accessible to everyone, while a nonprofit might be dedicated to eradicating hunger in their community. This vision becomes a source of inspiration, helping to attract people who are passionate about the cause.

A compelling vision also helps to *align efforts*. When everyone in an organization understands the vision, they can see how their work contributes to the larger goal. This alignment ensures that everyone is pulling in the same direction, making it easier to achieve ambitious objectives. For example, a company with a vision of creating the most user-friendly software might ensure that every department, from engineering to customer support, is focused on improving the user experience. This alignment creates a sense of cohesion, where every action is connected to the broader mission.

Creating a vision that inspires also involves *communicating it effectively*. A vision is only powerful if it's understood and embraced by the people it's meant to inspire. This means communicating the vision clearly, consistently, and in a way that resonates with your audience. For example, a company might share stories of how their products have positively impacted customers, or a nonprofit might highlight the progress they've made towards their mission. By bringing the vision to life through stories and examples, leaders can create an emotional connection that inspires people to get involved.

An inspiring vision also encourages people to *dream big*. Innovation is often born from ambitious goals—those that seem impossible at first but become achievable through hard work and creativity. For example, the vision of putting a man on the moon seemed out of reach when it was first proposed, but it inspired scientists, engineers, and astronauts to push the boundaries of what was possible. This same spirit of bold ambition drives innovation in business, motivating people to think beyond what is currently possible and to strive for something greater.

Creating a vision that inspires is not just about setting goals—it's about *creating a sense of purpose that resonates with people on a personal level*. Purpose gives people a reason to show up every day, to put in the effort, and to stay committed even when things get tough. It goes beyond profit margins and market share; it's about the positive impact that an organization can make in the world. For example, a renewable energy company might have a purpose centered around reducing the world's reliance on fossil fuels, making the planet a healthier place for future generations. This sense of purpose can become a powerful motivator, driving innovation and commitment throughout the organization.

A purpose-driven vision also helps to *attract like-minded talent*. People want to work for organizations that align with their values and offer them a chance to be part of something meaningful. When a company's vision is clearly articulated and authentically pursued, it becomes a magnet for individuals who share the same passion. For example, a social enterprise that focuses on providing clean water solutions to communities might attract employees who are passionate about sustainability and global development. This alignment between the company's vision and the personal values of its employees creates a strong sense of unity and dedication, making it easier to work towards ambitious goals.

Purpose-driven companies also *build deeper connections with their customers*. Today's consumers are increasingly looking to support brands that stand for something they believe in. When a company's vision aligns with the values of its customers, it creates a bond that goes beyond the transaction. For example, a brand that commits to ethical sourcing and transparency might attract customers who are conscious about the origins of the products they purchase. This shared sense of purpose can turn customers into brand advocates, willing to spread the word about the company's mission and values.

Building a purpose-driven vision also means *being true to your values, even when it's challenging*. There will be times when sticking to your principles may seem at odds with short-term gains, but those who build a lasting legacy understand that integrity is non-negotiable. For example, a company that prioritizes fair labor practices might face pressure to cut costs by outsourcing to a supplier with lower standards. However, by staying true to its commitment to ethical practices, the company maintains the trust of its customers and its integrity as a brand. This consistency is what builds long-term loyalty and respect, both within and outside of the organization.

Another critical aspect of innovation is *fostering a mindset of continuous improvement*. Continuous improvement is about always looking for ways to enhance products, processes, and customer experiences, even when things are going well. It's the belief that there is always room for growth, and that innovation is not a one-time event but a continuous journey. Companies that embrace this mindset are never satisfied with the status quo—they are always asking, "How can we make this better?"

Continuous improvement often starts with *encouraging feedback at every level of the organization*. When feedback is welcomed and valued, it creates a culture where people feel comfortable sharing their observations and suggestions. For example, frontline employees often have direct insights into customer needs and frustrations, making their feedback invaluable for product development. By creating channels for gathering and acting on feedback, companies can identify areas where improvements can be made, leading to better products and services.

Another key to continuous improvement is *embracing small, incremental changes*. While many people think of innovation as a radical transformation, some of the most effective improvements come from making small tweaks over time. This might involve streamlining a process, adjusting a product feature, or finding a more efficient way to deliver a service. For example, a company that manages a large customer support team might implement a small change in the way tickets are prioritized, resulting in faster response times and improved customer satisfaction. By focusing on incremental improvements, businesses can make steady progress towards their goals without the disruption that often comes with larger changes.

Continuous improvement also involves *learning from every experience*. Whether a project is a success or a failure, there are always lessons to be learned. Those who are committed to continuous improvement take the time to analyze their results, reflect on what worked well, and identify areas for growth. For example, after launching a new product, a team might conduct a retrospective meeting to discuss the strengths of their approach and the challenges they encountered. This reflection helps them improve their process for future launches, ensuring that they are always getting better at what they do.

A mindset of continuous improvement also involves *embracing the power of iteration*. Iteration is the process of refining an idea or product through repeated testing and adjustment. It's a cycle of developing, testing, learning, and refining that allows companies to adapt their offerings to better meet customer needs. For example, a software company might release a beta version of an app to a small group of users, gather feedback, and use that feedback to improve the user experience before the full launch. This iterative process ensures that the final product is as user-friendly and effective as possible.

Iteration is particularly valuable in a fast-changing market, where customer preferences and technological capabilities can shift rapidly. By adopting an iterative approach, businesses can stay responsive to these changes, adjusting their products and services based on real-time feedback. This approach is often used in agile development, where teams work in short sprints to produce incremental improvements. It's about being willing to release a minimum viable product (MVP) and then make adjustments based on user feedback, rather than waiting until a product is "perfect" to launch.

In addition to iteration, continuous improvement requires a focus on *efficiency and productivity*. Innovators understand that finding more efficient ways to work can free up time and resources for creative projects. This might involve automating routine tasks, optimizing workflows, or using technology to streamline operations. For example, a company might implement project management software that allows teams to collaborate more effectively, reducing the time spent on status meetings and email threads. By focusing on efficiency, businesses can ensure that their teams have the bandwidth to focus on high-value, innovative work.

Continuous improvement also means *celebrating progress, no matter how small*. Innovation can be a long and challenging journey, and it's important to recognize the wins along the way. Celebrating progress helps to maintain momentum and keeps the team motivated. For example, a company might celebrate the completion of a successful pilot program, even if it's just one step towards a larger goal. This recognition reinforces the value of continuous improvement, reminding everyone that each step forward, no matter how small, brings them closer to their vision.

Another powerful driver of innovation is *building an ecosystem of support*. An innovation ecosystem is a network of partners, resources, and infrastructure that supports the development of new ideas. This ecosystem might include academic institutions, research organizations, government agencies, and other businesses that share a commitment to fostering innovation. By building an ecosystem, companies can leverage the expertise and resources of others, making it easier to bring new ideas to life. For example, a biotech startup might partner with a university to conduct clinical trials, or a tech company might collaborate with a government agency to secure funding for a research initiative.

Building an innovation ecosystem also involves *connecting with industry experts and thought leaders.* These connections can provide valuable insights, mentorship, and access to new opportunities. For example, a company that wants to explore new markets might join an industry association or attend conferences where they can network with potential partners and learn about the latest trends. By staying connected to the broader industry, businesses can ensure that they are aware of emerging opportunities and best practices, positioning themselves as leaders in their field.

Another important aspect of building an ecosystem is *nurturing relationships with startups and small businesses.* Startups often have a fresh perspective and a willingness to take risks that larger companies might not. By partnering with startups, established businesses can access new ideas and technologies, while startups benefit from the resources and market reach of their larger partners. For example, a large consumer goods company might partner with a startup that has developed a new eco-friendly packaging solution, integrating the innovation into its product lines. This kind of collaboration can accelerate the pace of innovation for both parties.

Building an ecosystem of support also means *contributing to the innovation community.* Just as businesses benefit from the support of others, they also have a role to play in giving back to the community. This might involve sharing research findings, providing mentorship to early-stage entrepreneurs, or supporting educational programs that prepare the next generation of innovators. For example, a tech company might create an internship program that gives students hands-on experience with new technologies, or a manufacturing company might host workshops for local entrepreneurs. By contributing to the innovation community, businesses help to create an environment where new ideas can flourish.

The final piece of innovation is about *embracing the journey.* Innovation is not a destination—it's a way of thinking, a way of working, and a way of approaching the world. It's about constantly seeking out new challenges, being willing to take risks, and finding joy in the process of discovery. Those who embrace the journey of innovation understand that it's not just about the results; it's about the growth, the learning, and the impact they make along the way.

Embracing the journey means *finding meaning in the process.* It's easy to get caught up in the pressure to achieve immediate success, but true innovators understand that each step of the journey has value. For example, a team working on a challenging project might celebrate the progress they make each week, recognizing that even the small wins bring them closer to their goal. By focusing on the journey rather than just the outcome, innovators stay motivated and engaged, even when the path is uncertain.

The journey of innovation also involves *building a culture of curiosity.* Curiosity is the spark that drives innovation—it's the desire to understand how things work, to explore new ideas, and to find better ways of doing things. When people are curious, they ask questions, they challenge assumptions, and they are open to new possibilities. For example, a curious team might explore how new technologies like AI or blockchain could be applied to their industry, even if they are not yet mainstream. This curiosity ensures that they are always learning and evolving, keeping their innovation engine running.

Embracing the journey means *celebrating the unique path of each innovator.* Everyone's journey is different, and there is no single formula for success. Some innovators may find success quickly, while others may spend years refining their ideas before they reach their breakthrough. What matters is the persistence, the creativity, and the willingness to keep pushing forward, no matter how long it takes. By celebrating the unique path of each innovator, businesses create an environment where everyone feels empowered to pursue their own journey of growth and discovery.

CHAPTER 7: OVERCOMING OBSTACLES— TURNING CHALLENGES INTO OPPORTUNITIES

Challenges are an inevitable part of any journey, especially when it comes to innovation and personal growth. Whether you're starting a new venture, trying to break into a competitive market, or simply working towards self-improvement, obstacles will always be there. But the difference between those who succeed and those who don't often comes down to how they view and respond to those challenges. Instead of seeing obstacles as barriers, successful people see them as opportunities for growth, learning, and transformation.

Every obstacle has the potential to teach you something new. It could be about your own resilience, the gaps in your knowledge, or the need to adapt your approach. For example, an entrepreneur facing financial challenges might learn how to manage resources more effectively, or a creative professional struggling with a project might discover a new way to approach their work. Each challenge presents a chance to gain insights and develop skills that will serve you in the long run.

A key part of overcoming obstacles is *changing your mindset*. It's easy to become discouraged when things don't go according to plan, but those who thrive in the face of adversity have learned to view setbacks as temporary and solvable. This mindset shift from "I can't" to "How can I?" opens up new possibilities. For example, a tech startup that faces competition from larger players might focus on its unique strengths, such as offering a more personalized customer experience or innovating in a niche market. By asking the right questions, you can find new ways to tackle challenges.

The power of mindset is especially important when dealing with *self-doubt and fear*. Many people have great ideas and ambitions but hold themselves back because they are afraid of failing or being judged. But overcoming obstacles often means pushing through those fears and taking action, even when you're unsure of the outcome. For example, a public speaker who is nervous about presenting might practice in front of small groups until they build confidence. By facing fears head-on, you gain the courage to tackle bigger challenges over time.

Overcoming obstacles also requires *resilience*. Resilience is the ability to keep going when things get tough, to pick yourself up after a setback, and to maintain a positive attitude in the face of adversity. Resilience is not about ignoring problems or pretending everything is fine—it's about acknowledging challenges and then taking proactive steps to overcome them. For example, a business that experiences a sudden drop in sales might analyze the reasons behind it, adjust its strategy, and focus on building stronger relationships with customers. This proactive approach helps turn a setback into a stepping stone for future growth.

Resilience is often built through *practicing gratitude*. When facing difficulties, it's easy to focus on what's going wrong. But by taking the time to reflect on what's going well, you can shift your perspective and regain a sense of balance. For example, during a tough business quarter, an entrepreneur might focus on the loyal customers they have, the team's efforts, and the progress they've made, even if the numbers aren't where they want them to be. Gratitude doesn't change the challenges, but it changes how you feel about them, giving you the energy and optimism needed to keep pushing forward.

Another important aspect of overcoming obstacles is *seeking support from others*. No one has to face their challenges alone. Whether it's friends, mentors, colleagues, or family, having a support system can make all the difference when times get tough. For example, a writer facing creative block might find inspiration through conversations with other writers or attend workshops to gain new perspectives. Similarly, a business leader struggling with strategic decisions might seek advice from mentors who have navigated similar challenges before. Reaching out for help isn't a sign of weakness—it's a way to strengthen your resilience.

Support can also come from *building a positive community*. Being surrounded by people who encourage, inspire, and believe in you can be incredibly powerful when facing obstacles. For example, a startup founder might join a local entrepreneur group where members share their challenges and successes, creating a sense of camaraderie. This community provides not only practical advice but also the motivation to keep going. Being part of a positive community reminds you that you're not alone in your struggles and that others have faced similar challenges and come out stronger.

To overcome obstacles, it's also important to *take responsibility for your actions*. Blaming external circumstances, other people, or bad luck for your setbacks only takes away your power. True growth comes from recognizing where you have control and taking ownership of the situation. For example, if a project at work doesn't meet its goals, instead of blaming the team or external factors, you might ask yourself, "What could I have done differently?" This self-reflection allows you to learn from your mistakes and make better decisions moving forward.

Taking responsibility doesn't mean beating yourself up for every mistake—it means *focusing on what you can change*. It's about looking for actionable steps you can take to improve the situation. For example, if a product launch doesn't go as planned, a company might analyze customer feedback, identify where expectations weren't met, and make improvements before the next release. This approach turns setbacks into learning opportunities, allowing you to continuously improve. By taking ownership of your challenges, you reclaim the power to shape your own outcomes.

Another key to overcoming obstacles is *staying focused on your long-term vision*. When you're facing difficulties, it's easy to get caught up in the immediate struggle and lose sight of the bigger picture. But those who succeed are the ones who keep their eyes on their long-term goals, using their vision as a source of motivation. For example, an athlete training for a major competition might experience injuries or setbacks along the way, but they stay focused on their ultimate goal of reaching peak performance. This long-term focus helps them push through the tough days, knowing that each step brings them closer to their dream.

Staying focused on your vision doesn't mean ignoring the present—it means *using your vision as a guide*. When challenges arise, you can ask yourself, "How does this fit into my long-term plan?" This question helps you prioritize your actions and make decisions that align with your goals. For example, a business owner facing cash flow challenges might decide to invest in marketing rather than cutting costs, knowing that building brand awareness is essential for long-term growth. This strategic thinking allows you to navigate obstacles without losing sight of what matters most.

Overcoming obstacles is also about *developing problem-solving skills*. Problem-solving is the ability to analyze a situation, identify potential solutions, and choose the best course of action. It's a skill that can be developed through practice, and it's especially valuable when facing challenges. For example, a product manager dealing with supply chain disruptions might analyze different suppliers, negotiate new terms, or adjust the product design to accommodate available materials. This problem-solving approach allows them to find a solution rather than being paralyzed by the challenge.

Problem-solving often requires *thinking creatively*. Creativity isn't just for artists—it's a valuable skill in any field, allowing you to come up with innovative solutions when traditional approaches don't work. For example, a restaurant owner facing a decline in foot traffic might pivot to offering online cooking classes or meal kits, creating a new revenue stream. This creative thinking allows them to adapt to changing circumstances and turn challenges into new opportunities. By approaching problems with an open mind, you can find solutions that others might overlook.

Another important part of problem-solving is *breaking down big challenges into smaller, manageable steps*. When faced with a complex problem, it can feel overwhelming to try and solve it all at once. But by breaking it down into smaller tasks, you make it more approachable. For example, a student struggling with a challenging course might break down their study sessions into smaller, focused blocks, tackling one chapter or concept at a time. This approach makes progress more tangible and keeps you from feeling overwhelmed, making it easier to stay on track.

Effective problem-solving also involves *staying calm under pressure*. When you're stressed or anxious, it's difficult to think clearly and make rational decisions. That's why learning to manage your emotions is an essential part of overcoming obstacles. Techniques like deep breathing, mindfulness, or taking short breaks can help you maintain a sense of calm, even in difficult situations. For example, a manager dealing with a crisis might take a few minutes to step away from the situation, collect their thoughts, and return with a clear mind. This calmness allows them to think more strategically, making it easier to find a solution.

Another crucial aspect of overcoming obstacles is *maintaining a growth mindset*. A growth mindset is the belief that abilities and intelligence can be developed through effort, learning, and perseverance. People with a growth mindset view challenges as opportunities to learn and grow, rather than as threats to their competence. For example, an artist who receives criticism about their work might see it as a chance to improve their technique, rather than as a sign that they're not talented. This mindset shift transforms obstacles from roadblocks into stepping stones for personal development.

A growth mindset is also about *being open to feedback*. Feedback, whether from mentors, peers, or customers, provides valuable insights into where you can improve. Instead of taking feedback personally, those with a growth mindset see it as a tool for growth. For example, a writer who receives constructive criticism from an editor might use it to refine their writing style, resulting in a stronger manuscript. This willingness to learn from feedback makes it easier to overcome challenges, as you're constantly refining your approach and improving your skills.

Maintaining a growth mindset also involves *embracing the power of yet*. The power of yet is the idea that just because you haven't achieved something yet doesn't mean you never will. It's about recognizing that progress takes time and that setbacks are part of the learning process. For example, a student who struggles with a new subject might remind themselves that they haven't mastered it yet, but with effort and practice, they will improve. This perspective helps to keep frustration at bay, allowing you to stay motivated and keep pushing forward, even when the journey is difficult.

A growth mindset is also about *focusing on effort rather than outcomes*. While it's important to have goals, it's equally important to recognize the value of the effort you put in, even if the results aren't immediate. For example, a job seeker who spends months applying to positions might remind themselves that each application and interview is a step closer to their goal, even if they haven't received an offer yet. This focus on effort allows you to stay persistent, knowing that the progress you're making will eventually lead to success.

Another critical aspect of overcoming obstacles is *learning to manage your time effectively*. Time management is a skill that becomes especially important when you're faced with challenges, as it allows you to prioritize tasks, focus on what's most important, and ensure that you're making steady progress even when the path isn't clear. Effective time management is not about working longer hours—it's about working smarter, making sure that your energy is directed towards activities that will have the biggest impact.

One strategy for better time management is *prioritizing tasks using the Eisenhower Matrix*. This tool helps you categorize tasks into four quadrants: urgent and important, important but not urgent, urgent but not important, and neither urgent nor important. For example, a business owner dealing with a crisis might focus on urgent and important tasks, like resolving a customer complaint, while scheduling time for important but not urgent tasks, such as planning for future growth. By organizing tasks this way, you can focus on what truly matters without getting overwhelmed by less critical demands.

Time management also involves *setting clear and achievable goals*. When you're facing challenges, it's important to break down your goals into smaller, manageable steps. This makes it easier to track your progress and stay motivated. For example, a writer working on a large project might set a goal of writing 500 words a day. This smaller target makes the task less intimidating and helps them build momentum over time. Achieving these smaller milestones creates a sense of accomplishment, helping you stay on track even when the bigger goal feels far away.

Another key to effective time management is *minimizing distractions*.

Distractions can drain your focus and make it difficult to maintain momentum when you're facing a challenge. This might mean setting boundaries around your time, such as turning off notifications during focused work periods or setting specific times for checking emails. For example, an entrepreneur might dedicate the first two hours of each day to strategic planning, free from interruptions. This focus time allows them to work on the most critical tasks without being pulled in different directions.

In addition to managing time, overcoming obstacles requires *maintaining a strong sense of self-discipline*. Self-discipline is the ability to stay committed to your goals even when motivation wanes or when distractions arise. It's about doing what needs to be done, even when it's not easy or convenient. For example, an athlete training for a marathon might wake up early every morning to run, even when they'd rather stay in bed. This discipline is what helps them push through the tough days and make consistent progress towards their goal.

Self-discipline can be developed through *establishing routines*. Routines provide structure and make it easier to stick to your commitments, especially when you're dealing with challenges. For example, a student preparing for exams might establish a daily study routine, setting aside a specific time each day for focused study. This routine helps to create a habit, making it easier to stay disciplined even when distractions are tempting. Routines also reduce decision fatigue, as you don't have to constantly decide when or how to tackle a task.

Another aspect of self-discipline is *holding yourself accountable*. Accountability is about being honest with yourself about your progress, your setbacks, and your commitment to your goals. For example, a person who is trying to develop a new skill might keep a journal where they track their practice sessions, reflecting on what they've learned and where they need to improve. This practice of self-reflection helps to reinforce discipline, as it allows you to see where you're making progress and where you need to adjust your efforts.

Self-discipline is also strengthened by *celebrating small victories*. Recognizing your achievements, no matter how small, helps to reinforce positive behaviors and keeps you motivated. For example, a business owner who successfully navigates a challenging negotiation might take a moment to acknowledge the effort and skill that went into reaching an agreement. This celebration doesn't have to be grand—it could be as simple as treating yourself to your favorite meal or taking a short break. By celebrating your progress, you maintain a positive attitude and the energy needed to keep pushing through obstacles.

Another powerful strategy for overcoming obstacles is *embracing adaptability*. Adaptability is the ability to adjust your approach when circumstances change, allowing you to navigate new challenges with flexibility and creativity. Adaptability is essential in a world that is constantly evolving, where the ability to pivot can make the difference between success and failure. For example, a small business facing a decline in foot traffic might adapt by developing an online presence, reaching customers through social media and e-commerce platforms.

Adaptability often requires *letting go of rigid plans*. While it's important to have a strategy, those who are adaptable understand that plans may need to change as new information comes to light. This means being willing to adjust your approach, even if it means abandoning a strategy that you've invested time and effort into. For example, a product development team might have a vision for a new feature but adjust their direction based on user feedback. By remaining open to change, they ensure that their efforts are aligned with customer needs, rather than clinging to a plan that no longer serves its purpose.

Adaptability also involves *being open to new opportunities*. When you're focused on overcoming a particular challenge, it's easy to overlook opportunities that arise along the way. But those who are adaptable keep their eyes open for unexpected chances to grow, learn, and pivot. For example, a professional who loses their job might see it as an opportunity to explore a new industry or develop a passion project. This willingness to seize new opportunities allows them to turn setbacks into stepping stones for future success.

Another aspect of adaptability is *learning to manage uncertainty*. Uncertainty can be uncomfortable, but those who are adaptable learn to embrace it as a natural part of the process. This might involve taking calculated risks, experimenting with new approaches, or being comfortable with not having all the answers. For example, a startup founder might launch a new product without knowing exactly how the market will respond, but they use data and customer feedback to adjust their strategy as they go. This approach allows them to navigate uncertainty with confidence, rather than being paralyzed by the fear of the unknown.

Adaptability is also closely tied to *continuous learning*. When you're constantly learning, you're better equipped to adapt to new situations and find creative solutions to challenges. Continuous learning means staying curious, seeking out new information, and being open to changing your perspective. For example, a leader facing a new market trend might take online courses, read industry reports, or attend webinars to deepen their understanding of the change. This learning helps them make informed decisions, allowing them to adapt their strategy with confidence.

Continuous learning also involves *learning from your experiences*. Every challenge you face is an opportunity to learn something new, whether it's about your industry, your customers, or yourself. For example, a project that doesn't go as planned can provide valuable lessons about what works and what doesn't. By reflecting on your experiences and taking note of what you've learned, you can avoid repeating the same mistakes and apply your insights to future challenges. This learning mindset ensures that every setback contributes to your growth.

Another important part of continuous learning is *seeking out diverse perspectives*. When you expose yourself to different viewpoints, you gain new insights that can help you tackle challenges in more innovative ways. For example, a business leader might invite team members from different departments to share their ideas on how to solve a company-wide issue. This diversity of thought helps to ensure that all angles are considered, leading to more effective solutions. By seeking out diverse perspectives, you become better at adapting to new situations and finding creative ways to overcome obstacles.

Continuous learning also means *staying updated on industry trends*. In a rapidly changing world, staying informed about the latest developments in your field can help you anticipate challenges before they arise. For example, a marketer might stay updated on changes in social media algorithms or new digital marketing tools, ensuring that their campaigns remain effective. This proactive approach to learning allows you to stay ahead of the curve, adapting your strategy to meet new challenges as they come.

A critical aspect of overcoming obstacles is *building a strong support network*. Your network can be a source of encouragement, practical advice, and new opportunities when you're facing challenges. A strong support network is made up of people who believe in your potential, offer constructive feedback, and provide guidance when you're navigating difficult situations. For example, a mentor who has experience in your industry can offer insights that help you avoid common pitfalls and find new paths forward.

Building a support network often involves *investing in relationships*. Strong relationships don't happen overnight—they require time, effort, and a genuine interest in helping others succeed. For example, an entrepreneur might build relationships with other business owners by attending industry events, joining online communities, and offering help when they can. This investment in relationships creates a foundation of trust and reciprocity, making it easier to ask for support when you need it.

Another important part of building a support network is *knowing when to ask for help*. Many people hesitate to reach out for support because they don't want to seem like a burden, but those who build strong networks understand that asking for help is a sign of strength, not weakness. For example, a project manager who is feeling overwhelmed might ask a colleague for advice on prioritizing tasks, or an artist struggling with a creative block might reach out to a friend for feedback on their work. These connections provide fresh perspectives and remind you that you're not alone in your journey.

A support network is also about *giving back to others*. Relationships are a two-way street, and those who build strong networks are generous with their time, knowledge, and resources. By offering help to others, you build goodwill and create a culture of mutual support. For example, a tech professional might offer to mentor a student interested in entering the field, or a business owner might share advice with someone starting their first venture. This generosity not only strengthens your network but also reinforces the values of collaboration and community.

A crucial component of overcoming obstacles is *developing emotional intelligence.* Emotional intelligence, or EQ, is the ability to recognize and manage your own emotions, as well as understand and influence the emotions of others. This skill becomes especially valuable when facing challenges, as it helps you stay calm, make better decisions, and build stronger relationships. People with high emotional intelligence are more resilient, adaptable, and effective at navigating difficult situations.

One aspect of emotional intelligence is *self-awareness.* Self-awareness means understanding your emotional triggers, knowing how stress affects you, and being mindful of how your emotions influence your behavior. For example, a leader who feels overwhelmed by a tight deadline might recognize that stress is causing them to become short-tempered with their team. By acknowledging this, they can take a step back, manage their stress, and communicate more effectively. This self-awareness prevents emotions from controlling their actions, allowing them to lead with clarity and focus.

Self-awareness also involves *understanding your strengths and weaknesses.* When you know your strengths, you can leverage them to overcome obstacles, while recognizing your weaknesses allows you to seek help or improve in areas where you're struggling. For example, a marketer might be great at creative strategy but less skilled at data analysis. By acknowledging this, they can partner with a data expert or invest in learning new skills, rather than trying to do everything themselves. This self-awareness allows you to play to your strengths while addressing areas for growth.

Another important aspect of emotional intelligence is *self-regulation.* Self-regulation is the ability to manage your emotions, especially in stressful situations. This doesn't mean suppressing your feelings but rather controlling how you respond to them. For example, a manager who receives unexpected negative feedback might feel defensive at first, but instead of reacting impulsively, they take time to process the information, ask clarifying questions, and respond thoughtfully. This measured approach allows them to handle the situation with professionalism, rather than letting emotions dictate their actions.

Emotional intelligence also involves *empathy*, which is the ability to understand and share the feelings of others. Empathy allows you to connect with people on a deeper level, making it easier to build trust, resolve conflicts, and offer support when needed. For example, a leader who practices empathy might notice that a team member is struggling with their workload and take the time to ask how they're doing, offering help or adjusting expectations as needed.

This empathy not only strengthens the relationship but also creates an environment where people feel valued and supported.

Empathy is especially important when overcoming obstacles as a team. Challenges can create tension, stress, and frustration, but when people feel that their emotions are understood and respected, they are more likely to work together to find solutions. For example, a team facing a tight deadline might feel overwhelmed, but a leader who acknowledges their stress and offers encouragement can help them stay motivated and focused. This empathy-driven approach fosters collaboration and resilience, even in the face of significant challenges.

Another element of emotional intelligence is *social skills*, which include communication, conflict resolution, and relationship-building. Strong social skills are essential for navigating obstacles, as they allow you to work effectively with others, share ideas, and find common ground. For example, a business owner negotiating a difficult contract might use their communication skills to explain their position clearly, while also listening to the concerns of the other party. This open and respectful dialogue helps to resolve conflicts and reach mutually beneficial agreements.

Building strong social skills also involves *practicing active listening*. Active listening means fully focusing on the person speaking, understanding their message, and responding thoughtfully. For example, during a team meeting, a manager might listen carefully to each team member's input, ask follow-up questions, and acknowledge their contributions. This active listening ensures that everyone feels heard and valued, creating a more inclusive and supportive environment. Strong social skills, combined with emotional intelligence, are powerful tools for overcoming obstacles, as they strengthen relationships and foster collaboration.

Another key to overcoming obstacles is *embracing flexibility in your approach to problem-solving*. While having a plan is important, it's equally crucial to remain open to new ideas, feedback, and alternative solutions. Flexibility in problem-solving means being willing to adjust your strategy as needed, based on the information you gather along the way. For example, a software developer working on a project might receive feedback that certain features are not user-friendly. Instead of stubbornly sticking to the original design, they adapt their approach, redesigning the features to meet the users' needs.

Flexibility also involves *being comfortable with experimentation*. Sometimes, the best way to solve a problem is to try different approaches and see what works. This might involve testing new strategies, exploring creative solutions, or piloting a small-scale version of a project before fully committing. For example, a business launching a new product might conduct a limited release to gather customer feedback before expanding to a wider market. This willingness to experiment allows them to make adjustments based on real-world data, reducing the risk of failure and increasing the chances of success.

Experimentation is also closely tied to *embracing failure as part of the process*. Not every idea or strategy will work, but those who succeed are the ones who learn from their failures and use them to improve. For example, an entrepreneur who launches a product that doesn't sell well might analyze the reasons for the failure—whether it was poor marketing, pricing issues, or a lack of demand—and apply those lessons to their next venture. This iterative approach turns failure into a valuable learning experience, making it easier to overcome future obstacles.

Flexibility in problem-solving also means *being open to collaboration*. Sometimes, the best solutions come from working with others who bring different perspectives, skills, or experiences. For example, a healthcare provider facing a complex patient care issue might collaborate with specialists from different fields to develop a more comprehensive treatment plan. By seeking input from others, they are able to find a solution that they might not have considered on their own. This collaborative approach not only strengthens problem-solving but also fosters innovation and creativity.

Overcoming obstacles also requires *building mental toughness*. Mental toughness is the ability to stay focused, determined, and resilient, even in the face of challenges. It's about pushing through discomfort, setbacks, and uncertainty without losing sight of your goals. Those with mental toughness are able to persevere when others give up, and this quality is essential for overcoming obstacles in any field, whether it's business, sports, or personal development.

Mental toughness is developed through *setting and achieving small goals*. Each time you achieve a goal, no matter how small, it builds your confidence and reinforces your belief in your ability to succeed. For example, an athlete training for a marathon might start by setting a goal to run a certain distance each day, gradually increasing the difficulty as they build endurance. These small victories create momentum, helping them stay motivated even when the training becomes physically and mentally challenging.

Another way to build mental toughness is by *focusing on what you can control*. When facing obstacles, it's easy to become overwhelmed by factors outside of your control, such as market conditions, other people's actions, or unexpected events. But those with mental toughness focus on what they can control—such as their effort, attitude, and response to challenges. For example, a sales professional dealing with a downturn in the market might focus on improving their sales pitch, networking, and following up with potential leads, rather than worrying about the broader economy. This focus on controllable factors helps them maintain a sense of agency and progress.

Mental toughness also involves *developing a positive inner dialogue*. The way you talk to yourself can have a powerful impact on your ability to overcome challenges. Those with mental toughness use positive self-talk to stay focused, motivated, and confident, even when things get difficult. For example, a student facing a difficult exam might remind themselves of the hard work they've put in and the skills they've developed, rather than focusing on the fear of failure. This positive inner dialogue helps to reduce anxiety and build the confidence needed to tackle challenges head-on.

Another important aspect of mental toughness is *staying committed to your long-term vision, even when progress is slow*. It's easy to stay motivated when things are going well, but the true test of mental toughness comes when progress is slow, or when setbacks threaten to derail your efforts. Those who succeed are the ones who stay focused on their long-term goals, even when the journey feels difficult or uncertain. For example, a startup founder facing months of slow sales might stay committed to their vision, knowing that building a successful business takes time. This long-term focus helps them push through the tough times and keep working towards their goals.

Mental toughness is also built through *developing a strong sense of purpose*. When you have a clear sense of purpose, it gives you the motivation and resilience needed to overcome challenges. Purpose provides a reason to keep going, even when things get tough. For example, a social entrepreneur working to solve a community issue might stay motivated by their desire to make a positive impact, even when they face financial difficulties or setbacks. This sense of purpose gives them the mental strength to keep pushing forward, knowing that their work is making a difference.

Building mental toughness also involves *practicing mindfulness and stress management techniques*. Mindfulness helps you stay present, manage stress, and maintain a clear focus, even when faced with difficult challenges. For example, a professional dealing with a high-stress work environment might practice mindfulness meditation to stay calm and focused, rather than becoming overwhelmed by the pressure. This practice helps them manage their emotions, stay productive, and approach problems with a clear mind.

Finally, mental toughness is strengthened by *surrounding yourself with positive influences*. The people you spend time with can have a significant impact on your mindset, motivation, and resilience. Those with mental toughness choose to surround themselves with people who support their goals, believe in their potential, and encourage them to keep going, even when things get tough. For example, an artist might join a creative community where members support each other through critiques and feedback. This positive environment provides the encouragement needed to stay focused and resilient in the face of challenges.

Mental toughness is also deeply connected to the ability to *cultivate patience*. In an age where instant gratification is the norm, patience has become an underrated but crucial skill. It's about understanding that some challenges take time to overcome and that progress isn't always immediate. Those who develop patience can endure the slow grind of hard work, knowing that consistent effort will eventually pay off. For example, an artist working on a large-scale mural might spend weeks or even months perfecting each detail.

This patience allows them to create a masterpiece, where rushing the process would only compromise the final result.

Patience is not about being passive—it's about *taking deliberate, steady action while waiting for results*. It's about knowing when to push forward and when to let things unfold at their own pace. For instance, an entrepreneur launching a new product might set realistic timelines for market penetration, knowing that building a customer base takes time. Instead of expecting overnight success, they focus on consistently improving the product, refining their marketing strategy, and engaging with their audience. This steady approach allows them to build a foundation for long-term success, rather than being discouraged by initial slow growth.

Patience is also important when it comes to *navigating complex problems*. Some challenges don't have quick fixes, and it can take time to find the right solution. For example, a researcher working on a scientific breakthrough might spend years conducting experiments, analyzing data, and revising hypotheses. This patience allows them to pursue their work with persistence, knowing that each step brings them closer to a solution. By embracing the process rather than rushing towards the outcome, they are able to achieve a deeper level of understanding and create more impactful results.

Developing patience also involves *managing expectations*. Many people struggle with patience because they set unrealistic expectations for how quickly they should see results. By adjusting your expectations, you can approach challenges with a more balanced perspective, reducing frustration and anxiety. For example, a writer who expects to finish a novel in a month might become discouraged when progress is slow, but by setting a more realistic timeline, they can focus on the quality of their work rather than the speed of completion. This shift in perspective makes it easier to maintain patience and stay committed to the goal.

Another powerful strategy for overcoming obstacles is *learning how to adapt your mindset when faced with challenges*. Mindset is a powerful tool that shapes how you perceive and respond to difficulties. A fixed mindset sees challenges as insurmountable obstacles, while a growth mindset sees them as opportunities for learning and improvement. Cultivating a growth mindset is essential for anyone looking to overcome challenges, as it allows you to approach problems with curiosity and resilience.

One way to cultivate a growth mindset is by *embracing the concept of lifelong learning*. Lifelong learning means being open to new ideas, skills, and experiences, regardless of age or background. It's about seeing every challenge as a chance to expand your knowledge and abilities. For example, a seasoned professional facing a new technological shift might enroll in an online course to better understand the changes, rather than resisting them. This openness to learning allows them to stay relevant and adapt to new industry trends, turning challenges into opportunities for growth.

A growth mindset also involves *reframing failures as learning experiences*. Instead of seeing failures as a reflection of your abilities, a growth mindset views them as valuable feedback that can guide future efforts. For example, an athlete who loses a competition might analyze what went wrong and adjust their training accordingly. By focusing on what they can learn from the experience, they turn the setback into a stepping stone for future success. This approach not only reduces the fear of failure but also encourages a more proactive attitude towards overcoming challenges.

Reframing challenges also means *focusing on progress rather than perfection*. Many people get discouraged because they expect themselves to be perfect, but those with a growth mindset understand that progress is the true measure of success. For example, a musician learning a new instrument might celebrate each small improvement, even if they haven't mastered the piece yet. This focus on progress keeps them motivated and allows them to enjoy the learning process, rather than becoming frustrated by their imperfections. By embracing progress, you can maintain a positive attitude even when the journey is difficult.

A growth mindset also encourages *taking calculated risks*. Challenges often require stepping outside of your comfort zone, and those who are willing to take risks are better equipped to find creative solutions. Calculated risk-taking means evaluating the potential outcomes, considering the worst-case scenarios, and deciding to move forward when the potential rewards outweigh the risks. For example, a business leader considering an expansion into a new market might conduct thorough research, create a strategic plan, and then take the leap. This willingness to take risks, combined with careful planning, allows them to navigate uncertainties with confidence.

Taking risks also means *embracing uncertainty*. Many people shy away from challenges because they fear the unknown, but a growth mindset allows you to see uncertainty as a space for possibility and exploration. For example, a recent graduate entering a competitive job market might be unsure of where they'll end up, but they remain open to different opportunities, trusting that each experience will bring them closer to their career goals. By embracing uncertainty, they can remain flexible and adaptable, making it easier to navigate unexpected challenges.

Another key aspect of a growth mindset is *focusing on your internal locus of control*. An internal locus of control is the belief that you have control over your own actions and decisions, rather than being at the mercy of external forces. This perspective empowers you to take responsibility for your life and your challenges, making it easier to find solutions. For example, a writer facing rejection from publishers might focus on improving their craft, self-publishing their work, or building an audience online, rather than feeling defeated by the traditional publishing process. This sense of control allows them to remain proactive and optimistic, even in the face of setbacks.

A growth mindset is also about *celebrating effort as much as results*. When you value effort, you recognize that success is not just about reaching the destination but about the journey itself. For example, a student who spends hours mastering a difficult subject might feel proud of their effort, even if their test scores don't reflect it yet. This focus on effort helps to build resilience, as it reinforces the idea that hard work is worthwhile, regardless of immediate outcomes. By valuing the process, you stay motivated and committed to your goals, even when the path is challenging.

Overcoming obstacles also requires *building a culture of perseverance within yourself or your team*. Perseverance is the ability to keep going despite difficulties, setbacks, and delays. It's about maintaining a steady effort, even when progress is slow or uncertain. Perseverance is not just about working hard—it's about staying committed to your vision, even when the journey is longer and more challenging than expected. For example, a nonprofit organization working to address a social issue might spend years building partnerships, raising funds, and advocating for change. Their perseverance allows them to make a meaningful impact, even when progress feels slow.

Building perseverance starts with *defining your "why"*. Knowing why you're working towards a particular goal gives you the motivation to keep going, even when things get tough. For example, an athlete training for a world championship might remind themselves of their love for the sport, their desire to inspire others, or their commitment to personal growth. This "why" serves as a guiding light, helping them stay focused and driven, even when the training is grueling. By connecting with your deeper purpose, you can find the inner strength to push through obstacles.

Perseverance also involves *developing a routine of consistency*. Consistency means showing up and putting in the effort day after day, even when you don't see immediate results. It's about trusting that small, consistent actions will add up over time. For example, a content creator who posts regularly, even when their audience is small, is building the foundation for future growth. Each piece of content contributes to their body of work, helping them reach a wider audience and improve their skills. This consistent effort is what eventually leads to breakthroughs, making perseverance a critical part of success.

Another aspect of perseverance is *embracing setbacks as part of the journey*. Setbacks are a natural part of any challenging endeavor, and those who persevere understand that setbacks do not define their worth or potential. For example, a business owner facing unexpected costs might see it as a temporary setback, rather than a failure. They adjust their budget, find new ways to generate revenue, and keep moving forward. This ability to bounce back from setbacks is what distinguishes those who achieve long-term success from those who give up too soon.

Perseverance is also about *celebrating resilience and progress*. When you face challenges, it's important to recognize and appreciate the progress you've made, no matter how small. Celebrating progress helps to build a sense of accomplishment, reinforcing the belief that you are capable of overcoming obstacles. For example, a student struggling with a difficult subject might celebrate each improved quiz score, even if they haven't yet mastered the material. This celebration helps them stay motivated, reminding them that every step forward is a victory.

Building a culture of perseverance also means *surrounding yourself with role models who inspire persistence*. Role models can serve as examples of what's possible, showing you that challenges can be overcome with effort and determination. For example, a young entrepreneur might be inspired by the story of someone who built a successful business despite facing significant setbacks. This inspiration helps them see their own challenges in a new light, reinforcing the belief that persistence pays off.

In addition to role models, perseverance is reinforced by *creating a supportive environment*. When you're surrounded by people who believe in your potential and encourage you to keep going, it becomes easier to maintain your commitment. For example, a writer working on their first novel might join a writers' group where members share feedback, offer encouragement, and celebrate each other's progress. This supportive environment provides the strength needed to keep pushing through the difficult moments.

Finally, perseverance is about *embracing the idea that success is a marathon, not a sprint*. Many people give up on their goals because they expect results too quickly, but those who persevere understand that success is a long-term game. It's about staying committed, even when progress is slow, and trusting that your efforts will pay off in the end. For example, a musician trying to build a following might spend years playing small gigs, sharing their work online, and refining their craft. This long-term focus allows them to enjoy the journey and appreciate the growth that comes with each step.

A key element in overcoming obstacles is *understanding the power of reflection*. Reflection is the process of looking back on your experiences to understand what worked, what didn't, and how you can improve moving forward. It's about learning from each step of your journey and using those insights to refine your approach. For example, a business leader might reflect on a challenging quarter by analyzing their strategies, identifying areas for improvement, and setting new goals based on those lessons. This process of self-assessment helps them grow as a leader and make more informed decisions in the future.

Reflection is not about dwelling on mistakes—it's about *gaining clarity on the path ahead*. When you take the time to reflect, you can identify patterns in your behavior, recognize your strengths, and become aware of areas where you might need to adjust. For example, an athlete training for a competition might review videos of their performance to see where they can improve their technique. This clarity helps them focus their training on specific areas, turning reflection into a tool for continuous growth.

Another aspect of effective reflection is *journaling*. Journaling allows you to record your thoughts, feelings, and observations, providing a space to process your experiences. For example, an entrepreneur might use a journal to track their progress, record key learnings from each business decision, and reflect on the emotional highs and lows of their journey. By putting their thoughts into words, they gain a deeper understanding of their motivations, challenges, and achievements. This practice of journaling serves as a personal guide, helping them stay aligned with their goals and values.

Reflection also involves *celebrating your wins*. It's easy to focus solely on what went wrong, but true reflection includes acknowledging what you did right. Celebrating your successes, no matter how small, helps to build confidence and reminds you that you are making progress. For example, a student who has been working hard to improve their grades might take a moment to celebrate each time they achieve a new personal best. This positive reinforcement creates a sense of accomplishment, making it easier to stay motivated when facing new challenges.

Overcoming obstacles also means *learning how to manage stress effectively*. Stress is a natural response to challenges, but unmanaged stress can lead to burnout and make it difficult to stay focused. Those who overcome obstacles understand that managing stress is not about avoiding pressure, but about finding healthy ways to cope with it. For example, a professional facing a high-stakes project might practice stress-relief techniques like deep breathing, exercise, or meditation to maintain their mental and physical well-being. These techniques help them stay calm and focused, even when the pressure is on.

One effective way to manage stress is through *physical activity*. Exercise is a powerful stress reliever because it releases endorphins, which improve your mood and increase your sense of well-being. For example, a busy entrepreneur might make time for a morning jog or a quick workout session between meetings. This physical activity not only boosts their energy levels but also provides a mental break, helping them return to their work with a fresh perspective. By making exercise a regular part of their routine, they create a powerful tool for managing stress and maintaining resilience.

Another important aspect of stress management is *practicing mindfulness*. Mindfulness involves focusing your attention on the present moment, without judgment. It helps you become aware of your thoughts and feelings, allowing you to respond to stress in a more balanced way. For example, a manager dealing with a challenging team dynamic might use mindfulness techniques to stay grounded during difficult conversations, allowing them to listen more effectively and respond with empathy. This mindful approach helps to reduce reactive behavior and creates a sense of calm, even in high-pressure situations.

Stress management also involves *setting healthy boundaries*. When you're facing challenges, it's important to know your limits and make time for rest and recovery. For example, a project manager working on a demanding deadline might set boundaries around their work hours, ensuring that they take breaks and get enough sleep. By setting boundaries, they protect their energy and avoid burnout, making it easier to maintain focus and productivity over the long term. Healthy boundaries create a balance between work and personal life, allowing you to approach challenges with renewed energy.

Another powerful strategy for overcoming obstacles is *focusing on solutions rather than problems*. It's natural to feel overwhelmed when faced with challenges, but those who succeed are the ones who shift their focus from the problem to the solution. This solution-oriented mindset involves asking yourself, "What can I do to improve this situation?" rather than dwelling on what's going wrong. For example, a customer service team dealing with a high volume of complaints might focus on streamlining their response process, rather than feeling frustrated by the influx of issues. This shift in perspective allows them to find practical solutions and improve customer satisfaction.

A solution-oriented mindset is also about *seeing challenges as opportunities for innovation*. Many of the world's greatest inventions and breakthroughs came about because someone saw a problem and asked, "How can we solve this?" For example, a tech startup might recognize that users are struggling with a particular feature and use that feedback to develop a new, more user-friendly version. By focusing on how to make things better, they turn a challenge into a chance to innovate and create value for their customers.

Focusing on solutions also involves *being resourceful*. Resourcefulness is the ability to make the most of the resources you have, even when they are limited. For example, an artist working with a small budget might find creative ways to source materials, repurpose existing supplies, or collaborate with other artists to bring their vision to life. This resourcefulness allows them to overcome financial constraints and continue pursuing their passion. By focusing on what you can do with the resources available, you can find ways to move forward, even when the path isn't clear.

A solution-oriented mindset also means *encouraging creative problem-solving*. Creativity allows you to think outside the box and find solutions that others might overlook. For example, a community leader facing a lack of funding for a local project might organize a crowdfunding campaign or seek partnerships with local businesses. This creative approach allows them to overcome the funding gap and bring their vision to life. By encouraging yourself and others to think creatively, you can find new ways to navigate challenges and achieve your goals.

Overcoming obstacles also requires *developing a sense of adaptability in the face of changing circumstances*. Adaptability is the ability to adjust your plans and strategies as new information becomes available, allowing you to stay agile in a dynamic environment. Those who are adaptable are not tied to a single way of doing things—they are willing to pivot when necessary to achieve their goals. For example, a business facing shifts in consumer behavior might adapt by exploring new marketing channels, adjusting their product offerings, or rebranding to better connect with their audience.

Adaptability often involves *embracing a mindset of continuous iteration*. Iteration means making small adjustments, testing their impact, and refining your approach based on what you learn. For example, a software development team might release updates to their app based on user feedback, continuously improving the user experience. This iterative process allows them to adapt quickly to changes and ensure that their product remains relevant and effective. By focusing on iteration, you can make progress even in uncertain conditions, knowing that each adjustment brings you closer to the desired outcome.

Another important aspect of adaptability is *letting go of perfectionism*. Perfectionism can be a major barrier when facing challenges because it makes you afraid to take action until everything is "just right." But those who are adaptable understand that progress is more important than perfection. For example, a content creator might focus on producing consistent content, even if each piece isn't perfect, knowing that they will improve over time. This willingness to take imperfect action allows them to adapt quickly, respond to feedback, and continue growing.

Adaptability also involves *being open to new ways of thinking*. When you're faced with a challenge, it's easy to become attached to your current perspective, but those who are adaptable are willing to question their assumptions and explore different viewpoints. For example, a team working on a product launch might bring in outside experts to challenge their approach and provide fresh insights. This openness to new ideas ensures that they are not limited by their own biases, allowing them to find solutions that are more innovative and effective.

Another essential element of overcoming obstacles is *developing strong communication skills*. Clear and effective communication is crucial when navigating challenges, as it helps to align expectations, resolve conflicts, and build consensus around a shared vision. Those who communicate effectively are able to articulate their ideas, listen to others, and foster an environment where everyone feels heard. For example, a team leader working through a difficult project might hold regular check-ins with their team, ensuring that everyone is on the same page and that any concerns are addressed promptly.

Strong communication also involves *being transparent about challenges*. Transparency builds trust, especially when things are difficult. For example, a CEO facing a downturn in the business might openly share the challenges with their team, explaining the steps they are taking to address the situation. This transparency creates a sense of unity, as everyone understands what is at stake and feels empowered to contribute to the solution. It also prevents misunderstandings, as people are more likely to trust leaders who are honest about the difficulties they face.

In addition to transparency, effective communication requires *active listening*. Active listening means fully engaging with the speaker, asking questions for clarification, and responding thoughtfully. For example, a manager who practices active listening might give their full attention during one-on-one meetings, allowing team members to share their concerns and ideas without interruption. This active listening fosters a sense of respect and collaboration, making it easier to find solutions that work for everyone involved.

Another key to strong communication is *tailoring your message to your audience*. Different people have different needs and perspectives, and effective communicators know how to adjust their approach to ensure their message is understood. For example, a teacher explaining a concept to young students might use simple language and visual aids, while a scientist presenting research to colleagues might focus on technical details and data. By considering the needs of your audience, you can ensure that your message resonates and achieves the desired impact.

Overcoming obstacles is also about *embracing the power of perseverance*. Perseverance means staying dedicated to your goals, even when the going gets tough, and finding the strength to continue despite setbacks. It's about being relentless in your pursuit of growth, knowing that every step forward brings you closer to achieving your dreams. Perseverance is what separates those who give up at the first sign of trouble from those who push through and eventually reach their goals.

Perseverance is often built through *setting small, achievable goals*. These goals act as stepping stones, providing a clear path forward even when the ultimate goal feels far away. For example, an aspiring author working on their first novel might set a goal to write 500 words each day. This daily practice not only makes the task of writing a book more manageable but also creates a sense of progress and momentum. Each small goal achieved builds confidence, making it easier to tackle the next challenge.

Another critical aspect of perseverance is *developing mental resilience*. Mental resilience is the ability to stay positive and maintain a strong mindset, even when facing difficulties. It's about bouncing back from setbacks and maintaining the belief that you have the strength to overcome whatever comes your way. For example, a student who fails an important exam might use it as an opportunity to reflect on their study habits, seek additional support, and come back stronger for the next attempt. This resilience allows them to view setbacks as temporary and motivates them to keep pushing forward.

Perseverance is also about *building endurance through consistent effort*. Consistency is key when it comes to overcoming obstacles. It means showing up every day, putting in the work, and maintaining your focus, even when you don't see immediate results. For example, an athlete training for a competition might face days when their performance is below expectations, but they keep training with the understanding that consistency will lead to gradual improvement. This steady effort builds the endurance needed to overcome both physical and mental challenges.

Another aspect of perseverance is *learning how to manage negative thoughts*. When facing challenges, it's common for negative thoughts to creep in, telling you that you're not good enough, that your efforts are futile, or that you'll never succeed. But those who persevere learn how to recognize these thoughts and challenge them. They replace negative self-talk with positive affirmations, reminding themselves of their strengths and past achievements. For example, a business owner who feels overwhelmed by a dip in sales might remind themselves of past successes, the loyalty of their customers, and their ability to adapt to change.

Managing negative thoughts also involves *practicing self-compassion*. Self-compassion means being kind to yourself, especially when things don't go as planned. It's about treating yourself with the same understanding and empathy that you would offer a friend. For example, a musician struggling with stage fright might remind themselves that nerves are a normal part of performing and that each performance is an opportunity to improve. This self-compassion helps to reduce the pressure to be perfect, making it easier to persevere through challenges.

Another tool for perseverance is *visualizing success*. Visualization is a powerful technique where you imagine yourself achieving your goals, overcoming challenges, and feeling the satisfaction of success. For example, an athlete might visualize themselves crossing the finish line in a race, feeling strong and triumphant. This mental imagery helps to reinforce their belief in their ability to succeed, making it easier to stay motivated during tough training sessions. Visualization creates a mental map of success, guiding you through the obstacles with a sense of clarity and purpose.

Perseverance is also strengthened by *embracing a long-term perspective*. When you're in the midst of a challenge, it's easy to become fixated on the immediate difficulties. But those who persevere understand that challenges are just one part of a larger journey. They keep their eyes on the bigger picture, knowing that setbacks today don't define their future. For example, an entrepreneur facing cash flow issues might remind themselves that building a successful business takes time, and that each challenge is an opportunity to strengthen their foundation. This long-term perspective allows them to maintain hope and determination, even when the road is rocky.

Overcoming obstacles also involves *learning how to adapt your strategies*. Adaptation is crucial because it allows you to adjust your approach when things aren't working as expected. It's about being willing to pivot, try new methods, and keep an open mind. For example, a teacher struggling to engage their students with a particular lesson plan might try using interactive activities or technology to make the material more engaging. This willingness to adapt ensures that they can reach their students, even if the initial approach didn't work.

Adaptation also means *staying flexible in your expectations*. When you set out to achieve a goal, you might have a specific vision of how things should unfold. But the reality is that obstacles can change the course of your journey, requiring you to adjust your expectations. For example, a startup founder might initially plan for rapid growth but find that it takes longer than expected to build a customer base. By adjusting their timeline and focusing on sustainable growth, they can adapt to the reality of their situation without giving up on their vision.

Adapting your strategies also involves *seeking out new information and perspectives*. When you encounter a challenge, it's often because you're facing a problem that requires new knowledge or skills. For example, a writer facing a creative block might read books outside their usual genre, attend workshops, or seek feedback from peers. This infusion of new ideas helps to break through mental roadblocks and inspires fresh solutions. By actively seeking out new perspectives, you can find the insights needed to overcome challenges and continue making progress.

Adaptation is also about *embracing a mindset of curiosity*. When you approach challenges with curiosity, you see them as puzzles to be solved rather than obstacles to be feared. For example, a scientist conducting research might encounter unexpected results in their experiments. Instead of seeing this as a failure, they approach it with curiosity, asking questions and exploring new hypotheses. This mindset allows them to remain open to new possibilities, making it easier to adapt their approach and continue their work with enthusiasm.

A key part of overcoming obstacles is *learning to focus on what you can control*. When faced with challenges, it's easy to become overwhelmed by factors outside of your control, such as market conditions, economic shifts, or other people's decisions. But those who succeed are the ones who focus on their own actions and decisions, rather than worrying about what they can't change. For example, a job seeker facing a tough job market might focus on improving their skills, networking with industry professionals, and tailoring their applications. By concentrating on what they can control, they maintain a sense of agency and purpose.

Focusing on what you can control also means *setting realistic goals*. When you're facing a challenge, it's important to set goals that are within your reach, rather than aiming for perfection. For example, a student struggling with a difficult course might set a goal to improve their grade by one letter, rather than expecting to become an expert overnight. This focus on attainable goals helps to build confidence and momentum, making it easier to keep going when progress is slow.

Another aspect of focusing on what you can control is *taking responsibility for your actions*. Taking responsibility means acknowledging your role in the situation and actively working to improve it. For example, a manager who notices that their team is struggling with communication might take the initiative to organize team-building exercises or introduce new tools for collaboration. By taking ownership of the problem, they create an environment where solutions can flourish, rather than waiting for someone else to step in.

Focusing on what you can control also involves *developing a proactive mindset*. A proactive mindset means anticipating challenges before they become problems and taking steps to address them. For example, a small business owner might monitor cash flow closely and set aside funds for unexpected expenses, rather than waiting until a financial crisis hits. This proactive approach ensures that they are always prepared to handle challenges, making it easier to adapt and thrive in a changing environment.

Another vital aspect of overcoming obstacles is *building a strong sense of purpose*. Purpose gives you a reason to keep going, even when the journey is difficult. It's about understanding the "why" behind your goals and using that sense of purpose as a source of motivation. When you have a clear purpose, it becomes easier to push through setbacks and stay focused on your long-term vision. For example, a doctor working in an underserved community might stay motivated by their desire to provide quality healthcare to those who need it most. This sense of purpose helps them stay committed, even when resources are limited and challenges are abundant.

Building a sense of purpose often involves *connecting your work to a larger mission*. It's about seeing how your efforts contribute to a broader impact, whether it's helping others, advancing a cause, or creating something meaningful. For example, a software developer working on an educational app might be motivated by the knowledge that their product can help students learn more effectively. This connection to a larger mission provides a sense of fulfillment and makes it easier to overcome the inevitable challenges of product development.

A sense of purpose also helps you *maintain perspective*. When you face setbacks, it's easy to become consumed by the immediate difficulties. But a strong sense of purpose allows you to take a step back and remember why you started in the first place. For example, an activist working towards social change might face opposition or slow progress, but their belief in the importance of their cause helps them stay resilient. This perspective keeps them focused on the bigger picture, rather than getting discouraged by the challenges of the moment.

Building a sense of purpose is also about *staying true to your values*. When you're aligned with your core values, it's easier to make decisions, set priorities, and stay motivated. For example, a business owner who values sustainability might focus on building an eco-friendly brand, even if it means facing challenges in sourcing materials or competing with less sustainable products. This alignment with their values gives them the strength to persevere, knowing that their work is a reflection of what they believe in.

Another essential element in overcoming obstacles is *cultivating optimism*. Optimism is the belief that positive outcomes are possible, even when faced with adversity. It doesn't mean ignoring challenges or pretending everything is perfect—it means choosing to focus on solutions, believing in your capacity to overcome difficulties, and maintaining hope for a better future. Optimism acts as a buffer against stress and helps you maintain the energy needed to keep moving forward.

Optimism is closely tied to *practicing gratitude*. Gratitude involves recognizing the good things in your life, even when things aren't going as planned. By focusing on what you are thankful for, you shift your perspective away from what's missing or going wrong. For example, an entrepreneur struggling to secure funding for their startup might take a moment to appreciate the support of their team, the progress they've made so far, and the passion that drives their vision. This practice of gratitude doesn't erase the challenges but provides a mental and emotional balance that makes it easier to keep going.

Another way to cultivate optimism is through *positive self-talk*. The way you talk to yourself can significantly impact your mindset and resilience. Those who overcome obstacles often use positive affirmations to remind themselves of their strengths, their past successes, and their ability to navigate difficult situations. For example, a public speaker preparing for a big event might tell themselves, "I am prepared, I have valuable insights to share, and I am capable of delivering a great presentation." This kind of self-encouragement helps to counteract anxiety and builds confidence, making it easier to face challenges with a positive outlook.

Optimism also involves *focusing on possibilities rather than limitations*. When you encounter a problem, it's easy to get stuck in a mindset that focuses on what you can't do or what's holding you back. But those who succeed in overcoming obstacles shift their focus to what is possible, even within the constraints they face. For example, a small business owner dealing with limited resources might focus on building a loyal customer base through excellent service, rather than lamenting their inability to compete with larger brands on price. This focus on possibilities allows them to find creative ways to succeed, even in challenging conditions.

Another critical aspect of overcoming obstacles is *building a support system that encourages accountability*. Accountability means taking responsibility for your commitments and following through on your goals, and having people around you who hold you accountable can make a big difference. Accountability partners, mentors, or peer groups can provide the encouragement, feedback, and reality checks needed to stay on track when challenges arise.

Accountability often starts with *sharing your goals with others*. When you let someone else know what you're working towards, it creates a sense of responsibility to follow through. For example, a fitness enthusiast might share their training goals with a friend, agreeing to check in with each other weekly on their progress. This shared commitment creates a sense of accountability that helps them stay disciplined, even when motivation wanes. Knowing that someone else is aware of your efforts can be a powerful motivator to keep going.

Another aspect of accountability is *seeking feedback and guidance from mentors*. Mentors offer valuable insights based on their own experiences, helping you navigate challenges with greater confidence. For example, a young entrepreneur might seek advice from a more seasoned business owner when facing difficulties in scaling their business. This mentor can offer advice on common pitfalls, provide encouragement, and hold them accountable for taking the necessary steps to overcome their challenges. This kind of support ensures that they have someone in their corner who believes in their potential and helps them stay focused on their goals.

Accountability can also come from *joining a community with shared goals*. Being part of a group where everyone is working towards similar objectives can provide a sense of camaraderie and shared motivation. For example, a writer might join a writing group where members set weekly word count goals and provide feedback on each other's work. This community creates a supportive environment where members hold each other accountable, celebrate progress, and push each other to improve. Being part of such a community makes it easier to stay committed to your goals, even when the journey becomes difficult.

Overcoming obstacles is also about *embracing the power of creative thinking*. Creative thinking is the ability to look at problems from new angles and come up with unconventional solutions. When you think creatively, you open up new possibilities and break free from the limitations of traditional approaches. For example, a nonprofit organization facing funding cuts might explore creative partnerships with local businesses, offering marketing exposure in exchange for support. This outside-the-box approach allows them to secure the resources they need while creating value for their partners.

Creative thinking often involves *challenging assumptions*. When you face a challenge, it's easy to fall into the trap of thinking that there is only one way to solve it. But those who think creatively are willing to question their assumptions and explore new perspectives. For example, a teacher struggling to engage students with traditional methods might experiment with project-based learning or gamification, turning lessons into interactive experiences. By challenging the assumption that learning has to follow a certain format, they create a more engaging classroom environment.

Another important part of creative thinking is *being open to experimentation*. Experimentation allows you to test different ideas, learn from the results, and refine your approach based on what you discover. For example, a content creator might try out different formats—such as videos, podcasts, and blogs—to see which resonates most with their audience. This willingness to experiment helps them discover what works best, allowing them to adapt their content strategy in response to their audience's preferences. Experimentation creates a culture of learning, where each attempt brings you closer to a solution.

Creative thinking also involves *embracing a playful mindset*. Playfulness is often associated with childhood, but it's a valuable quality for anyone facing challenges. When you approach problems with a sense of play, you allow yourself to explore possibilities without fear of failure. For example, an engineer developing a new product might create prototypes using unconventional materials, just to see what happens. This playful approach helps to generate new ideas and keeps the process enjoyable, making it easier to stay motivated when the challenges become complex.

Overcoming obstacles also requires *cultivating a mindset of resilience and growth*. Resilience is the ability to bounce back from setbacks, while a growth mindset is the belief that your abilities can be developed through hard work and learning. When you combine resilience with a growth mindset, you become unstoppable, able to face challenges head-on and turn them into opportunities for growth. For example, a student who struggles with a challenging subject might persist through extra study sessions, seeking out additional resources until they begin to improve. This resilience and belief in their ability to grow help them overcome the initial difficulty.

Resilience is built through *practicing self-care*. Taking care of your physical and emotional well-being is essential for maintaining the energy and focus needed to tackle challenges. For example, a professional facing burnout might prioritize getting enough sleep, eating nutritious meals, and engaging in activities that bring them joy. This self-care helps to replenish their energy and maintain their resilience, making it easier to bounce back from setbacks and stay committed to their goals.

A growth mindset involves *embracing challenges as a path to mastery*. Instead of avoiding difficult tasks, those with a growth mindset see them as opportunities to develop new skills and improve. For example, a coder who is learning a new programming language might struggle with complex concepts at first, but they embrace the challenge, knowing that each problem they solve brings them closer to mastery. This mindset encourages persistence, making it easier to push through the initial difficulties and continue learning.

Resilience is also about *staying connected to your inner motivation*. When you have a strong internal drive, it gives you the strength to keep going, even when external rewards are not immediately visible. For example, an artist creating a new series of paintings might not see immediate recognition or sales, but their love for the creative process keeps them inspired. This inner motivation helps them remain resilient through the ups and downs of the creative journey, allowing them to produce work that is authentic and meaningful.

Another crucial element of overcoming obstacles is *embracing the power of small steps*. When faced with a big challenge, it can feel overwhelming to think about everything that needs to be done. But breaking down the challenge into smaller, more manageable steps makes it easier to get started and maintain momentum. For example, an entrepreneur launching a new business might start by setting small goals, such as designing a logo, building a website, and reaching out to potential clients. Each small step moves them closer to their larger goal, creating a sense of progress that keeps them motivated.

Taking small steps also allows you to *build momentum*. Momentum is the energy that comes from making progress, and it can be a powerful force when you're facing challenges. For example, a runner training for a marathon might start by running short distances each day, gradually increasing their endurance over time. This steady progress helps them build the physical and mental stamina needed to reach their goal. By focusing on small, achievable steps, they avoid feeling overwhelmed and create a positive cycle of effort and reward.

Small steps also help to *build confidence*. When you accomplish a small goal, it reinforces the belief that you are capable of achieving your larger objectives. For example, a student preparing for a major exam might focus on mastering one chapter at a time, rather than trying to study the entire textbook at once. Each chapter they master boosts their confidence, making it easier to tackle the next one. This incremental approach ensures that they build a solid foundation of knowledge, making the larger challenge more manageable.

Another benefit of focusing on small steps is that it allows you to *adjust your approach as you go*. When you're working towards a big goal, it's important to remain flexible and be willing to make adjustments based on what you learn. For example, a business owner launching a new product might test it with a small group of customers before a full-scale release, using the feedback to refine the product. This iterative process allows them to improve the product based on real-world data, increasing the chances of success. By taking small, deliberate steps, you create a path forward that is adaptable and responsive to change.

A vital strategy for overcoming obstacles is *cultivating self-belief*. Self-belief is the confidence in your own abilities and the conviction that you have what it takes to achieve your goals. This inner confidence is not about being arrogant or dismissing the challenges you face—it's about having a quiet but firm assurance that you can figure things out, no matter how difficult the situation may be. When you believe in yourself, you're more likely to take action, persist through setbacks, and push beyond your comfort zone.

Building self-belief often starts with *acknowledging your past successes*. Reflecting on the challenges you've already overcome can remind you of your resilience and capabilities. For example, an entrepreneur who has faced and navigated financial difficulties in the past might remind themselves of how they managed to stabilize their business through tough times. This reminder serves as evidence of their ability to overcome adversity, making it easier to trust themselves when facing new challenges. By keeping a record of your achievements, no matter how small, you create a personal toolkit of successes that can boost your confidence in tough moments.

Self-belief is also strengthened through *positive visualization*. Visualization involves imagining yourself succeeding, seeing yourself achieving your goals, and feeling the emotions associated with that success. For example, a public speaker preparing for an important presentation might visualize themselves speaking confidently, connecting with the audience, and receiving positive feedback. This mental rehearsal helps to build self-confidence, making it easier to step onto the stage with a sense of assurance. Visualization trains your mind to expect success, which in turn influences your actions and attitude.

Another way to build self-belief is by *focusing on progress rather than perfection*. Perfectionism can undermine your confidence because it creates unrealistic standards that are impossible to meet. Instead of aiming for perfection, focus on making steady progress. For example, a writer working on a book might remind themselves that a rough first draft is still an important step towards a polished manuscript. This shift in focus from perfection to progress allows them to celebrate each step forward, reinforcing their belief in their ability to finish the project.

Self-belief also involves *surrounding yourself with people who uplift you*. The people you spend time with can have a significant impact on how you see yourself. When you are surrounded by individuals who believe in you, support your goals, and encourage you to keep going, it becomes easier to believe in yourself. For example, a young artist might find support in a community of fellow creatives who appreciate their work and provide constructive feedback. This positive environment helps to build their confidence, making it easier to trust their creative instincts and pursue their artistic vision.

Surrounding yourself with positive influences also means *setting boundaries with those who undermine your confidence*. Sometimes, well-meaning people may project their own fears and doubts onto you, making it harder to maintain your self-belief. Learning to set boundaries allows you to protect your mental and emotional space, focusing instead on the voices that uplift and inspire you. For example, a student pursuing an unconventional career path might limit conversations with family members who doubt their choices, choosing instead to seek out mentors and peers who understand their aspirations.

Self-belief is also reinforced through *taking consistent action*. When you take action, even small steps, you build a sense of momentum that reinforces your belief in your abilities. For example, a fitness enthusiast might start with a simple goal of walking for 10 minutes each day, gradually building up to more intense workouts. Each small action taken strengthens their belief that they are capable of achieving their fitness goals. This consistency creates a feedback loop, where action builds confidence, which in turn encourages more action.

Taking consistent action also involves *embracing discomfort as a sign of growth*. Growth doesn't happen in the comfort zone—it happens when you push yourself to try new things, take risks, and challenge your limits. For example, a musician learning a new instrument might struggle with difficult pieces at first, but they recognize that this discomfort is part of the learning process. By leaning into the discomfort, they build their skills and gain confidence in their ability to master the instrument. Embracing discomfort allows you to see challenges as opportunities for growth, rather than as threats to your self-belief.

Overcoming obstacles also requires *developing a habit of resourcefulness*. Resourcefulness is the ability to find quick and clever ways to overcome difficulties, especially when resources are limited. It's about making the most of what you have and finding creative solutions when faced with constraints. Resourceful individuals don't dwell on what they lack; instead, they focus on what they can do with the tools and opportunities available to them.

Resourcefulness often involves *thinking outside the box*. When faced with a challenge, resourceful people don't just rely on conventional methods—they explore alternative approaches and think creatively about how to solve the problem. For example, a small business owner with a limited marketing budget might leverage social media platforms and engage with influencers to reach a wider audience without spending heavily on advertising. By thinking creatively, they find ways to achieve their goals despite financial constraints.

Another aspect of resourcefulness is *being willing to ask for help when needed*. Resourceful people know that they don't have to solve every problem on their own. They understand the value of reaching out to others for guidance, advice, or collaboration. For example, a nonprofit leader working on a community project might reach out to local businesses for partnerships, tapping into resources like venues, volunteers, or expertise. By leveraging the strengths and resources of others, they are able to amplify their impact and overcome challenges more effectively.

Resourcefulness also means *learning how to repurpose and adapt existing resources*. Sometimes, you may not have access to the ideal tools or materials, but you can adapt what you have to meet your needs. For example, a filmmaker with a limited budget might use a smartphone to shoot a high-quality short film, finding innovative ways to create compelling visuals with minimal equipment. This ability to adapt allows them to turn constraints into opportunities for creativity, proving that great work can be done even without perfect conditions.

A key part of being resourceful is *embracing a mindset of abundance rather than scarcity*. When you adopt an abundance mindset, you focus on the possibilities and opportunities around you, rather than fixating on what you lack. This mindset shift helps you see challenges as opportunities to grow, learn, and innovate, rather than as roadblocks. For example, an entrepreneur facing tough competition might focus on the unique value they can offer to customers, rather than worrying about being outmatched by larger companies. This abundance mindset allows them to find creative ways to stand out in the market.

Adopting an abundance mindset also means *celebrating the success of others*. When you believe that there is enough opportunity to go around, you can be genuinely happy for others' achievements, knowing that their success doesn't take away from your own. For example, a writer who sees a fellow author's book gaining popularity might see it as proof that there is a strong demand for fresh ideas and new perspectives. This perspective helps them stay inspired and motivated, rather than feeling threatened by the achievements of their peers.

Resourcefulness is also strengthened by *maintaining a willingness to learn*. Learning new skills, seeking out knowledge, and staying curious allow you to become more adaptable and capable of solving a wider range of problems. For example, a chef who learns about different culinary techniques from around the world expands their ability to create unique dishes, even with limited ingredients. This commitment to learning ensures that they always have new ideas and tools at their disposal, making it easier to overcome challenges in the kitchen.

Another aspect of resourcefulness is *embracing a do-it-yourself (DIY) attitude*. When you're willing to roll up your sleeves and learn how to do things yourself, you become more self-reliant and capable of tackling challenges head-on. For example, a startup founder might learn the basics of website design to create a simple but effective online presence before they have the resources to hire a professional designer. This DIY approach allows them to make progress even when budgets are tight, proving that a lack of resources doesn't have to be a barrier to success.

The final aspect of overcoming obstacles is *developing a relentless focus on growth*. Growth is about constantly pushing yourself to improve, expand your skills, and challenge your limits. It's about never being satisfied with where you are but always striving to become a better version of yourself. Those who are committed to growth see challenges as opportunities to refine their abilities, learn new things, and achieve greater heights.

A growth-focused mindset involves *setting ambitious but realistic goals*. When you set goals that stretch your abilities, you create a sense of urgency and purpose that drives you forward. For example, a sales professional might set a goal to reach a new revenue milestone, knowing that it will require them to step outside their comfort zone and develop new strategies. This ambition helps them stay focused, even when faced with setbacks, because they understand that growth comes from embracing challenges.

Developing a focus on growth also means *investing in personal development*. Personal development is about taking the time to cultivate skills, build new habits, and expand your knowledge. For example, a professional looking to advance in their career might invest in leadership training, read books on their industry, or seek out mentors who can guide them. This commitment to continuous improvement ensures that they are always evolving, making it easier to adapt to new challenges and seize opportunities as they arise.

A relentless focus on growth is also about *cultivating resilience through setbacks*. Setbacks are a natural part of the growth process, and those who focus on growth understand that each setback is an opportunity to learn and improve. For example, an athlete who suffers an injury might use the recovery period to work on their mental game, study techniques, and come back stronger than before. This resilience allows them to keep moving forward, even when progress is slow or difficult, because they see setbacks as a temporary part of their journey rather than as a reason to give up.

CHAPTER 8: GETTING STARTED—TURNING IDEAS INTO REALITY

Getting started is often the most challenging step in any journey. It's the moment when you have to shift from dreaming to doing, from planning to action. But taking that first step is also the most important because it sets everything else in motion. Many people have great ideas, big dreams, and ambitious goals, but what separates those who succeed from those who don't is the ability to take action, even when it feels daunting. This chapter focuses on the mindset, strategies, and actions needed to get started and turn your ideas into tangible results.

The first key to getting started is *clarity of vision*. Clarity is knowing exactly what you want to achieve and why it matters to you. It's about having a clear picture of your destination, even if you don't yet know every detail of the path that will take you there. For example, an entrepreneur who wants to launch a new product might start by defining what problem their product solves, who their ideal customers are, and what success looks like. This clarity gives them a sense of direction and purpose, making it easier to take the first steps towards their goal.

Clarity also involves *breaking down your vision into smaller, actionable steps*. A big goal can feel overwhelming, but by dividing it into smaller tasks, you create a roadmap that makes the journey more manageable. For example, an author who dreams of writing a book might break the process down into writing a few pages each day, researching, and outlining chapters. This step-by-step approach allows them to focus on the immediate task at hand rather than feeling overwhelmed by the scale of the entire project. Each small step builds momentum, turning a big dream into a series of achievable actions.

Another important part of getting started is *embracing the mindset of a beginner*. When you start something new, you won't have all the answers, and that's okay. It's about being open to learning, making mistakes, and improving along the way. For example, a new coder learning to build their first app might struggle with bugs and errors, but instead of getting discouraged, they see it as an opportunity to learn. This beginner's mindset keeps them curious and willing to try new things, which is essential for making progress.

Getting started also means *letting go of perfectionism*. Perfectionism is the enemy of action because it creates the belief that everything needs to be flawless before you can begin. But the truth is, progress is more important than perfection. For example, a content creator launching a podcast might feel nervous about releasing their first episode because it's not as polished as they'd like. But by focusing on the value they are providing to their audience rather than the imperfections, they take that crucial first step. This focus on progress allows them to improve with each episode, rather than waiting for the perfect moment to start.

Letting go of perfectionism also involves *understanding that mistakes are part of the process*. No one gets everything right on the first try, and that's okay. Mistakes are opportunities to learn, adjust, and grow. For example, a small business owner might make a pricing mistake that leads to lower-than-expected sales. Instead of seeing this as a failure, they analyze the feedback, adjust their pricing strategy, and come back stronger. This willingness to make mistakes without fear creates a learning environment where progress can flourish.

Another key to getting started is *finding your inner motivation*. Motivation is what drives you to take action, even when it's difficult or uncomfortable. It's about connecting with the deeper reasons why you want to achieve your goals. For example, a fitness coach starting their own gym might be motivated by their passion for helping others live healthier lives and their desire to create a positive impact in their community. This motivation keeps them energized, helping them push through the challenges that come with building a business from the ground up.

Finding your inner motivation also involves *identifying your "why"*. Your "why" is the core reason that drives your goals and actions. It's what keeps you going when the initial excitement fades and the hard work begins. For example, a student working towards a degree might be driven by their desire to create a better future for themselves and their family. This "why" serves as a source of strength, reminding them of the importance of their journey. By connecting with this deeper purpose, they find the resilience needed to take those first steps and stay committed to their path.

Another essential aspect of getting started is *building momentum through action*. Momentum is the force that keeps you moving forward, and it's created by taking consistent action, no matter how small. The hardest part is often getting started, but once you're in motion, it becomes easier to maintain that forward momentum. For example, an artist who commits to creating one piece of art every day, even if it's just a quick sketch, gradually builds a habit that makes creating a natural part of their routine. This daily practice helps them improve their skills and stay motivated, turning their passion into a sustainable practice.

Building momentum also involves *celebrating small wins*. Each time you reach a milestone, no matter how small, it's important to acknowledge your progress. For example, a startup founder might celebrate signing their first client, even if it's a small contract. This celebration boosts their morale and reminds them that their hard work is paying off. Recognizing these small wins helps to maintain enthusiasm and encourages you to keep moving forward, even when the ultimate goal still seems far away.

Momentum is also about *developing a routine that supports your goals*. Routines create structure, making it easier to take consistent action even when motivation is low. For example, a writer might establish a daily routine of writing for 30 minutes each morning before starting their day. This routine ensures that they make steady progress, even when they don't feel particularly inspired. By creating a routine, you turn the act of working towards your goals into a habit, making it easier to stay on track and maintain momentum.

Another important aspect of building momentum is *starting before you feel ready*. Waiting until you feel completely ready often leads to endless delays and missed opportunities. Those who succeed understand that readiness comes from action, not from waiting. For example, an entrepreneur with a product idea might start by creating a simple prototype and gathering feedback, rather than waiting until they have the perfect version. This approach allows them to test their ideas, learn from real-world feedback, and refine their product based on experience. By starting before they feel fully ready, they create momentum that helps to propel their vision forward.

Getting started also means *embracing the power of action over planning*. Planning is important, but it's easy to get stuck in a cycle of overthinking and analyzing every detail. While having a plan is crucial, action is what turns plans into reality. For example, a musician dreaming of releasing an album might spend months planning the perfect tracklist, cover art, and marketing strategy. But it's only when they actually start recording the songs that their vision begins to take shape. This shift from planning to action is what separates ideas from results.

Action over planning also means *being willing to take the first imperfect step*. The first version of anything you create will rarely be perfect, but it's the starting point that allows you to learn and improve. For example, a new YouTuber might feel nervous about posting their first video because it doesn't match the quality of established creators. But by posting that first video, they gain experience, receive feedback, and improve their content over time. This willingness to take imperfect action helps them build confidence and refine their skills, turning their initial efforts into something more polished.

Another way to embrace action is through *setting deadlines for yourself*. Deadlines create a sense of urgency, helping you avoid procrastination and stay focused. For example, a designer working on their first portfolio might set a deadline to have their website live within a month. This deadline helps them stay on track, ensuring that they prioritize the necessary tasks and avoid getting bogged down in endless revisions. By setting realistic deadlines, you create a timeline that keeps you accountable and moves you closer to your goals.

Action is also about *being willing to pivot when necessary*. Sometimes, the first steps you take might reveal that a different approach is needed. Being open to pivoting means adjusting your strategy without losing sight of your ultimate goal. For example, a startup founder who launches a product might discover that customers are more interested in a feature they hadn't initially focused on. By pivoting to prioritize that feature, they adapt to the market's needs and increase their chances of success. This flexibility allows them to stay on the path to success, even when the initial plan needs to change.

Another crucial part of getting started is *learning how to deal with self-doubt*. Self-doubt is a natural part of starting something new, especially when you're stepping outside your comfort zone. It's that voice in your head that questions whether you're good enough, ready, or capable. But those who succeed learn how to manage their self-doubt rather than letting it control their actions. For example, a new coach might feel insecure about offering their services, but they remind themselves of the value they bring and the difference they can make in their clients' lives. By focusing on the impact they want to have, they quiet the voice of doubt and take action.

Dealing with self-doubt also involves *practicing self-compassion*. Self-compassion means treating yourself with kindness, especially when you make mistakes or feel unsure. For example, a programmer learning a new coding language might make several errors as they get started. Instead of being harsh on themselves, they acknowledge that learning takes time and that every mistake is a step towards improvement. This self-compassion allows them to keep trying without feeling discouraged, making it easier to build confidence over time.

Self-doubt can also be managed by *surrounding yourself with supportive people*. When you have a network of friends, mentors, or peers who believe in your potential, it becomes easier to counteract the negative voice of self-doubt. For example, an artist struggling to share their work publicly might find encouragement from a group of fellow artists who appreciate their unique style and perspective. This support helps to build their confidence, making it easier to take the first steps towards sharing their creations with a wider audience.

Another way to overcome self-doubt is by *focusing on the value you provide*. When you shift your attention from yourself to the people you want to help, it reduces the pressure to be perfect. For example, a writer working on their first self-help book might focus on the impact their words could have on someone struggling with a similar challenge. This focus on providing value makes it easier to take action, as it shifts the emphasis from self-criticism to the positive difference they want to make. By focusing on serving others, they find the courage to take those first steps.

Getting started also requires *cultivating a mindset of persistence*. Persistence is about staying committed to your goals, even when progress is slow or obstacles arise. It's the determination to keep moving forward, one step at a time, regardless of setbacks. For example, an entrepreneur trying to secure investors for their new business might face multiple rejections, but instead of giving up, they keep refining their pitch, learning from each meeting, and reaching out to new contacts. This persistence eventually leads them to find the right partner who believes in their vision.

Persistence is built through *embracing the process rather than focusing solely on the outcome*. When you become too fixated on the end result, it's easy to feel frustrated by how far you still have to go. But by focusing on the daily actions that move you closer to your goal, you find satisfaction in the progress you're making. For example, a musician learning a challenging new piece might focus on mastering just a few bars each day, enjoying the process of improving rather than worrying about when they'll be able to perform the entire piece. This shift in perspective makes it easier to stay motivated over the long term.

Another aspect of persistence is *developing resilience against criticism and rejection*. When you start something new, especially in a public space, criticism is often inevitable. But those who succeed learn how to distinguish between constructive feedback and negativity. For example, a photographer sharing their work online might receive critical comments, but they choose to focus on the feedback that helps them grow, rather than dwelling on unkind words. This resilience helps them continue sharing their art, learning from their audience, and improving their craft.

Persistence is also about *being willing to adjust your approach*. If one strategy isn't working, it doesn't mean that you should abandon your goal—it means that it's time to try a different method. For example, a small business owner struggling to attract customers through traditional advertising might pivot to social media marketing, where they find a more engaged audience. This willingness to adapt ensures that they keep moving forward, even when the initial plan needs to change. Persistence, combined with flexibility, creates a powerful combination that makes it possible to overcome obstacles and achieve long-term success.

Another critical part of getting started is *taking ownership of your time*. Time is one of the most valuable resources you have, and how you use it can determine your progress. When you take ownership of your time, you become intentional about how you spend each hour, focusing on activities that bring you closer to your goals. For example, a student balancing a full-time job with their studies might use time-blocking techniques to dedicate specific hours each day to coursework, work responsibilities, and self-care. This structure helps them make the most of their limited time, ensuring that they stay on track without feeling overwhelmed.

Taking ownership of your time also means *eliminating time-wasters*. It's easy to get caught up in activities that don't contribute to your goals, such as mindless scrolling through social media or procrastinating on important tasks. For example, a writer working on a manuscript might realize that they're spending too much time browsing the internet instead of writing. By setting boundaries around their online time, such as using website blockers during writing sessions, they free up more time for focused work. This conscious choice to cut out distractions helps them stay disciplined and maintain momentum.

Another aspect of time ownership is *prioritizing tasks based on their impact*. Not all tasks are created equal—some will have a greater impact on your progress than others. Those who make the most of their time learn to focus on high-priority tasks that move the needle, rather than getting bogged down in busywork. For example, a startup founder might prioritize tasks like building relationships with key partners and refining their product offering over less critical tasks like tweaking their website's design. By focusing on what truly matters, they ensure that their time is spent on actions that create the most value.

Time ownership is also about *learning to say no*. When you're starting something new, it's tempting to say yes to every opportunity, but overcommitting can quickly drain your energy and focus. Learning to say no means protecting your time for the things that align with your goals. For example, a graphic designer who is building their own business might decline a freelance project that doesn't align with their brand, even if it offers a good payout. This decision allows them to focus on clients and projects that align with their vision, ensuring that their time is invested in building the future they want.

Getting started also means *creating an environment that supports your goals*. Your environment can have a significant impact on your ability to focus, stay motivated, and maintain discipline. Creating a space that is conducive to your work can help you get into the right mindset and make it easier to take action. For example, a student preparing for exams might set up a quiet study space with all the materials they need, free from distractions. This dedicated environment helps them concentrate and make the most of their study time.

Creating a supportive environment also involves *surrounding yourself with like-minded individuals*. The people around you can either uplift you or hold you back, so it's important to seek out those who share your ambition and support your goals. For example, an aspiring entrepreneur might join a local startup community or online groups where they can connect with others who are on a similar journey. These connections provide encouragement, accountability, and opportunities to learn from those who have been through similar challenges. Being part of a supportive community helps you stay motivated, especially when the path gets tough.

Another important aspect of creating a supportive environment is *minimizing negative influences*. Sometimes, the people or situations around you can drain your energy or make you doubt your abilities. Learning to recognize and distance yourself from these negative influences is key to maintaining your focus and drive. For example, a creative professional might choose to spend less time with friends who constantly criticize their career choices and instead seek out mentors who provide constructive feedback. This shift in their environment helps them build a more positive mindset, making it easier to stay committed to their creative goals.

A supportive environment also includes *building routines that align with your goals*. Routines provide structure, helping you turn your goals into daily habits. For example, a writer who dreams of completing a novel might establish a morning routine that includes 30 minutes of uninterrupted writing. This routine ensures that writing becomes a non-negotiable part of their day, making progress towards their goal a daily habit. Routines turn your goals into something you work on consistently, rather than sporadically, allowing you to build momentum over time.

Another crucial element of getting started is *learning how to overcome the fear of failure*. Fear of failure can be paralyzing, preventing you from taking action because you're afraid of making mistakes or facing rejection. But those who get started understand that failure is not the end—it's a part of the process. For example, a startup founder might fear that their product won't resonate with the market, but instead of letting that fear hold them back, they launch a minimum viable product (MVP) and use customer feedback to improve. This willingness to embrace the possibility of failure allows them to learn faster and make adjustments along the way.

Overcoming the fear of failure also means *redefining what failure means to you*. Instead of seeing failure as a reflection of your worth, you can choose to see it as a learning experience. For example, an athlete who loses a competition might analyze their performance to identify areas for improvement. Rather than seeing the loss as a failure, they see it as an opportunity to grow stronger. This shift in perspective allows them to approach future challenges with greater confidence, knowing that each setback brings valuable lessons.

Another way to overcome the fear of failure is by *focusing on the process rather than the outcome*. When you become too attached to a specific result, the fear of not achieving it can make it difficult to take action. But by focusing on the process and the actions you can control, you reduce the pressure and make it easier to move forward. For example, a content creator might focus on producing high-quality videos consistently, rather than fixating on how many followers they gain each week. This focus on the process helps them stay motivated and continue improving, even if the results take time to manifest.

The fear of failure can also be managed by *building a mindset of resilience*. Resilience means being able to recover quickly from setbacks and maintain a positive outlook, even when things don't go as planned. For example, a salesperson facing a tough month with fewer sales might use the setback as motivation to refine their pitch, learn new strategies, and reach out to new prospects. This resilience helps them maintain a proactive attitude, turning challenges into opportunities for growth rather than reasons to give up.

Getting started also involves *embracing the mindset of a lifelong learner*. Lifelong learning means being open to new ideas, skills, and experiences, no matter where you are in your journey. When you approach challenges with the mindset that there is always something new to learn, it becomes easier to adapt and grow. For example, a digital marketer who is launching their own agency might take online courses, attend webinars, and stay updated on industry trends to ensure they are offering the best services to their clients. This commitment to learning helps them stay competitive and confident, even in a rapidly changing field.

Lifelong learning is also about *seeking out mentors and role models*. Mentors can provide guidance, share their experiences, and help you avoid common pitfalls. For example, a chef opening their first restaurant might seek advice from experienced restaurateurs who can offer insights into managing a kitchen, hiring staff, and building a loyal customer base. This mentorship provides a valuable perspective, making it easier to navigate the challenges of entrepreneurship. Mentors can act as a sounding board, helping you refine your vision and take action with greater confidence.

Embracing lifelong learning also means *learning from your peers*. Sometimes, the people who are on a similar journey can offer the most relevant insights, as they are navigating similar challenges. For example, a software developer attending a hackathon might collaborate with peers who have different areas of expertise, learning new coding techniques and problem-solving strategies. This peer-to-peer learning creates a sense of camaraderie and collective growth, making it easier to overcome technical challenges and stay inspired.

Another aspect of lifelong learning is *keeping a curious mindset*. Curiosity leads you to explore new ideas, ask questions, and challenge assumptions. For example, a designer working on a new project might research design trends from different cultures, gaining fresh inspiration that informs their work. This curiosity helps them stay innovative and ensures that their work remains relevant and engaging. A curious mindset turns every challenge into an opportunity to discover something new, making it easier to stay motivated and take action.

A crucial aspect of getting started is *developing discipline*. Discipline is the ability to stay focused and committed to your goals, even when motivation wanes or distractions arise. It's about building the habits that ensure you keep making progress, regardless of how you feel on any given day. For example, an athlete training for a marathon might wake up early every morning to run, even when they don't feel like it. This discipline allows them to keep improving their stamina and endurance, bringing them closer to their goal with each run.

Discipline is often built through *establishing non-negotiable habits*. These are the daily or weekly actions that become a part of your routine, no matter what. For example, a content creator might make it a non-negotiable habit to post one video each week, ensuring that they continue to produce content even when they're busy or uninspired. By making certain actions non-negotiable, they create a sense of accountability to themselves, making it easier to stay consistent and maintain progress over time.

Another key to developing discipline is *removing temptations and distractions*. When you eliminate distractions from your environment, it becomes easier to stay focused on the task at hand. For example, a writer working on a novel might create a distraction-free workspace by turning off notifications, using noise-canceling headphones, and setting aside specific times for writing. This intentional setup helps them create a flow state where they can focus deeply on their work, allowing them to produce high-quality content without interruptions.

Discipline also involves *mastering time management*. Effective time management means understanding how to allocate your time to different tasks in a way that aligns with your priorities. For example, a business owner might use a time-blocking system, dedicating specific hours to tasks like client meetings, product development, and strategic planning. This structured approach ensures that they are making progress in all areas of their business without feeling overwhelmed. Time management is a powerful tool for maintaining discipline because it helps you create a balanced routine that supports sustained effort.

Another essential aspect of getting started is *embracing uncertainty with confidence*. When you start something new, there will always be elements you can't control or predict. Embracing uncertainty means being willing to take action even when the path ahead isn't fully clear. It's about having faith in your ability to adapt, learn, and find solutions as you go. For example, a student applying to study abroad might face uncertainty about adapting to a new culture, making friends, and succeeding in a different academic environment. But by focusing on the adventure and growth opportunities, they take that leap, trusting that they will find their way once they arrive.

Embracing uncertainty also involves *developing a flexible mindset*. A flexible mindset allows you to adapt your plans without feeling discouraged when things don't go as expected. For example, a startup founder might have a clear vision for their product, but they remain open to pivoting based on customer feedback. This flexibility allows them to adjust their approach and create a product that truly meets market needs, even if it differs from their initial idea. Flexibility ensures that you remain resilient in the face of unexpected changes, making it easier to stay on track.

Another way to embrace uncertainty is through *practicing mindfulness*. Mindfulness is the practice of staying present and focused on the current moment, rather than getting lost in worries about the future. For example, a project manager overseeing a complex project might use mindfulness techniques to stay calm during stressful periods, allowing them to make better decisions and remain focused on what they can control. This focus on the present helps them navigate uncertainty without being overwhelmed by what lies ahead.

Embracing uncertainty also means *being willing to ask for help*. When you're venturing into the unknown, it's valuable to seek guidance from those who have experience in the areas where you feel uncertain. For example, a first-time investor might reach out to seasoned financial advisors to better understand the risks and opportunities in the market. By seeking out mentorship, they gain insights that help them navigate uncertainty with greater confidence. Asking for help is a sign of strength because it shows a willingness to learn and adapt, making it easier to make progress even in unfamiliar territory.

Getting started also involves *creating a strong support system*. A support system consists of the people who believe in you, encourage you, and offer guidance when you face challenges. It can include mentors, friends, family, peers, or colleagues who understand your goals and are invested in your success. A strong support system helps you stay motivated, provides a sounding board for your ideas, and offers emotional support during difficult times. For example, a designer launching their first product line might rely on a close group of friends for feedback and encouragement as they refine their designs and market their brand.

Creating a support system often starts with *building relationships with people who share similar goals*. When you surround yourself with individuals who are on a similar journey, it creates a sense of camaraderie and shared accountability. For example, a software developer learning a new programming language might join an online community where other developers share resources, tips, and success stories. This community not only provides technical support but also creates a sense of belonging, making it easier to stay committed to their learning journey.

Another important part of building a support system is *being willing to offer support to others*. Supportive relationships are reciprocal, meaning that the encouragement and help you offer others often comes back to you when you need it most. For example, an entrepreneur who takes the time to mentor younger startups might find that their mentees become valuable connections as they grow their businesses. This reciprocity creates a network of people who are willing to lend a hand, making it easier to overcome challenges and take bold steps.

A strong support system also involves *finding people who challenge you to grow*.

It's important to have people in your life who push you out of your comfort zone and encourage you to aim higher. For example, an athlete training with a coach who sets ambitious goals for them might discover that they are capable of much more than they initially believed. This encouragement to stretch beyond perceived limits helps them achieve new levels of performance. Having people who believe in your potential can be a powerful motivator, making it easier to take on challenges that feel intimidating.

Another vital aspect of getting started is *understanding the importance of consistency*. Consistency is about showing up every day and putting in the work, even when it feels tedious or progress seems slow. It's the small, consistent actions that accumulate over time and lead to big results. For example, a musician practicing their instrument for an hour every day might not see immediate improvement, but over months and years, this consistency leads to mastery. Consistency is the secret to turning effort into skill and persistence into success.

Consistency also involves *building habits that align with your goals*. Habits are powerful because they automate positive behaviors, making it easier to stay on track without relying on willpower alone. For example, a writer who makes it a habit to write every morning before checking their email is more likely to finish their manuscript than someone who writes sporadically. This habit ensures that writing becomes a daily priority, rather than something that only happens when inspiration strikes. By building habits, you create a routine that supports continuous progress.

Another important part of consistency is *tracking your progress*. Tracking your progress helps you stay aware of how far you've come, even when the day-to-day changes feel small. For example, an athlete training for a marathon might keep a log of their daily runs, recording the distance, time, and how they felt during each session. This log not only provides a sense of accomplishment but also helps them identify patterns and adjust their training plan as needed. Tracking progress creates a sense of accountability and allows you to celebrate your growth over time.

Consistency is also about *embracing the concept of "showing up," even on tough days*. Not every day will be easy, and there will be times when motivation is low or distractions abound. But those who succeed understand that showing up, even when it's difficult, is what builds discipline and resilience. For example, a student studying for a difficult exam might have days when they feel tired or overwhelmed, but by committing to studying for just 15 minutes, they keep the momentum going. This act of showing up, even in small ways, makes it easier to maintain progress, turning effort into results over the long term.

Getting started also involves *embracing the power of commitment*. Commitment is about making a decision to pursue your goals wholeheartedly, without wavering when challenges arise. It's about being all-in, knowing that you're willing to do whatever it takes to achieve your vision. For example, a social entrepreneur working on a community initiative might face bureaucratic hurdles, funding challenges, and skepticism from others, but their commitment to their cause keeps them moving forward. This unwavering dedication gives them the strength to persist, even when the journey is difficult.

Commitment is often tested during *moments of doubt or difficulty*. These moments are when you must reaffirm your commitment and remind yourself why you started in the first place. For example, a musician who faces criticism after their first live performance might feel discouraged, but their commitment to sharing their art with the world helps them continue practicing and improving. By reconnecting with their passion, they find the determination to keep going, turning criticism into fuel for growth.

Commitment is also about *making sacrifices for the sake of your goals*. Achieving something meaningful often requires giving up certain comforts, habits, or activities that don't align with your vision. For example, an entrepreneur who is serious about building their business might sacrifice weekend social gatherings to focus on product development or market research. These sacrifices are not about deprivation—they are about prioritizing what matters most. By choosing to focus on their long-term vision, they create the conditions for success.

Another aspect of commitment is *staying true to your values and principles*. When you align your actions with your core values, it gives you a sense of purpose and integrity. For example, a filmmaker committed to creating meaningful stories might turn down projects that don't resonate with their vision, even if they offer financial gain. This commitment to authenticity allows them to build a body of work that reflects their true passion and purpose. By staying true to their values, they attract opportunities that align with their vision, making it easier to achieve their goals in a way that feels fulfilling.

Getting started also means *learning to take calculated risks*. Risk-taking is often necessary when pursuing a new goal, but it doesn't have to be reckless. Calculated risks involve carefully evaluating the potential outcomes and making decisions that have the highest chance of leading to success while minimizing potential downsides. For example, an investor looking to grow their portfolio might diversify their investments to balance riskier assets with more stable ones. This strategy allows them to take advantage of growth opportunities without exposing themselves to unnecessary financial loss.

Calculated risk-taking involves *weighing the pros and cons of each decision*. Before taking a leap, it's essential to consider what could go right, what could go wrong, and whether the potential reward justifies the risk. For example, a freelance graphic designer considering a shift to full-time entrepreneurship might assess their current client base, savings, and market demand before making the switch. By carefully evaluating these factors, they make an informed decision that increases their chances of success while ensuring they are prepared for potential challenges.

Another important part of taking calculated risks is *embracing the mindset that failure is a part of growth*. When you view failure as a learning experience rather than a setback, it becomes easier to take risks without fear. For example, a startup founder might launch a beta version of their app, knowing that it may not be perfect. If users point out flaws or suggest improvements, they use that feedback to refine the product, turning the initial risk into valuable insights. This willingness to take risks and learn from the outcome helps them create a product that better meets users' needs.

Calculated risk-taking also involves *creating a plan for different scenarios*. This means thinking about what you would do if things don't go as expected and having a backup plan ready. For example, an artist planning a large-scale exhibition might secure a smaller gallery as an alternative venue in case the primary space becomes unavailable. This contingency planning allows them to adapt to unexpected changes without abandoning their goal. By preparing for different outcomes, they feel more confident taking risks, knowing that they have a plan for handling potential setbacks.

Another crucial part of getting started is *developing a strong work ethic*. A strong work ethic means being willing to put in the effort required to achieve your goals, even when it's not easy or glamorous. It's about showing up consistently, staying focused, and being willing to do the hard work that others might shy away from. For example, a musician working to master a new instrument might spend hours practicing scales, refining their technique, and building muscle memory. This dedication to the craft, even when the work is repetitive, is what leads to mastery over time.

Developing a strong work ethic also involves *embracing the idea that hard work and talent go hand in hand*. While natural talent can give you a head start, it's consistent effort that ultimately leads to success. For example, a student with a natural aptitude for math might still spend time practicing complex problems to ensure they fully understand the concepts. This combination of talent and effort allows them to excel beyond those who rely solely on innate ability. By valuing hard work, you build the persistence needed to tackle challenges and make continuous progress.

A strong work ethic is also about *taking pride in the quality of your work*. It's not just about completing tasks but about doing them to the best of your ability, no matter how small they may seem. For example, a chef preparing meals at a busy restaurant might take the time to ensure each dish is plated beautifully, even during a rush. This attention to detail reflects their commitment to excellence, making them stand out in their field. By taking pride in your work, you create a reputation for reliability and quality that opens up more opportunities over time.

Building a strong work ethic also means *being proactive rather than reactive*. Proactive people anticipate challenges and take steps to address them before they become major obstacles. For example, a project manager overseeing a large team might schedule regular check-ins to ensure that everyone is on track and identify potential issues early. This proactive approach helps to prevent problems from escalating and ensures that the team remains focused on their goals. Being proactive allows you to maintain control over your progress, making it easier to navigate the challenges that come with pursuing big ambitions.

Getting started also involves *learning the art of focus*. Focus is the ability to direct your attention towards what matters most, filtering out distractions and staying on task. In a world filled with constant notifications and endless information, the ability to focus has become a superpower. For example, a writer working on a novel might use techniques like the Pomodoro method—working for 25 minutes followed by a 5-minute break—to maintain deep focus during writing sessions. This structured approach helps them enter a flow state, where they can produce their best work without interruption.

Focus also means *setting clear boundaries around your time and attention*. When you're clear about what you need to accomplish, it becomes easier to say no to distractions and commitments that don't align with your goals. For example, an entrepreneur building their business might set aside specific hours each day for deep work, turning off their phone and letting others know that they are unavailable during this time. These boundaries create a space where they can fully immerse themselves in their work, leading to higher productivity and better results.

Another aspect of focus is *learning to prioritize your energy*. Different tasks require different levels of mental energy, and it's important to tackle the most challenging tasks when you're at your peak. For example, a software engineer might schedule their most complex coding sessions in the morning when their mind is freshest, leaving administrative tasks for the afternoon. This approach allows them to use their peak focus periods for the work that requires the most concentration, ensuring that they make the most of their mental energy each day.

Focus is also about *eliminating the things that drain your attention*. This might involve decluttering your workspace, reducing your digital distractions, or simplifying your to-do list to focus on what truly matters. For example, a designer working on a big project might clean up their workspace, remove unnecessary apps from their phone, and create a simple list of priorities for the week. This minimalist approach helps them focus on the task at hand, making it easier to maintain momentum without getting overwhelmed. By creating a focused environment, they set themselves up for success.

Another key aspect of getting started is *embracing the power of networking*.

Networking is about building relationships with people who can offer support, guidance, and opportunities. It's not just about what others can do for you but also about how you can provide value to others. For example, a freelancer looking to expand their client base might attend industry events, connect with potential clients on social media, and offer free workshops to showcase their expertise. This proactive approach to networking helps them build a strong reputation and opens up new opportunities for collaboration.

Networking also involves *finding mentors who can guide you on your journey*. Mentors provide valuable insights based on their own experiences, helping you avoid common pitfalls and make informed decisions. For example, a young entrepreneur might seek mentorship from a seasoned business leader who has navigated the challenges of scaling a company. This mentor can offer advice on everything from building a team to managing cash flow, making it easier for the entrepreneur to overcome obstacles. Mentorship creates a pathway for learning and growth, providing the support needed to reach the next level.

Another important aspect of networking is *building relationships with peers who share your vision*. Your peers can provide encouragement, share knowledge, and collaborate on projects that benefit both of you. For example, a filmmaker working on a new project might team up with a sound designer who has a similar passion for storytelling. This collaboration allows them to combine their strengths, creating a final product that is richer and more impactful. Building relationships with like-minded peers creates a network of people who can support each other's growth, making it easier to achieve shared goals.

Networking also means *giving back to your community*. When you share your knowledge, offer mentorship, or support others in their journey, you build goodwill and create a positive impact. For example, a digital marketer who offers free webinars on social media strategies helps small business owners improve their online presence. This act of giving not only builds their reputation as an expert but also fosters a sense of community. By contributing to the success of others, you build a network of people who are eager to support you in return.

Another critical element of getting started is *embracing the mindset of a problem solver*. Problem-solving is about approaching challenges with curiosity, creativity, and a willingness to find solutions. When you view obstacles as puzzles to be solved rather than roadblocks, you become more resilient and resourceful. For example, a software developer encountering a bug in their code might see it as an opportunity to deepen their understanding of the programming language, rather than as a setback. This mindset allows them to approach challenges with a sense of excitement, making it easier to keep moving forward.

Problem-solving also involves *breaking down complex problems into smaller parts*. When a challenge feels too big to tackle, it helps to break it down into smaller, more manageable pieces. For example, a startup founder working on a new product might divide the development process into stages: research, prototyping, user testing, and final adjustments. This approach makes it easier to focus on one aspect of the problem at a time, reducing the sense of overwhelm and allowing for more efficient progress.

Another important part of problem-solving is *seeking out new perspectives*. Sometimes, the best solutions come from looking at a problem from a different angle. For example, a teacher struggling to engage their students might seek advice from colleagues, attend professional development workshops, or explore new teaching methods. This openness to new ideas allows them to find creative ways to connect with their students, turning a challenge into an opportunity for innovation.

Problem-solving also involves *embracing a mindset of experimentation*. Experimentation means trying out different solutions, learning from the results, and refining your approach. For example, a content creator might test different formats—such as blogs, videos, or podcasts—to see which resonates most with their audience. This willingness to experiment allows them to adapt their content strategy based on real-world feedback, rather than sticking rigidly to a single approach. By embracing experimentation, they remain adaptable and open to new possibilities, making it easier to find solutions that work.

A fundamental part of getting started is *building self-discipline*. Self-discipline is the ability to control your impulses, stay focused on your goals, and make decisions that align with your long-term vision, even when it's not easy. It's about having the inner strength to prioritize your commitments over momentary distractions. For example, a student preparing for a major exam might resist the temptation to binge-watch their favorite series, choosing instead to dedicate time to study. This self-discipline allows them to stay on course, making steady progress toward their academic goals.

Self-discipline is built through *setting clear rules for yourself*. These rules act as personal boundaries that help you stay aligned with your goals. For example, an entrepreneur might establish a rule that they won't check emails after a certain time in the evening, allowing them to focus on deep work or spend quality time with their family. This kind of self-imposed structure helps to minimize distractions and keeps them focused on what truly matters. By setting rules, you create a framework that makes it easier to stay disciplined and committed.

Another important aspect of self-discipline is *practicing delayed gratification*. Delayed gratification means resisting the urge for an immediate reward in favor of a bigger payoff in the future. For example, a content creator might choose to invest time in learning new skills, like video editing or SEO, even though they won't see immediate results. This investment in their skills pays off in the long run, as they are able to produce higher-quality content that reaches a larger audience. Embracing delayed gratification helps to build patience, making it easier to stay focused on the long-term vision.

Self-discipline also involves *being aware of your habits*. Your habits can either support your goals or hold you back, and self-discipline is about consciously choosing habits that align with your aspirations. For example, a writer who aims to finish a book might develop the habit of writing for 30 minutes every morning, turning it into a daily ritual. By making this habit non-negotiable, they ensure that writing becomes a consistent part of their routine, even on days when motivation is low. This awareness of habits allows them to shape their behavior in a way that supports their creative process.

Another crucial part of getting started is *learning to manage your energy, not just your time*. While time management is important, energy management is what determines your ability to perform at your best. Different activities require different levels of mental and physical energy, and understanding when you are most energetic allows you to plan your day more effectively. For example, a marketer who finds that their creative energy peaks in the morning might schedule brainstorming sessions or content creation during those hours, leaving administrative tasks for the afternoon when their energy naturally dips. This approach ensures that they are using their peak energy for the work that matters most.

Energy management also involves *incorporating rest and recovery into your routine*. Just as athletes need rest days to allow their muscles to recover, those pursuing ambitious goals need to build time for rest into their schedules. For example, an entrepreneur working long hours to launch a startup might take one day off each week to disconnect from work, spend time with loved ones, or engage in a hobby that rejuvenates them. This rest period helps to prevent burnout, ensuring that they can return to their work with renewed focus and creativity.

Another way to manage energy is through *practicing mindfulness and meditation*. Mindfulness practices help to clear mental clutter, making it easier to focus on the present moment. For example, a software engineer who spends a few minutes each day practicing deep breathing might find that it helps them stay calm during complex coding sessions. This sense of calmness prevents mental exhaustion, allowing them to maintain clarity and productivity throughout the day. By incorporating mindfulness into their routine, they create a mental space that supports sustained focus.

Energy management also means *fueling your body with the right nutrition*. The food you eat has a direct impact on your energy levels and mental clarity. For example, a designer working on a creative project might choose to start their day with a balanced breakfast rich in protein and healthy fats, which provides sustained energy throughout the morning. By paying attention to their diet, they ensure that they are physically prepared to tackle demanding tasks, making it easier to stay productive and focused. This holistic approach to energy management creates a foundation for long-term success.

Getting started also involves *embracing the power of goal-setting*. Goals give you a clear direction, helping you understand what you want to achieve and why it's important to you. When you set clear, specific goals, it becomes easier to create a roadmap for how to reach them. For example, a personal trainer who wants to help their clients achieve better results might set a goal to complete a certification in advanced training techniques within six months. This goal provides a clear target to work towards, making it easier to plan the steps they need to take to reach it.

Effective goal-setting often involves *using the SMART framework—Specific, Measurable, Achievable, Relevant, and Time-bound*. SMART goals help to ensure that your goals are clear and realistic, providing a solid foundation for action. For example, a content creator might set a SMART goal to gain 1,000 new subscribers on their YouTube channel by posting two high-quality videos each week for the next three months. This goal is specific (gaining subscribers), measurable (1,000 new subscribers), achievable (based on past growth rates), relevant (aligned with their desire to grow their channel), and time-bound (three months). SMART goals make it easier to track progress and adjust your approach as needed.

Another important aspect of goal-setting is *writing down your goals*. Writing down your goals makes them tangible and creates a sense of accountability. For example, an author working on their first book might write down their goal of completing the first draft by a specific date, placing it somewhere they see every day. This physical reminder keeps the goal top of mind, making it easier to stay focused and motivated. The act of writing down your goals also serves as a commitment to yourself, reinforcing your determination to achieve them.

Goal-setting also involves *breaking down larger goals into smaller milestones*. When a goal feels too big or distant, it can be overwhelming, but by breaking it down into smaller milestones, you create a series of manageable steps. For example, a software developer aiming to build a new app might set milestones for each stage of development—research, wireframing, coding, testing, and launch. These smaller milestones provide a sense of progress, making it easier to maintain momentum and stay motivated throughout the project. This approach turns big goals into a series of smaller victories.

Another crucial part of getting started is *overcoming the fear of starting small*. Many people hesitate to start because they feel that their initial efforts won't be impressive or significant enough. But those who achieve great things understand that every journey begins with small, imperfect steps. For example, a podcast host might start with a simple recording setup and a few episodes, even if they dream of having a professional studio and a large audience. By starting small, they gain experience, refine their skills, and gradually build a loyal listener base.

Starting small also means *focusing on building a solid foundation*. When you start with small, manageable projects, you give yourself the space to learn, experiment, and make mistakes without overwhelming yourself. For example, a photographer who dreams of running their own studio might begin by offering portrait sessions for friends and family. This experience helps them develop their style, build a portfolio, and gain confidence in their craft before taking on larger projects. By starting small, they create a foundation of experience that prepares them for bigger opportunities.

Overcoming the fear of starting small also involves *recognizing the value of incremental progress*. It's easy to overlook small gains when you're focused on a big goal, but those small steps are what eventually lead to significant achievements. For example, a fitness enthusiast who begins by adding just 10 minutes of exercise to their daily routine might not see dramatic changes immediately, but over time, those extra minutes add up to a healthier lifestyle. This focus on incremental progress helps them stay patient and committed, knowing that each small step brings them closer to their goal.

Another way to embrace starting small is through *celebrating early wins*. When you start something new, even small victories deserve recognition because they represent the courage it took to begin. For example, an artist who sells their first piece of artwork might take a moment to appreciate the achievement, even if it's a small sale. This celebration of early wins helps to build confidence and create a positive association with the journey, making it easier to continue taking steps forward. By appreciating the small successes, you create a mindset that values progress over perfection.

Getting started also means *developing the skill of active learning*. Active learning is about taking a hands-on approach to acquiring new skills, rather than passively consuming information. It's about engaging with the material, asking questions, experimenting, and applying what you learn in real-world situations. For example, a graphic designer learning a new software might create mock projects or volunteer for small gigs to practice using the tools they are studying. This active engagement allows them to learn more effectively than simply watching tutorials, building a deeper understanding of the software's capabilities.

Active learning also involves *seeking out opportunities for feedback*. Feedback helps you understand what you're doing well and where you can improve, making it an essential part of the learning process. For example, a speaker practicing for an important presentation might seek feedback from friends or colleagues, using their input to refine their delivery and message. This willingness to seek feedback helps them improve more quickly, allowing them to address weak areas before stepping onto the stage. By embracing feedback, they turn learning into a collaborative process that accelerates their growth.

Another aspect of active learning is *embracing a mindset of curiosity*. Curiosity is what drives you to explore new ideas, question assumptions, and push beyond what you already know. For example, a digital marketer might explore emerging social media platforms, experiment with new content formats, and study case studies from other industries to discover new strategies. This curiosity keeps them adaptable, allowing them to stay ahead of trends and bring fresh ideas to their work. A curious mindset makes learning a continuous journey, ensuring that you are always growing and evolving.

Active learning also means *turning theory into practice*. It's one thing to read about a concept, but it's another to apply it in real-life situations. For example, a chef studying a new cooking technique might practice it in their own kitchen, experimenting with different ingredients and methods to master the skill. This hands-on practice helps them understand the nuances that aren't always covered in textbooks or tutorials. By turning knowledge into action, they develop a deeper mastery of their craft, making it easier to innovate and adapt to new challenges.

Another vital aspect of getting started is *embracing the power of persistence*. Persistence is the ability to keep pushing forward, even when progress seems slow or obstacles seem insurmountable. It's about having the mental toughness to continue on your path, no matter how many times you encounter setbacks. For example, a writer aiming to publish a novel might face rejection from publishers, but instead of giving up, they use each rejection as an opportunity to refine their manuscript and improve their pitch. This persistence allows them to eventually find a publisher who believes in their work.

Persistence is not just about brute force; it also involves *learning to adapt when things don't go as planned*. Sometimes, the path to success requires you to adjust your strategy rather than giving up. For example, a startup founder might realize that their initial product isn't resonating with customers as expected. Instead of shutting down the business, they might pivot, using customer feedback to create a new version of the product that better meets market needs. This willingness to adapt allows them to turn setbacks into valuable lessons, making it easier to persist through challenges.

Another way to cultivate persistence is by *finding inspiration in others who have overcome similar challenges*. Stories of perseverance can provide the motivation you need to keep going when the going gets tough. For example, an athlete recovering from an injury might find encouragement in the story of a fellow athlete who overcame a similar setback and went on to achieve great things. This reminder that others have faced and conquered challenges can reignite your own determination, making it easier to maintain a persistent mindset.

Persistence is also about *maintaining a sense of optimism*. While persistence is often about grit and hard work, optimism helps to keep your spirits high. For example, a sales professional who faces frequent rejections might maintain an optimistic outlook by focusing on the potential success that could come from the next client they reach out to. This positive mindset keeps them motivated to keep making calls and reaching out, even when it feels difficult. Optimism fuels persistence, turning challenges into opportunities and setbacks into stepping stones.

Getting started also involves *learning to trust the process*. Trusting the process means having faith that the actions you are taking will eventually lead to the results you desire, even if progress is not immediately visible. It's about understanding that growth often happens gradually, and success is the result of consistent effort over time. For example, a gardener planting a new tree might not see visible growth for the first few months, but they trust that the roots are developing beneath the surface. This trust allows them to continue nurturing the tree, knowing that their efforts will pay off in time.

Trusting the process also means *letting go of the need for instant results*. In today's fast-paced world, it's easy to become impatient when things don't happen as quickly as you'd like. But those who trust the process understand that meaningful achievements take time. For example, a musician learning a new instrument might feel frustrated when they don't master a piece right away. But by focusing on the practice rather than the outcome, they develop the patience needed to keep improving. This patience helps them enjoy the journey, making it easier to stay committed to their goals.

Another aspect of trusting the process is *embracing uncertainty with faith in your abilities*. When you start something new, there will always be unknowns, but trusting the process means believing that you have the skills and resilience to handle whatever comes your way. For example, an entrepreneur launching a new product might face uncertainty about how the market will respond, but they trust that their research, preparation, and passion will guide them through any challenges. This trust allows them to take bold steps, knowing that each action brings them closer to their vision.

Trusting the process also involves *celebrating small milestones along the way*. When you acknowledge the progress you've made, even if it seems small, it reinforces your belief in the journey. For example, a student studying for a challenging exam might celebrate each time they master a difficult concept or improve their practice test scores. This recognition of progress helps to maintain morale, making it easier to stay focused and motivated throughout the study period. Celebrating small milestones is a way of acknowledging that the process is working, which keeps you engaged and enthusiastic about the journey.

Another key to getting started is *embracing the power of collaboration*. Collaboration is the art of working with others to achieve a common goal, and it can significantly accelerate your progress. By combining skills, perspectives, and resources, collaborative efforts can lead to creative solutions that you might not have discovered on your own. For example, a tech entrepreneur developing a new app might partner with a designer and a marketing expert, leveraging their expertise to create a product that is both user-friendly and marketable. This collaborative approach allows them to bring a well-rounded product to market faster.

Collaboration is also about *being open to feedback and new ideas*. When you collaborate with others, you have the opportunity to learn from their experiences and gain insights that can improve your own approach. For example, a writer working with an editor might receive suggestions on how to refine their story, making it more engaging for readers. This feedback helps them see their work from a different perspective, leading to a stronger final product. Being open to feedback makes collaboration a learning experience, allowing you to grow and improve more quickly.

Another important aspect of collaboration is *building strong relationships based on trust and mutual respect*. Successful collaborations are built on a foundation of clear communication, shared values, and a commitment to working towards a common goal. For example, a nonprofit leader working with community partners to organize an event might focus on building trust through transparent communication and a shared vision for the event's impact. This trust ensures that everyone involved is working towards the same goal, making it easier to overcome challenges and achieve success together.

Collaboration also involves *knowing when to ask for help*. When you're starting something new, it's easy to feel like you have to figure everything out on your own, but seeking help can save time and lead to better outcomes. For example, a small business owner struggling with bookkeeping might reach out to an accountant for guidance, allowing them to focus on growing their business while ensuring that their finances are in order. This willingness to ask for help makes it easier to overcome roadblocks and continue moving forward. Collaboration, when done well, turns individual efforts into collective achievements.

Getting started also means *embracing a growth mindset*. A growth mindset is the belief that your abilities can be developed through effort, learning, and perseverance. It's about seeing challenges as opportunities to grow rather than as fixed limitations. For example, a graphic designer who encounters a difficult client request might see it as an opportunity to develop new skills or explore creative solutions, rather than as an insurmountable problem. This mindset allows them to turn challenges into valuable learning experiences, making it easier to continue growing in their field.

A growth mindset also involves *being willing to step outside your comfort zone*. Growth doesn't happen when you're doing the same things you've always done; it happens when you push yourself to try new things and take on challenges that stretch your abilities. For example, a public speaker who is used to speaking to small groups might challenge themselves to present at a larger conference, knowing that it will help them develop their confidence and skills. By stepping outside their comfort zone, they create new opportunities for growth and improvement.

Another key to cultivating a growth mindset is *embracing the idea that effort is more important than innate talent.* When you focus on the value of hard work and persistence, you become less concerned with how naturally talented you are and more focused on how much effort you're willing to put in. For example, a coder learning a new programming language might remind themselves that the key to mastery is practice, not just natural aptitude. This focus on effort helps them stay motivated through the initial learning curve, knowing that consistent practice will lead to progress.

A growth mindset also means *being open to continuous learning and self-improvement.* It's about seeing every experience, both good and bad, as an opportunity to become better. For example, a manager who receives criticism from their team might use it as a chance to improve their leadership style and communication skills. By embracing feedback as a tool for growth rather than as a personal attack, they turn a challenging situation into an opportunity for self-improvement. A commitment to lifelong learning ensures that you are always evolving, making it easier to adapt to new challenges and take on bigger goals.

Getting started also involves *building a strong sense of accountability.* Accountability means taking responsibility for your actions, commitments, and progress. It's about holding yourself to the promises you make, even when no one else is watching. For example, a fitness enthusiast who sets a goal to run a certain distance each week might use a running app to track their progress, holding themselves accountable for each run. This sense of accountability ensures that they stay committed to their goals, making it easier to push through difficult workouts and maintain a consistent routine.

Accountability can also be strengthened through *finding an accountability partner.* An accountability partner is someone who shares their goals with you and checks in regularly to ensure that you're staying on track. For example, a writer aiming to complete a manuscript might team up with another writer, agreeing to exchange updates on their word count each week. This partnership provides a sense of support and accountability, making it harder to procrastinate and easier to stay focused on the goal.

Another way to build accountability is through *creating a system for tracking your progress.* Tracking your progress helps you stay aware of where you are in relation to your goals, making it easier to adjust your approach as needed. For example, a student preparing for an important exam might create a study schedule and use a checklist to mark off completed topics. This visual representation of their progress provides a sense of accomplishment and helps them stay motivated, even when the material is challenging. By keeping track of your actions, you create a clear path towards your goals.

Building accountability also involves *being honest with yourself about your strengths and weaknesses.* When you acknowledge areas where you need to improve, it becomes easier to seek out the resources or support needed to grow. For example, an entrepreneur who recognizes that they struggle with time management might take a course on productivity techniques or hire a business coach to help them improve. This willingness to confront weaknesses with honesty allows them to turn challenges into opportunities for growth, ensuring that they remain accountable to their vision.

A crucial aspect of getting started is *embracing the role of consistency in building habits*. Consistency is not about doing something perfectly; it's about doing it regularly, even when it's hard. When you are consistent, you build momentum, and that momentum makes it easier to continue working towards your goals. For example, a musician who practices their instrument every day, even for just 20 minutes, builds a habit that gradually improves their skill level. Over time, these small, consistent efforts compound, turning practice into mastery.

Building consistency starts with *setting realistic expectations*. It's tempting to set overly ambitious goals, but those who succeed understand that starting small and building up is often more sustainable. For example, someone new to fitness might start with short workouts, gradually increasing their intensity and duration as they build strength and endurance. This gradual approach prevents burnout and ensures that the habit becomes a natural part of their daily routine. By setting realistic goals, you create a foundation for consistency that can be maintained over the long term.

Another important part of building consistency is *tracking your daily habits*. Tracking helps you see your progress and hold yourself accountable, even when motivation dips. For example, a writer working on a novel might keep a daily word count tracker, celebrating each time they meet their goal. This visual reminder of their progress helps them stay committed, making it easier to keep showing up to write, even on days when inspiration is lacking. Tracking your habits creates a sense of accomplishment, reinforcing the positive behaviors that support your goals.

Consistency is also about *developing routines that support your success*. A well-structured routine minimizes decision fatigue and ensures that you dedicate time to the things that matter most. For example, an entrepreneur might start each morning with a routine that includes goal-setting, reviewing key tasks, and a quick meditation session to focus their mind. This routine sets the tone for the day, making it easier to prioritize important tasks and maintain focus throughout the day. Routines create a rhythm that keeps you moving forward, turning daily actions into progress.

Getting started also involves *overcoming the fear of failure*. Fear of failure is one of the biggest barriers that holds people back from taking action, but those who succeed learn to reframe their fear. They understand that failure is not a sign of weakness but a sign that they are pushing their limits and trying new things. For example, an inventor working on a new product might face multiple prototypes that don't work as planned, but they see each failure as a step closer to the final design. This mindset allows them to approach challenges with curiosity and resilience, rather than with anxiety.

Overcoming the fear of failure starts with *developing a growth-oriented perspective*. When you focus on learning and growth, rather than on achieving a perfect result, it becomes easier to take risks and try new things. For example, a student learning a new language might make mistakes in pronunciation, but instead of feeling embarrassed, they focus on how each mistake helps them improve. This focus on growth rather than perfection helps them stay open to feedback and willing to keep practicing. A growth mindset turns failure into a valuable part of the learning process, making it easier to stay motivated.

Another way to overcome the fear of failure is through *visualizing success and managing self-doubt*. Visualization involves imagining yourself succeeding, seeing yourself overcoming challenges, and experiencing the emotions of accomplishment. For example, a public speaker preparing for their first large audience might spend a few minutes each day visualizing themselves delivering their speech confidently and engaging with the crowd. This mental rehearsal helps to build confidence, making it easier to face the actual event without being overwhelmed by nerves. Visualization helps to shift your focus from fear to the possibilities of success.

Overcoming fear also involves *surrounding yourself with a positive support network*. When you have people in your corner who believe in you, it becomes easier to take risks because you know that you have a support system to fall back on. For example, an artist struggling with self-doubt might find encouragement in a group of fellow creatives who remind them of their unique vision and talents. This positive reinforcement helps to quiet the voice of doubt, making it easier to take bold steps and explore new creative ideas. A supportive network creates a safety net that makes it less intimidating to venture outside of your comfort zone.

Another critical part of getting started is *embracing the power of intention*. Intention is the force that drives your actions, giving you a sense of purpose and direction. When you act with intention, you make decisions that are aligned with your long-term vision, rather than being swayed by short-term distractions. For example, an entrepreneur aiming to build a sustainable business might make intentional choices about the materials they use, prioritizing eco-friendly options even if they come with higher costs. This intention shapes their business identity and builds trust with customers who share their values.

Acting with intention often involves *defining your core values*. Your values are the principles that guide your decisions and actions, and they act as a compass when you face difficult choices. For example, a writer who values authenticity might choose to focus on creating content that resonates with their true voice, rather than following trends that don't align with their beliefs. This commitment to authenticity helps them build a loyal audience that appreciates their genuine approach. By aligning your actions with your values, you create a sense of integrity that makes it easier to stay true to your path.

Another way to embrace intention is through *setting clear daily priorities*. When you know what your most important tasks are, it becomes easier to focus your energy on the things that matter most. For example, a student preparing for finals might prioritize studying difficult subjects in the morning when their concentration is at its peak, leaving easier tasks for later in the day. This prioritization helps them make the most of their study time, ensuring that they are prepared when exams come around. Setting daily priorities helps to turn intention into action, making it easier to make progress every day.

Intention is also about *being mindful of how you spend your time and energy*. It's easy to get caught up in activities that don't align with your goals, but when you act with intention, you choose to invest your time in ways that bring you closer to your vision. For example, a digital marketer building their online presence might spend time engaging with their audience on social media, sharing valuable content and responding to comments, rather than getting lost in endless scrolling. This mindful approach to time management ensures that their actions are always moving them towards their goals.

Another crucial aspect of getting started is *learning how to push through resistance*. Resistance is that inner voice that tells you to procrastinate, to delay, or to avoid tasks that feel challenging or uncomfortable. It's a natural part of the creative process, but those who succeed learn how to push through it rather than letting it hold them back. For example, a writer might feel resistance when sitting down to draft a difficult chapter, but by committing to write for just 15 minutes, they find that the initial discomfort fades, and they get into a flow. This small push helps them overcome the mental barrier and make progress.

Pushing through resistance often involves *creating rituals that signal it's time to work*. Rituals can help you transition from a state of distraction into a focused mindset. For example, a designer might start each work session by organizing their workspace and listening to a specific playlist that helps them concentrate. This ritual serves as a cue that it's time to focus, making it easier to overcome the initial resistance and dive into the work. Rituals create a sense of familiarity that makes it easier to get started, even when motivation is low.

Another way to push through resistance is through *breaking large tasks into smaller, manageable pieces*. When a task feels overwhelming, breaking it down into smaller parts makes it more approachable. For example, an entrepreneur working on a business plan might start by drafting just one section each day, such as the market analysis or the mission statement. By focusing on one small part at a time, they reduce the mental resistance that comes with tackling a big project all at once. This incremental approach makes it easier to stay consistent and maintain momentum.

Pushing through resistance also involves *acknowledging and reframing negative thoughts*. It's common to have thoughts like "I'm not good enough" or "This is too hard" when facing a challenge, but those who push through resistance learn to recognize these thoughts without letting them dictate their actions. For example, a musician struggling with self-doubt might remind themselves that every artist goes through periods of struggle and that their effort is what will ultimately lead to improvement. This reframing helps them push past the negative thoughts and continue practicing, even when it feels difficult.

Getting started also means *learning to embrace imperfection*. Perfectionism can be a major barrier to taking action because it creates unrealistic standards that are impossible to meet. Those who succeed understand that it's better to take imperfect action than to wait for the perfect moment. For example, a photographer who wants to build their portfolio might start by taking photos with the equipment they already have, rather than waiting until they can afford the best camera. This willingness to start with what they have allows them to build skills and experience, eventually leading to the quality they aspire to.

Embracing imperfection involves *focusing on progress rather than perfection*. Progress is about making improvements, learning from mistakes, and getting a little better each day. For example, a software developer learning a new coding language might focus on writing functional code rather than perfect code, knowing that each attempt helps them understand the language better. This focus on progress helps them stay motivated, as they can see how far they've come, even if the final product isn't flawless yet. Progress is a more realistic and rewarding goal, making it easier to stay committed.

Another way to embrace imperfection is through *releasing the need for constant validation*. When you're starting something new, it's easy to seek approval from others, but those who succeed learn to value their own progress over external validation. For example, a blogger sharing their first posts might focus on creating content that they are passionate about, rather than worrying about likes or comments. This focus on self-expression allows them to enjoy the process of creating, making it easier to continue sharing their work even when recognition is slow to come.

Embracing imperfection also means *accepting that mistakes are part of the journey*. Mistakes are not failures; they are opportunities to learn and grow. For example, an entrepreneur who launches a marketing campaign that doesn't perform as expected might analyze the data, learn what went wrong, and use those insights to improve their next campaign. This acceptance of mistakes as part of the process allows them to move forward with confidence, knowing that each mistake brings them closer to success. By embracing imperfection, they free themselves to take action without fear.

A key part of getting started is *understanding the value of adaptability*. Adaptability is the ability to adjust your plans and approach when circumstances change or when you encounter new information. It's about being flexible enough to pivot without losing sight of your core goal. For example, a business owner who planned to open a physical store might adapt to changing market conditions by launching an online shop instead. This ability to adjust their strategy ensures that they continue to move forward, even when the original plan needs to change.

Adaptability often involves *being open to feedback and new perspectives*. When you're willing to listen to others and consider their insights, you gain a better understanding of how to navigate challenges. For example, an artist trying to reach a larger audience might seek feedback from peers or mentors who have successfully marketed their work. By listening to their advice, they might discover new ways to present their art or find platforms that better suit their style. This openness to feedback allows them to adapt their approach, making it easier to achieve their goals.

Another aspect of adaptability is *learning to let go of rigid expectations*. While having a plan is important, those who succeed understand that clinging too tightly to specific outcomes can limit their potential. For example, a startup founder might have a clear vision for their product, but they remain open to changing features or target markets based on customer feedback. This willingness to adjust their vision allows them to create a product that truly meets market needs, rather than sticking to an idea that doesn't resonate with users. Letting go of rigid expectations makes it easier to stay resilient in the face of change.

Adaptability is also about *embracing change as an opportunity for growth*. Instead of seeing changes as disruptions, adaptable people see them as chances to learn, grow, and explore new possibilities. For example, a teacher who is asked to switch to online classes might use the opportunity to learn new digital tools and create innovative ways to engage their students. This positive attitude towards change helps them remain enthusiastic and proactive, even when the learning curve is steep. By embracing change, they turn challenges into stepping stones, making it easier to continue moving forward.

Another essential aspect of getting started is *cultivating patience*. Patience is the ability to stay calm and focused, even when progress feels slow or obstacles seem overwhelming. It's about understanding that good things take time and that success is often the result of long-term effort. For example, a gardener planting a new crop might know that it will take weeks or even months before they see any growth. This understanding allows them to continue watering and nurturing the plants, trusting that their efforts will eventually bear fruit. Patience ensures that they stay committed, even when immediate results aren't visible.

Patience also involves *embracing the process of growth*. Growth often happens slowly and in stages, and those who succeed learn to appreciate each phase of the journey. For example, an artist working on a large painting might focus on enjoying the process of each brushstroke, rather than rushing to complete the piece. This focus on the process helps them stay present in the moment, allowing them to create a more thoughtful and detailed final product. Embracing the process allows them to find joy in the act of creation, making it easier to stay motivated over time.

Another way to cultivate patience is through *setting long-term goals*. Long-term goals help you maintain a sense of perspective, making it easier to stay focused on the bigger picture rather than getting discouraged by short-term setbacks. For example, a student aiming to become a doctor might remind themselves of their ultimate goal during challenging study sessions, keeping their sights set on the impact they want to make in the medical field. This focus on the long-term vision helps them remain patient through the difficult moments, knowing that each step brings them closer to their dream.

Patience is also about *understanding that setbacks are part of the journey*. When you expect setbacks and view them as a natural part of the process, it becomes easier to handle them without losing motivation. For example, a startup founder who experiences a dip in sales might use the time to analyze customer feedback and refine their marketing strategy, rather than becoming disheartened. This understanding that setbacks are temporary helps them maintain a steady pace, allowing them to continue moving forward with resilience and optimism.

Getting started also means *developing a sense of accountability to yourself*. Accountability is about holding yourself responsible for the commitments you've made and ensuring that you follow through. It's about treating your goals with the same seriousness that you would treat a promise to someone else. For example, an entrepreneur working to launch their first product might set weekly milestones and review their progress at the end of each week. This self-reflection ensures that they stay on track, making it easier to identify areas for improvement and celebrate small victories.

Self-accountability often involves *creating systems that help you stay organized*. Organization helps to keep your tasks, goals, and progress clear, making it easier to stay focused on what needs to be done. For example, a freelancer juggling multiple clients might use project management software to track deadlines, client feedback, and deliverables. This organized approach allows them to manage their time effectively, ensuring that they meet client expectations and maintain a high standard of work. By creating systems, they make it easier to hold themselves accountable and deliver consistent results.

Another important part of self-accountability is *setting clear intentions for each day*. When you start each day with a sense of purpose, it becomes easier to focus on the actions that will move you closer to your goals. For example, a writer might start their morning by setting an intention to complete a certain number of pages before lunch. This intention serves as a guide throughout the day, helping them stay on task even when distractions arise. Setting daily intentions creates a sense of direction, making it easier to stay committed to your goals.

Self-accountability is also about *taking responsibility for your actions and decisions*. When things don't go as planned, it's easy to place blame on external factors, but those who succeed understand the importance of owning their mistakes. For example, a business owner who misses a deadline might reflect on how they managed their time and identify ways to improve in the future. This willingness to take responsibility allows them to learn from their mistakes, making it easier to avoid similar issues down the road. By taking ownership of their actions, they create a sense of control over their progress.

Another essential aspect of getting started is *embracing the power of self-reflection*. Self-reflection is the practice of looking inward, assessing your actions, and evaluating your progress. It's about asking yourself tough questions and being honest about where you are in relation to your goals. For example, a graphic designer aiming to build their brand might regularly review their portfolio, asking themselves which projects align most with their vision and where they can improve. This self-reflection helps them stay aligned with their creative direction, making it easier to refine their skills and grow their brand.

Self-reflection often involves *keeping a journal or written record of your thoughts and progress*. Writing down your experiences, challenges, and successes can provide valuable insights into your journey. For example, a student preparing for a major exam might keep a study journal where they record what study techniques work best and where they struggle. This written record allows them to identify patterns and adjust their study habits, leading to more effective learning. Journaling creates a space for self-reflection, helping you gain clarity on what's working and what needs to change.

Another important aspect of self-reflection is *taking the time to celebrate your progress*. When you're focused on achieving big goals, it's easy to overlook the progress you've already made. But by pausing to acknowledge your achievements, no matter how small, you create a sense of fulfillment that keeps you motivated. For example, an entrepreneur might celebrate each new client they bring on board, even if their ultimate goal is to build a much larger customer base. This celebration of progress reinforces the value of their efforts, making it easier to maintain momentum.

Self-reflection is also about *asking yourself what you've learned from each experience*. When you take the time to extract lessons from your successes and setbacks, you gain a deeper understanding of what works for you. For example, a runner training for a marathon might reflect on what types of training sessions improve their endurance the most and which ones leave them feeling fatigued. This insight allows them to adjust their training plan, ensuring that they continue to improve. By focusing on the lessons learned, you turn every experience into an opportunity for growth.

A crucial part of getting started is *understanding that progress is not always linear*. It's natural to expect that your journey will move forward in a straight line, but the reality is that progress often comes with ups and downs. There will be moments of rapid growth, followed by plateaus where it feels like nothing is changing. Those who succeed understand that these plateaus are not signs of failure—they are part of the process. For example, an athlete who hits a performance plateau might use the time to focus on recovery, allowing their body to adapt before pushing for new personal records. This understanding helps them stay patient and avoid burnout.

Progress being non-linear also means *embracing the idea of taking one step back to take two steps forward*. Sometimes, making a temporary retreat or change of direction is necessary to achieve a greater gain. For example, an entrepreneur who experiences a downturn in sales might take the time to re-evaluate their business model, adjust their marketing strategies, and focus on building stronger customer relationships. This period of adjustment allows them to come back stronger, with a clearer understanding of what their market needs. By recognizing that setbacks can lead to greater breakthroughs, they maintain a long-term perspective.

Another aspect of non-linear progress is *focusing on the journey rather than just the destination*. When you appreciate the lessons, experiences, and growth that come with each stage of your journey, it becomes easier to stay engaged, even during challenging times. For example, a musician practicing a difficult piece might focus on the joy of each practice session, rather than only thinking about the final performance. This focus on the process helps them remain passionate and committed, making it easier to push through the tough parts of learning.

Understanding that progress is non-linear also means *giving yourself grace during slow periods*. It's natural to feel frustrated when you're not seeing immediate results, but those who succeed learn to trust that their efforts are building a foundation for future growth. For example, a writer who experiences writer's block might use the time to read, research, or take walks to recharge their creativity. This period of rest helps them come back to their writing with fresh ideas, allowing them to create with renewed energy. By being kind to themselves during slow periods, they make it easier to stay resilient and keep moving forward.

CHAPTER 9: STILL WANT MORE? HERE ARE SOME TO DO'S

Taking your journey to the next level is all about action. Once you've laid the foundation, built habits, and started moving towards your goals, there's always room to elevate your game. It's about turning your ambitions into a structured plan and ensuring you continue to challenge yourself.

The first step in advancing your progress is *embracing the power of continuous learning*. The world is constantly evolving, and those who stay ahead are the ones who commit to learning, even after they've mastered the basics. For example, a marketer who stays up to date with new digital trends, algorithms, and platforms will always have an edge over those who stick to outdated strategies. This approach means dedicating time to reading industry blogs, taking online courses, and attending webinars. Learning keeps your mind sharp, making you adaptable and ready for any changes that come your way.

Continuous learning also means *learning from those who have walked the path before you*. Studying the success stories and experiences of others helps you gain insights into what works and what doesn't. For example, an entrepreneur might read biographies of successful business leaders, learning how they navigated challenges, built resilience, and scaled their ventures. This process helps them avoid common pitfalls and find inspiration in the achievements of others. By staying curious and open to new ideas, you ensure that you're always growing, always adapting, and always finding new ways to reach your goals.

Another way to continue your growth is through *setting new challenges for yourself*. Complacency is the enemy of progress, and the only way to keep moving forward is to keep raising the bar. For example, a runner who has reached their goal of completing a 5K might set their sights on a 10K or even a half marathon. These new challenges push them out of their comfort zone, making them stronger, more resilient, and more confident. Setting challenges is about daring yourself to see what you're truly capable of, proving to yourself that there's always more to achieve.

Elevating your journey also involves *building a network of mentors and peers*. Surrounding yourself with people who have the knowledge, experience, and perspective you aspire to can be a game-changer. Mentors provide guidance and wisdom, helping you avoid mistakes and make informed decisions. For example, a creative writer who connects with a published author gains access to insights about the publishing industry, tips for marketing their book, and strategies for refining their craft. This mentorship creates a support system that provides direction and encouragement.

Finding peers who are on a similar journey is equally important. These are the people who understand your struggles, celebrate your wins, and provide a sense of camaraderie. For example, a digital artist might join an online community where they share their work, exchange feedback, and learn new techniques from fellow creators. This peer network becomes a source of motivation, making it easier to stay committed to daily practice. Building a community of mentors and peers ensures that you are always learning, always improving, and never facing challenges alone.

Expanding your network also means *seeking opportunities to collaborate*. Collaboration can open doors to new experiences, new skills, and new perspectives. For example, a tech entrepreneur might collaborate with a designer to create a user-friendly interface for their app, combining their technical skills with the designer's eye for aesthetics. This collaboration results in a better product and a broader understanding of what makes an app successful. When you work with others, you gain access to skills and knowledge that complement your own, making it easier to reach new heights.

Another powerful step is *creating a personal brand that reflects your unique strengths and values*. Your personal brand is how you present yourself to the world, and it's what sets you apart in a crowded market. For example, a fitness coach might build a brand around a specific training philosophy, using social media to share their approach, client transformations, and personal journey. This brand becomes a magnet for people who resonate with their message, creating opportunities for growth and connection. Building a personal brand helps you attract the right opportunities, making it easier to stand out and build a loyal following.

Continuing your progress also involves *mastering the art of focus and eliminating distractions*. It's easy to get sidetracked by things that don't align with your goals, but those who stay on top learn how to maintain laser-sharp focus. For example, a student preparing for a scholarship exam might create a distraction-free study environment, turn off notifications, and set specific study hours. This commitment to focus ensures that they make the most of their study time, allowing them to grasp complex topics and perform better during the exam.

Focus also means *learning how to say no to opportunities that don't align with your vision*. It's tempting to say yes to every project or request, but not all opportunities are created equal. For example, a freelancer who wants to specialize in web development might decline projects that involve unrelated tasks, like graphic design or social media management. This choice allows them to focus on building expertise in their niche, making them more attractive to clients who need their specific skills. By saying no to distractions, you create space for the opportunities that truly align with your goals.

Eliminating distractions also involves *setting boundaries with your time and energy*. Time is a finite resource, and how you manage it determines your ability to make progress. For example, an entrepreneur who blocks out time for focused work in the morning ensures that they are tackling their most important tasks when their energy is at its peak. This structure helps them avoid burnout and maintain a healthy work-life balance, ensuring that they stay productive over the long haul. By setting boundaries, you protect your time for the things that matter most, making it easier to stay on track.

Focus is also about *developing deep work habits*. Deep work means engaging in tasks that require intense concentration, allowing you to produce high-quality work. For example, a software developer working on a complex project might set aside uninterrupted time to focus solely on coding, avoiding meetings and distractions during these sessions. This focus on deep work helps them solve problems more efficiently, leading to breakthroughs that wouldn't be possible with a distracted mind. By prioritizing deep work, you create a habit of excellence, making it easier to achieve your highest potential.

Elevating your journey also involves *developing a strategic mindset*. A strategic mindset is about thinking ahead, anticipating challenges, and planning your moves with intention. It's about seeing the bigger picture and understanding how each action contributes to your long-term vision. For example, a startup founder might develop a strategic plan that outlines their goals for the next year, including key milestones, revenue targets, and market expansion plans. This plan serves as a roadmap, guiding their actions and ensuring that they stay focused on their long-term objectives.

Having a strategic mindset also means *being proactive rather than reactive*. Instead of waiting for opportunities to come to you, you take the initiative to create them. For example, a job seeker might reach out to companies they admire, offering to work on specific projects, rather than waiting for job openings to be posted. This proactive approach helps them stand out, making it easier to land opportunities that align with their passion and skills. By taking charge of your journey, you create a path that is uniquely tailored to your goals.

A strategic mindset also involves *understanding the importance of diversification*. Just as a diversified investment portfolio can help manage risk, diversifying your skills and income streams can make you more resilient. For example, a musician who relies on live performances might diversify by offering online music lessons, creating a YouTube channel, and licensing their music for films. This diversification ensures that they have multiple ways to earn income, making it easier to weather changes in the industry. By thinking strategically, you create a plan that keeps you adaptable and prepared for whatever comes your way.

Another aspect of a strategic mindset is *embracing the power of leverage*. Leverage means using the resources you have—whether time, skills, technology, or relationships—to achieve more with less effort. For example, an author who automates their email list management can focus more time on writing, while still staying connected with their readers. This use of technology as leverage allows them to scale their reach without burning out. By finding ways to leverage your resources, you multiply your impact, making it easier to achieve your goals efficiently.

Taking your journey to the next level also involves *setting ambitious goals that push your limits*. Ambitious goals are the ones that make you uncomfortable, the ones that challenge you to grow beyond what you thought was possible. For example, a graphic designer who has been freelancing might set a goal to land a contract with a major brand, even if it feels intimidating. This goal pushes them to refine their portfolio, reach out to industry contacts, and elevate their work to a new standard. By setting goals that scare you a little, you discover new strengths and capabilities.

Ambitious goals also require *breaking free from self-imposed limitations*. Sometimes, the biggest obstacles are the beliefs you hold about what you can or cannot do. For example, a content creator who doubts their ability to build a large following might set a goal to post consistently for six months, focusing on providing value rather than worrying about the numbers. This shift in mindset allows them to focus on what they can control, making it easier to overcome self-doubt and take action. By challenging your own limitations, you open the door to new possibilities.

Achieving ambitious goals also means *committing to a plan of action*. Once you've set a big goal, it's important to break it down into smaller steps and create a timeline for achieving each milestone. For example, an athlete training for a triathlon might create a plan that includes weekly goals for swimming, cycling, and running, building up their endurance over time. This structured approach ensures that they make steady progress, making the big goal feel more achievable. A commitment to action turns ambition into reality, making it easier to see results.

Ambitious goals also involve *staying adaptable and willing to adjust your approach*. Sometimes, the path to your goal will require you to make changes along the way. For example, a startup founder might realize that their initial business model isn't working, but instead of abandoning their goal, they pivot to a new strategy that better serves their customers. This willingness to adapt ensures that they stay focused on the end result, even if the journey looks different than they initially imagined. By remaining flexible, you maintain momentum, no matter what challenges arise.

Continuing your journey to new heights requires *embracing the power of visualization*. Visualization is more than just imagining success—it's about creating a clear mental picture of what you want to achieve and how you'll get there. When you visualize your goals vividly, you activate the same neural pathways that you use when you're actually performing those actions. For example, an athlete preparing for a competition might spend time each day visualizing their race, picturing every stride, every breath, and the feeling of crossing the finish line. This mental rehearsal helps them feel more confident and focused when the actual race day arrives.

Visualization can be especially powerful when it's paired with *specific, sensory-rich details*. The more detailed your mental image, the more real it feels, and the more your mind believes that the outcome is achievable. For example, an entrepreneur visualizing the launch of their new product might imagine the sound of applause as they present it to an audience, the expressions of excitement on people's faces, and the messages of praise they receive afterward. This detailed vision makes the goal feel tangible and inspires them to put in the work needed to make it a reality.

Another important aspect of visualization is *using it to prepare for challenges*. It's not just about picturing smooth sailing; it's also about imagining how you'll handle setbacks and obstacles. For example, a public speaker might visualize themselves staying calm and composed if the microphone cuts out during their presentation. This mental preparation helps them feel ready for whatever happens, reducing anxiety and increasing their ability to adapt on the spot. By visualizing both success and potential challenges, you create a mental blueprint that helps you navigate the journey with confidence.

Visualization is also a powerful tool for *reinforcing your commitment to your goals*. When you regularly spend time visualizing the life you want, it keeps your vision fresh in your mind, making it easier to stay motivated through the day-to-day grind. For example, a student aiming to graduate with honors might start each morning by visualizing themselves walking across the stage, receiving their diploma, and feeling proud of their hard work. This daily practice reminds them of why they're studying so hard, helping them push through late nights and challenging exams. Visualization keeps your motivation alive, making it easier to stay on track.

Another key element of taking your journey further is *developing a mindset of abundance*. An abundance mindset is about believing that there are enough opportunities, resources, and success for everyone. It's the opposite of a scarcity mindset, which focuses on limitations and competition. For example, an artist with an abundance mindset might believe that their unique perspective and style will attract the right audience, even if the art world seems crowded. This belief allows them to create freely, without worrying about competition, and to find their own space in the market.

Developing an abundance mindset also means *being generous with your knowledge and skills*. When you share what you know, you build a reputation as someone who provides value, which can lead to unexpected opportunities. For example, a graphic designer who offers free design tips on social media might attract potential clients who appreciate their expertise and want to hire them for custom work. This act of generosity doesn't diminish their value; it enhances it, building trust and credibility in their field. By focusing on what you can give, rather than what you might lose, you open yourself up to greater possibilities.

Another way to cultivate an abundance mindset is through *reframing challenges as opportunities*. When you view challenges as barriers, it's easy to feel discouraged, but when you see them as opportunities for growth, you become more resilient. For example, a software developer facing a complex coding problem might view it as a chance to learn a new algorithm or deepen their understanding of a programming language. This shift in perspective turns frustration into curiosity, making it easier to approach the problem with an open mind. An abundance mindset allows you to see potential where others see limitations.

An abundance mindset also means *celebrating the success of others*. When you genuinely feel happy for the achievements of those around you, it reinforces the belief that success is not a zero-sum game. For example, a startup founder who sees a competitor raising funds might reach out with a congratulatory message, knowing that their own time will come. This positive attitude fosters a sense of community, creating relationships that can lead to collaboration and mutual support. By celebrating others' successes, you reinforce the belief that there is enough room for everyone to thrive.

Taking your journey further also involves *developing resilience*. Resilience is the ability to bounce back from setbacks, stay strong under pressure, and continue moving forward, even when things get tough. It's about having the inner strength to keep going, no matter how many times you get knocked down. For example, a writer who receives critical reviews on their first book might use the feedback to refine their writing style, turning the criticism into a tool for growth rather than a reason to quit. This resilience helps them continue creating, knowing that each new piece of work is a step toward improvement.

Resilience is often built through *practicing self-compassion*. Being kind to yourself when you make mistakes or face setbacks helps you recover more quickly. For example, a business owner who experiences a financial loss might remind themselves that setbacks are a normal part of entrepreneurship and that they have the skills to overcome it. This self-compassion allows them to avoid getting stuck in self-blame and instead focus on finding solutions. By treating yourself with the same kindness you would offer a friend, you build the emotional resilience needed to keep moving forward.

Another important aspect of resilience is *developing a solution-oriented mindset*. When you focus on solutions rather than problems, it becomes easier to find a way through difficult situations. For example, a teacher struggling to engage their students in a virtual classroom might brainstorm new ways to make lessons interactive, rather than dwelling on the challenges of online learning. This shift in focus helps them find creative solutions, turning obstacles into opportunities for innovation. A solution-oriented mindset keeps you looking forward, making it easier to adapt to change.

Resilience also involves *building a support system that lifts you up*. Surrounding yourself with people who believe in you and offer encouragement can make all the difference when you're facing challenges. For example, an athlete recovering from an injury might find strength in their coach's belief in their ability to return to the sport. This support helps them stay motivated during difficult rehab sessions, making it easier to push through pain and setbacks. A strong support system provides the emotional backing that makes resilience possible, helping you rise above the tough times.

Another powerful way to elevate your journey is through *mastering the art of storytelling*. Storytelling is a skill that helps you connect with others, convey your message, and make your ideas resonate. Whether you're an entrepreneur pitching a product, a leader inspiring your team, or a content creator building an audience, storytelling can be a game-changer. For example, a brand that shares the story behind their mission and values can create a deeper connection with their customers, making them feel like they're part of something bigger. This storytelling approach builds loyalty and makes the brand memorable.

Mastering storytelling often involves *learning how to tap into emotions*. Emotions are what make stories relatable and impactful. For example, a non-profit organization raising funds for a cause might share the story of an individual whose life was changed by their work, highlighting the challenges they faced and the hope that the organization brought. This emotional connection makes potential donors feel more invested in the cause, increasing their willingness to contribute. By telling stories that evoke emotions, you make your message more powerful and persuasive.

Another important aspect of storytelling is *being authentic*. Authentic stories are the ones that come from the heart, reflecting your true experiences, values, and vision. For example, a musician sharing the story behind their latest song might talk about the personal struggles that inspired the lyrics, creating a connection with listeners who have faced similar challenges. This authenticity makes the story resonate more deeply, creating a sense of shared experience. Being true to yourself in your storytelling helps you build trust with your audience, making it easier to connect with those who appreciate your message.

Storytelling is also about *knowing how to craft a narrative that inspires action*. A great story doesn't just entertain—it motivates people to take action, whether that's buying a product, joining a movement, or pursuing their own goals. For example, a coach sharing their journey from struggling to stay fit to becoming a successful athlete might inspire others to start their own fitness journey. This narrative shows what's possible, making the listener believe that they, too, can achieve their goals. A well-crafted story turns ideas into movements, helping you create change and leave a lasting impact.

Elevating your journey also involves *embracing financial literacy*. Financial literacy is the understanding of how money works—how to earn it, save it, invest it, and make it grow. It's about having the knowledge and skills to make informed decisions about your finances, ensuring that you're building a secure future. For example, an individual who understands the basics of investing can use that knowledge to build a diverse portfolio, creating multiple streams of income that grow over time. This financial awareness provides the foundation for financial independence.

Financial literacy often involves *learning to create and stick to a budget*. A budget is a tool that helps you understand where your money is going and how you can allocate it more effectively. For example, a freelancer with fluctuating income might create a budget that accounts for their essential expenses, savings goals, and a buffer for lean months. This budget helps them avoid financial stress, making it easier to focus on their work without worrying about money. Budgeting creates a sense of control over your finances, helping you make decisions that support your long-term goals.

Another aspect of financial literacy is *understanding the power of compound interest*. Compound interest is the concept that allows your money to grow exponentially over time. For example, an investor who starts contributing to a retirement account in their twenties might see their investments grow significantly over a few decades, thanks to the compounding effect. This understanding motivates them to start saving early, knowing that each dollar they invest today will be worth much more in the future. By leveraging compound interest, you create a path to financial stability and security.

Financial literacy is also about *learning how to minimize debt and build credit wisely*. Good credit opens doors to opportunities, such as lower interest rates on loans and better terms for mortgages. For example, a young professional who uses a credit card responsibly—paying off the balance each month—builds a strong credit history, making it easier to qualify for loans when they want to buy a home. Understanding how to manage credit helps you avoid financial pitfalls, ensuring that you are in control of your financial future. By prioritizing financial literacy, you empower yourself to make decisions that lead to long-term success.

An essential part of advancing your journey is *learning how to build multiple streams of income*. Relying on a single source of income can be risky, especially in uncertain economic times. Diversifying your income means that you have more than one way to earn, which provides greater financial stability. For example, a teacher might continue their day job while creating an online course that they sell on educational platforms. This additional income stream allows them to earn money even outside of school hours, making it easier to save and invest in their long-term goals.

Creating multiple streams of income often involves *leveraging your existing skills in new ways*. You might have talents or knowledge that can be repurposed into new ventures. For example, a software developer could use their coding skills to build a simple mobile app while continuing their full-time job. Once the app is live and gains traction, it provides an additional revenue stream through in-app purchases or ads. By finding creative ways to use what you already know, you open up opportunities for income that can grow over time, turning side projects into significant contributors to your financial well-being.

Another way to build multiple income streams is through *exploring passive income opportunities*. Passive income is money that you earn without actively working for it once the initial setup is complete. For example, an author might write an eBook and make it available for sale on platforms like Amazon Kindle. Once the book is published, it continues to generate royalties without requiring ongoing effort. This passive income allows the author to focus on new projects while still earning from their previous work. Passive income streams provide a sense of financial freedom, making it easier to pursue passions without being tied to a 9-to-5 job.

Building multiple streams of income also involves *investing in assets that appreciate over time*. Assets like real estate, stocks, and mutual funds can provide returns that grow your wealth over the long term. For example, a young professional might invest in a rental property that provides a steady flow of rental income while also appreciating in value. This investment becomes a source of ongoing income, while the property's increasing value builds wealth. By focusing on assets that appreciate, you create a financial cushion that allows you to take risks, explore new ventures, and enjoy greater stability.

Taking your journey further also means *mastering the art of time management*. Time is one of the most valuable resources you have, and learning how to manage it effectively can make a huge difference in your productivity and success. Time management is not just about being busy; it's about focusing on the right tasks that bring you closer to your goals. For example, a business owner might use time-blocking techniques to dedicate specific hours of the day to different tasks like marketing, product development, and customer service. This structured approach ensures that they make progress in all areas without feeling overwhelmed.

One effective time management strategy is *prioritizing tasks using the Eisenhower Matrix*. This tool helps you categorize tasks based on their urgency and importance, allowing you to focus on what truly matters. For example, an entrepreneur might use the matrix to identify tasks that are urgent and important, such as addressing a client issue, while scheduling tasks that are important but not urgent, like strategic planning, for later in the week. This method ensures that urgent matters are handled promptly, while important long-term tasks receive the attention they deserve.

Another key to time management is *eliminating distractions that steal your focus*. In a world filled with constant notifications and social media updates, it's easy to lose track of time. For example, a writer might use website blockers to prevent access to social media during their writing sessions, allowing them to focus solely on their manuscript. This approach helps them maintain a flow state, where they can produce their best work without interruptions. By creating a distraction-free environment, you make it easier to stay on task and get more done in less time.

Time management is also about *understanding when to delegate tasks*. You don't have to do everything yourself, and learning to delegate can free up time for the things that require your unique skills and expertise. For example, a business owner might hire a virtual assistant to handle routine administrative tasks, allowing them to focus on high-level strategy and decision-making. This delegation ensures that tasks are completed efficiently while enabling the owner to use their time more effectively. By learning to let go of tasks that others can handle, you create space for innovation and growth.

Another crucial aspect of advancing your journey is *cultivating emotional intelligence*. Emotional intelligence (EQ) is the ability to understand and manage your own emotions while also recognizing and influencing the emotions of others. It's a key skill for building strong relationships, leading teams, and navigating complex social situations. For example, a manager with high emotional intelligence might notice when a team member is feeling overwhelmed and offer support or adjust their workload. This empathetic approach helps to build trust and creates a positive work environment where people feel valued.

Emotional intelligence also involves *learning to control your reactions*. It's natural to feel frustration, anger, or anxiety in challenging situations, but those with high EQ learn to pause before reacting. For example, an entrepreneur dealing with a difficult client might take a moment to breathe and consider their response, rather than reacting defensively. This ability to manage emotions allows them to maintain professionalism and find solutions that keep clients satisfied. By mastering your emotional responses, you create better outcomes in both personal and professional interactions.

Another important part of emotional intelligence is *developing active listening skills*. Active listening means fully focusing on what the other person is saying, without planning your response while they speak. For example, a team leader in a creative agency might practice active listening during brainstorming sessions, ensuring that each team member feels heard and valued. This approach fosters collaboration and leads to more innovative ideas. By listening with the intent to understand, rather than just to reply, you build deeper connections and gain insights that you might have missed otherwise.

Emotional intelligence also involves *practicing self-awareness*. Self-awareness means understanding your strengths, weaknesses, triggers, and motivations. For example, a coach who knows that they tend to become impatient under pressure might develop strategies to stay calm during intense situations, such as using deep-breathing exercises or taking short breaks. This self-awareness allows them to manage their own emotions, making them a more effective leader. By being in tune with yourself, you become better equipped to handle stress, make thoughtful decisions, and navigate the ups and downs of your journey.

Taking your progress to new levels also involves *embracing the concept of mindful productivity*. Mindful productivity is about focusing on being present and fully engaged in the task at hand, rather than just rushing through to check things off a list. It's about quality over quantity, ensuring that each action you take is aligned with your bigger goals. For example, a designer working on a new project might set aside time for deep focus sessions, where they immerse themselves in the creative process without distractions. This mindful approach allows them to produce work that is thoughtful and innovative.

Mindful productivity is also about *recognizing when to slow down*. Sometimes, taking a break or slowing down can actually improve your productivity. For example, a writer experiencing creative block might take a walk outside or spend time reading, allowing their mind to reset before returning to their work. This break helps them return with fresh ideas and a renewed sense of energy. By listening to your mind and body's need for rest, you prevent burnout and maintain a steady pace of progress.

Another aspect of mindful productivity is *practicing gratitude for your achievements*. When you take time to appreciate the progress you've made, it creates a sense of fulfillment that keeps you motivated. For example, an entrepreneur might reflect on how far their business has come since its launch, appreciating the clients they've served and the milestones they've reached. This gratitude creates a positive mindset, making it easier to face new challenges with optimism. By focusing on what you've accomplished, rather than what's left to do, you stay connected to your purpose and enjoy the journey.

Mindful productivity also means *being intentional with your daily routines*. Instead of letting your day be dictated by outside demands, you set intentions for how you want to spend your time and energy. For example, a software developer might start their day with a 10-minute meditation session, followed by a review of their top priorities for the day. This routine helps them enter their work with clarity and focus, making it easier to tackle complex problems without feeling overwhelmed. By designing your day with intention, you create a life that aligns with your values and goals.

Advancing your journey further involves *developing a legacy mindset*. A legacy mindset means thinking beyond immediate success and considering the long-term impact you want to have on the world. It's about asking yourself, "How will my actions today shape the future?" For example, a teacher might think about how the lessons they teach their students will influence their lives for years to come, striving to instill values that go beyond academics. This mindset helps them focus on making a lasting difference, rather than just achieving short-term goals.

A legacy mindset also involves *contributing to something bigger than yourself*. This could mean giving back to your community, mentoring others, or using your skills to support a cause you care about. For example, an architect who designs sustainable buildings might see their work as part of a larger movement towards environmental responsibility. This sense of purpose motivates them to push boundaries and create innovative designs that leave a positive mark on the world. By aligning your work with a greater purpose, you create a sense of meaning that fuels your dedication.

Another important aspect of a legacy mindset is *building systems that outlast you*. Whether you're leading a team, building a business, or creating art, those with a legacy mindset think about how to create something that endures. For example, a nonprofit founder might focus on building a strong organizational structure that can continue to serve its mission even after they step down. This focus on sustainability ensures that their impact lasts long after they are gone, creating a ripple effect that continues to benefit others.

A legacy mindset is also about *inspiring the next generation*. It's about passing on the knowledge, skills, and values that have helped you succeed, so that others can build on what you've created. For example, a successful chef might mentor young culinary students, sharing not just their techniques but also their passion for the craft. This mentorship creates a legacy of knowledge and inspiration that shapes the future of the industry. By focusing on what you can leave behind, you create a path that others can follow, ensuring that your impact is felt for years to come.

A crucial part of taking your journey further is *building a habit of daily reflection*. Reflection helps you gain clarity on what's working, what isn't, and where you need to make adjustments. It's a practice that ensures you're not just moving forward but moving forward in the right direction. For example, an entrepreneur might end each day by asking themselves, "What did I accomplish today?" and "What could I improve tomorrow?" This daily practice allows them to course-correct quickly, making it easier to stay aligned with their goals.

Daily reflection is not just about assessing productivity; it's also about *tuning into your emotional and mental state*. Understanding how you feel about your progress can reveal hidden stressors or unmet needs. For example, a musician who spends time reflecting might realize that they feel most creative in the mornings and adjust their schedule to prioritize songwriting during those hours. This self-awareness helps them make decisions that optimize their time and energy, leading to better creative output. By paying attention to your inner state, you ensure that your journey remains fulfilling, not just productive.

Another powerful aspect of daily reflection is *celebrating small wins*. Progress can sometimes feel slow, but by recognizing the small victories, you maintain a sense of momentum and motivation. For example, a student preparing for a tough exam might celebrate completing a chapter or mastering a difficult concept, even if they still have more to cover. This recognition of progress helps them stay positive and focused, making it easier to keep pushing through the study sessions. Celebrating small wins is a way of reminding yourself that you are moving forward, even when the bigger goal seems distant.

Daily reflection is also about *identifying areas for growth*. When you regularly assess your performance, you gain a clearer understanding of where you can improve. For example, a sales professional might reflect on a challenging client call and identify ways to handle similar situations more effectively in the future. This focus on continuous improvement ensures that they are always learning and adapting, making them more skilled over time. Reflection turns every experience into a lesson, helping you grow and adapt more quickly.

Taking your journey to the next level also involves *embracing the art of strategic risk-taking*. Risk-taking is an essential part of growth, but it's important to approach it with a strategy that balances boldness with caution. Strategic risk-taking means evaluating potential outcomes, weighing the benefits and drawbacks, and making informed decisions. For example, an investor looking to diversify their portfolio might research new markets or emerging technologies before committing funds, ensuring that their risks are calculated. This approach allows them to seize opportunities without jeopardizing their financial stability.

Strategic risk-taking often involves *knowing when to take the leap and when to hold back*. Timing is crucial when it comes to taking risks. For example, an entrepreneur might decide to launch a new product after observing market trends that indicate a growing demand, rather than rushing to release it without proper market research. This timing ensures that they enter the market when conditions are favorable, increasing their chances of success. By paying attention to timing, you make decisions that maximize the potential for positive outcomes.

Another aspect of strategic risk-taking is *learning to trust your intuition while backing it up with data*. Intuition is often informed by your experiences, and it can guide you toward opportunities that others might overlook. For example, a creative director who feels strongly that a particular advertising campaign will resonate with audiences might use data from past campaigns to support their instincts, ensuring that their decision is both creative and grounded. This combination of intuition and data creates a balanced approach that allows you to take bold steps with confidence.

Risk-taking is also about *embracing failure as a learning tool*. Not every risk will pay off, but each one provides valuable lessons that can inform your next move. For example, a startup founder who launches a product that doesn't gain traction might use customer feedback to identify what went wrong and pivot to a new approach. This willingness to learn from failure ensures that each setback is a step toward greater understanding and improvement. By viewing failure as a necessary part of the process, you build the resilience needed to keep taking risks.

Another key element of advancing your progress is *building a habit of giving back*. Giving back is not just about charity; it's about creating a positive impact in the communities and industries that have supported your growth. It's about using your skills, time, and resources to make a difference. For example, a business owner who has achieved success might mentor aspiring entrepreneurs, sharing the lessons they've learned and helping others navigate challenges. This act of mentorship creates a ripple effect, fostering a culture of support and collaboration.

Giving back also means *recognizing the power of social responsibility*. As you grow, your influence expands, and with that comes the opportunity to create change on a larger scale. For example, a tech company that prioritizes environmental sustainability might adopt eco-friendly practices, such as reducing waste or using renewable energy sources. This commitment to social responsibility not only benefits the environment but also attracts customers who share those values. By integrating social responsibility into your business or personal mission, you contribute to a better world while building a positive reputation.

Another way to give back is through *sharing your knowledge freely*. Whether it's through writing, speaking, or creating online content, sharing what you know can empower others to pursue their own goals. For example, a graphic designer might create free tutorials on design principles, helping beginners learn the basics. This act of sharing not only builds their online presence but also creates a community of learners who appreciate their generosity. By focusing on what you can offer to others, you create a legacy of knowledge and inspiration.

Giving back is also about *being a source of encouragement and support for others on their journey*. Sometimes, a few words of encouragement can make all the difference in someone's life. For example, a coach who takes the time to uplift their team members when they're feeling discouraged fosters a culture of resilience and positivity. This encouragement helps others push through difficult times, creating a supportive environment where everyone feels valued. By being a source of positivity, you create a space where others can thrive and grow.

Elevating your journey further means *embracing the power of gratitude*. Gratitude is more than just saying thank you; it's about recognizing and appreciating the positive aspects of your life and the people who contribute to it. Practicing gratitude shifts your focus from what's lacking to what's abundant, creating a mindset of contentment and fulfillment. For example, a busy professional might start each day by writing down three things they're grateful for, such as supportive colleagues, a new client, or simply the opportunity to do work they love. This practice helps them maintain a positive outlook, even during challenging times.

Gratitude also involves *expressing appreciation to those who have helped you along the way*. Acknowledging the contributions of others strengthens your relationships and builds a network of support. For example, an artist who takes the time to thank their early supporters, whether through personal messages or public shout-outs, creates a sense of loyalty and connection. This expression of gratitude makes people feel valued, encouraging them to continue supporting your journey. By showing appreciation, you build a community that stands by you through ups and downs.

Another important aspect of gratitude is *using it as a tool for resilience*. When you focus on what you're grateful for, it becomes easier to find strength during difficult times. For example, an athlete recovering from an injury might focus on being grateful for the progress they've made and the support they've received, rather than dwelling on what they can't do yet. This shift in perspective helps them maintain a sense of hope and determination, making it easier to stay committed to their recovery. Gratitude helps you stay grounded, allowing you to navigate challenges with grace.

Gratitude is also about *celebrating the journey, not just the destination*. When you appreciate the small moments of joy and growth along the way, you create a sense of satisfaction that sustains you through the long haul. For example, a startup founder might take time to appreciate the milestones they've reached, such as hiring their first employee or receiving positive feedback from customers. This celebration of progress creates a sense of fulfillment that makes the work feel meaningful. By focusing on gratitude, you create a journey that is as rewarding as the goals you're working towards.

Taking your journey to the next level involves *embracing the mindset of being a lifelong learner*. A commitment to lifelong learning means being open to new knowledge, skills, and experiences, no matter how much you've already achieved. It's about recognizing that there's always more to explore and that growth never stops. For example, a successful chef might continue to attend culinary workshops, learning new techniques and experimenting with different cuisines. This mindset keeps their passion for cooking alive, allowing them to stay innovative in a competitive industry.

Lifelong learning also means *seeking out new perspectives and ideas*. It's easy to get comfortable with what you know, but those who remain curious never stop exploring. For example, a writer might read books from different genres or attend lectures outside of their field to gain fresh insights. This exposure to new ideas helps them avoid creative stagnation, allowing them to bring unique elements into their work. By staying curious, you ensure that you are always growing, evolving, and staying relevant.

Another way to cultivate lifelong learning is through *embracing challenges that stretch your skills*. Challenges are opportunities to push your limits and discover new strengths. For example, a designer might take on a project that requires learning a new software or working in a style they've never tried before. This challenge forces them to think differently and develop new skills, making them more versatile and adaptable. Embracing challenges as learning opportunities keeps your mind sharp, ensuring that you're always prepared for the next big thing.

Lifelong learning is also about *sharing what you learn with others*. Teaching is one of the most effective ways to solidify your own understanding while helping others grow. For example, a developer who learns a new programming language might create tutorials or host workshops to help others master the skill. This act of teaching not only benefits their peers but also deepens their own expertise. By sharing knowledge, you create a cycle of learning that enriches both your journey and the journeys of those around you.

A vital aspect of pushing your journey forward is *learning to embrace vulnerability*. Vulnerability is often misunderstood as a weakness, but in reality, it is a source of strength. It's about being open, honest, and true to yourself, even when it feels uncomfortable. For example, an entrepreneur sharing their struggles and failures publicly can build a stronger connection with their audience, showing that success isn't always a straight path. This authenticity makes them more relatable, creating trust and loyalty among their followers who appreciate the honesty.

Embracing vulnerability means *being willing to ask for help when you need it*. It's easy to feel like you have to figure everything out on your own, but those who embrace vulnerability understand that asking for help is a sign of strength, not weakness. For example, a business owner might seek advice from a mentor when facing a tough decision, knowing that the mentor's experience can provide valuable insights. This willingness to reach out for support ensures that they don't waste time on avoidable mistakes, making it easier to navigate challenges and stay focused on their goals.

Another key aspect of vulnerability is *sharing your true story*. Everyone has a unique journey, and sharing the real story behind your successes and struggles can inspire others and make your work more impactful. For example, a writer who openly discusses the years of rejection they faced before publishing their first book can inspire aspiring authors to keep going, even when the path feels difficult. This transparency shows that success is built on persistence and resilience, encouraging others to persevere through their own challenges.

Vulnerability is also about *allowing yourself to feel and express emotions*. In a world that often glorifies stoicism, those who succeed understand that emotions are a natural part of the human experience. For example, a leader who acknowledges their team's hard work and expresses genuine gratitude creates a culture of appreciation and respect. This emotional openness makes it easier for team members to feel valued and engaged, leading to better collaboration and morale. By embracing vulnerability, you build deeper relationships and create an environment where people feel safe to be themselves.

Taking your journey to new heights also involves *understanding the power of community building*. Building a community around your work, mission, or passion can amplify your impact and provide a support network that encourages growth. It's about creating a space where people can connect, share ideas, and find inspiration. For example, a fitness coach might create an online community where clients share their progress, support each other's goals, and access exclusive content. This community becomes a source of motivation and accountability, making it easier for members to stay committed to their fitness journeys.

Community building often involves *fostering a sense of belonging*. When people feel like they are part of something bigger than themselves, they are more likely to stay engaged and contribute positively. For example, a nonprofit organization that creates volunteer groups centered around shared values and goals can build a strong sense of unity among its members. This sense of belonging keeps volunteers passionate about the cause, making it easier for the organization to achieve its mission. By creating an environment where people feel valued and connected, you cultivate a community that thrives.

Another key aspect of community building is *encouraging collaboration and shared learning*. A strong community is one where knowledge and resources flow freely, allowing everyone to grow together. For example, an entrepreneur leading a mastermind group might facilitate discussions where members share their experiences, challenges, and strategies. This collaborative approach helps each member learn from others' successes and mistakes, creating a collective wisdom that benefits everyone. By fostering a spirit of collaboration, you ensure that your community becomes a place of continuous growth and innovation.

Community building is also about *giving people a voice and a platform*. When people feel heard and seen, they are more likely to stay engaged and invested in the community. For example, a content creator might invite followers to share their stories or experiences related to the topics they discuss, featuring these stories in their content. This approach not only makes the community feel more inclusive but also enriches the creator's content with diverse perspectives. By providing a platform for others, you create a space where everyone's voice matters, making the community stronger and more vibrant.

Another crucial part of elevating your progress is *developing resilience in the face of criticism*. Criticism is inevitable when you put yourself out there, especially if you're doing something new or unconventional. But those who thrive understand how to use criticism as a tool for growth rather than letting it become a source of self-doubt. For example, a startup founder might receive harsh feedback from early users, but instead of taking it personally, they analyze the feedback to improve their product. This ability to separate constructive feedback from negativity helps them adapt and make their offering better.

Resilience to criticism also involves *learning to filter out noise*. Not all feedback is useful, and knowing how to distinguish between helpful insights and unconstructive negativity is essential. For example, a public figure might receive a lot of unsolicited opinions on social media, but they focus on the feedback from trusted mentors and industry experts who understand their vision. This ability to focus on meaningful feedback helps them stay true to their goals while remaining open to improvement. By filtering out the noise, you protect your confidence and stay on the path that aligns with your values.

Another way to build resilience to criticism is through *practicing self-validation*. While external feedback can be valuable, it's important to develop the ability to validate your own progress and achievements. For example, a graphic designer might remind themselves of the positive reviews from clients and the creative breakthroughs they've experienced, rather than dwelling on a single piece of negative feedback. This focus on self-validation helps them maintain a balanced perspective, ensuring that their self-worth is not solely dependent on others' opinions.

Resilience to criticism is also about *using negative feedback as fuel for improvement*. Instead of letting criticism discourage you, those who succeed use it as motivation to work harder and refine their skills. For example, an athlete who receives feedback about their technique might double down on their training, using the criticism as a challenge to prove their capabilities. This mindset transforms setbacks into opportunities for growth, ensuring that criticism becomes a stepping stone rather than a stumbling block. By embracing criticism with a positive attitude, you build the resilience needed to keep moving forward.

Taking your progress further also involves *understanding the importance of mental and physical well-being*. Success is not just about achieving external goals; it's also about maintaining balance and taking care of your overall well-being. When you prioritize your health, you ensure that you have the energy, focus, and resilience needed to tackle challenges. For example, an entrepreneur who sets aside time for daily exercise and meditation creates a routine that helps them manage stress and stay energized. This focus on well-being allows them to maintain high levels of productivity without burning out.

Mental well-being often involves *practicing mindfulness and stress management techniques*. Mindfulness is the practice of being fully present in the moment, which can help reduce anxiety and increase focus. For example, a student dealing with exam stress might practice mindfulness by taking deep breaths and focusing on each breath, calming their mind before starting their studies. This simple practice helps them enter a state of calm, making it easier to concentrate on the task at hand. By incorporating mindfulness into your daily routine, you create a mental space that supports clarity and peace.

Physical well-being is equally important and involves *building habits that support your body's needs*. This could mean eating a balanced diet, staying active, and ensuring that you get enough rest. For example, a musician who spends hours practicing might focus on maintaining good posture and stretching regularly to prevent strain injuries. This attention to physical well-being ensures that they can continue playing without pain or injury, allowing them to sustain their passion over the long term. By taking care of your body, you ensure that you have the stamina needed to pursue your goals with vigor.

Another aspect of well-being is *creating a work-life balance that allows you to recharge*. It's easy to become consumed by your ambitions, but those who maintain their success understand the importance of making time for hobbies, relationships, and relaxation. For example, a writer might set boundaries around their work hours, ensuring that they have time to spend with family or enjoy nature walks. This balance helps them return to their writing with a fresh perspective, making it easier to produce quality work. By prioritizing balance, you create a sustainable approach to success that supports both your professional and personal fulfillment.

Advancing your journey further means *developing a vision for your future*. A vision is more than just a goal—it's a clear and compelling picture of the life you want to create. It's about knowing what kind of impact you want to have, what values you want to uphold, and what legacy you want to leave behind. For example, an environmental activist might have a vision of a world where clean energy is accessible to everyone, and their actions, projects, and partnerships all align with this vision. This clarity of vision guides their decisions and keeps them focused on making a meaningful impact.

Having a vision also involves *breaking it down into actionable steps*. A vision provides the direction, but it's the daily actions that turn it into reality. For example, a musician who dreams of performing at major venues might set smaller goals like releasing an album, building a social media following, and collaborating with other artists. Each of these steps brings them closer to their ultimate vision, creating a roadmap that guides their progress. By breaking down your vision into specific actions, you create a path that makes the big dream feel achievable.

A strong vision also means *being willing to adapt and evolve*. As you grow and learn, your vision might shift, and that's a natural part of the journey. For example, a tech entrepreneur might start with a vision of creating a product that solves a specific problem but later discover new needs that inspire them to pivot. This flexibility ensures that their vision stays relevant and impactful, allowing them to continue making a difference even as the world changes. By being open to evolution, you ensure that your vision remains a source of inspiration, not a rigid set of rules.

Developing a vision is also about *staying connected to your "why."* Your "why" is the deeper reason behind your goals, the purpose that drives you even when the work is challenging. For example, a teacher who is passionate about inspiring young minds might remind themselves of the joy they feel when a student has a breakthrough moment in understanding. This connection to their "why" keeps them motivated, even during difficult days. By staying connected to your purpose, you create a sense of fulfillment that makes the journey worth every effort.

Another powerful way to continue advancing your journey is *mastering the art of self-discipline*. Self-discipline is the ability to do what needs to be done, even when you don't feel like doing it. It's the skill that separates those who achieve their goals from those who simply dream about them. For example, an athlete training for a marathon might get up early every morning to run, even on days when they feel tired or unmotivated. This consistency is what prepares them for race day, ensuring that they're ready to perform at their best.

Self-discipline is not about deprivation or harsh self-control; it's about *building habits that align with your goals*. For example, a musician aiming to master a new instrument might set a rule to practice for 30 minutes every day, no matter what. This small daily habit becomes second nature over time, making it easier to improve steadily without relying on bursts of motivation. By focusing on consistency rather than intensity, they create a practice routine that leads to long-term growth. Self-discipline helps you stay committed, ensuring that progress continues even when enthusiasm fades.

Another key aspect of self-discipline is *learning to delay gratification*. The ability to resist short-term temptations in favor of long-term rewards is a critical part of achieving lasting success. For example, a student preparing for final exams might choose to study on a Saturday instead of going out with friends, knowing that their efforts will pay off in better grades and future opportunities. This ability to prioritize what matters most allows them to stay focused, even when distractions are tempting. Delaying gratification is a way of investing in your future, making it easier to achieve bigger goals.

Self-discipline also means *holding yourself accountable to the standards you've set*. When you commit to a goal, you set expectations for yourself, and self-discipline is about living up to those expectations. For example, an entrepreneur who sets a goal to launch a new product by a certain date might create a detailed project plan and track their progress weekly. This accountability helps them stay on schedule, ensuring that they meet their deadlines and deliver on their promises. By holding yourself accountable, you create a sense of integrity that builds trust in your own abilities.

Taking your journey further also means *embracing the power of creativity*. Creativity isn't just for artists; it's a mindset that allows you to see possibilities where others see obstacles. It's about thinking outside the box, finding new solutions, and bringing fresh ideas into everything you do. For example, a marketer who takes a creative approach might find unique ways to engage their audience, such as creating interactive social media campaigns that encourage followers to participate. This creativity helps them stand out in a crowded market, attracting more attention and building a loyal community.

Creativity often involves *embracing curiosity and exploring new interests*. The more you expose yourself to different fields, experiences, and ideas, the more connections you can make between them. For example, a software developer who takes up photography as a hobby might discover new ways to visualize data or design more user-friendly interfaces. This cross-pollination of ideas can lead to breakthroughs that wouldn't have been possible within a single field. By staying curious and open to new experiences, you expand your creative potential, making it easier to innovate.

Another aspect of creativity is *learning to play with ideas without fear of failure*. Creativity thrives when you give yourself permission to experiment, even if the outcome is uncertain. For example, a writer might explore a new genre or writing style without worrying about whether it will be well-received. This willingness to take creative risks helps them discover new aspects of their voice, making their work more dynamic and engaging. By focusing on the process of creation rather than the end result, you free yourself to explore ideas that might lead to unexpected success.

Creativity is also about *solving problems with a fresh perspective*. When you approach challenges with a creative mindset, you look for innovative solutions that go beyond the obvious. For example, a startup founder facing cash flow issues might come up with a creative pricing model that allows customers to pay over time, making their product more accessible. This problem-solving approach allows them to adapt to market needs and stay competitive. By using creativity as a tool for innovation, you ensure that you're always finding new ways to grow and succeed.

Another crucial aspect of advancing your progress is *building emotional resilience*. Emotional resilience is the ability to manage stress, adapt to change, and maintain a positive outlook even during tough times. It's about understanding that setbacks and challenges are a natural part of life and learning how to bounce back from them. For example, a teacher adapting to remote learning during a pandemic might face technical difficulties and disruptions, but by focusing on what they can control and maintaining a positive attitude, they continue to support their students effectively.

Building emotional resilience often involves *developing healthy coping mechanisms*. When you encounter stress, having constructive ways to deal with it ensures that you can maintain your focus and well-being. For example, a business owner might cope with stress by practicing mindfulness, journaling, or engaging in physical activity. These practices help them process their emotions and keep stress from overwhelming them, allowing them to stay focused on their goals. By developing healthy coping strategies, you create a mental toolkit that helps you stay strong in the face of adversity.

Another important aspect of emotional resilience is *embracing flexibility in your thinking*. Life is unpredictable, and those who succeed are the ones who can adapt their mindset when things don't go as planned. For example, a creative professional who faces unexpected delays in a project might use the time to explore new skills or ideas that can enrich their work. This flexibility allows them to see setbacks as opportunities for growth, rather than as failures. By staying adaptable, you ensure that you can find a way forward, no matter what challenges arise.

Emotional resilience is also about *building a support network that lifts you up during difficult times*. When you have people you can rely on for encouragement and understanding, it becomes easier to stay motivated, even when facing setbacks. For example, an athlete going through a tough season might lean on their coach, teammates, and family for support, knowing that they have a community that believes in their potential. This network provides the emotional strength needed to keep pushing forward. By building relationships with people who uplift you, you create a safety net that helps you navigate challenges with confidence.

Taking your journey to the next level involves *embracing the concept of lifelong impact*. Lifelong impact means thinking about how your actions, choices, and contributions will shape the world beyond your immediate goals. It's about creating a ripple effect that influences others in a positive way. For example, a mentor who invests time in guiding young professionals not only helps them succeed but also inspires them to become mentors themselves, creating a chain reaction of support and growth. This focus on impact ensures that your work continues to resonate, even after you've moved on to new ventures.

Lifelong impact also involves *being intentional about the legacy you want to leave*. A legacy is not just about wealth or achievements; it's about the values, lessons, and changes you bring into the world. For example, a scientist who focuses on making sustainable advancements in their field might leave behind a legacy of innovation that inspires future generations to continue their research. This focus on long-term impact guides their decisions, ensuring that their work leaves a lasting mark. By thinking about the bigger picture, you create a vision that extends beyond your own lifetime.

Another aspect of creating lifelong impact is *using your platform to amplify important causes*. When you have a voice or influence in a community, you have the opportunity to use that influence for good. For example, a content creator with a large following might use their platform to raise awareness about social issues, encourage charitable giving, or promote positive change. This use of influence creates a community that values more than just entertainment, fostering a culture of awareness and action. By using your platform responsibly, you make a difference that reaches far beyond your immediate audience.

Lifelong impact is also about *teaching others to become leaders in their own right*. When you share your knowledge, empower others, and encourage them to take initiative, you create a new generation of changemakers. For example, a business leader who takes the time to develop leadership skills in their team ensures that the organization remains strong and adaptable, even as new challenges arise. This focus on leadership development creates a culture of growth that outlasts any single person's contribution. By inspiring others to lead, you create a legacy that continues to shape the future.

Elevating your journey also involves *embracing the power of self-reinvention*. Reinvention is about being willing to change directions, adapt to new opportunities, and redefine yourself when the time is right. It's about letting go of old labels and embracing the potential for new beginnings. For example, a successful corporate executive might decide to pivot into a completely different field, such as becoming a wellness coach or starting a nonprofit. This willingness to reinvent themselves allows them to explore new passions and make a difference in new ways, even if it means stepping outside of their comfort zone.

Self-reinvention often involves *letting go of the fear of judgment*. It's natural to worry about what others might think when you make a major change, but those who embrace reinvention understand that their true potential lies beyond others' opinions. For example, an artist who decides to shift their style might face criticism from their existing audience, but by staying true to their new vision, they attract a new audience that appreciates their evolution. This focus on authenticity allows them to continue growing creatively, making it easier to explore new forms of expression without being held back by fear.

Another important aspect of self-reinvention is *embracing a beginner's mindset*. When you're starting something new, it's important to stay humble and open to learning, even if you're already an expert in another area. For example, a seasoned entrepreneur who decides to learn coding might approach it with the same curiosity and eagerness as a newcomer, knowing that this openness will help them learn faster. This beginner's mindset allows them to stay adaptable and open to new insights, making it easier to master new skills and thrive in unfamiliar territory.

Self-reinvention is also about *being willing to challenge your own beliefs and assumptions*. Growth often requires questioning the beliefs that have kept you comfortable. For example, a writer who has always focused on fiction might decide to explore nonfiction, challenging themselves to think in new ways and address different audiences. This willingness to step outside of their usual approach allows them to expand their creative boundaries and discover new strengths. By challenging yourself, you ensure that your journey is never stagnant, always evolving towards new possibilities.

A key aspect of advancing your journey is *developing a mindset of proactive problem-solving*. Being proactive means anticipating challenges before they arise and taking action to address them. It's about seeing potential obstacles as opportunities for preparation rather than roadblocks. For example, a project manager might create contingency plans for potential delays in a project timeline, ensuring that if issues do arise, they already have a strategy in place to minimize the impact. This proactive approach helps them stay on track and reduces stress when unexpected events occur.

Proactive problem-solving is about *taking initiative rather than waiting for problems to be handed to you*. When you see an area that could be improved or an issue that could be resolved, stepping up to take action is what sets successful people apart. For example, an employee who notices inefficiencies in their department might suggest new tools or workflows to their manager, demonstrating leadership and a commitment to continuous improvement. This initiative not only solves immediate problems but also builds a reputation as someone who adds value to the team.

Another important element of proactive problem-solving is *developing critical thinking skills*. Critical thinking allows you to analyze situations, identify underlying issues, and come up with innovative solutions. For example, an entrepreneur facing a downturn in sales might dig into the data to understand customer behavior, identifying patterns that point to the need for a new marketing approach. This analytical mindset helps them find targeted solutions, rather than relying on guesswork. By thinking critically about challenges, you create more effective strategies and become more resilient in the face of complexity.

Proactive problem-solving also involves *embracing a mindset of continuous improvement*. Instead of settling for good enough, those who succeed are always looking for ways to refine and optimize their approach. For example, a software developer might regularly review their code to identify ways to make it more efficient, even after the initial release. This focus on improvement ensures that their work remains at the cutting edge, making them a valuable asset to their team. By striving for excellence, you keep raising the bar for yourself and those around you, making it easier to achieve sustained growth.

Taking your journey further also involves *learning the art of negotiation*. Negotiation is a critical skill that can open doors to better opportunities, partnerships, and outcomes. It's about finding a win-win solution that meets both your needs and those of the other party. For example, a freelancer negotiating a contract might focus on understanding the client's budget and priorities, then finding a way to offer a service package that aligns with both. This approach ensures that they create a relationship where both parties feel valued and satisfied, making it easier to secure repeat business.

Negotiation is not just about asking for what you want; it's also about *understanding the value you bring to the table*. When you know your worth, you can advocate for yourself confidently, whether it's in salary discussions, client contracts, or partnerships. For example, an artist negotiating a gallery show might emphasize the unique perspective and audience reach they offer, positioning themselves as an asset to the gallery. This understanding of their value helps them negotiate terms that reflect their contributions, ensuring that they are compensated fairly.

Another important aspect of negotiation is *developing active listening skills*. Effective negotiators know that understanding the other party's perspective is key to finding common ground. For example, a sales professional negotiating with a new client might listen carefully to their concerns and priorities, using that information to tailor their proposal. This approach helps them address the client's needs directly, making it easier to reach an agreement. By listening actively, you show respect for the other party's viewpoint, building trust and creating a foundation for successful negotiations.

Negotiation also involves *staying calm under pressure*. When stakes are high, it's easy to let emotions take over, but those who succeed in negotiations maintain their composure. For example, a business leader negotiating a major partnership might face aggressive tactics from the other side, but by staying calm and focused on their objectives, they can navigate the situation effectively. This ability to manage emotions ensures that they remain clear-headed, allowing them to make decisions that serve their best interests. By mastering the art of negotiation, you open up new possibilities for growth and success.

Another critical aspect of taking your journey to the next level is *building a habit of setting boundaries*. Boundaries are essential for maintaining a healthy balance between your personal and professional life. They protect your time, energy, and mental well-being, ensuring that you don't burn out. For example, a digital marketer who sets boundaries around their work hours ensures that they have time for family, hobbies, and relaxation, even during busy campaign seasons. This balance helps them recharge, making it easier to maintain high levels of creativity and focus.

Setting boundaries also means *knowing when to say no*. It's easy to overcommit, especially when you're passionate about what you do, but learning to decline opportunities that don't align with your goals is crucial. For example, a consultant who is focused on scaling their own business might say no to requests for free advice, knowing that their time is better spent on clients who value their expertise. This ability to say no allows them to stay focused on their priorities, ensuring that they use their time and energy in the most effective way.

Another aspect of setting boundaries is *communicating your limits clearly*. When you let others know your availability, expectations, and preferences, it prevents misunderstandings and sets the tone for respectful interactions. For example, a remote worker might communicate to their team that they are available for meetings during specific hours, but they use the mornings for focused work. This clarity helps their team understand when they can expect responses, reducing frustration and improving collaboration. By communicating boundaries, you create a work environment that respects your needs and supports productivity.

Boundaries are also about *protecting your time for deep work and rest*. Deep work is the focused, undistracted time you spend on tasks that require intense concentration, while rest is the time you spend recharging. For example, an author might set aside blocks of time where they turn off their phone and focus solely on writing, followed by time for leisurely walks or reading to rest their mind. This balance ensures that they remain productive without sacrificing their well-being. By creating time for both work and rest, you sustain your energy and creativity, making it easier to continue pushing forward.

Elevating your journey also involves *learning how to pivot when necessary*. Pivoting means being willing to change your direction when new information or circumstances require it. It's about staying committed to your overall vision while being flexible about how you achieve it. For example, a startup founder who realizes that their initial product isn't meeting market needs might pivot to focus on a new feature that resonates more with users. This willingness to adapt allows them to stay relevant and keep growing, even when the original plan doesn't work out as expected.

Pivoting often requires *letting go of sunk costs*. Sunk costs are investments of time, money, or effort that you can't recover, and it's easy to feel like you have to keep going just because you've already put so much in. However, those who succeed understand that it's better to adjust course than to continue down a path that isn't working. For example, a content creator who has invested in a particular platform might realize that their audience engagement is much higher on another platform and decide to shift their focus. This decision allows them to maximize their impact, even if it means abandoning the time invested in the previous platform.

Pivoting also involves *staying open to new opportunities that align with your evolving goals*. Sometimes, a pivot can lead to opportunities that you hadn't initially considered but are better aligned with your strengths and passions. For example, a graphic designer who starts offering branding workshops might find that they enjoy teaching and decide to pivot into educational content. This new direction not only aligns with their passion but also allows them to reach a wider audience. By staying open to new possibilities, you ensure that your journey remains dynamic and fulfilling.

Another important aspect of pivoting is *having the courage to take risks, even when the outcome is uncertain*. Pivoting often involves stepping into unknown territory, and it can feel risky to leave behind what is familiar. For example, a consultant who has built a reputation in one industry might decide to pivot into a new field where they see emerging opportunities. This leap requires confidence in their ability to adapt, even if it means starting over in some ways. By embracing the uncertainty that comes with change, you create the possibility for greater growth and new adventures.

Another powerful way to advance your journey is *cultivating the habit of gratitude as a daily practice*. Gratitude isn't just a feeling—it's a practice that can transform the way you experience the world. When you actively look for things to be grateful for, you shift your focus from what's lacking to what's abundant. For example, an artist might make it a habit to write down three things they're grateful for every morning, such as the support of their fans, the opportunity to create, and the inspiration they find in everyday life. This practice helps them start each day with a positive mindset.

Gratitude can also be a powerful tool for *strengthening relationships*. When you express gratitude to others, it fosters a sense of connection and appreciation. For example, a manager who regularly thanks their team members for their contributions creates a work environment where people feel valued and motivated. This expression of gratitude makes it easier for team members to go the extra mile, knowing that their efforts are recognized. By making gratitude a habit, you build stronger relationships and a more supportive community.

Another important aspect of gratitude is *using it to stay grounded during challenges*. When things aren't going your way, focusing on what you're grateful for can help you maintain perspective and resilience. For example, a business owner facing a tough quarter might focus on being grateful for their team's dedication, the loyal customers they have, and the lessons they've learned. This focus on gratitude helps them stay hopeful, making it easier to navigate through difficult times with a positive outlook. Gratitude becomes a source of strength, helping you keep moving forward.

Gratitude is also about *celebrating progress, no matter how small*. It's easy to get caught up in the hustle and forget to appreciate how far you've come. For example, a student working towards a degree might take time to celebrate completing each semester, recognizing the hard work and growth that got them there. This celebration of small wins creates a sense of accomplishment that fuels their motivation for the next challenge. By focusing on gratitude, you create a mindset that values the journey, not just the destination, making the entire process more rewarding.

A key to taking your journey to new heights is *building resilience through embracing uncertainty*. Life is inherently unpredictable, and success often hinges on your ability to adapt to the unknown. Embracing uncertainty means leaning into challenges and seeing them as opportunities for growth, rather than sources of fear. For example, a tech entrepreneur might face sudden changes in market trends that render their original business model obsolete. Instead of giving up, they see it as a chance to explore new products or services that better meet evolving customer needs. This mindset allows them to thrive in dynamic environments where others might struggle.

Resilience in the face of uncertainty often involves *developing a mindset of adaptability*. Adaptability is the ability to change your approach when circumstances shift, ensuring that you can continue moving toward your goals even when the path isn't straightforward. For example, a teacher might adapt their lesson plans for remote learning, finding creative ways to keep students engaged through online platforms. This flexibility ensures that they continue to deliver quality education, regardless of the medium. By embracing adaptability, you ensure that setbacks and changes don't derail your progress but instead become opportunities to innovate.

Another critical aspect of resilience is *maintaining a sense of optimism, even when facing challenges*. Optimism doesn't mean ignoring difficulties; it means believing that you have the ability to overcome them. For example, a musician who has faced multiple rejections from record labels might maintain hope by focusing on the positive feedback from their audience and the improvements in their craft. This positive outlook keeps them motivated to keep creating and pursuing new opportunities. By maintaining a hopeful perspective, you build the emotional stamina needed to keep moving forward, no matter what obstacles arise.

Resilience through uncertainty also involves *taking calculated risks without fear of failure*. When you accept that failure is a natural part of the process, it becomes easier to take the bold steps needed to reach your goals. For example, a freelance writer might decide to pitch a high-profile magazine, knowing that rejection is a possibility but also recognizing that acceptance could significantly boost their career. This willingness to risk failure opens up new opportunities that wouldn't be available to those who play it safe. By taking calculated risks, you position yourself to seize the moments that can change everything.

Another essential part of advancing your journey is *cultivating a habit of self-care*. Self-care is more than just pampering yourself; it's about ensuring that your mind, body, and spirit are in a state that allows you to perform at your best. It's about recognizing when you need rest, when you need to slow down, and when you need to push yourself. For example, an entrepreneur who is burning the candle at both ends might realize that taking regular breaks for exercise and spending time with loved ones helps them maintain their focus and creativity. This balance between work and rest ensures that they don't burn out before they reach their goals.

Self-care often involves *listening to your body's signals and responding to its needs*. It's easy to ignore signs of exhaustion or stress when you're chasing big goals, but those who prioritize self-care understand that these signals are their body's way of asking for support. For example, a writer might take a day off when they feel mentally drained, allowing themselves to recharge through reading, taking a walk, or simply resting. This break helps them return to their work with renewed energy and a fresh perspective, making it easier to produce high-quality content. By listening to your body, you ensure that your journey is sustainable and fulfilling.

Another key aspect of self-care is *practicing mindfulness and being present in the moment*. Mindfulness helps you slow down, appreciate where you are, and find joy in the simple things, even during busy times. For example, a student preparing for exams might practice mindfulness by taking a few minutes each day to focus on their breathing, letting go of worries about the future or regrets about the past. This practice helps them stay calm and focused, making it easier to study effectively. By incorporating mindfulness into your routine, you create a sense of peace that supports both your well-being and your productivity.

Self-care also means *establishing boundaries that protect your time for rest and rejuvenation*. It's about making sure that you have time for the things that nourish your spirit, whether that's spending time with family, pursuing hobbies, or simply enjoying a quiet moment. For example, a digital creator might set a rule to unplug from social media for an hour each evening, using that time to read, meditate, or reflect on their day. This boundary ensures that they have time to recharge, making it easier to stay inspired and creative in their work. By prioritizing self-care, you create a foundation that allows you to thrive in every area of your life.

Taking your progress further also involves *embracing the concept of being a lifelong student*. Being a lifelong student means maintaining an open mind and a willingness to learn from everyone and everything around you. It's about recognizing that no matter how much you know, there is always more to discover. For example, a business leader might attend workshops outside of their industry, learning new approaches to leadership, communication, or innovation. This openness to new knowledge ensures that they remain adaptable and can bring fresh ideas into their work.

Being a lifelong student also means *learning from your mistakes and successes alike*. Each experience, whether positive or negative, holds lessons that can inform your next steps. For example, a public speaker who has experienced both successful and difficult presentations might reflect on what made the difference—perhaps it was the way they engaged with the audience or the stories they chose to share. This reflection helps them refine their approach, ensuring that they continue to improve. By seeing every experience as an opportunity to learn, you ensure that your journey is one of constant growth.

Another important aspect of being a lifelong student is *seeking out diverse perspectives*. It's easy to stay within the comfort zone of familiar ideas, but those who continue growing make a point of exploring different viewpoints. For example, a filmmaker might study storytelling techniques from cultures and genres that differ from their own, finding new ways to approach their craft. This exposure to different ideas broadens their creative horizons, making it easier to create work that is rich and multi-dimensional. By embracing diverse perspectives, you ensure that your thinking remains fresh and innovative.

Being a lifelong student also involves *staying humble and recognizing that there is always more to learn*. Humility is what keeps you open to feedback and willing to challenge your assumptions. For example, a seasoned entrepreneur might invite feedback from their younger employees, recognizing that they have insights into new market trends and technologies. This humility allows them to stay relevant in a fast-changing industry, ensuring that they don't become complacent. By staying humble, you create a mindset that is always open to new possibilities, making it easier to adapt and grow.

Another powerful way to elevate your journey is through *fostering a spirit of generosity*. Generosity is not just about giving money; it's about giving your time, energy, and skills to uplift others. It's about recognizing that success is more fulfilling when you help others succeed as well. For example, a mentor who takes time out of their schedule to guide young professionals not only helps them grow but also finds a deeper sense of purpose in their own journey. This act of giving creates a positive cycle, where generosity leads to stronger relationships and a sense of community.

Generosity often involves *sharing your knowledge freely with those who can benefit from it*. When you share what you've learned, you empower others to navigate their own paths more effectively. For example, a financial advisor might offer free workshops on personal finance for young adults, teaching them how to budget, invest, and plan for the future. This act of sharing not only builds their reputation as a knowledgeable professional but also creates a ripple effect, helping others make smarter financial decisions. By sharing your expertise, you make a lasting impact that extends beyond your own success.

Another aspect of generosity is *being a source of encouragement and support for others*. Sometimes, a simple word of encouragement can make all the difference in someone's life. For example, a coach who believes in their team's potential might take time to acknowledge each member's strengths, inspiring them to push beyond their perceived limits. This encouragement creates a positive environment where everyone feels capable of achieving great things. By being a source of positivity, you lift others up, making it easier for them to overcome challenges and strive for their best.

Generosity also means *practicing kindness in everyday interactions*. Small acts of kindness can create a big impact, whether it's offering a listening ear, lending a hand, or showing appreciation. For example, a leader who makes a habit of checking in on their team members' well-being fosters a culture of care and mutual respect. This kindness helps to build trust, making it easier for people to work together and support one another. By focusing on how you can serve others, you create a legacy of goodwill that enriches both your life and the lives of those around you.

Advancing your journey also means *embracing the idea of leaving a legacy of wisdom*. A legacy of wisdom is about passing on the insights, values, and knowledge that have guided your own journey so that others can benefit from them. It's about creating something that endures beyond your own lifetime, offering guidance to future generations. For example, an author might write a book that distills the lessons they've learned in their field, providing a roadmap for those who come after them. This book becomes a source of inspiration and guidance, continuing to make an impact long after the author's active career has ended.

Leaving a legacy of wisdom often involves *mentoring others and helping them develop their own skills*. When you invest in others, you create a ripple effect that extends your influence far beyond your immediate reach. For example, a scientist who mentors young researchers not only helps them develop their technical skills but also instills in them a sense of curiosity and integrity. This mentorship shapes the way those researchers approach their work, ensuring that the values of exploration and ethical conduct continue in the field. By mentoring others, you create a legacy that shapes the future.

Another important aspect of leaving a legacy of wisdom is *documenting your journey and the lessons you've learned along the way*. Whether through writing, speaking, or creating content, sharing your story allows others to learn from your experiences. For example, a business leader might create a podcast where they discuss the highs and lows of building a company, offering practical advice to aspiring entrepreneurs. This documentation becomes a resource that others can turn to, helping them navigate their own challenges. By sharing your journey, you create a lasting impact that continues to guide others.

Leaving a legacy of wisdom also involves *encouraging others to think for themselves and seek their own truth*. True wisdom is not about giving all the answers; it's about inspiring others to ask questions and explore their own paths. For example, a teacher who challenges their students to think critically and form their own opinions creates a culture of independent thought. This approach helps students develop the skills they need to navigate a complex world with confidence. By encouraging curiosity and independent thinking, you create a legacy that empowers others to find their own way.

FINAL CHAPTER: THE PATH FORWARD

True growth comes from *understanding that the journey never really ends*. It's about realizing that every milestone is just the beginning of a new phase, a new challenge, and a new lesson to learn. Success isn't a destination—it's a mindset, a continuous state of evolving, adapting, and reaching for new heights. For example, a musician who releases their first hit song understands that the work doesn't stop there; it's about creating a body of work that continues to push boundaries, exploring new sounds, and connecting with audiences in different ways. This perspective keeps them moving forward, even after achieving significant recognition.

Understanding that the journey continues allows you to *approach each day with a sense of purpose and curiosity*. Instead of looking back at what's been accomplished, you focus on what can be done today to make an impact. For example, a startup founder who has raised their first round of funding might immediately start thinking about how they can scale operations and improve customer satisfaction. This focus on the present moment keeps them grounded, making it easier to identify opportunities and adapt to changes in real time. By treating each day as a new chance to grow, you maintain momentum without becoming complacent.

Another powerful aspect of embracing the continuous journey is *staying open to reinvention*. Reinvention is the art of starting anew, of shedding old skins and stepping into a new identity when the time is right. It's about not being afraid to change your path or explore a different aspect of yourself. For example, an athlete who retires from competitive sports might find fulfillment in becoming a coach, using their experience to guide others toward success. This ability to pivot and redefine yourself ensures that life remains exciting and dynamic, offering new challenges that keep you engaged.

Embracing the path forward also means *taking time to appreciate the lessons you've learned along the way*. Every setback, every victory, and every unexpected twist holds valuable insights that shape who you are. For example, a writer who has faced rejection from multiple publishers might look back and realize how those experiences pushed them to refine their craft and find their unique voice. This appreciation for the process creates a sense of gratitude that makes the future feel full of promise. By focusing on the lessons gained, you build a foundation that supports the next stage of your journey.

Another aspect of moving forward is *building a vision that evolves as you grow*. Your vision doesn't have to be set in stone; it can change as you learn more about yourself and the world around you. It's about creating a vision that is both inspiring and flexible, allowing you to adapt without losing sight of your core values. For example, a social entrepreneur might start with a vision of solving a specific problem in their community, but as they gain experience, they expand that vision to address similar challenges in other regions. This evolving vision keeps them motivated, ensuring that their work remains relevant and impactful.

Creating a dynamic vision often involves *setting new challenges that stretch your abilities*. When you push yourself beyond what you thought was possible, you discover new strengths and capacities. For example, a graphic designer who has mastered digital art might challenge themselves to explore traditional painting, using it as a way to refresh their creativity and bring new perspectives into their digital work. This willingness to explore new areas ensures that their skills continue to grow, keeping their work innovative and exciting. By continually setting new challenges, you ensure that your vision remains a living, breathing part of your journey.

Another powerful element of moving forward is *surrounding yourself with people who inspire growth*. The right community can fuel your motivation, keep you accountable, and provide the encouragement you need to stay on track. For example, a tech entrepreneur might join a mastermind group of fellow founders who share their ambition and commitment to innovation. This community becomes a source of ideas, support, and constructive feedback, making it easier to navigate the ups and downs of building a business. By choosing to be around people who inspire you, you ensure that you're always learning and growing.

Building a vision that evolves also means *being willing to question your own assumptions*. Growth often requires challenging the beliefs that have kept you comfortable and being open to new ways of thinking. For example, a researcher who has always relied on traditional methods might embrace new technologies like AI and machine learning to enhance their work. This willingness to step outside of their comfort zone allows them to stay at the forefront of their field, ensuring that their work continues to make an impact. By staying curious and open-minded, you create a vision that evolves alongside your journey.

Another key to advancing on your path is *embracing the power of giving back as a guiding principle*. Giving back is not just a way to help others; it's a way to create meaning and purpose in your own life. It's about recognizing that the more you grow, the more you have to offer to those who are just starting their journeys. For example, a successful business owner might create a scholarship program for young entrepreneurs, helping them access education and resources that were crucial to their own success. This act of giving creates a ripple effect, ensuring that their impact extends far beyond their immediate circle.

Giving back also means *sharing the lessons you've learned with those who can benefit from them*. Everyone has something valuable to share, whether it's practical skills, insights from past experiences, or even the encouragement to keep going when times get tough. For example, a writer who has published multiple books might host free workshops for aspiring authors, offering guidance on everything from finding their voice to navigating the publishing industry. This willingness to share not only helps others but also reinforces their own understanding of their craft. By focusing on how you can serve others, you create a legacy that continues to inspire.

Another important aspect of giving back is *creating opportunities for those who might not have them otherwise*. When you use your influence or resources to lift others up, you create a more inclusive and equitable world. For example, a tech founder might make it a priority to hire interns from underrepresented backgrounds, offering mentorship and training that helps them build successful careers. This focus on creating opportunities helps to build a diverse and dynamic team, bringing new perspectives into the organization. By making giving back a core part of your vision, you create a sense of purpose that keeps you inspired.

Giving back also involves *being a positive role model in both small and large ways*. It's about showing through your actions what it means to live with integrity, kindness, and a commitment to growth. For example, a community leader might make it a habit to volunteer their time to local projects, showing others that success is not just about personal achievement but also about contributing to the common good. This example inspires others to follow in their footsteps, creating a culture of giving that extends far beyond one person's efforts. By leading with generosity, you create a path that others are eager to follow.

Taking your journey to new heights means *embracing the practice of continuous reflection*. Reflection is about looking back not to dwell on the past, but to understand how far you've come and where you still want to go. It's about taking stock of your achievements, your growth, and the lessons you've learned along the way. For example, an artist might take time each year to review their portfolio, noticing the evolution of their style and technique. This reflection helps them see the progress they've made, giving them the confidence to take on even bigger challenges in the future.

Continuous reflection often involves *asking yourself meaningful questions*. Questions like "What did I learn from my biggest challenges?" or "How have my priorities changed over time?" help you gain clarity on your journey and identify areas for improvement. For example, a business leader might reflect on how their approach to leadership has evolved, identifying ways to become even more effective in guiding their team. This process of self-inquiry ensures that they remain aligned with their core values, making it easier to stay true to their vision while adapting to new situations.

Reflection is also about *recognizing the moments of joy and fulfillment that make the journey worthwhile*. It's easy to get caught up in the hustle and forget to appreciate the small victories, but those who succeed make a habit of celebrating the moments that matter. For example, a startup founder might take time to appreciate the first positive review from a customer, the excitement of launching a new product, or the pride in seeing their team come together. This focus on moments of joy helps them maintain a sense of balance, ensuring that the pursuit of growth never overshadows the experience of living.

Another aspect of continuous reflection is *using what you learn to set new intentions for the future*. Reflection helps you identify what's working, what's not, and what you want to change. For example, an athlete who reflects on their performance over the past season might set new goals for their training, focusing on areas where they want to improve. This process of setting new intentions keeps them focused and motivated, making it easier to continue making progress. By using reflection as a tool for growth, you ensure that your journey remains dynamic, purposeful, and deeply rewarding.

Another important aspect of moving forward on your journey is *embracing change as an inevitable part of growth*. Change is often uncomfortable, but it is also necessary if you want to evolve and reach new heights. Whether it's a shift in your career, relationships, or personal goals, being open to change allows you to adapt and thrive in new environments. For example, a digital marketer who built a career on social media might embrace the rise of new platforms, learning how to leverage them for their clients instead of resisting the change.

This adaptability ensures that they remain relevant and continue to grow as the industry evolves.

Change often comes with uncertainty, but *learning to find comfort in discomfort* is what separates those who succeed from those who stay stagnant. When you push beyond your comfort zone, you discover new abilities and strengths that you never knew you had. For example, a professional speaker who is used to delivering keynotes in person might find themselves uncomfortable with the idea of virtual presentations. However, by embracing the change and mastering the technology needed to deliver engaging online speeches, they open themselves up to new audiences and opportunities. This willingness to embrace discomfort leads to growth that wouldn't have been possible within the boundaries of comfort.

Another critical element of embracing change is *understanding that it often leads to personal transformation*. When you allow yourself to flow with the changes in life, you not only grow in your career or personal life but also evolve as a person. For example, an entrepreneur who faces a major business setback might initially feel defeated, but through the process of rebuilding, they may discover new strengths in leadership, creativity, and resilience. This transformation shapes them into a stronger and more adaptable leader, ready to take on future challenges with confidence. By seeing change as a catalyst for transformation, you ensure that each new phase of life brings valuable lessons and growth.

Embracing change also involves *letting go of what no longer serves you*. Growth often requires releasing old habits, beliefs, or relationships that are holding you back. For example, an artist who clings to their early style might find themselves stuck in a creative rut, unable to explore new forms of expression. By letting go of the need to stay within their comfort zone, they open themselves up to new creative possibilities that reignite their passion. This ability to let go creates space for new experiences, ideas, and opportunities, allowing you to continue moving forward with clarity and purpose.

Moving forward on your journey also involves *developing emotional intelligence*. Emotional intelligence (EQ) is the ability to understand and manage your own emotions while also being attuned to the emotions of others. It's a crucial skill for building strong relationships, leading teams, and navigating the complexities of life. For example, a manager with high EQ might notice when a team member is feeling overwhelmed and offer support, either by lightening their workload or providing resources to help them manage stress. This empathetic approach not only strengthens the team dynamic but also creates a work environment where people feel valued and supported.

Emotional intelligence also means *recognizing and managing your own emotional triggers*. It's natural to experience frustration, anger, or disappointment, but those with high EQ learn to pause and reflect before reacting. For example, an entrepreneur who receives critical feedback from a client might initially feel defensive, but by taking a moment to breathe and consider the feedback objectively, they can respond in a way that addresses the client's concerns and strengthens the relationship. This ability to regulate emotions ensures that conflicts are resolved constructively, rather than escalating unnecessarily. By practicing emotional regulation, you create better outcomes both personally and professionally.

Another important aspect of emotional intelligence is *practicing active listening*. Active listening means fully focusing on what the other person is saying, without planning your response while they speak. For example, a leader in a brainstorming session might practice active listening by asking clarifying questions and encouraging everyone to share their ideas, rather than dominating the conversation. This approach fosters collaboration and creates an environment where people feel heard and valued. By listening deeply and empathetically, you build stronger relationships and make more informed decisions.

Emotional intelligence also involves *being aware of your emotional impact on others*. Every interaction you have leaves an impression, and those with high EQ are mindful of how their words and actions affect the people around them. For example, a teacher who is aware of the power of their words might offer constructive feedback to a struggling student in a way that builds confidence rather than discouragement. This awareness helps to create positive, supportive environments where people feel empowered to grow. By being mindful of your emotional influence, you ensure that your interactions uplift others, contributing to a more harmonious and productive environment.

Taking your journey further means *cultivating a sense of purpose that drives your actions*. Purpose is the underlying motivation that gives your life direction and meaning. It's what keeps you going during difficult times and what makes success feel fulfilling. For example, a nonprofit founder who is passionate about reducing homelessness in their city might find purpose in every small victory, whether it's securing funding for a new shelter or helping a single family find permanent housing. This sense of purpose fuels their persistence and resilience, making it easier to push through setbacks and continue working toward their mission.

Having a sense of purpose also involves *aligning your daily actions with your long-term goals*. When you're clear on what you want to achieve, it becomes easier to prioritize tasks and make decisions that bring you closer to your vision. For example, an aspiring author might set a goal to write a certain number of words each day, knowing that consistent progress will eventually lead to a finished manuscript. This alignment between purpose and action ensures that their efforts are always moving them in the right direction, even when progress feels slow. By staying focused on your purpose, you create a sense of momentum that keeps you motivated.

Another important aspect of purpose is *recognizing that it can evolve over time*. As you grow and learn more about yourself and the world, your sense of purpose may shift. For example, a doctor who starts their career focused on clinical practice might discover a passion for medical research later in life, realizing that their purpose is to contribute to advancements in healthcare rather than direct patient care. This willingness to let your purpose evolve ensures that it remains authentic and meaningful, even as your circumstances change. By being open to new directions, you ensure that your sense of purpose remains a source of inspiration and motivation.

Cultivating purpose also means *finding ways to integrate your passions into your work*. When your work aligns with what you love, it becomes more than just a job—it becomes a calling. For example, a graphic designer who is passionate about environmental issues might seek out clients who are working on sustainability initiatives, using their skills to contribute to causes they care about. This integration of passion and purpose makes the work more fulfilling and enjoyable, ensuring that it remains a source of joy rather than stress. By aligning your work with your passions, you create a life that feels meaningful and rewarding.

Another essential aspect of moving forward is *developing a growth mindset*. A growth mindset is the belief that your abilities, intelligence, and talents can be developed through dedication and hard work. It's the opposite of a fixed mindset, which assumes that these traits are static and unchangeable. For example, a student who embraces a growth mindset might approach a difficult subject with curiosity and persistence, believing that they can improve their understanding through practice and effort. This mindset not only helps them overcome challenges but also fosters a love of learning that extends beyond the classroom.

Developing a growth mindset often involves *embracing failure as a valuable part of the learning process*. Those with a growth mindset understand that failure is not a reflection of their abilities but rather an opportunity to learn and improve. For example, an entrepreneur who launches a product that doesn't perform well might analyze the feedback and use it to refine their approach, viewing the failure as a stepping stone to eventual success. This willingness to learn from mistakes ensures that they continue to grow, even when things don't go as planned. By seeing failure as a teacher, you build resilience and adaptability that serve you in every area of life.

Another key element of a growth mindset is *staying open to feedback and constructive criticism*. Those with a growth mindset actively seek out feedback, knowing that it can help them identify areas for improvement. For example, a professional athlete might work closely with their coach to fine-tune their performance, using every piece of feedback as a tool for growth. This openness to criticism ensures that they are always improving, making it easier to reach new levels of achievement. By embracing feedback, you create a continuous loop of learning and growth that propels you forward.

A growth mindset also involves *celebrating effort and persistence, not just outcomes*. When you focus on the process rather than the result, you build the internal motivation needed to keep going, even when success feels distant. For example, an artist who is working on a challenging piece might take pride in the hours they've spent refining their technique, even if the final product isn't perfect. This focus on effort helps them stay engaged with their craft, making it easier to continue improving. By valuing persistence and hard work, you cultivate a mindset that thrives in the face of challenges.

An essential aspect of continuing your journey is *embracing the power of self-belief*. Self-belief is the foundation upon which all your efforts are built. It's the conviction that you have the ability to achieve your goals, even when the road is tough and the outcome uncertain. For example, a new entrepreneur might face skepticism from those around them, but their unwavering belief in their vision keeps them moving forward, taking risks, and making sacrifices to turn that vision into reality. This self-belief acts as a shield against doubt, giving them the courage to pursue opportunities that others might shy away from.

Self-belief is not just about thinking positively; it's about *recognizing your strengths and trusting your instincts*. When you know what you bring to the table, you're more likely to take on challenges that others might avoid. For example, a software developer who believes in their coding skills might take on a complex project that requires learning new frameworks, trusting that their problem-solving abilities will help them figure it out. This willingness to bet on themselves allows them to push their limits, growing their skills and confidence with each new challenge. By trusting in your own capabilities, you give yourself the freedom to explore new horizons.

Another important aspect of self-belief is *building a mindset of resilience in the face of setbacks*. Even when things don't go as planned, those with strong self-belief understand that failure is temporary and that their potential remains intact. For example, a writer who faces rejection from multiple publishers might remind themselves of the positive feedback they've received from readers, using it as a reminder that their work has value. This focus on their strengths helps them stay motivated, even when facing obstacles. By believing in yourself, you create a buffer against the discouragement that can come with setbacks.

Self-belief also means *taking responsibility for your growth and development*. Instead of waiting for opportunities to come to you, self-belief empowers you to create your own opportunities. For example, a musician who believes in their talent might start performing at local venues and sharing their music online, instead of waiting for a record label to discover them. This proactive approach ensures that they are always moving forward, creating their own path to success. By taking ownership of your journey, you position yourself as the driver of your destiny, rather than a passenger waiting for directions.

Moving forward on your journey also involves *learning the art of balance*. Balance is about finding a harmony between your ambitions and your personal well-being, between your work and your relationships, and between your drive for success and your need for rest. It's about understanding that each aspect of your life is interconnected, and that neglecting one area can impact the others. For example, a high-achieving executive might learn that taking time to disconnect from work and spend time with their family not only improves their personal relationships but also enhances their focus and productivity when they return to work. This balance ensures that they are able to sustain their success over the long term.

The art of balance often involves *setting boundaries that protect your time and energy*. Boundaries are not walls; they are guidelines that help you prioritize what truly matters. For example, a freelancer who works from home might set specific work hours and dedicate evenings to personal hobbies and family time. This separation ensures that they can be fully present in each area of their life, reducing the risk of burnout and maintaining a sense of fulfillment. By setting boundaries, you create a structure that allows you to give your best to each aspect of your life.

Another important element of balance is *learning to prioritize your mental and emotional health*. Success can bring pressure, and those who thrive are the ones who make time for activities that recharge their minds and spirits. For example, a scientist working on a demanding research project might schedule time for daily walks in nature, using these moments of quiet reflection to relieve stress and gain new insights. This focus on mental and emotional well-being ensures that they remain passionate about their work, rather than feeling overwhelmed. By making self-care a priority, you create a balance that supports both your goals and your happiness.

The art of balance also involves *knowing when to push forward and when to slow down*. There will be times when you need to give everything you have, and times when you need to step back and let things unfold naturally. For example, an artist preparing for an exhibition might work late nights to complete their pieces, but after the show, they might take a few days off to rest and recharge. This ability to listen to your own needs ensures that you remain energized and motivated, making it easier to sustain high levels of creativity and productivity. By learning to balance your efforts with rest, you ensure that your journey remains fulfilling and sustainable.

Taking your journey further also involves *developing a sense of gratitude for every stage of your progress*. Gratitude is not just about appreciating the good times; it's about finding value in every experience, even the challenging ones. When you cultivate gratitude, you shift your focus from what you lack to what you have, creating a mindset of abundance. For example, a startup founder who faces a tough quarter might focus on being grateful for the loyal customers they have, the lessons they've learned, and the dedication of their team. This gratitude helps them maintain a positive outlook, making it easier to navigate through difficult times with resilience.

Gratitude also involves *expressing appreciation to those who have helped you along the way*. Acknowledging the support, mentorship, and encouragement you've received strengthens your relationships and builds a network of allies. For example, a filmmaker might take time to thank their crew, the cast, and the supporters who believed in their vision, creating a culture of appreciation that fosters loyalty and trust. This expression of gratitude makes it easier for people to feel valued and motivated, ensuring that they continue to support your journey. By recognizing the contributions of others, you create a community that grows alongside you.

Another aspect of gratitude is *using it as a tool to stay grounded and focused*. When you take time to appreciate the progress you've made, it helps you stay present and connected to your purpose. For example, a teacher who feels overwhelmed by their workload might pause to reflect on the impact they've had on their students, finding fulfillment in the moments when they've made a difference. This focus on the positive aspects of their work helps them stay motivated, even when facing challenges. By practicing gratitude regularly, you create a sense of contentment that sustains your drive.

Gratitude also involves *finding joy in the simple moments that make life meaningful*. It's easy to get caught up in the big goals, but those who embrace gratitude find value in the everyday experiences that bring happiness. For example, a designer working on a tight deadline might take a moment to enjoy a cup of coffee and appreciate the sunrise before starting their day. This small act of gratitude helps them start the day with a positive mindset, making it easier to tackle challenges with enthusiasm. By focusing on the beauty of everyday moments, you create a journey that is rich in meaning and joy.

Advancing your journey further means *understanding the power of small, consistent actions*. Big dreams are built on the foundation of small steps taken consistently over time. It's about realizing that each small effort, each daily habit, and each seemingly insignificant decision contributes to the larger picture. For example, a musician who practices their instrument for just 30 minutes every day will see significant improvement over time, even if the progress feels slow in the moment. This focus on consistency helps them build the discipline needed to achieve mastery, making their big goals feel more attainable.

Consistency often involves *building routines that align with your goals*. When you create routines, you reduce the friction that comes with decision-making, making it easier to stay on track. For example, a writer who sets a routine to write every morning before starting other tasks creates a habit that ensures they make progress on their manuscript each day. This routine becomes a source of stability, helping them stay focused and productive, even when motivation is low. By creating routines that support your goals, you ensure that progress becomes a part of your daily life.

Another important aspect of consistency is *understanding that progress is often invisible in the short term*. It's easy to feel discouraged when you don't see immediate results, but those who succeed understand that growth happens gradually. For example, a personal trainer who works with clients might remind them that building strength and endurance takes time, even if the changes aren't immediately visible. This focus on long-term progress helps their clients stay committed, making it easier for them to reach their fitness goals. By staying patient and trusting the process, you ensure that your efforts compound over time.

Consistency is also about *being willing to show up even when the work is hard or unexciting*. It's easy to stay motivated when things are going well, but true progress comes from showing up during the tough times. For example, an artist working on a large commission might find themselves frustrated or creatively drained, but by continuing to put in the work each day, they eventually break through the creative block. This perseverance ensures that they complete the project with integrity, maintaining the quality of their work. By committing to consistency, you create a path that leads to sustained growth and achievement.

An integral part of moving forward is *embracing the power of self-awareness*. Self-awareness is the ability to see yourself clearly and objectively through reflection and introspection. It means understanding your strengths, recognizing your weaknesses, and being aware of how your actions affect those around you. For example, a leader who is self-aware might realize that their decision-making style can be intimidating to newer team members and make an effort to foster a more inclusive atmosphere. This awareness allows them to adapt their approach, creating a healthier work environment that encourages collaboration and growth.

Self-awareness also involves *being honest with yourself about where you are and where you want to go*. It's about acknowledging your current reality without judgment while keeping a clear vision of your desired future. For example, an athlete who dreams of competing at a professional level might recognize that they need to improve their endurance and strength before they can reach that goal. This honest assessment helps them create a targeted training plan that addresses their weaknesses while building on their strengths. By understanding your starting point, you make it easier to map out the path to your destination.

Another key aspect of self-awareness is *learning to manage your ego*. Ego can often cloud judgment and prevent growth by making it difficult to accept feedback or admit mistakes. For example, a business owner who lets their ego dictate decisions might refuse to listen to customer feedback, believing that they know best. In contrast, a self-aware business owner understands that their perspective is not always complete and welcomes input that can improve their product or service. This humility ensures that they continue to grow and adapt, even when faced with criticism. By managing your ego, you create space for genuine learning and improvement.

Self-awareness is also about *understanding your emotional triggers and how they influence your behavior*. When you recognize what triggers stress, frustration, or anxiety, you can take proactive steps to manage those emotions before they escalate. For example, a teacher who knows that last-minute changes to their schedule create stress might plan buffer time between classes to prepare for unexpected adjustments. This foresight helps them maintain a calm and positive demeanor, even when things don't go as planned. By understanding your emotional responses, you create a more balanced and resilient mindset, making it easier to navigate challenges.

Taking your journey further involves *embracing the art of strategic planning*. Strategic planning is about looking beyond the immediate and focusing on the bigger picture. It's about setting clear, long-term goals and developing a roadmap that guides you toward those objectives. For example, a tech startup founder might set a five-year vision for their company, including growth targets, product development goals, and market expansion plans. This long-term focus ensures that daily decisions align with the broader vision, making it easier to stay on track and achieve sustained success.

Strategic planning often involves *breaking down big goals into smaller, manageable steps*. When you divide a large objective into smaller milestones, it becomes less overwhelming and more achievable. For example, a writer working on a 300-page novel might break down their writing process into daily word count goals, focusing on completing one chapter at a time. This approach allows them to track progress and maintain momentum without getting discouraged by the scale of the project. By focusing on incremental progress, you make it easier to reach even the most ambitious goals.

Another important aspect of strategic planning is *anticipating potential challenges and preparing for them*. Being able to foresee obstacles allows you to develop contingency plans, making it easier to navigate difficulties without losing sight of your objectives. For example, a nonprofit organization planning a fundraising campaign might consider potential roadblocks like economic downturns or donor fatigue, and develop alternative strategies for reaching their funding goals. This preparedness ensures that they remain resilient and adaptable, even when facing setbacks. By planning strategically, you create a roadmap that helps you stay focused and prepared for whatever comes your way.

Strategic planning is also about *aligning your resources and efforts with your priorities*. It's easy to get caught up in busywork that doesn't contribute to your long-term goals, but those who succeed are intentional about where they focus their time and energy. For example, a designer who wants to build their portfolio might prioritize client projects that align with their creative vision, rather than taking on every job that comes their way. This focus on quality over quantity ensures that their portfolio represents the type of work they want to attract. By aligning your actions with your strategic vision, you make every effort count toward achieving your goals.

A crucial part of advancing your journey is *developing the habit of resilience*. Resilience is the ability to bounce back from setbacks, adapt to change, and keep moving forward despite challenges. It's about building a mental and emotional toolkit that allows you to maintain your focus and positivity, even in the face of adversity. For example, a student who fails an important exam might use the experience as a learning opportunity, identifying areas for improvement and developing a new study plan. This ability to turn setbacks into stepping stones ensures that they continue to progress, even when the road is difficult.

Resilience often involves *developing a positive inner dialogue*. The way you talk to yourself can have a significant impact on your ability to overcome obstacles. For example, an entrepreneur facing a tough financial period might remind themselves that they've overcome challenges before and that this is just another opportunity to grow stronger. This self-encouragement helps them maintain a hopeful outlook, making it easier to stay motivated and focused on finding solutions. By cultivating a positive inner voice, you create a source of strength that keeps you going during tough times.

Another key aspect of resilience is *embracing a growth mindset when faced with challenges*. A growth mindset sees failure not as a defeat but as a chance to learn and improve. For example, a public speaker who experiences a difficult presentation might reflect on what went wrong and practice new techniques for engaging the audience. This focus on learning helps them become a better speaker, rather than being discouraged by the setback. By approaching challenges with a willingness to learn, you transform obstacles into opportunities for growth.

Resilience is also about *building routines that support your well-being and help you recover from stress*. Routines create a sense of stability and predictability, which can be comforting during uncertain times. For example, a professional athlete might have a post-game routine that includes stretching, hydration, and meditation to help them recover both physically and mentally. This routine ensures that they maintain their peak performance while also taking care of their health. By establishing routines that support resilience, you create a foundation that helps you navigate challenges with greater ease and confidence.

Taking your progress further means *focusing on building a legacy of integrity*. Integrity is about being true to your values, even when it's difficult, and making decisions that reflect your principles. It's about understanding that success is not just about what you achieve but how you achieve it. For example, a business owner who prioritizes ethical practices, even when it means turning down lucrative but questionable opportunities, builds a reputation for trustworthiness that attracts loyal customers. This commitment to doing the right thing ensures that their success is sustainable and respected.

Building a legacy of integrity often involves *making decisions that align with your core values*. When you have a clear sense of what you stand for, it becomes easier to navigate difficult choices. For example, a journalist who values truth and transparency might choose to pursue a story that exposes wrongdoing, even if it means facing pushback from powerful interests. This adherence to their values ensures that they maintain their credibility and earn the trust of their audience. By staying true to your principles, you create a legacy that reflects your commitment to integrity.

Another important aspect of integrity is *being consistent in your actions and words*. Consistency builds trust, both in yourself and in others. When people know that they can rely on you to keep your promises and act with integrity, it creates a foundation of mutual respect. For example, a mentor who consistently shows up for their mentees and provides honest, thoughtful guidance earns their mentees' trust and admiration. This consistency helps to build strong, lasting relationships that are based on mutual respect. By being consistent in your actions, you create a legacy that others can believe in.

Integrity also means *holding yourself accountable for your actions*. It's about being willing to admit when you've made a mistake and taking responsibility for your actions. For example, a team leader who acknowledges a misstep in a project and works to correct it sets a powerful example for their team, showing that accountability is a part of growth. This willingness to take responsibility fosters a culture of openness and learning, where mistakes are seen as opportunities for improvement. By holding yourself accountable, you demonstrate a commitment to growth that inspires those around you.

An essential aspect of moving forward is *embracing the concept of lifelong curiosity*. Curiosity is the spark that keeps your mind open to new ideas and your heart open to new experiences. It's about maintaining a childlike wonder about the world, even as you grow older and gain more experience. For example, an engineer who remains curious might explore new technologies and approaches, constantly seeking ways to improve their designs or solve problems more efficiently. This curiosity ensures that they stay at the forefront of innovation, continually evolving their skills and expertise.

Curiosity is not just about learning new facts; it's about *asking questions that challenge your assumptions and broaden your perspective*. When you cultivate curiosity, you become comfortable with uncertainty and willing to explore unfamiliar territory. For example, a writer might push themselves to read books outside of their usual genres, finding inspiration in stories and styles that are different from their own. This willingness to explore new ideas helps them break out of creative ruts and discover fresh approaches to their work. By asking questions and seeking new perspectives, you ensure that your journey remains dynamic and full of possibilities.

Another key aspect of curiosity is *being open to learning from others, regardless of their background or experience level*. Everyone you meet has something valuable to teach you, and those who embrace curiosity understand the power of listening. For example, a seasoned entrepreneur might learn valuable lessons from a young startup founder who has a different approach to social media marketing. This openness to learning creates a reciprocal exchange of knowledge, where both parties benefit from each other's experiences. By staying curious about people and their stories, you build a network of insights that enrich your own perspective.

Curiosity also involves *embracing the joy of exploring new interests and hobbies*. When you allow yourself to pursue interests purely for the love of learning, you keep your mind engaged and your creativity flowing. For example, a busy professional might take up gardening as a hobby, finding peace and inspiration in the process of nurturing plants. This new interest might seem unrelated to their career, but it provides a sense of balance and perspective that enriches their overall well-being. By embracing curiosity, you create a life that is full of passion and discovery, making each day an opportunity to learn something new.

Taking your journey further means *cultivating the habit of intentionality*. Intentionality is about being purposeful in your actions and decisions, ensuring that everything you do aligns with your values and long-term vision. It's about moving through life with clarity and focus, rather than drifting aimlessly. For example, a designer who is intentional about their career might choose projects that align with their passion for sustainability, rather than taking on every opportunity that comes their way. This focus ensures that their work feels meaningful and that each project contributes to their greater goals. By being intentional, you create a path that is aligned with your true self.

Intentionality often involves *setting clear priorities and being willing to say no to distractions*. It's easy to become overwhelmed by endless to-do lists and external demands, but those who are intentional understand the importance of focusing on what matters most. For example, a parent who values quality time with their children might set aside specific evenings where they disconnect from work and engage in activities together, such as reading or playing games. This intentional focus on family time ensures that their relationships remain strong, even amidst a busy schedule. By prioritizing what truly matters, you ensure that your time and energy are spent in ways that align with your values.

Another important aspect of intentionality is *being mindful of your environment and the influences you allow into your life*. The people, media, and activities that surround you have a profound impact on your mindset and motivation. For example, a creative professional might choose to spend time with other artists and innovators who inspire them, rather than engaging with negative influences that drain their energy. This intentional curation of their environment helps them stay motivated and focused on their creative goals. By being selective about what you surround yourself with, you create an environment that supports your growth.

Intentionality also means *creating rituals and practices that reinforce your purpose*. Rituals are habits that hold special meaning and keep you connected to your deeper intentions. For example, a social entrepreneur who values giving back might start each day by writing down one act of kindness they plan to do, whether it's mentoring a colleague or volunteering their time. This daily practice keeps them grounded in their purpose, ensuring that each day contributes to their greater mission. By building rituals that align with your intentions, you create a sense of continuity and focus that helps you stay on course.

Another crucial aspect of advancing your journey is *developing a mindset of abundance*. An abundance mindset is the belief that there is more than enough success, love, and opportunity to go around. It's the opposite of a scarcity mindset, which is rooted in fear and the belief that resources are limited. For example, an artist with an abundance mindset might celebrate the successes of their peers, knowing that their own path to success is unique and unaffected by others' achievements. This mindset allows them to build supportive relationships within their industry, creating a network of encouragement and collaboration.

An abundance mindset also involves *focusing on possibilities rather than limitations*. When you approach challenges with the belief that there is always a solution, you open yourself up to creative problem-solving and new opportunities. For example, a business owner facing a decline in sales might see it as an opportunity to explore new markets, develop innovative products, or strengthen their customer relationships. This focus on possibilities ensures that they remain proactive, turning challenges into opportunities for growth. By embracing the mindset of abundance, you ensure that setbacks become springboards for new success.

Another key aspect of an abundance mindset is *being generous with your time, energy, and resources*. When you believe that there is enough for everyone, you become more willing to share your knowledge and support others. For example, a financial advisor who is confident in their ability to attract clients might offer free workshops to help young people understand the basics of budgeting and investing. This act of generosity builds trust and goodwill, attracting clients who appreciate their willingness to give. By focusing on giving rather than hoarding, you create a network of support that lifts everyone up.

An abundance mindset also involves *practicing gratitude for what you have while still striving for more*. It's about recognizing the blessings in your life without becoming complacent. For example, a teacher who is grateful for their supportive school environment and the progress of their students might still set goals to improve their teaching methods and reach more students. This balance between gratitude and ambition keeps them motivated, ensuring that they continue to grow without losing sight of the good things they already have. By embracing abundance, you create a mindset that is both content and driven, allowing you to appreciate the journey while striving for new heights.

Moving forward on your journey also involves *embracing the power of storytelling*. Storytelling is a way of connecting with others, sharing your experiences, and leaving a lasting impact. It's about turning your journey into a narrative that others can relate to and learn from. For example, a community activist might use storytelling to share the challenges and triumphs of their advocacy work, inspiring others to get involved and make a difference. This storytelling helps to build empathy and understanding, creating a shared sense of purpose that motivates collective action.

Storytelling is not just about sharing your successes; it's about *being vulnerable and honest about your struggles as well*. When you share the challenges you've faced, you show others that they are not alone in their struggles. For example, a small business owner might share the story of how they overcame a near-failure, including the doubts and fears they experienced along the way. This honesty makes their story more relatable, allowing others to see that setbacks are a natural part of the journey. By being open about your experiences, you create a narrative that is authentic and inspiring.

Another important aspect of storytelling is *using your story to teach and uplift others*. Your experiences hold valuable lessons that can help others avoid the same mistakes or find the courage to pursue their dreams. For example, a mentor might share the story of their early career struggles with a mentee, offering insights on how they navigated the challenges and found their path. This act of sharing helps the mentee gain perspective and confidence, making it easier for them to overcome their own obstacles. By using storytelling as a tool for teaching, you create a legacy of wisdom that reaches far beyond your immediate circle.

Storytelling also involves *creating a narrative that evolves as you grow*. Your story is not fixed; it changes with each new experience and lesson learned. For example, a musician who started out playing in local venues might expand their story to include touring the world, collaborating with other artists, and exploring new genres. This evolving narrative keeps their journey exciting and dynamic, allowing them to connect with new audiences while staying true to their roots. By embracing the evolution of your story, you ensure that it remains a source of inspiration for both yourself and others.

A vital aspect of moving forward is *embracing humility*. Humility is the recognition that no matter how much you achieve, there is always more to learn and room to grow. It's about understanding that success is not an end point but a stepping stone to greater wisdom and understanding. For example, a successful entrepreneur might remain humble by recognizing that their achievements were not only the result of their hard work but also the support, guidance, and opportunities they received along the way. This humility keeps them grounded, allowing them to continue learning and connecting with others on a deeper level.

Humility also means *being open to feedback and recognizing that others have valuable perspectives*. It's about understanding that you don't have all the answers and being willing to learn from those around you. For example, a seasoned artist might seek feedback from younger creators, recognizing that new perspectives can bring fresh energy into their work. This openness to learning from others ensures that their art remains vibrant and relevant, allowing them to grow alongside the changing creative landscape. By embracing humility, you create a mindset that is receptive to growth and innovation.

Another important aspect of humility is *giving credit where it's due*. Acknowledging the contributions of others shows that you value their efforts and recognize that success is often a collaborative effort. For example, a team leader who takes time to publicly appreciate the hard work of their team members fosters a culture of recognition and respect. This act of giving credit builds trust and morale, making it easier for the team to stay motivated and engaged. By celebrating the successes of others, you create an environment where everyone feels valued and inspired to contribute their best.

Humility also involves *being willing to admit when you're wrong*. It's easy to get caught up in pride, but those who embrace humility understand that admitting mistakes is a sign of strength, not weakness. For example, a teacher who realizes they've misunderstood a student's needs might apologize and adjust their approach, showing that they prioritize the student's success over their own ego. This willingness to correct course creates a culture of growth and continuous improvement, where mistakes are seen as opportunities for learning rather than failures. By embracing humility, you ensure that your journey is one of constant evolution.

Another crucial part of advancing your journey is *embracing collaboration over competition*. Collaboration is about recognizing that when you work with others, you can achieve far more than you could alone. It's about finding common goals and working together to create something greater than the sum of its parts. For example, a filmmaker might collaborate with musicians, designers, and writers to create a movie that combines each person's strengths, resulting in a more immersive and impactful experience for the audience. This spirit of collaboration enriches the creative process, making it possible to reach new levels of excellence.

Collaboration is also about *being open to learning from others and allowing their strengths to complement your own*. When you collaborate, you acknowledge that no one is an expert in everything, and that each person brings unique skills and insights to the table. For example, a startup founder might work closely with a marketing expert to build a brand that resonates with their target audience, recognizing that the marketer's expertise can help them reach new customers. This openness to learning creates a partnership where both parties grow and succeed together. By focusing on collaboration, you create a network of support that makes it easier to overcome challenges.

Another important aspect of collaboration is *embracing diversity of thought*. When you bring together people with different backgrounds, experiences, and perspectives, you create a richer environment for innovation. For example, a research team that includes scientists from different disciplines might come up with more comprehensive solutions to complex problems, drawing on their diverse expertise. This diversity ensures that no angle is overlooked, leading to more robust and creative outcomes. By valuing diverse perspectives, you ensure that your journey is one of continuous discovery and growth.

Collaboration also involves *building relationships based on mutual respect and trust*. Successful collaborations are not just about sharing ideas; they're about creating an environment where everyone feels heard, valued, and empowered to contribute. For example, a community organizer who works with local leaders to address social issues might ensure that every voice is included in the decision-making process, fostering a sense of ownership and shared responsibility. This approach builds a stronger, more cohesive community, making it easier to achieve common goals. By focusing on building respectful relationships, you create a foundation for long-lasting partnerships that drive success.

Taking your journey further means *developing a habit of boldness*. Boldness is the willingness to take risks, to step into the unknown, and to pursue your dreams with unwavering determination. It's about not letting fear hold you back from doing what you know is right. For example, a social entrepreneur might take a bold step by launching a program in a community that others have overlooked, believing that their efforts can make a difference. This courage to act, even when the outcome is uncertain, is what sets them apart and allows them to create meaningful change.

Boldness often involves *challenging the status quo and pushing boundaries*. It's about refusing to accept limitations and instead, asking "What if?" For example, a technologist might push the boundaries of what's possible by developing a new app that addresses a common problem in a unique way. This willingness to innovate and take on challenges that others might shy away from helps them create solutions that make a real impact. By being bold, you open yourself up to new possibilities and create a path that is uniquely your own.

Another important aspect of boldness is *embracing the possibility of failure*. Those who are bold understand that taking risks means sometimes missing the mark, but they don't let that deter them. For example, a writer who self-publishes their first book might face rejection or criticism, but they see it as an opportunity to learn and improve. This willingness to put themselves out there, even when success is not guaranteed, allows them to grow stronger and more resilient. By embracing the potential for failure, you create a mindset that is focused on growth rather than fear.

Boldness also means *being true to yourself, even when it's not the popular choice*. It's about having the confidence to pursue your vision, even when others don't understand it. For example, an artist who experiments with unconventional styles might face skepticism from critics, but by staying true to their creative vision, they attract an audience that values their authenticity. This focus on being true to themselves ensures that their work remains original and impactful. By being bold, you give yourself the freedom to create, explore, and express yourself fully, making your journey a true reflection of who you are.

Another essential part of moving forward is *embracing the power of focus*. Focus is the ability to direct your attention toward what matters most, filtering out distractions and noise. It's about concentrating your energy on the tasks and goals that have the greatest potential to move you forward. For example, a scientist working on a groundbreaking research project might limit their time on social media and dedicate specific hours to deep, uninterrupted work. This focus allows them to make meaningful progress, ensuring that their time is spent on what truly matters.

Focus is also about *prioritizing depth over breadth*. It's easy to spread yourself too thin by trying to do too many things at once, but those who succeed understand the value of diving deep into their chosen path. For example, a photographer who specializes in portrait photography might focus on mastering lighting techniques, rather than trying to excel in every type of photography. This focus on depth ensures that they become an expert in their field, attracting clients who appreciate their unique style. By focusing on what you do best, you create a reputation for excellence that sets you apart.

Another key aspect of focus is *learning to manage your time effectively*. Time is a finite resource, and those who master the art of time management are better equipped to achieve their goals. For example, a student balancing classes, a part-time job, and extracurricular activities might use time-blocking to ensure that each commitment gets the attention it deserves. This focus on scheduling helps them maintain a balance while making steady progress toward their academic and personal goals. By managing your time with intention, you create a structure that supports your focus and productivity.

Focus also involves *eliminating distractions that pull you away from your priorities*. Distractions can come in many forms—social media, endless notifications, or even negative self-talk. For example, an entrepreneur who wants to focus on scaling their business might set boundaries around their digital habits, such as turning off notifications during work hours or using productivity apps that limit social media usage. This reduction of distractions helps them stay engaged with their work, making it easier to reach their targets. By protecting your focus, you ensure that your time and energy are dedicated to what truly moves you forward.

A key element of advancing on your path is *embracing the importance of continuous improvement*. Continuous improvement is about always looking for ways to become better, whether in your skills, your mindset, or your approach to challenges. It's the idea that there is always room to grow, no matter how much you've already accomplished. For example, a chef might constantly refine their recipes, seeking feedback from diners and experimenting with new ingredients to create the perfect dish. This dedication to improvement ensures that their work remains fresh and innovative, attracting customers who appreciate their commitment to quality.

Continuous improvement often involves *seeking out feedback and being willing to adjust your approach*. Those who are committed to growth understand that feedback is not a criticism of their worth but a tool for becoming better. For example, a public speaker who receives feedback about their delivery style might practice adjusting their tone and pacing, using the feedback as a guide to enhance their impact on the audience. This willingness to adapt ensures that they continue to evolve, making their presentations more engaging and effective. By embracing feedback, you create a culture of growth that encourages constant learning.

Another aspect of continuous improvement is *focusing on incremental progress rather than drastic changes*. Growth is often a series of small steps rather than giant leaps, and those who embrace this understand that each small improvement adds up over time. For example, a fitness enthusiast who wants to improve their strength might start by adding just a few extra reps to their workout each week. This focus on gradual progress helps them build strength without the risk of burnout or injury. By valuing the small wins, you create a journey that is sustainable and rewarding.

Continuous improvement also means *staying curious about new trends, tools, and techniques in your field*. The world is always changing, and those who are committed to growth understand the importance of staying up to date. For example, a graphic designer who learns new design software might find new ways to bring their creative vision to life, staying ahead of industry trends. This openness to learning ensures that they remain competitive, making it easier to attract clients who are looking for cutting-edge designs. By keeping an open mind, you ensure that your skills and knowledge remain relevant in an ever-evolving world.

Another crucial aspect of moving forward is *embracing the power of adaptability*. Adaptability is the ability to adjust to new conditions, whether they are changes in your environment, industry, or personal circumstances. It's about maintaining flexibility and openness, even when things don't go as planned. For example, a software developer who is used to working with a particular programming language might find that the market is shifting toward a newer, more efficient language. Instead of resisting this change, they take the time to learn the new language, positioning themselves as a valuable asset in a rapidly evolving industry. This adaptability ensures that they remain relevant and continue to grow in their career.

Adaptability often involves *rethinking your approach when faced with unexpected challenges*. When you encounter obstacles, being adaptable allows you to find new ways to reach your goals without being tied to a specific plan. For example, a small business owner who faces supply chain disruptions might find alternative suppliers or adjust their product offerings to maintain sales. This willingness to adjust ensures that they remain resilient, even when external factors threaten their business. By being flexible in your approach, you ensure that setbacks don't derail your progress but instead become opportunities for innovation.

Another key aspect of adaptability is *learning to let go of rigid expectations*. Sometimes, our own expectations can limit our ability to see new possibilities. For example, an artist who expects to achieve success in a specific style might find that their audience responds more enthusiastically to their experimental work. By letting go of the expectation that they must stick to one style, they allow themselves to explore new creative directions that lead to even greater success. This openness to change creates a sense of freedom, making it easier to embrace opportunities that don't fit neatly into the original plan.

Adaptability also means *cultivating a mindset of experimentation*. When you view life as a series of experiments, you become less afraid of making mistakes, knowing that each experiment brings you closer to finding what works. For example, a marketer testing different strategies for a new campaign might try various approaches, from video content to influencer partnerships, analyzing what resonates best with their audience. This experimental mindset allows them to adapt quickly, optimizing their efforts based on real-world feedback. By approaching challenges with curiosity and a willingness to try new things, you create a journey that is dynamic and full of potential.

Taking your journey further involves *embracing the power of empathy*. Empathy is the ability to understand and share the feelings of others. It's about seeing the world through someone else's eyes and recognizing the challenges, joys, and fears they experience. For example, a manager who practices empathy might take the time to listen to an employee who is struggling with a heavy workload, offering support and understanding rather than criticism. This empathy creates a sense of trust and connection, making it easier for the employee to feel valued and motivated. By practicing empathy, you build relationships that are based on mutual respect and understanding.

Empathy is not just about understanding others' emotions; it's also about *taking compassionate action*. When you act on your empathy, you create real change in the lives of those around you. For example, a community leader who understands the struggles of local families might organize a food drive or create educational programs to support them. This action-oriented approach ensures that empathy goes beyond words, making a tangible impact on the community. By turning empathy into action, you create a ripple effect that extends far beyond your immediate circle.

Another important aspect of empathy is *using it to improve communication*. When you understand where someone else is coming from, you can communicate more effectively, even when discussing difficult topics. For example, a business owner negotiating a contract with a supplier might take the time to understand the supplier's challenges, finding a solution that benefits both parties. This empathetic approach creates a sense of partnership, making it easier to reach agreements that are mutually beneficial. By using empathy in your interactions, you build stronger relationships and create a more collaborative environment.

Empathy also involves *being kind to yourself as well as to others*. It's easy to be your own harshest critic, but those who practice self-empathy understand the importance of self-compassion. For example, an artist who struggles with creative block might remind themselves that it's okay to take a break and recharge, rather than pushing through exhaustion. This self-kindness helps them maintain a positive mindset, making it easier to return to their work with renewed energy. By being empathetic with yourself, you create a foundation of self-respect that supports your overall well-being.

Moving forward on your journey also means *embracing the importance of creating value*. Creating value is about focusing on how your work, actions, and presence can make a positive impact on others. It's about looking beyond your own needs and thinking about how you can contribute to the well-being and success of those around you. For example, a product designer who focuses on creating value might design products that solve real problems for their users, making their lives easier or more enjoyable. This focus on value ensures that their work remains in demand, as customers appreciate the thoughtfulness behind each design.

Creating value often involves *listening to what others need and finding ways to meet those needs*. When you take the time to understand what your audience, clients, or community is looking for, you can tailor your efforts to provide solutions that resonate. For example, a coach who listens to their clients' challenges might develop personalized strategies that address their specific goals, rather than offering generic advice. This focus on meeting individual needs ensures that their clients feel heard and supported, making it easier to build lasting relationships. By focusing on creating value, you ensure that your efforts are always aligned with what matters most to those you serve.

Another key aspect of creating value is *focusing on quality over quantity*. It's easy to get caught up in producing more, but those who focus on value understand that quality leaves a lasting impression. For example, a content creator who focuses on producing a few high-quality videos that deeply engage their audience is likely to build a loyal following, rather than spreading themselves thin by producing numerous but less impactful videos. This focus on quality ensures that their work stands out in a crowded market, attracting viewers who appreciate their dedication. By prioritizing quality, you create a lasting impact that sets you apart from the competition.

Creating value also means *being willing to go the extra mile to make a difference*. Sometimes, it's the little things that make the biggest difference in how others perceive your work. For example, a customer service representative who takes an extra moment to follow up with a customer to ensure their issue is resolved creates a memorable experience that builds loyalty. This attention to detail shows that they genuinely care about the customer's experience, making it easier to build a reputation for excellence. By going the extra mile, you create value that is felt deeply and remembered long after the interaction ends.

Another powerful way to advance on your path is *embracing the importance of self-discipline*. Self-discipline is the ability to stay committed to your goals and maintain consistency in your efforts, even when motivation wanes. It's about developing habits that support your long-term success and resisting the urge to give up when things get tough. For example, a writer who dreams of finishing a novel might set a daily writing goal and stick to it, even on days when inspiration is lacking. This self-discipline ensures that they make steady progress, turning their dream into a reality one page at a time.

Self-discipline often involves *mastering the art of delayed gratification*. Those who are self-disciplined understand that true success requires patience and perseverance, and they are willing to make sacrifices today for a better tomorrow. For example, an athlete training for a competition might skip social events or stick to a strict diet, knowing that these sacrifices will pay off when they reach their peak performance. This focus on long-term rewards helps them stay committed, even when the immediate payoff is not apparent. By mastering delayed gratification, you build the resilience needed to achieve your most ambitious goals.

Another key aspect of self-discipline is *creating routines that support your goals*. Routines are a powerful way to automate your discipline, reducing the mental effort needed to stay on track. For example, a student preparing for a major exam might create a study routine that includes specific times for reviewing different subjects, ensuring that they cover all the material systematically. This routine helps them stay organized and focused, making it easier to avoid procrastination. By building routines that align with your goals, you make discipline a natural part of your daily life.

Self-discipline also involves *resisting distractions and staying focused on your priorities*. In a world full of constant stimuli, those who are disciplined know how to create environments that minimize distractions. For example, a remote worker who needs to concentrate on an important project might create a dedicated workspace free from interruptions, setting boundaries around their time. This focus on minimizing distractions ensures that they can fully engage with their work, making it easier to reach their goals. By being intentional about where you place your focus, you make it easier to maintain discipline and stay on course.

A key element of advancing on your journey is *embracing the power of visualization*. Visualization is the practice of imagining yourself achieving your goals, feeling the emotions of success, and seeing yourself overcome challenges before they happen. It's about creating a mental image of your desired future and using that image as a source of motivation. For example, an athlete preparing for a big game might visualize themselves making the perfect play, feeling the rush of adrenaline and the satisfaction of victory. This mental rehearsal helps them build confidence, making it easier to perform at their best when the moment arrives.

Visualization also involves *using your imagination to explore possibilities and envision new paths*. When you allow yourself to dream freely, you create a vision that pulls you forward, making it easier to take bold steps. For example, an entrepreneur who envisions their company expanding globally might use that vision as a guide, motivating them to seek out partnerships, explore new markets, and build a scalable business model. This focus on what could be helps them stay motivated, even when facing the inevitable ups and downs of entrepreneurship. By embracing visualization, you create a clear picture of where you want to go, making it easier to map out the steps to get there.

Another key aspect of visualization is *using it to cultivate a positive mindset*. When you visualize success, you train your mind to focus on what is possible rather than what could go wrong. For example, a student preparing for a presentation might visualize themselves speaking confidently and receiving positive feedback from their peers. This positive imagery helps to reduce anxiety and build a sense of readiness, making it easier to deliver the presentation with poise. By focusing on positive outcomes, you create a mental environment that supports your success.

Visualization is also about *revisiting your vision regularly to keep it fresh and inspiring*. It's easy to lose sight of your goals amidst daily challenges, but those who succeed make a habit of returning to their vision to remind themselves of why they started. For example, a musician who is in the middle of a challenging recording process might take a moment to visualize their finished album and imagine the joy it will bring to their listeners. This renewed connection to their vision helps them push through the hard work, making it easier to stay focused. By keeping your vision in sight, you create a constant source of motivation that guides you through every step of your journey.

An essential part of advancing on your journey is *embracing the power of consistency*. Consistency is the discipline of showing up every day, regardless of the circumstances, and putting in the work required to achieve your goals. It's about realizing that progress doesn't happen overnight, but through small, steady efforts over time. For example, a musician aiming to master an instrument might practice for an hour each day, building their skills gradually. This consistency ensures that they make progress, even if the improvements are incremental at first. By showing up consistently, you create a foundation for success that compounds over time.

Consistency is often challenging because it requires *commitment even when motivation fades*. It's easy to stay focused when you're excited about a new project, but the real test comes when the initial enthusiasm wears off. For example, a fitness enthusiast who commits to a workout regimen might find it difficult to maintain their routine during busy or stressful periods. However, by staying disciplined and showing up to the gym even when they're tired, they ensure that their long-term goals remain within reach. This ability to stay consistent, even in the face of challenges, is what separates those who achieve lasting success from those who give up too soon.

Another key aspect of consistency is *building habits that support your goals*. Habits are the building blocks of consistency because they allow you to automate your actions, reducing the mental effort required to stay on track. For example, a writer who sets aside time to write every morning creates a habit that ensures they make daily progress on their manuscript, without needing to rely on willpower alone. This focus on creating productive habits ensures that their writing becomes a regular part of their routine, making it easier to reach their goals. By building habits that align with your vision, you create a structure that supports consistent progress.

Consistency also means *focusing on long-term results rather than seeking immediate gratification*. Those who understand the value of consistency know that the most meaningful progress often takes time, and they are willing to stay the course. For example, an entrepreneur who is building a brand might focus on providing value to their customers over years, knowing that this long-term commitment will lead to a loyal customer base. This focus on the bigger picture helps them stay motivated, even when immediate results are slow to appear. By embracing a long-term perspective, you ensure that your efforts are directed toward sustainable success rather than short-lived gains.

Taking your journey further involves *embracing the importance of resilience in the face of adversity*. Resilience is the ability to bounce back from setbacks and continue moving forward, even when things don't go as planned. It's about maintaining your focus and drive, despite obstacles and disappointments. For example, a small business owner who faces a financial downturn might pivot their business model or explore new markets, using the setback as an opportunity to innovate. This resilience allows them to stay afloat, even during challenging times, and ultimately emerge stronger. By developing resilience, you ensure that challenges become stepping stones rather than roadblocks.

Resilience often involves *cultivating a growth mindset*. Those with a growth mindset see challenges as opportunities to learn and improve, rather than as failures. For example, a student who struggles with a difficult subject might use the experience to develop better study habits and time management skills, rather than viewing their struggle as a sign of inability. This focus on learning ensures that they continue to grow, even when progress is slow or difficult. By adopting a growth mindset, you create a mental framework that supports resilience, making it easier to push through tough times.

Another important aspect of resilience is *developing emotional endurance*. Emotional endurance is the ability to manage your emotions during stressful or difficult situations, ensuring that you remain calm and focused. For example, a leader who faces a crisis at work might feel overwhelmed, but by practicing mindfulness and emotional regulation techniques, they are able to stay composed and make clear-headed decisions. This emotional stability helps them navigate the crisis more effectively, ensuring that their team remains confident and supported. By building emotional endurance, you create the mental fortitude needed to weather life's storms.

Resilience also involves *seeking support when needed*. Those who are truly resilient understand that they don't have to go through challenges alone. For example, a writer experiencing creative block might reach out to fellow writers for advice or join a writing group for encouragement. This willingness to seek help ensures that they don't become isolated in their struggle, making it easier to regain momentum. By building a support network, you create a safety net that helps you stay resilient, even when times are tough. By relying on the strength of others, you reinforce your own ability to persevere.

Another crucial element of advancing on your path is *embracing the concept of lifelong learning*. Lifelong learning is the practice of continuously seeking knowledge and developing new skills throughout your life. It's about recognizing that there is always more to learn, regardless of how much you've already achieved. For example, a seasoned professional who remains curious about new developments in their field might attend workshops, take online courses, or read books to stay up to date. This commitment to learning ensures that they remain competitive and open to new ideas, even as their career evolves. By embracing lifelong learning, you keep your mind sharp and your skills relevant.

Lifelong learning also involves *being open to learning from a variety of sources*. Knowledge doesn't always come from formal education—it can be found in conversations, experiences, and even failures. For example, an entrepreneur might learn valuable lessons from a failed business venture, gaining insights that help them succeed in future endeavors. This openness to learning from diverse sources ensures that they continue to grow, even when things don't go as planned. By remaining curious and open-minded, you create a mindset that is always ready to absorb new information and apply it to your journey.

Another key aspect of lifelong learning is *cultivating a sense of curiosity*. Curiosity is the engine that drives lifelong learning, pushing you to explore new ideas and challenge your assumptions. For example, a scientist who is curious about the natural world might spend their free time conducting independent research or experimenting with new theories. This curiosity keeps them engaged and excited about their work, ensuring that they never stop learning. By staying curious, you create a journey that is rich with discovery and growth.

Lifelong learning also involves *adapting to new technologies and trends*. The world is constantly changing, and those who succeed are the ones who stay ahead of the curve by embracing new tools and techniques. For example, a teacher who adopts new educational technologies might find more effective ways to engage their students, keeping their lessons relevant in a rapidly evolving field. This willingness to adapt ensures that they remain effective and innovative, even as the world around them changes. By staying open to new technologies, you ensure that your skills and knowledge remain current, making it easier to thrive in a fast-paced environment.

Taking your journey further means *embracing the power of intention*. Intention is about being purposeful in your actions and decisions, ensuring that everything you do aligns with your values and long-term goals. It's about moving through life with clarity and focus, rather than being reactive to external circumstances. For example, an artist who is intentional about their work might choose projects that align with their creative vision, rather than taking on every opportunity that comes their way. This focus on intention ensures that their work remains authentic and fulfilling, allowing them to stay true to their artistic identity. By acting with intention, you create a path that is aligned with your core values.

Intention often involves *setting clear goals and breaking them down into actionable steps*. When you have a clear sense of what you want to achieve, it becomes easier to prioritize your time and energy in ways that move you closer to your goals. For example, a student who wants to graduate with honors might set specific academic and personal goals for each semester, tracking their progress and adjusting their efforts as needed. This focus on intention helps them stay motivated, making it easier to achieve their desired outcomes. By setting clear goals and acting with purpose, you create a sense of direction that guides you forward.

Another important aspect of intention is *being mindful of your daily actions and how they contribute to your long-term vision*. It's easy to get caught up in the busyness of life, but those who act with intention understand the importance of aligning their actions with their larger goals. For example, a business owner who is intentional about building a strong company culture might prioritize regular team meetings, employee development programs, and open communication. This intentional focus on culture ensures that their company grows in a way that reflects their values, attracting like-minded employees and clients. By being mindful of your actions, you ensure that every step you take contributes to your greater vision.

Intention also means *being proactive rather than reactive*. Instead of waiting for opportunities to come to you, acting with intention means seeking out opportunities that align with your goals. For example, a graphic designer who wants to expand their portfolio might proactively reach out to potential clients or collaborate with other creatives, rather than waiting for projects to appear. This proactive approach ensures that they stay in control of their journey, making it easier to reach their goals. By being intentional in your efforts, you create a journey that is focused, purposeful, and aligned with your aspirations.

Another key element of advancing your journey is *embracing the importance of contribution*. Contribution is about giving back to others and making a positive impact on the world around you. It's about using your skills, talents, and resources to uplift those who need it most. For example, a software developer who volunteers their time to teach coding to underprivileged youth creates opportunities for others to succeed, while also finding fulfillment in making a difference. This focus on contribution ensures that their work is not just about personal success but also about leaving a lasting legacy of impact. By contributing to the well-being of others, you create a life that is rich in meaning.

Contribution often involves *recognizing the unique gifts you have to offer*. Everyone has something valuable to share, whether it's knowledge, experience, or simply a listening ear. For example, a retiree who has spent decades in the workforce might volunteer as a mentor for young professionals, offering guidance on career development and work-life balance. This act of sharing their wisdom helps others navigate the challenges of their own careers, creating a sense of community and support. By recognizing your own unique gifts, you ensure that your contributions have a lasting impact.

Another important aspect of contribution is *being willing to step outside your comfort zone to help others*. Sometimes, making a meaningful difference requires taking risks or making sacrifices. For example, a business leader who advocates for fair wages in their industry might face pushback from competitors, but their efforts create a better standard of living for their employees. This willingness to take a stand ensures that their contributions go beyond the status quo, creating real change in the lives of others. By embracing the courage to make a difference, you create a legacy that is both bold and compassionate.

Contribution also means *focusing on the ripple effect of your actions*. Every act of kindness, support, or encouragement has the potential to create positive ripples that extend far beyond what you can see. For example, a teacher who inspires a love of learning in their students might not see the full impact of their work, but those students may go on to achieve great things, inspired by the seeds of curiosity planted in the classroom. This focus on the ripple effect ensures that you never underestimate the power of your contributions. By understanding the far-reaching impact of your actions, you create a journey that is focused on creating a better world for others.

A crucial element of advancing your journey is *embracing the power of gratitude*. Gratitude is the practice of acknowledging the good in your life, regardless of the challenges you face. It's about focusing on the positive aspects of your experiences, which helps shift your perspective from what is lacking to what is abundant. For example, a startup founder who experiences setbacks might focus on being grateful for the lessons learned, the support from their team, and the opportunity to pursue their vision. This focus on gratitude helps them maintain a positive outlook, even when things don't go as planned. By practicing gratitude, you create a mindset that finds joy and meaning in every moment.

Gratitude also involves *appreciating the journey, not just the destination*. It's easy to become so focused on your goals that you forget to enjoy the process of getting there. For example, an athlete training for a marathon might take time to appreciate the small victories along the way—each mile run, each improvement in speed, each day of discipline. This appreciation for the process ensures that they remain motivated and engaged, even when the end goal feels distant. By focusing on the journey, you create a sense of fulfillment that makes every step worthwhile.

Another important aspect of gratitude is *expressing appreciation to those who have supported you*. When you take the time to thank the people who have helped you along the way, you strengthen your relationships and build a community of support. For example, an artist who acknowledges their mentors, collaborators, and even their audience creates a sense of connection and appreciation that enhances their creative work. This gratitude creates a positive cycle, where support and encouragement flow both ways, making it easier to thrive. By expressing gratitude to those around you, you create a culture of positivity that uplifts everyone involved.

Gratitude also means *finding beauty in the simple, everyday moments*. It's about recognizing that joy doesn't always come from grand achievements but can be found in the quiet, ordinary experiences that make life meaningful. For example, a writer might find gratitude in the peaceful morning hours when they sit down with a cup of coffee and let their thoughts flow onto the page. This focus on simple pleasures helps them maintain a sense of balance and contentment, even amidst the pressures of deadlines and expectations. By finding gratitude in the little things, you create a life that feels rich and fulfilling, no matter what challenges come your way.

Taking your journey further involves *embracing the power of reflection*. Reflection is the process of looking back on your experiences to gain insights, understand your growth, and identify areas for improvement. It's about taking time to pause and think deeply about where you've been, where you are, and where you want to go. For example, a business leader might reflect on the past year, considering the successes, setbacks, and decisions that shaped their company's trajectory. This reflection helps them see patterns, recognize strengths, and identify opportunities for change. By making reflection a regular part of your journey, you ensure that each experience becomes a stepping stone toward greater wisdom.

Reflection often involves *asking yourself meaningful questions*. Questions like "What did I learn from this experience?" or "How have my priorities changed over time?" help you gain clarity and perspective. For example, a teacher who reflects on a challenging semester might realize that their greatest moments of growth came from adapting to unexpected changes, such as shifting to online learning. This insight helps them appreciate their own resilience and prepares them to tackle future challenges with confidence. By asking the right questions, you turn reflection into a tool for growth that deepens your understanding of yourself.

Another important aspect of reflection is *celebrating your progress*. It's easy to focus on what you have yet to accomplish, but those who practice reflection understand the importance of recognizing how far they've come. For example, a musician who looks back on their early recordings might notice how much their style and skill have evolved over the years. This appreciation for progress helps them stay motivated, making it easier to keep pushing forward. By taking time to celebrate your achievements, you build a sense of self-confidence that fuels your continued growth.

Reflection also involves *using the lessons of the past to guide your future actions*. When you reflect on your experiences, you gain valuable insights that help you make better decisions moving forward. For example, an entrepreneur who reflects on a failed product launch might identify what went wrong and use that knowledge to develop a more effective strategy for their next project. This focus on learning from the past ensures that each setback becomes an opportunity for improvement. By applying the lessons of reflection, you create a path that is informed by experience and driven by continuous growth.

Another essential aspect of advancing your journey is *embracing the power of connection*. Connection is about building relationships with others that are based on trust, understanding, and mutual support. It's about recognizing that no one achieves success alone, and that the relationships you cultivate along the way play a crucial role in your growth. For example, a community organizer who builds strong connections with local leaders and residents creates a network of support that makes it easier to address community challenges. This focus on connection ensures that they have allies who share their vision and are willing to work together toward common goals.

Connection also means *being genuinely interested in the stories and experiences of others*. When you take the time to listen to others and understand their perspectives, you create a sense of empathy and understanding that deepens your relationships. For example, a mentor who listens attentively to the struggles of their mentee can offer more relevant guidance, helping them navigate challenges with greater clarity. This focus on understanding creates a relationship that is based on trust and respect, making it easier for both parties to grow together. By building connections that are rooted in empathy, you create a sense of community that enriches your journey.

Another key aspect of connection is *offering support to others without expecting anything in return.* True connection is built on generosity and a willingness to uplift others, even when there is no immediate benefit to yourself. For example, a writer who offers feedback to fellow writers, sharing their insights and encouraging their peers, creates a supportive community where everyone can thrive. This focus on giving builds a network of trust and collaboration that becomes a source of strength during difficult times. By offering support to others, you create a sense of connection that is based on mutual respect and a shared commitment to growth.

Connection also involves *being willing to ask for help when you need it.* It's easy to feel like you have to do everything on your own, but those who value connection understand that reaching out for support is a sign of strength, not weakness. For example, an entrepreneur who faces a challenging market might seek advice from industry experts or join a network of like-minded professionals who can provide guidance. This willingness to lean on others ensures that they have the support they need to overcome obstacles and continue moving forward. By building a network of trusted connections, you ensure that your journey is supported by a community of allies.

Taking your journey further involves *embracing the power of self-care.* Self-care is about recognizing that you cannot pour from an empty cup, and that taking care of your physical, emotional, and mental well-being is essential for long-term success. It's about understanding that rest, relaxation, and rejuvenation are not luxuries, but necessities that allow you to maintain your energy and focus. For example, a lawyer who deals with high-stress cases might practice self-care by taking regular breaks, engaging in hobbies, or spending time in nature to recharge. This focus on self-care ensures that they can continue to perform at their best, without burning out.

Self-care also involves *setting boundaries that protect your time and energy.* It's easy to feel obligated to say yes to every request, but those who practice self-care understand the importance of saying no when necessary. For example, a freelancer who values their personal time might set clear boundaries around their work hours, ensuring that they have time to recharge and spend with loved ones. This focus on boundaries helps them maintain a healthy work-life balance, making it easier to stay engaged and productive during work hours. By setting boundaries, you create space for self-care that supports your overall well-being.

Another important aspect of self-care is *engaging in activities that bring you joy and relaxation.* Self-care is not just about managing stress; it's about doing things that make you feel alive and fulfilled. For example, a musician who loves hiking might make time to explore new trails, finding inspiration and peace in nature. This focus on joy ensures that their creative energy remains vibrant, making it easier to stay passionate about their work. By prioritizing activities that bring you happiness, you create a life that feels balanced and meaningful.

Self-care also means *being mindful of your mental and emotional health*. It's easy to get caught up in the demands of daily life, but those who value self-care understand the importance of checking in with themselves regularly. For example, a teacher who feels overwhelmed might practice mindfulness or journaling to process their emotions, finding clarity and calm amidst the chaos. This focus on mental and emotional well-being helps them stay resilient, making it easier to navigate challenges with grace. By taking care of your mind and heart, you create a foundation of strength that supports your journey through all its ups and downs.

A fundamental part of advancing your journey is *embracing the concept of purpose-driven living*. Purpose-driven living is about aligning your actions with a sense of greater meaning, allowing your values and beliefs to guide your choices. It's about recognizing that life is more than just a series of tasks, but a journey that holds the potential for impact and fulfillment. For example, a doctor who is driven by a desire to serve their community might go beyond their daily responsibilities, volunteering at local clinics or mentoring aspiring medical students. This focus on purpose gives their work a sense of depth, making each day feel meaningful.

Purpose-driven living often involves *defining your core values and using them as a compass*. When you are clear on what matters most to you, it becomes easier to make decisions that align with your beliefs. For example, a social entrepreneur who values environmental sustainability might choose to work with partners who share their commitment to ethical practices, even if it means turning down more profitable opportunities. This focus on values ensures that their journey remains true to their mission, creating a sense of integrity that resonates with others. By defining your purpose, you create a guiding light that keeps you focused on what truly matters.

Another important aspect of purpose-driven living is *finding ways to contribute to the well-being of others*. Purpose is often found in the impact you have on the lives of those around you. For example, a teacher who finds purpose in inspiring their students might take extra time to mentor those who need encouragement, knowing that their support can make a lasting difference. This focus on contributing to others' growth ensures that their work feels rewarding, making it easier to stay passionate about their role. By focusing on how you can make a positive impact, you create a sense of purpose that enriches your journey.

Purpose-driven living also involves *being open to the evolution of your purpose over time*. As you grow and learn, your sense of purpose may shift, revealing new passions and areas of interest. For example, an artist who starts out focused on self-expression might find that their purpose evolves into using their art to raise awareness for social issues. This willingness to let their purpose evolve ensures that they remain connected to their work in a deep and authentic way, even as their journey changes. By embracing the fluidity of purpose, you create a path that is always moving toward greater meaning and fulfillment.

ABOUT THE AUTHOR

Afjal Khan is a dedicated writer, educator, and passionate advocate for Gen Z empowerment. With a deep understanding of both the modern challenges and timeless wisdom, Afjal blends his expertise in Islamic studies and personal development to inspire young adults to master their financial lives while staying true to their values. His mission is to guide the next generation in navigating the complexities of the contemporary world, helping them build strong financial foundations without compromising on their faith or principles.

Drawing from the rich legacy of the Salaf and the core principles of Islamic teachings, Afjal aims to empower young people to thrive in all aspects of life—spiritually, financially, and morally. His work focuses on providing practical and actionable advice that aligns with Islamic values, encouraging readers to embrace the power of Tawheed, resilience, and a strong sense of identity in a fast-paced, ever-evolving world.

"As a humble student of knowledge, I (Afjal Khan) welcome any feedback or corrections. While I strive to ensure that everything I share aligns with the Qur'an and Sunnah, I am human and capable of making mistakes. If any part of my work inadvertently contradicts authentic Islamic teachings, I ask for your forgiveness. Please do not follow my words if they conflict with Islam, and I kindly request that you inform me of any errors so that I may correct them, inshaAllah, as long as I am alive. You are welcome to reach out to me at **mdafjalkhan29@gmail.com** for any corrections, insights, or questions."

Afjal Khan's work remains deeply rooted in the authentic traditions of Islam, while addressing the unique challenges faced by today's youth. His mission is to bridge the gap between Islamic values and modern life, offering a practical path to financial empowerment, personal growth, and spiritual fulfillment. Whether through his books, lectures, or digital content, Afjal is committed to supporting Gen Z as they strive to lead purposeful, successful lives grounded in faith.

To stay connected with Afjal Khan and access valuable resources, join his growing community. Sign up for exclusive content, including free guides and eBooks, all designed to help you level up in life while staying true to your principles.

@IQRAJOURNEY

www.ingramcontent.com/pod-product-compliance
Lightning Source LLC
Chambersburg PA
CBHW052141220526
45471CB00004B/1470